P9-DNK-720

Christianity IN CRISIS

HANK HANEGRAAFF

HARVEST HOUSE PUBLISHERS
Eugene, Oregon 97402

Except where otherwise indicated, all Scripture quotations in this book are taken from the Holy Bible, New International Version ®, Copyright © 1973, 1978, 1984 by the International Bible Society. Used by permission of Zondervan Bible Publishers. All rights reserved. The "NIV" and "New International Version" trademarks are registered in the United States Patent and Trademark Office by International Bible Society. Use of trademarks by permission of International Bible Society.

Verses marked NASB are taken from the New American Standard Bible, © 1960, 1962, 1963, 1968, 1971, 1972 1973, 1975, 1977 by The Lockman Foundation. Used by permission.

Verses marked NKJV are taken from the New King James Version, Copyright © 1979, 1980, 1982 by Thomas Nelson, Inc., Publishers. Used by permission.

Verses marked KJV are taken from the King James Version of the Bible.

CHRISTIANITY IN CRISIS

Copyright © 1997 by Hank Hanegraaff
Published by Harvest House Publishers
Eugene, Oregon 97402

Library of Congress Cataloging-in-Publication Data

Hanegraaff, Hank
    [Christianity in crisis]
    Christianity in crisis with study guide / Hank Hanegraaff.
      p. cm.
    Originally published under titles: Christianity in crisis and Christianity in
    crisis study guide.
    ISBN 1-56507-696-6
    1. Faith movement (Hagin)—Controversial literature.
  I. Hanegraaff, Hank. Christianity in crisis study guide.
  II. Title.
    BR1643.5.H36   1997   97-2656
    289.9'4—dc21   CIP

All rights reserved. No portion of this book may be reproduced in any form without the written permission of the Publisher.

Printed in the United States of America.

99 00 01 02 03 04 / BP / 12 11 10 9 8 7 6 5 4 3

To Erwin de Castro—
an example of a layman
who strives to serve God with all
his heart, soul, and mind.

Acknowledgments

I want to thank my heavenly Father for giving me the health, strength, and everything necessary to complete *Christianity in Crisis*. He has blessed me with a wonderful board and staff whose prayers and encouragement were crucial to the completion of this project.

I am especially appreciative for the insights and assistance of Bob Lyle and the research staff of the Christian Research Institute. A special thanks to Elliot Miller, Ron Rhodes, Ken Samples, Paul Carden, Brad Sparks, and B.J. Oropeza for critically reviewing the book manuscript prior to publication.

In addition, my gratitude knows no bounds for the tireless dedication of my personal assistant, Erwin de Castro. During the tough times he was always by my side. He is not only a trusted friend but a truly remarkable intellect.

Others deserving mention include:

Norman Geisler, for theologically reviewing the manuscript prior to publication.

Berit Kjos, for her insight, input, and especially her prayers.

Rolly DeVore, for diligently monitoring the teachings of the Faith movement (he has become an expert in this field).

Kathie Delph, for taking dictation when my fingers were too numb to type.

Ed Decker, for his constant encouragement and faithful prayer support.

Bob Hawkins Sr. and the staff of Harvest House Publishers, for their support and courageous commitment to publish this volume.

Steve Halliday, for not only lending his editorial skills to this project but also for the all-nighter he pulled to meet a pressing deadline.

Gretchen Passantino, for her editorial input.

And last, but not least, my wife Kathy and six children—Michelle, Katie, David, John Mark, Hank Jr., and Christy—who demonstrated remarkable patience and understanding right up to the end. David, in particular, let me know that the time to finish had come by relentlessly asking me, "How many more pages, Dad?"

CONTENTS

Before We Begin

*I*magine that late one evening you board a plane to take the long flight from Los Angeles to Atlanta.[1] As you look around the cabin, you notice that several passengers have begun to read magazines or newspapers. A man and his wife in the row in front of you are engaged in quiet conversation. Several passengers seem to be staring off into space, enveloped in a world of thought. Still others have already drifted off to sleep. You stretch sleepily and anticipate a quiet, peaceful trip.

Just before takeoff, however, the calm suddenly erupts into chaos as six screaming children and their mother board the aircraft. She sits across the aisle from you and appears oblivious to the disruption. Not only are her children loud and rambunctious, but they seem to vacillate wildly between nervous laughter and tears.

The anger and irritation etched on the faces of your fellow passengers is obvious. Yet no one seems willing to do anything. Finally you can no longer contain yourself. Leaning over to the mother, you blurt out, "Ma'am, can you please do something about your kids? They're out of control! Can't you see that people are trying to read? Don't you realize how late it is? We're tired! We need some peace and quiet!"

As though jolted back to reality, the woman looks into your eyes and in a shaky voice responds, "Yes, yes, you're right. I'm very sorry—forgive me! You see, I just received word that my husband was in a terrible automobile accident.

He's in a coma, and the doctors are not sure he'll live. I'm having a difficult time coping, and . . . and . . . I'm not sure the children are handling this very well either."

Imagine how you would feel at that moment! Suddenly you perceive reality from a whole new perspective. Irritation gives way to compassion. In an instant you view this woman and her circumstances through a whole new set of lenses. A macroshift in your perspective occurs in a microsecond.

We need exactly that kind of macroshift right now to avert a very real and present crisis in Christianity. Without such a megashift in both perception and perspective, the church is in horrifying danger. Allow me to explain.

In recent years, multitudes who name the name of Christ have adopted a wildly distorted perception of what it truly means to be a Christian. Perhaps even more alarming, millions more have been kept from seriously considering the claims of Christ because they perceive Christianity as a con and Christian leaders as con artists.

Under the banner "Jesus is Lord," multitudes are being duped by a gospel of greed and are embracing doctrines straight from the metaphysical cults. While convinced that what they hear is the real thing, they are in fact turning on to nothing more than a cheap counterfeit. Eternal truths from the Word of God are being perverted into bad mythology— and all the while Christianity is hurtling at breakneck speed into a crisis of unparalleled proportions.

That's quite a charge, I know. And I understand that it might be hard for you to swallow. So to prove that I'm no alarmist, allow me to give you a taste of what you're about to read in this book. The following quotes may appear so outrageous as to be fabricated, but every one of them—along with every other example in this book—has been carefully authenticated. These quotes have fallen directly from the lips or the pens of a handful of men and women who consider themselves to be modern-day prophets. It is these self-proclaimed apostles who are leading the church into the kingdom of the cults. But don't just take my word for it:

"Satan *conquered* Jesus on the Cross."

—*Kenneth Copeland*

"You're not looking at Morris Cerullo—
you're looking at God. You're looking at
Jesus."

—*Morris Cerullo*

"Never, ever, ever go to the Lord and say, 'If
it be thy will. . . .' Don't allow such faith-
destroying words to be spoken from your
mouth."

—*Benny Hinn*

"God has to be given permission to work in
this earth realm on behalf of man. . . . Yes!
You are in control! So, if man has control,
who no longer has it? God."

—*Frederick K.C. Price*

"Man was created on terms of equality with
God, and he could stand in God's presence
without any consciousness of inferiority."

—*Kenneth E. Hagin*

As you will see, this is just the tip of the iceberg. If
cultic and occultic systems like the New Age movement pose
the greatest threat to the body of Christ from without, the
deadly cancer represented by these quotes poses one of the
greatest threats to Christianity from within. The true Christ
and the true faith of the Bible are being replaced rapidly with
diseased substitutes offered by a group of teachers who
belong to what has been labeled the "Faith movement."

This cancer has been triggered by a steady diet of
"fast-food Christianity"—a Christianity long on looks but
short on substance. The dispensers of this carcinogenic diet
have utilized the power of the airwaves, as well as a plethora

of pleasantly packaged books and tapes, to lure their prey to dinner. The unsuspecting have been called not to love the Master, but to love what is on the Master's table.

For years I have preached on this subject with dramatic urgency. In addition, I recall countless hours spent with Dr. Walter Martin (founder of the Christian Research Institute) before his death, discussing this catastrophe and its implications for the historic Christian faith.

To avert this crisis, we must shift from perceiving God as a means to an end to recognizing that He *is* the end. We must shift from a theology based on *temporary* perspectives to one based on *eternal* perspectives.

And while change must come, it clearly will not come easily. Those who are feeding this cancer occupy some of the most powerful platforms within Christianity. They control vast resources and stand to lose multiplied millions of dollars if they are exposed.

The stakes are so high that those who are plunging Christianity into crisis seem willing to do and say virtually anything to silence opposition and rally support.

This book highlights the beliefs of about a dozen of the more influential Faith teachers on the scene today. While far more personalities could have been cited, I wanted to focus on those teachers who wield the largest influence within the movement. The individuals I repeatedly quote are those who tend to shape the development of the movement and who are responsible for spawning a host of imitators.

Because Faith teachers are part of a movement and are not members of a monolithic organization, not every Faith teacher holds to every doctrine examined in this book. But the spectrum of false teachings I analyze does accurately represent the entire Faith movement. In other words, not all Faith teachers subscribe to exactly the same beliefs on every point of doctrine, but they do hold to an aberrant core of doctrine that rightly places them within the broad outlines of the Faith movement.

Not everything these teachers espouse is wrong. If these men and women promoted nothing but error, their audiences would quickly shrink to insignificance. It is sometimes possible to watch 15 minutes of a Faith broadcast and wonder what the fuss is all about, since we may see and hear nothing worthy of censure. *But it is what occurs on minute 16 that ought to rock us on our heels, for it is the fatal error mixed in with the truth that makes the Faith movement so dangerous.* While supposedly lifting up the name of Jesus, Faith teachers ridicule the biblical Christ and replace Him with a creation of their own imaginations.

This book is focused on the deadly errors of the Faith movement. I would like nothing better than to spend my time painting the fresh, green pastures of biblical truth; but when a wolf prowls the landscape, it is time for me to put down my brush and take up a different tool. This book has one major concern: to expose heresy. I do not enjoy the task, but it must be done. To refuse this biblical duty in favor of more pleasant options is to demean Christ and to belittle the church He bought with His own blood. I had no choice but to write *Christianity in Crisis*.

My earnest prayer is not only that the readers of this book will sit up and take notice, but that this work might somehow be used by God to effect enduring change among all those who dare to take the sacred name "Christian" upon their lips.

The title of this book, *Christianity in Crisis*, is no exaggeration. The cancer which this book exposes is now reaching the critical stage and is spreading with such speed as to warrant the book's title. Yet, thankfully, I firmly believe that this is a cancer for which there is a cure.

This book is not merely about exposing darkness to light; it is about replacing the crisis in Christianity with a Christianity centered in Christ. It is not merely about cursing the darkness; it is about building a lighthouse in the midst of the gathering storm.

I had three categories of readers in mind as I sat down to pen this book. First, my heart goes out to those people who have been misled into joining the Faith movement. These dear people are sincere in their desire to serve the Lord, but have been directed into a pathway that leads directly to the kingdom of the cults. I desperately desire that these precious believers see the truth of the gospel and exchange a counterfeit faith for a real one—one that has encouraged and nurtured and strengthened men and women throughout the 2000-year history of the true Christian church.

Second, I write to Bible-believing Christians who may be either concerned or confused about the Faith movement. I hope this book forever settles whatever questions you may have about the true nature of the movement and where it fits on the Christian spectrum. The answer is: It doesn't. The Faith movement is every bit as cultic as the teachings of the Mormons, the Jehovah's Witnesses, and Christian Science. It is not worthy of a true Christian's support.

Third, I want to clearly show observers outside the church that the Faith movement does *not* represent biblical Christianity. In the past few months more than one Faith teacher has been exposed on national TV for questionable beliefs and practices, and I want to proclaim loudly and clearly that the Faith movement long ago departed from orthodox Christianity. It emphatically does *not* represent biblical Christians. We have enough problems of our own; we can't afford to be associated with the cultic aberrations of the Faith movement.

Perhaps the burden I feel in writing this book is best summarized through the warnings of Peter, Paul, and the master teacher, Jesus Christ Himself. Take a moment to hear their words as they echo through the ages.

- *The apostle Peter said:*

There were also false prophets among the people, just as there will be false teachers among you. They will secretly introduce destructive heresies, even denying the sovereign Lord who bought them. . . . Many will follow their shameful ways and will bring the way of truth into disrepute. In their greed these teachers will exploit you with stories they have made up (2 Peter 2:1-3).

- *To this warning the apostle Paul adds these words:*

  Even from your own number men will arise and distort the truth in order to draw away disciples after them. So be on your guard! Remember that for three years I never stopped warning each of you night and day with tears (Acts 20:30,31).

- *Now hear the words of the incarnate Christ Himself:*

  Watch out for false prophets. They come to you in sheep's clothing, but inwardly they are ferocious wolves (Matthew 7:15).

It is no great joy to sound the alarm, but it is necessary. I grieve over the spiritual damage that so many have already suffered, and it is my hope that this book may rescue at least some of Christ's sheep from a terrible destiny.

May God be pleased to use this book not only to expose the false teachers who are turning truth into mythology, but also to propose solutions for a Christianity in crisis.

PART ONE

Turning the Truth into Mythology

The following tale is a composite of the erroneous
teachings of individuals like Benny Hinn, Kenneth
Copeland, Kenneth Hagin, Frederick Price, and many
others. While not all the Faith teachers hold to every
aspect of this tale, they have all made substantial
contributions to both the production and proliferation
of these aberrations and heresies.

 NCE UPON A TIME, long long ago, on a faraway planet,[1] there lived a good God. This God was very much like you and me—a Being who stands about 6'2" to 6'3", weighs a couple of hundred pounds, and has a handspan of about 9 inches.[2]

God's wisdom and power were so great that He could visualize beautiful images and then turn the images into reality[3] by utilizing a special power called the force of faith.[4]

One day this God had a cosmic brainstorm. He decided to use the force of His faith to create something superb and special.[5] He decided to bring a whole new world into existence.[6] This was not going to be just any old world; it was going to be the most fantastic world imaginable. In fact, this world would become so wonderful that it would feature an exact duplicate of the Mother Planet where God lived.[7]

After carefully visualizing every detail of this wonderful world, God went into action. Releasing the force of His faith like a whirlwind, God spoke into existence the planet He saw in His mind's eye.[8] And was God excited! Looking down with fondness on this classic new creation, He named it planet Earth.

But this was only the beginning. Suddenly a host of brilliant new ideas began to flood God's creative consciousness. He began to visualize vast oceans and springs abounding with water. He saw magnificent mountains and fertile fields. His mind produced flashes of thunder and lightning. Plants, flowers, and trees blazed in rapid succession through His thoughts. God began to visualize life replete with beautiful birds and creatures of every size and shape.

Yet there was much more to come, for after five days of vivid visualizations, God's mind moved into yet another dimension. On day six, in His mind's eye, God saw the crowning jewel of His creation. As the details coalesced in His mind, God suddenly found Himself focused on an exact duplicate of Himself.[9]

So God spoke, and suddenly out of the pristine soil of planet Earth there arose another god—a god spelled with a small "g," but a god nonetheless.[10] As the image of this little god[11] took form, God saw that He had outdone Himself. For there, before His eyes, stood another god—with a body just like His own, including size and shape.[12]

God finally had done it! He had thought the unthinkable, and by His Word of faith God had created a
creature that was not even subordinate to Himself.[13]

And was God ever glad, for now He had a col-
league whose nature was identical to His own—a god
who could think like Him, be like Him, and do almost
(but not quite) everything that He could do. God called
His carbon copy "Adam," and gave him complete dominion and authority over the entire creation.[14] This
creature had so much power that his Creator could not do
anything in the earth realm without first obtaining his
permission.[15]

Adam was truly a super-being! He could fly like
the birds and swim underwater like a fish. And that's not
all. Even without a space suit, Adam could fly through
the universe. In fact, with a single thought he could
transport himself to the moon![16]

Yet, even after creating a super-being like Adam,
God was not fully satisfied. Somehow He just knew that
a piece of the puzzle was missing. So, putting His mind
into action, God began brainstorming once more.

In a flash it dawned on Him. Adam was made in
His image, so obviously he must be as much female as he
was male. So why not separate the male part from the
female part? Not willing to waste a single moment, God
charged into action! Causing a deep sleep to fall upon
Adam, God opened him up, removed the female part
from the male part, and made a being of surpassing
beauty. He made woman—man with a womb—and called
the womb-man "Eve."[17]

But this time God had gone too far, for He had brought into existence the very beings who would one day get Him thrown off the new planet He had created. As incredible as it may seem, these super-beings would one day soon turn on their Creator and relegate Him to the status of the greatest failure of all time.

You see, long before God had visualized planet Earth into existence, He had also created another world full of beings called angels. One of these angels was a being of such breathtaking beauty and brilliance that he was named "Lucifer," the Morning Star.

Lucifer had great ambitions. In fact, he wanted to take control of everything God had ever created; he wanted to become exactly like the Most High. Lucifer tried to overthrow God with the power of words, but ended up losing.[18] Because of his treason, Lucifer was cast out of heaven and was renamed "Satan," the deceiver.

Tumbling from the Mother Planet where God lived, Satan landed on the replica that God had spoken into existence. He landed on planet Earth, where Adam and Eve would one day live. There he lay in wait for the opportunity of the ages, the opportunity to get back at God.

And then, one day, opportunity came knocking. Not long after God had brought Adam and Eve into existence, Satan spied them standing naked in the middle of the Garden of Eden.

Satan instantly transformed himself into a serpent and cunningly tricked the two little gods into committing cosmic treason. For the price of an apple, Adam and

Eve sold their godhood to Satan. And the Devil, through Adam, became the god of this world.[19]

Alas, not only did Adam and Eve lose their nature as gods, but they were infused with the very nature of Satan.[20] Adam had become the first person to be born again; he was "born" with the nature of God and "born again" with the nature of Satan.[21]

In one blinding instant, the first man and woman were transformed from divine to demonic, becoming susceptible to sin, sickness, suffering—and, more importantly, spiritual death. In fact, Eve's body (which was originally designed to give birth out of the side), underwent a radical transformation. From that moment on, she and her female offspring would bring forth children from the lower region of their anatomies.[22]

In that fateful moment, Adam and Eve were barred from Eden and God was banished from the earth. Satan now had legal rights to the earth and all her inhabitants,[23] and God was left on the outside desperately searching for a way to get back in.[24]

God, in a flash, had become the greatest failure of all time. Not only had He lost His top-ranking angel as well as at least a third of His other angels, but now He had also lost the first man, the first woman, and the earth and all its fullness![25]

But God was not yet ready to throw in the towel. Realizing that He needed man's invitation to get back into the earth, God immediately went to work. After thousands of years God finally found a man named Abraham, who took the bait and became the vehicle through which God, if He was lucky, might one day win back the world He had lost.[26]

Through Abraham a second Adam would eventually come who, if all went according to plan, would return to man his godhood and to God His good earth.

Abraham could well have told God to "bug off."[27] Instead, he decided to buy into God's deal. In fact, God and Abraham became blood brothers.[28] They forged a covenant that would gain Abraham health and wealth, and regain for God a foothold in the world He had created.[29] God's plan was to make Abraham the father of all nations and to produce from his seed another Adam who would regain the turf lost by the first Adam.

In keeping with His Word, God made Abraham very, very wealthy. Then, once again, He proceeded to visualize. Through God's mind raced images of a brand-new Adam—a man who would one day restore Him to His rightful place in the universe and who would forever banish His archrival, Satan, from the kingdom.

And then it happened! One day the image of this Savior coalesced in God's mind. Without hesitation, God began speaking into existence the picture of the Redeemer He had painted on the canvas of His consciousness.[30] Excitedly, God positively confessed, "The Messiah is coming, the Messiah is coming!"[31]

As God's Spirit hovered over a young woman named Mary, the confession began to take shape before His very eyes.[32] The spoken Word became legs, arms, eyes, and hair. And then suddenly there emerged the body of the second Adam.[33]

The second Adam was named Jesus. As Abraham's descendant, Jesus was wealthy and prosperous. He lived in a big house,[34] handled big money,[35] and even wore designer clothes.[36] In fact, Jesus was so wealthy that He needed a treasurer to keep track of all His money.[37]

Jesus, who was a whiz at speaking things into existence,[38] showed His disciples how to master the art of positive confession.[39] Thus they too enjoyed unlimited health and wealth. Some of His followers caught on so well that they became rich beyond comprehension. The apostle Paul, for example, had so much money that government officials would work feverishly to try to get a bribe out of him.[40]

Jesus also overcame every trick and temptation that Satan could throw His way. Even though He never claimed to be God, Jesus succeeded in living a life of sinless perfection.[41] When all was said and done, Jesus passed the test that the first Adam had failed.

And then, in the prime of His life, Jesus entered a garden—a garden much like Eden, where the first Adam had lost his godhood. In this garden, called Gethsemane, Jesus moved into the final stages of a process that would transform Him from an immortal man to a satanic being[42] and would, in turn, recreate men as little gods[43] who would no longer be subject to the scourge of sin, sickness, and suffering.[44]

As part of the process, Jesus would have to die a double death on the cross. He would have to die spiritually as well as physically. If physical death had been enough, the two thieves on the cross could have atoned for the sins of mankind.[45] No, the real key was spiritual death and suffering in hell.

One day, upon a cruel cross, the crystal Christ—the paragon of virtue—was transformed into a defiled demoniac. The lamb became a serpent[46] and was ushered into the very bowels of the earth. There Christ was tortured by Satan and his minions.[47] And all hell laughed.[48]

Little did Satan know, however, that the last laugh would be on him. For just as Adam had fallen for Satan's trap in Eden, now Satan had fallen for God's trap in hell.[49]

You see, Satan had blown it on a technicality. He had dragged Jesus into hell illegally.[50] Satan had completely forgotten to consider that Jesus had not actually sinned. Jesus had merely become sin as a result of the sin of others. Alas, Satan and his demonic hosts had tortured the emaciated, poured out, little, wormy spirit of Christ without legal rights.[51]

This was exactly the opening God had been looking for. Seizing the moment, God spoke His faith-filled words into the bowels of the earth. Suddenly the twisted, death-wracked spirit of Jesus began to fill out and come back to life. He began to look like something the Devil had never before seen.[52]

There, in the sinister presence of the evil one himself, Jesus began to flex His spiritual muscles. As a horde of whimpering demons looked on, Jesus whipped the Devil in his own backyard. He snatched Satan's keys and emerged from hell as a born-again man.[53]

God had pulled off the coup of the ages. Not only had He tricked Satan out of his lordship by using Jesus as the bait, but He had also caught Satan on a technicality through which Jesus could be born again.

But that's not all. Because Jesus was re-created from a satanic being to an incarnation of God, you too can become an incarnation—as much an incarnation as Jesus Christ of Nazareth![54] And, as an incarnation of

God, you can have unlimited health and unlimited
wealth—a palace like the Taj Mahal with a Rolls Royce
in your driveway.[55] You are a little messiah running
around on earth![56]

All it takes is to recognize your own divinity. You
too can harness the force of faith. Never again will you
have to pray, "Thy will be done."[57] Rather, your Word
is God's command.[58] By using your tongue to release the
force of faith, you can speak whatsoever you desire into
existence.[59] Then you can live happily ever after on this
planet of prosperity.

———————————✍————————————

Well, there you have it—the skin of the truth stuffed
with a monstrous lie! What you have just read is a composite
of the writings and ramblings of some of the most powerful
teachers operating within the Christian church today—
people who have systematically turned God's truth into mythology.

What you will discover as you read on is so horrifying
that your natural inclination may be disbelief or even denial.
But I assure you that what I am communicating is not based
on hype or sensationalism. Rather, it is painstakingly accurate and thoroughly documented.

So prepare yourself as we descend for awhile into the
kingdom of the cults.

The Cast of Characters

*P*erhaps the best place to begin our investigation is with a brief examination of the chief teachers of the Faith message. It is important to note that the bulk of their theology can be traced directly to the cultic teachings of New Thought metaphysics. Much of the theology of the Faith movement can also be found in such cults as Religious Science, Christian Science, and the Unity School of Christianity.

Long before the Faith movement became a dominant force within the Christian church, Phineas Parkhurst Quimby (1802–1866), the father of New Thought, was popularizing the notion that sickness and suffering ultimately have their origin in incorrect thinking.[1] Quimby's followers held that man could create his own reality through the power of positive affirmation (confession).[2] Metaphysical practitioners have long taught adherents to visualize health and wealth, and then to affirm or confess them with their mouths so that the intangible images may be transformed into tangible realities.[3]

Although proponents of Faith theology have attempted to sanitize the metaphysical concept of the "power of mind" by substituting in its stead the "force of faith," for all practical purposes they have made a distinction without a true difference. New Thought writer Warren Felt Evans, for example, wrote that "faith is the most intense form of mental action."[4] In treating a patient, Evans commented that "the effect of the suggestion [or positive affirmation that the patient is well] is the result of the faith of the subject, for it is always proportioned to the degree in which the patient *believes* what you say."[5] Likewise, H. Emilie Cady, a well-known writer for Charles and Myrtle Fillmore's Unity School of Christianity, explained that "our affirming, backed by faith, is the link that connects our conscious human need with His power and supply."[6] Cady also claimed that "there is power in our word of faith to bring all good things right into our everyday life."[7] Such statements demonstrate that the distinction between the "mind" of metaphysics and the "faith" of Faith theology is little more than cosmetic.

There is no denying that much of Faith theology is derived directly from metaphysics. Some of the *substance*, *style*, and *scams* endemic to the movement, however, can be traced to teachings and practices expressed primarily by certain post-World-War-II faith healers and revivalists operating within Pentecostal circles.[8] With regard to *substance*, for example, both Kenneth Copeland and Kenneth Hagin point to T.L. Osborn and William Branham as true men of God who greatly influenced their lives and ministries. Of course, Osborn himself has consistently followed E.W. Kenyon's Scripture-twisting practices,[9] and Branham has (among other things) denounced the doctrine of the trinity as coming directly from the devil.[10]

Unfortunately, Hagin and Copeland are not alone in affirming Branham; Faith proponent Benny Hinn gives him hearty approval as well.[11] When it comes to *style*, however, Hinn gravitates more toward such faith healers as Aimee Semple McPherson and Kathryn Kuhlman. The influence of these women on Hinn's life and ministry is so great that he still visits their gravesites and experiences "the anointing," which he claims emanates from their bones.[12] In addition, Hinn has given his endorsement to notorious revivalist A.A. Allen,[13] a huckster if there ever was one.

This brings us to the third "s," the *scams*. Faith teachers such as Robert Tilton and Marilyn Hickey have embraced many of the practices pioneered by Pentecostal preachers such as Allen and Oral Roberts, as I will show later.

Oral Roberts, you may recall, is the man who claimed that Jesus told him God had chosen him to find an effective treatment for cancer. In a lengthy appeal, Roberts avowed that the Lord told him, "I would not have had you and your partners build the 20-story research tower unless I was going to give you a plan that will attack cancer." Roberts then said that Jesus instructed him to tell his partners that "this is not Oral Roberts asking [for the money] but their Lord."[14]

(The project was completed, but has since been "shut down and sold to a group of investors for commercial development."[15] And no cure for cancer was found.)

In like fashion, Allen scammed his followers by asserting that he could command God to "turn dollar bills into twenties."[16] He also was known to have urged his followers to send for his "prayer cloths anointed with the Miracle Oil"[17] and offered "Miracle tent shavings" as points of contact for personal miracles.[18] Allen even "launched a brief 'raise the dead' program."[19] Of course, it died.

Allen was eventually expelled from the Assemblies of God denomination when he jumped bail after being arrested for drunk driving.[20] In 1970 he died from what "news accounts report [as] sclerosis of the liver."[21]

As we examine the primary purveyors of Faith theology, we will see living proof of the maxim that "error begets error and heresy begets heresy." If, for example, you examine the cultic progression of E.W. Kenyon's theology, you will discover that his original deviations from orthodox Christianity were minor compared to those which characterized the later stages of his ministry. And with each of Kenyon's successive disciples, the errors become ever more pronounced.

Hagin, who popularized Kenyon, not only expanded Kenyon's errors but added to them as well. The progression from bad to worse has continued with people like Kenneth Copeland and Charles Capps, and is now sinking to new depths through ministry leaders such as Frederick Price, Benny Hinn, and Robert Tilton.

Twisted texts, make-believe miracles, and counterfeit Christs are common denominators of the Faith movement's cast of characters. Here is a brief overview,* with detailed information on each person appearing in subsequent chapters and in a special section of this book titled "Kenyon and the Leading Proponents of a Different Gospel."

Essek William Kenyon

Essek William Kenyon, whose life and ministry were enormously impacted by such cults as Science of Mind, the Unity School of Christianity, Christian Science, and New Thought metaphysics, is the true father of the modern-day Faith movement. Many of the phrases popularized by today's prosperity teachers, such as "What I confess, I possess," were originally coined by Kenyon. Kenneth Hagin drew heavily from Kenyon's work, including his statement, "Every man who has been born again is an incarnation, and Christianity is a miracle. The believer is as much an incarnation as was Jesus of Nazareth."

Kenneth E. Hagin

Not only does Hagin boast of alleged visits to heaven and hell, but he recounts numerous out-of-body experiences as well.

On one occasion, Hagin claims he was in the middle of a sermon when suddenly he was transported back in time.

---

* Because this section is intended as an overview, the direct quotations appearing here are not formally documented. All of them will appear later in the book in an expanded form and will be documented at that time.

He ended up in the backseat of a car and watched as a young woman from his church committed adultery with the driver. The entire experience lasted about 15 minutes, after which Hagin abruptly found himself back in church, summoning his parishioners to prayer.

Virtually every major Faith teacher has been impacted by Hagin, including one of his star pupils, Kenneth Copeland.

Kenneth Copeland

Kenneth Copeland got his start in ministry by memorizing Hagin's messages. It wasn't long before he had learned enough from Hagin to establish his own cult. To say his teachings are heretical would be an understatement. Copeland brashly pronounces God to be the greatest failure of all time, boldly proclaims that "Satan *conquered* Jesus on the Cross," and describes Christ in hell as an "emaciated, poured out, little, wormy spirit."

More of Copeland's cult and its occult connections are documented later in this book, including parallels between Copeland and Mormon founder Joseph Smith. Yet despite the evidence, Benny Hinn ominously warned that "those who attack Kenneth Copeland are attacking the very presence of God." (For further information regarding the definition of "cult" see chapter 2.)

Benny Hinn

Benny Hinn is one of the fastest-rising stars on the Faith circuit. According to an October 5, 1992, article in *Christianity Today*, sales of his books in the last year-and-a-half have exceeded those of James Dobson and Charles Swindoll combined. While claiming to be "under the anointing," Hinn has uttered some of the most unbelievable statements imaginable, including the claim that the Holy Spirit revealed to him that women were originally designed to give birth out of their sides.

Despite his outrageous antics, Hinn has managed to gain wide acceptance and visibility within the evangelical Christian church. His platform on the Trinity Broadcasting Network, as well as his promotion by a mainstream Christian publisher, has catapulted him into prime-time visibility.

Whether Hinn is referring to his family history or his rendezvous with the Holy Spirit, his stories seldom stack up with the facts. A case in point are the thousands of healings claimed by Hinn. Recently he sent me three examples—presumably, the cream of the crop—as proof of his miracle-working power. One of the cases involved a man who was supposedly healed of colon cancer. A medically naive person reading the pathology report may well see the notation "no evidence of malignancy" and be duped into thinking that a bona fide healing had indeed taken place. The Christian Research Institute's medical consultant, however, noted that the colon tumor in question was *surgically* removed rather than miraculously healed! The other two cases had comparably serious problems.

Frederick K.C. Price

Frederick Price is the most notable of a growing number of African-American prosperity preachers. His church in Los Angeles now claims some 16,000 members. He is seen nationally on television and has referred to himself as the "chief exponent of Name It and Claim It." Price has added his own unique twists to Faith theology by asserting that Jesus took on the nature of Satan *prior* to the crucifixion and by claiming that the Lord's Prayer is not for Christians today. Despite telling his followers that he doesn't allow sickness in his home, Price's wife has been treated for cancer in her pelvic area. Referring to his wealth, Price says the reason he drives a Rolls Royce is that he is following in Jesus' steps.

John Avanzini

John Avanzini is billed by his Faith peers as a recognized authority on biblical economics. The truth, however, is that he is an authority at separating poor people from their money. Whenever Faith teachers need money, they inevitably call on "Brother John." Armed with a full range of Bible-twisting tricks, he tells the unsuspecting that "a greater than a lottery has come. His name is Jesus!"

According to Avanzini, if Jesus was rich, we should be rich as well. He recasts Christ into a mirror image of himself—complete with designer clothes, a big house, and a wealthy, well-financed advance team. Thinking otherwise, Avanzini claims, will prevent Christians from reaping the prosperity God has laid out for them.

Avanzini runs the gamut from teaching people how to get their hands on the "wealth of the wicked" to what might best be described as his "hundredfold hoax." When it comes to taking money from God's people, few can match the effectiveness of John Avanzini. There is an exception, however; his name is Robert Tilton.

Robert Tilton

Robert Tilton hit the big time as a fisher of funds by developing a religious "infomercial" called "Success-N-Life." It all began when he traveled to Hawaii to hear from the Lord. Says Tilton, "If I'm going to go to the cross, I'm going to go in a pretty place. Not some dusty place like Jerusalem. That's gravel is all that place is." While languishing in his exotic wilderness, Tilton "realized his mission was to persuade the poor to give what they could to him—God's surrogate—so they too could be blessed."

Then, one day, Tilton tuned in to Dave Del Dotto's real estate infomercials. The rest is history. Tilton used what he saw as a prototype for building an empire that takes in as much as 65 million dollars per year.

It now appears that Tilton's empire may dwindle rapidly amid reports of scandal and a variety of lawsuits (additional information later). Responding to charges that the prayer request letters he promises to pray over end up in dumpsters, Tilton claims, "I laid on top of those prayer requests so much that the chemicals actually got into my blood stream, and . . . I had two small strokes in my brain." If that's not outrageous enough for you, read on.

Marilyn Hickey

Marilyn Hickey, much like Tilton, employs a broad range of tactics to induce followers into sending her money. Among her many ploys are anointed prayer cloths, ceremonial breastplates, and ropes that can be used as points of contact. In one of her appeal letters, Hickey promises she will slip into a ceremonial breastplate, "press your prayer request to [her] heart," and "place your requests on [her] shoulders"—all for a suggested donation.

For the most part, Hickey's teachings are recycled from other prosperity preachers such as Tilton, Hagin, and Copeland. Her message is peppered with such Faith jargon as "the God-kind of faith," "confession brings possession," and "receiving follows giving."

Paul Yonggi Cho (David Cho)

Paul Yonggi Cho—pastor of the world's largest church, located in Seoul, South Korea—claims to have received his call to preach from Jesus Christ Himself, who supposedly appeared to him dressed like a fireman. Cho has packaged his faith formulas under the label of "fourth-dimensional power." He is well aware of his link to occultism, arguing that if Buddhists and Yoga practitioners can accomplish their objectives through fourth-dimensional powers, then Christians should be able to accomplish much more by using the same means. In case you are tempted to confuse the size of

Cho's following with the truth of his teachings, understand that the Buddhist version of "name it and claim it" has an even larger following than does Cho's version.

Cho recently made the news by changing his name from Paul to David. As Cho tells the story, God showed him that Paul Cho had to die and David Cho was to be resurrected in his place. According to Cho, God Himself came up with his new name.

Charles Capps

Charles Capps was ordained a minister in the International Convention of Faith Churches and Ministers by Kenneth Copeland. He derived his teachings directly from Kenneth Hagin. This dangerous combination has led Capps to make some of the most blasphemous statements in Faith lore. Capps has gone so far as to teach that Jesus was the product of God's Positive Confession. When drawn to their logical conclusions, Capps's statements regarding the incarnation deny the very preexistence of Christ. Ironically, in the same chapter that Capps communicates this heresy, he writes, "If you continually sit under teaching that is wrong, the spirit of error will be transmitted to you."

Capps's teachings range from the blasphemous to the ridiculous. For example, he claims that if someone says, "I'm just dying to do that" or "That just tickled me to death," his or her statements will literally come true. According to Capps, this is precisely why members of the human race now live only about 70 years instead of 900 years, as was the case with Adam.

Jerry Savelle

Jerry Savelle has made his fortune by mimicking virtually all of the Faith teachers previously identified. His greatest claim to fame, however, may be his ability to imitate Kenneth Copeland. Savelle regurgitates virtually every heresy in the Faith movement.

With regard to health, Savelle boasts that sickness and disease cannot enter his world. As for wealth, he says that words can speak your world into existence. Savelle now peddles his books and tapes to 36 countries at the astonishing rate of some 300,000 copies per year.

Morris Cerullo

Morris Cerullo claims that he gave up a driving ambition to become Governor of New Jersey in order to become a minister of the gospel. He purports to have first met God at the age of eight. Since then his life has been one remarkable experience after another: He says he was taught by leading rabbis, led out of a Jewish orphanage by two angelic beings, transported to heaven for a face-to-face meeting with God, and told he would be capable of revealing the future.

Cerullo, you may recall, is the Faith teacher who boasted, "You're not looking at Morris Cerullo—you're looking at God. You're looking at Jesus." (More on this and other claims by Cerullo in later chapters.) On another occasion, Cerullo claimed God was directing him to say, "Would you surrender your pocketbooks unto Me, saith God, and let Me be the Lord of your pocketbooks. . . . Yea, so be thou obedient unto My voice."

Paul Crouch

Paul Crouch and his wife, Jan, are the founders of the Trinity Broadcasting Network (TBN), which today has an estimated net worth of half a billion dollars. As Crouch himself puts it, "God has, indeed, given us the MOST POWERFUL VOICE in the history of the WORLD." Unfortunately, that voice is frequently being used to promote teachings straight from the kingdom of the cults. Crouch's influence has become so vast that he can now raise as much as 50 million dollars during a single "Praise-a-Thon." What many of those who support TBN do not know, however, is that part of this money goes to promoting cultic groups and individuals who not only deny the trinity but claim that this essential of Christianity is a pagan doctrine. It is indeed ironic that a broadcasting network called "Trinity" would promote anti-trinitarian doctrine.

To those who would speak out against the false teachings proliferated on his network, Crouch has this to say: "I think they're damned and on their way to hell; and I don't think there's any redemption for them." Shortly after I met with Crouch to prove that the Faith movement compromises essential Christian doctrine, Crouch looked into the lens of the television camera and angrily declared, "If you want to criticize Ken Copeland for his preaching on faith, or Dad Hagin, get out of my life! I don't even want to talk to you or hear you. I don't want to see your ugly face. Get out of my face, in Jesus' name."

Sadly, Crouch refers to the Faith message as a "revival of truth . . . restored by a few precious men."

Conclusion

Tragically, these purveyors of error have become adept at misleading their followers with a message that sounds authentic but is in reality a counterfeit. They point to Scripture, produce "miracles," and operate under the banner "Jesus is Lord."

But think of the words of Jesus Himself when He proclaimed, "Many will say to me on that day, 'Lord, Lord, did we not prophesy in your name, and in your name drive out demons and perform many miracles?' Then I will tell them plainly, 'I never knew you. Away from me, you evildoers!' " (Matthew 7:22,23).

Cult or Cultic?

*W*hile the Faith movement is undeniably cultic—
and particular groups within the movement are clearly cults—
it should be pointed out that *there are many sincere, born-
again believers within the movement.* I cannot overemphasize
this crucial point. These believers, for the most part, seem to
be wholly unaware of the movement's cultic theology.

I have personally met several dear people who fall into
this category. I question neither their faith nor their devotion
to Christ. They represent that segment of the movement
which, for whatever reason, has not comprehended or internalized the heretical teachings set forth by the leadership of
their respective groups. In many instances, they are new
converts to Christianity who have not yet been grounded in
their faith. But this is not always the case.

I remember with great fondness, for example, the
kindred spirit I shared with two ladies who participated in my
Personal Witness Training program in Atlanta, Georgia. Year
in and year out, these ladies would diligently and faithfully
work to equip church members to effectively communicate
the good news of the gospel. They were as committed to
Christ as any two people I have ever met; yet they were both
staunch supporters of Kenneth Copeland and Kenneth Hagin.
I can still recall the conversations we had in 1985 concerning
this topic. What stands out most vividly in my mind was their

honest conviction that these men did not teach what I claimed they did.

Over the years I have received hundreds of letters from people immersed in the Faith movement who were completely oblivious to the rank heresy they were being fed—individuals who have said, "Until I saw the evidence with my very own eyes, I was not willing to accept it." For this reason, we must take care to judge the *theology* of the Faith movement rather than those being seduced by it.

What Makes a Cult?

Christ Himself, in His magnificent Sermon on the Mount, taught us not to judge self-righteously or hypocritically. As frail mortals, we can only look on the outside; it is God who discerns the intent of the heart (1 Chronicles 28:9; Jeremiah 17:10).

Having said that, however, let me reiterate that those who knowingly accept Faith theology are clearly embracing a different gospel, which is in reality no gospel at all. Let us never forget that Scripture admonishes us in the strongest of terms to test all things by the Word of God and to hold fast to that which is good (1 Thessalonians 5:21; cf. Acts 17:11). As Jude exhorts us, we must contend earnestly for the faith (Jude 3).

By the time you finish reading this book, you will have come face-to-face with detailed documentation which conclusively demonstrates that many of the groups within the Faith movement are cults. Therefore we need to understand exactly what is meant by the term "cult." For the purposes of this writing, I will focus on two primary ways in which a cult may be defined.

First, a cult may be defined from a sociological perspective. According to sociologist J. Milton Yinger, "The term cult is used in many different ways, usually with the connotations of small size, search for a mystical experience, lack of an organizational structure, and presence of a charismatic leader."[1] For the most part, sociologists have tried to avoid negative overtones in their descriptions of cults. The same cannot be said, however, for the media-driven public at large.

According to religion observer J. Gordon Melton, the 1970's saw the emergence of "secular anti-cultists" who "began to speak of 'destructive cults,' groups which hypnotized or brainwashed recruits, destroyed their ability to make rational judgments and turned them into slaves of the group's leader."[2] Cults of this variety are viewed as both deceptive and manipulative, with the groups' leadership exercising control over virtually every aspect of the members' lives. Furthermore, converts are typically cut off from all former associations—including relatives and friends—and are expected to give their complete devotion, loyalty, and commitment to the cult.[3] Examples of cults labeled as sociologically destructive range from the Hare Krishnas to Reverend Sun Myung Moon's Unification Church to the Family of Love led by "Moses" David Berg.

A second way to define a cult is from a theological perspective. A cult, in this sense, is deemed a pseudo-Christian group. As such, it claims to be Christian but denies one or more of the essential doctrines of historic Christianity; these doctrines focus on such matters as the meaning of faith, the nature of God, and the person and work of Jesus Christ. Denver Seminary professor Gordon Lewis succinctly summarizes it this way:

> A cult, then, is any religious movement which claims the backing of Christ or the Bible, but distorts the central message of Christianity by 1) an additional revelation, and 2) by displacing a fundamental tenet of the faith with a secondary matter.[4]

Christian Research Institute founder Walter Martin adds that "a cult might also be defined as a group of people gathered about a specific person or person's misinterpretation of the Bible."[5] From a theological perspective, cults include organizations such as the Church of Jesus Christ of Latter-day Saints, the Watchtower Bible and Tract Society, and the Church of Religious Science.

A primary characteristic of cults in general is the practice of taking biblical texts out of context in order to develop pretexts for their theological perversions.[6] In addition, cults have virtually made an art form out of using Christian terminology, all the while pouring their own meanings into the words.[7] For example, while practically all cults laud the name "Jesus," they preach a Jesus vastly different from the Jesus of the historic Christian faith. As Jesus Christ Himself put it, the real litmus test is "Who do you say I am?" (Matthew 16:15).

Mormons answer the question by saying that Jesus is merely the spirit-brother of Lucifer. Jehovah's Witnesses assert that Jesus is Michael the Archangel. New Agers often refer to Jesus as an avatar or mystical messenger. As blasphemous as all of this is, however, many Faith adherents actually reduce Jesus to an even lower level. For them, He is no more an incarnation of God than is any believer.

The Difference Between "Cultic" and a "Cult"

Given these definitions of a cult, it is completely justified to characterize *particular* groups within the Faith movement as cults—either theologically or sociologically or, in some cases, both. However, in classifying the Faith movement in general, it is more precise to use the term "cultic," which essentially means "cult-like."

This distinction clarifies that "cults" (from a theological perspective) refer to groups with uniform sets of doctrines and rigidly defined organizational structures; they are monolithic. *Movements*, on the other hand, are multi-faceted and diverse in their beliefs, teachings, and practices. Thus, while certain groups within the Faith movement can be properly classified as cults, the word "cultic" more aptly describes the movement as a whole.

To put it another way, the "Faith phenomena" collectively reflects the sort of diversity found in movements (like the New Age movement), as opposed to mirroring the homogeneous and relatively static character of cults like the Mormon Church and the Watchtower organization.

The Faith movement, as all other movements, is composed of various groups, each with its own distinctives, but which share a common theme, vision, and goal.[8] For this reason, the numerous Faith churches, teachers, and adherents should be judged on an individual basis. Each should rise or fall on his or her own merits.

Kenneth Copeland Ministries, headed by Kenneth and Gloria Copeland, for example, bears all the marks of a cult. First, it has a formalized hierarchical structure; it boasts a centralized organizational facility; and it is equipped with a publishing arm complete with a distribution mechanism. Additionally, as will be fully documented, the Copelands bludgeon many of the essentials of historic Christianity, preaching their own deviant brand of antibiblical theology that the vast majority of their devotees accept without question. Furthermore, fervent followers consider the Copelands to be the final authority in matters of faith and practice. Thus we can legitimately characterize the Copelands as being cult leaders who, in the vernacular of the apostle Paul, represent "a different gospel—which is really no gospel at all" (Galatians 1:6,7).

The Error Continuum

In combating the errors which confront Christianity,

it is important to understand that *all errors are not created equal*; some are clearly more damaging than others.

It may be helpful to picture these errors as resting on a continuum that stretches from the outright silly to the gravely serious. Benny Hinn's comment about women originally giving birth out of their sides, for example, can be considered a *silly* statement—which, while nonbiblical, poses no direct threat to essential Christian doctrine.[9]

On the other hand, such teachings as God possessing a physical body, humans created as exact duplicates of God, and Christ's transformation into a satanic being fall squarely on the other end of the "error spectrum." They are *heretical*, which is another way of saying that they directly oppose the clear teaching of Scripture on matters of essential importance as highlighted in the creeds and councils of the church.

Classifying errors can oftentimes be a tricky business, as a sizable gray area exists between the serious and the not-so-serious type of error. Nevertheless, such difficulties should not discourage us from judging whether certain teachings and practices are faithful to the Word of God and the doctrines of historic Christianity. If anything, they ought to move us to spend more time in carefully thinking about the things we hear daily and hold dearly.[10]

You, the reader, will inevitably need to decide whether you think the Faith movement is cultic or Christian. You must decide whether these doctrines are true or false or some muddy mixture of both.

If you decide that this movement is a valid expression of Christianity, then in all fairness you should also embrace as fellow believers the Mormons, the Jehovah's Witnesses, the Christian Scientists, and a host of other groups normally thought of as cults.

That is the choice before you.

3

Charismatic or Cultic?

I have become both weary and wary of those who use the perversions of the Faith movement to drive a wedge between charismatic and noncharismatic Christians.[1] Frankly, this is both counterproductive and divisive, for the Faith movement is not charismatic; it is cultic.

I want to make it crystal clear that the issues discussed in this book do not involve an "in-house" debate among committed Christians over such matters as the perpetuity of spiritual gifts. This book is not about whether you speak in tongues or whether God still heals today. It is not about the way you were baptized. It is not about whether you are "pre-trib," "mid-trib," or "post-trib."

I want to stress that sincere and dedicated believers can differ in good conscience when it comes to peripheral issues. They cannot do so, however, when it comes to the primary doctrines that separate Christianity from the kingdom of the cults. When it comes to such matters as the fabric of faith, the nature of God, and the atonement of Christ, there must be unity. As Saint Augustine so aptly put it: "In essentials, unity; in nonessentials, liberty; and in all things, charity."

For the most part, charismatics and noncharismatics are unified when it comes to the essentials of the historic

Christian faith. Their primary differences involve nonessential Christian doctrine. Therefore, while we may vigorously debate secondary matters within the faith, we must never divide over them.

Not so, however, when it comes to the Faith movement; there we must draw the line. The Faith movement has systematically subverted the very essence of Christianity so as to present us with a counterfeit Christ and a counterfeit Christianity. Therefore standing against the theology of the Faith movement does *not* divide; rather, it unites believers.

It would be a grave error to equate the Faith movement with the charismatic movement. It is indeed a travesty that the Faith teachers have been able to cleverly disguise themselves as charismatics, thereby tarnishing the reputation of a legitimate movement within Christianity.

Furthermore, it is tragic that a number of noncharismatics have attempted to use the Faith teachers to prove that the charismatic movement is in chaos. In fact, some have used the inane statements of the Faith teachers to label charismatics as having zeal without knowledge and enthusiasm without enlightenment—in short, being keen but clueless. This, of course, is clearly untrue.

Are we prepared to call a man like Dr. Gordon Fee, one of the foremost Bible scholars today, "keen but clueless"? Are we going to say that Dr. Walter Martin, founder of the Christian Research Institute and father of the modern-day countercult revolution, had zeal but not in accordance with knowledge? Do we really want to categorize Chuck Smith, pastor of Calvary Chapel of Costa Mesa, California, and founder of one of the largest and most effective Christian movements in modern-day history, as having enthusiasm without enlightenment?

Some of today's clearest thinkers are charismatic Christians: men like Dr. Paul Walker of the Mount Paran Church of God in Atlanta, Georgia; Dr. Mark Rutland of

Calvary Assembly in Orlando, Florida; Elliot Miller, editor of the *Christian Research Journal* and author of *A Crash Course on the New Age Movement*, considered by many to be the definitive work on the subject; Michael Green, noted author and rector of St. Aldate's in Oxford; and George Carey, respected theologian and Archbishop of Canterbury; along with a host of others.

Moreover, some of the most scholarly rebuttals of Faith theology have come from within the charismatic movement itself. Notable examples include the works of Walter Martin,[2] Gordon Fee,[3] Dan McConnell,[4] Charles Farah,[5] Elliot Miller,[6] H. Terris Neuman,[7] and Dale H. Simmons.[8]

What is especially tragic, however, is that a wide assortment of Christian men and women (both charismatic and noncharismatic) are endorsing leaders within the Faith movement. It is incredible to think that this cultic system has become so powerful that otherwise credible Christians have given it carte blanche to proliferate its poisonous doctrinal perversions to an unsuspecting public.

It is mind-boggling that some Christian publishers will not only publish but defend the cultic teachings of Faith preachers. Perhaps even worse, Christian broadcasters are all too eager to bring some of these men and women, live and in color, into the homes of millions of viewers every day. If Christians are going to publish and promote such teachings, they might as well begin broadcasting programs produced by the Unity School of Christianity or the Church of Religious Science.

Years ago, when Moody Press realized that one of its authors had traded Christianity for the kingdom of the cults, they immediately pulled his book from circulation. They prudently refused to promote a man whose teachings were at least indirectly responsible for tragic physical consequences toward as many as 90 men, women, and children.[9]

In sharp contrast, when certain publishers and producers are warned about the cultic theology of people like Benny Hinn, they immediately come to their defense.

One is left to wonder where the heroes of the faith are. Where are those who are willing to stand for integrity? Where are those men and women who, like the saints of old, are willing to face "the tyrant's brandished steel, the lion's gory mane, and the fires of a thousand deaths" to preserve the faith once for all delivered to the saints? If Christians were willing to give their very lives in days gone by, shouldn't we be willing to sacrifice our positions, platforms, and popularity in order to preserve the faith?

We are currently faced with a crisis within Christianity. But this crisis is not the fault of the charismatic renewal. Rather, it is focused on a life-and-death struggle between orthodoxy and heresy—between the kingdom of Christ and the kingdom of the cults.

4

Charting the Course

*A*s I began writing *Christianity in Crisis*, I had three basic objectives in mind: 1) To pen this book in a readable style so you not only begin, but finish; 2) To provide you with complete and accurate documentation; 3) To present this information in a memorable format.

All of memory can be boiled down to the process of making associations. Simply stated, making an association means joining or connecting two pieces of information so that when you think of one, the other also comes to mind. It could be a name and a face, a state and its capital, or a chapter in the Bible and what is contained in it.

There are many ways to make memorable associations. One way is to use acronyms. The word H-O-M-E-S, for example, can be used in the following way to remind you of the names of the Great Lakes.

H uron

O ntario

M ichigan

E rie

S uperior

In a similar way I developed the acronym F-L-A-W-S to make the material in *Christianity in Crisis* memorable.*

In each of the next five parts I will use one letter from the acronym F-L-A-W-S to contrast "four spiritual laws" of the Christian faith with "four spiritual flaws" of the Faith movement. The diagram on the next page will help us chart our course through the remainder of the book.

Part 2: Faith in Faith

The "F" in F-L-A-W-S will serve to remind you of the word *Faith*. In chapters 5-8 we will look at the Faith movement's metaphysical concept of faith. The four spiritual flaws in this regard can be summarized as follows:

▪ *The force of faith.* Faith is a force and words are the containers of the force. Thus, through the power of words, you create your own reality.

▪ *The formula of faith.* Formulas are the name of the game in Faith theology. Through them you can literally "write your own ticket with God."

▪ *The faith of God.* The god of the Faith movement is no god at all. You may be amazed to learn that he is a mere faith being who has to operate in accordance with universal laws of faith.

▪ *The Faith Hall of Fame.* For the Faith teachers to stand, Job has to fall. Thus they induct Job into the "Faith Hall of Shame" and induct themselves into the "Faith Hall of Fame."

Part 3: Little Gods or Little Frauds?

The "L" in F-L-A-W-S will remind you of the words *Little gods*. In chapters 9–12 we will take a look at the

---

* For more information on how you can learn to remember things quickly and retain them forever, contact Memory Dynamics, Box 667, San Juan Capistrano, CA 92693-0667. Phone (714) 589-1504.

FLAWS

F AITH IN FAITH	L ITTLE GODS OR LITTLE FRAUDS	A TONEMENT ATROCITIES	W EALTH & WANT	S ICKNESS & SUFFERING
FORCE OF FAITH	DEIFICATION OF MAN	RE-CREATION ON THE CROSS	CULTURAL CONFORMITY	SYMPTOMS & SICKNESS
FORMULA OF FAITH	DEMOTION OF GOD	REDEMPTION IN HELL	CONS AND COVER-UPS	SATAN & SICKNESS
FAITH OF FAITH	DEIFICATION OF SATAN	REBIRTH IN HELL	COVENANT CONTRACT	SIN & SICKNESS
FAITH OF GOD	DEMOTION OF SATAN			SOVEREIGNTY & SICKNESS
FAITH HALL OF FAME	DEMOTION OF CHRIST	REINCARNATION	CONTEXT CONTEXT CONTEXT	SICKNESS

FLAWS

54

Faith movement's concept of men as little gods. The four spiritual flaws can be summarized as follows:

- *The deification of man.* In Faith theology man was created as an exact duplicate of God, including size and shape.

- *The demotion of God.* The Faith movement not only deifies man but also demotes God to the status of a bumbling bellhop at the beck and call of His creation.

- *The deification of Satan.* Satan is deified as the God of this world and is positioned with so much power that he could manage to "turn the light off in God."

- *The demotion of Christ.* All cults and world religions compromise the deity of the Lord Jesus Christ. The Faith movement is no exception.

Part 4: Atonement Atrocities

The "A" in F-L-A-W-S will remind you of Atonement Atrocities. In chapters 13–16 you will get a full-orbed perspective of how the Faith movement has trashed the crux of Christianity—the atonement of the Lord Jesus Christ. The four spiritual flaws can be summarized as follows:

- *Re-creation on the cross.* On the cross, Jesus was re-created from divine to demonic, taking on the very nature of Satan.

- *Redemption in hell.* In the words of one Faith teacher, "Satan *conquered* Jesus on the Cross." In the words of yet another, "If the punishment for sin was to die on a cross . . . the two thieves could have paid your price."

- *Rebirth in hell.* In hell, the "emaciated, poured out, little, wormy spirit" of Jesus was born again. "The trap was set for Satan and Jesus was the bait."

- *Reincarnation.* Jesus was reincarnated from demonic to divine and then emerged from hell as an incarnation of

God. When you are born again, you too are reincarnated from demonic to divine, becoming "as much an incarnation as was Jesus of Nazareth."

Part 5: Wealth and Want

The "W" in F-L-A-W-S will remind you of Wealth and Want. In chapters 17–20 we will see that Faith theology transforms Christianity from a gospel of grace to a gospel of greed. The four spiritual flaws in this regard are as follows:

▪ *Cultural conformity.* Rather than transforming our culture to Christ, prosperity preachers are hawking a Jesus who "wears designer clothes."

▪ *Cons and cover-ups.* The cons and cover-ups of the Faith movement are so outrageous that you have to read them yourself to believe them.

▪ *Covenant-contract.* The Faith concept of Wealth and Want finds its genesis in a covenant that God made with Abram. God supposedly told Abram, "I'm making a proposition to you. You can tell me to bug off if you don't like it."

▪ *Context, context, context.* Faith teachers are masters at attributing esoteric or mystical meanings to biblical passages. Among other things, they claim to prove that Jesus and the disciples were fabulously wealthy. To give you a handle on sorting out truth from error in the process of interpreting Scripture, I have developed the acronym L-I-G-H-T-S.

Part 6: Sickness and Suffering

The "S" in F-L-A-W-S will remind you of Sickness and Suffering. In chapters 21–24 you will learn that devastation and death have followed in the wake of the false teachings of the Faith movement. The Faith movement's four spiritual flaws on sickness and suffering are as follows:

▪ *Symptoms and sickness.* Are symptoms merely tricks used by the devil to steal our guarantee of divine health and healing?

▪ *Satan and sickness.* The cruelty displayed by the Faith movement when it comes to the sick is almost beyond comprehension. Arguably, the most famous of all Faith teachers today writes, "If your body belongs to God, it does not and cannot belong to sickness."

▪ *Sin and sickness.* It is not enjoyable to read the stories of people who lost their loved ones and were told that it was a direct result of sin, but it may be necessary. Perhaps we will wake up to the fact that the kingdom of the cults is now within the very walls of the church itself.

▪ *Sovereignty and sickness.* One of our bestselling "evangelical" authors writes, "Never, ever, ever, go to the Lord and say, 'If it be thy will.' . . . Don't allow such faith-destroying words to be spoken from your mouth." And that's just the beginning. The sovereignty of God is the first casualty in the cultic theology of the Faith movement.

Part 7: Back to Basics

I happen to love the game of golf. Although it has brought me great satisfaction over the years, it has been extremely frustrating as well. After many years of practice and playing, I have finally stumbled upon a secret: When things go wrong, it is usually not because I am failing to follow some newfangled formula, but because I have begun to compromise the essentials. I never cease to be amazed at how quickly things fall into place when I get back to basics.

What's true in golf is applicable to a Christianity in crisis as well. Everything can quickly come back into focus by getting back to basics. It may not sound exciting, but this is truly where the real experience of victorious Christian living can be found! In chapters 25–29 we will focus our attention on getting back to basics by following five basic steps. Fortunately, they are as easy to remember as A-B-C-D-E.

- *Amen.* We begin with the letter "A," which represents the word "Amen." Amen traditionally comes at the end of every prayer, and prayer is our primary way of communicating with God. To help you separate fact from fiction regarding prayer, I've developed the acronym F-A-C-T-S. It should provide you with a good handle on the purpose, the power, and the provision of prayer.

- *Bible.* "B" stands for Bible. While prayer is our primary way of communicating with God, the Bible is God's primary way of communicating with us. Thus nothing should take precedence over spending time in the Word. If we fail to eat well-balanced meals, we will eventually suffer physically. Likewise, if we do not regularly feed on the Word of God, we will suffer spiritually. The acronym M-E-A-L-S will give you a handle on getting into the Word and getting the Word into you.

- *Church.* "C" stands for Church. Scripture exhorts us not to neglect the gathering of ourselves together, as is the custom of some (Hebrews 10:25). Today, however, multitudes are turning from the church and tuning into television. We are being conformed to the ways of our culture rather than to the will of God. The acronym G-O-D will give us a good grasp of what it means to get back to the basics of vital church life.

- *Defense.* "D" stands for Defense. Getting back to basics means equipping yourself for the defense of the faith. The Cold War may be over, but the need to defend the faith is just beginning to heat up. The defense of the faith is not just a suggestion; it is basic training for every Christian. And that means you! Thankfully, learning to defend your faith is not as difficult as you may think. It all boils down to being able to answer three key questions.

▪ *Essentials.* "E" stands for Essentials. Much is being said today about unity. Unity, however, cannot truly exist apart from the essentials on which the Christian faith is founded. The essentials are an abiding reference point which have guided Christ's body through the storms that have sought to sink it throughout the church age. Christ promised He would be with us always, "to the very end of the age" (Matthew 28:20). In getting back to essential Christianity, we will use the acronym A-G-E as our point of reference.

E.W. Kenyon and the Leading Proponents of a Different Gospel

A special section called "Kenyon and the Leading Proponents of a Different Gospel" (pp. 331-361) gives a more detailed look at the primary figures of the Faith movement. What you will discover is so shocking that your natural inclination may well be disbelief or even denial. But everything I report is accurate and thoroughly documented.

With all this in mind, let us press forward and turn our attention to the Faith movement's false teaching of having "faith in faith."

Christianity in CRISIS

PART TWO

Faith
in
Faith

*T*alk about providence! On the very week I began this chapter on faith I was poised on the precipice of what could be the greatest step of faith in the 33-year history of the Christian Research Institute. Overnight this move would double the outreach capacity of what was already the largest evangelical countercult ministry in the world. And so as I prepared to make the move, I trusted that there was no safer action than a step of faith.

So what is faith? Is faith merely a blind step into the dark, or can faith be considered a leap into the light? Is faith a force? Are words the containers for the force?

And how should I direct my faith? Should it be directed inward—faith in my own faith? Or is God to be the object of my faith?

Speaking of God, is God a faith-being? Would He know of any good faith formulas? While I'm asking, can someone please tell me how to get to the Faith Hall of Fame?

Larry and Lucky Parker thought they knew the way to the Faith Hall of Fame. They had listened to the Faith message for years. They knew the Faith formulas practically by heart. But this time when a Faith peddler rode through town, they swallowed more of his spiritual cyanide than they could safely digest. They charged in the wrong direction down a one-way street of faith.

Their tragic tale was courageously published in 1980 by Harvest House. Their book, *We Let Our Son Die*, recounts the tragic details of a misguided trip of faith. In painful and painstaking detail, Larry and his wife paint the picture of how they withheld insulin from their diabetic son. Predictably, Wesley lapsed into a diabetic coma.

The Parkers, warned about the impropriety of making a "negative confession," continued to "positively confess" Wesley's healing until the time of his death. Even after Wesley's demise, the Parkers, undaunted in their "faith," conducted a resurrection service rather than a funeral. In fact, for more than a year following his death, they refused to abandon their firmly held faith that Wesley, like Jesus, would rise from the dead. Eventually, both Larry and Lucky were tried and convicted of manslaughter and child abuse.

A tragic tale? Yes. But even more tragic is that countless other stories like this could be painfully retold. In each case the moral is always the same: A flawed concept of faith inevitably leads to shipwreck—sometimes spiritually, in other cases physically, and in still other scenarios, both.

Since faith helps to weave Christianity into an exquisite tapestry, it will serve us well to carefully consider the false doctrines which are systematically unraveling the fabric of our faith.

Many people who espouse Faith doctrines have embraced concepts that are so unbiblical that they boggle the mind. In some cases these concepts find their genesis in the kingdom of the cults; in other cases they are firmly rooted in the world of the occult.

In the following pages you will come face-to-face with Faith teachers who have completely redefined the biblical concept of faith. They define faith as a force and claim that words are the containers for the force.

You will learn to detect flawed faith formulas which have been virtually canonized by the Faith movement.

You will discover that the "God" of the Faith movement is not the true God at all. He is merely a pathetic puppet governed by the impersonal force of faith.

Finally, it is my hope that you will be equipped to contrast true heroes of the faith, past and present, with the spiritual charlatans who have inducted themselves into what might best be characterized as their own "Faith Hall of Shame."

When it comes to Faith theology, truth is often stranger than fiction. While millions of Faith adherents have not let their children die, they do continue to applaud doctrines that lead to devastating consequences. Marilyn Hickey, for example, teaches people to speak to their bodies:

> Say to your body, "You're whole, body! Why, you just function so beautifully and so well. Why, body, you never have any problems. You're a strong, healthy body." Or speak to your leg, or speak at your foot, or speak to your neck, or speak to your back; and once you have spoken and believe that you have received, and don't go back on it. Speak to your wife, speak to your husband, speak to your circumstances; and speak faith to them to create in them and God will create what you are speaking.[1]

Many Faith teachers elaborate on such doctrines with devastating consequences. It is precisely here that many Faith teachers have taken a dramatic U-turn from Christianity into the world of the occult.

The Force of Faith

I have spent hundreds of hours reading and researching the concepts of the Faith teachers who daily parade through our living rooms via the airwaves. Through it all, a significant theme has emerged. That theme, buried in the message of Faith teaching, is that faith is a force.

Kenneth Copeland, considered a leading Faith authority, believes so strongly in this concept that he has made the phrase "force of faith" famous through constant repetition. He even wrote a book titled *The Force of Faith* to propagate this deadly error.

As Copeland puts it, "Faith is a power force. It is a tangible force. It is a conductive force."[1] He further says that in much the same way that the force of gravity makes the law of gravity work, "it is this force of faith which makes the laws of the spirit world function."[2]

According to Copeland, "This force originates from God, out of His unlimited heart."[3] In fact, he says, the world "was born out of the force of faith that was resident inside the being of God."[4]

Copeland even claims that "God cannot do anything for you apart or separate from faith" because "faith is God's source of power."[5]

Just think of it—God *cannot* do anything for you apart from the force! Without the force of faith, God has no power at all toward you. Already one thing should be clear: Copeland's God is no God at all. The true omnipotent God of Scripture is not the God of Copeland's teaching.

Copeland likens "God's source of power" to a coin. This coin has both a positive and a negative side. The positive side, or "heads," represents faith. Faith activates God. The negative side, or "tails," represents fear. Fear activates Satan. Copeland puts it like this: "Fear activates Satan, the way faith activates God."[6]

To use another analogy, you might picture "God's source of power" as a giant battery in the sky. This battery has both a positive and a negative pole. The positive pole represents "faith" while the negative pole represents "fear."

As Charles Capps puts it, "Job activated Satan by his fear when he said, 'the thing which I greatly feared is come upon me' (Job 3:25). Active faith in the Word brings God onto the scene. Fear brings Satan on the scene."[7]

So how does God activate the force of faith? The answer is *through words*.

The Containers of Faith

Words are the containers that carry the substance of faith. In Faith theology, if you speak words of faith, you activate the positive side of the force; if you speak words of fear, you activate the negative side of the force. In Faith vernacular this is called "making positive or negative confessions." The Faith movement would have us believe that everything that happens to us is a direct result of our words: "Words are spiritual containers, and the force of faith is released by words."[8] As Copeland explains it:

> God used words when He created the heaven and the earth. . . . Each time God spoke, He released His faith—the creative power to bring His words to pass.[9]

Copeland claims that words were also the vehicle God used to "paint a picture of a Redeemer, a man who would be the manifestation of His Word in the earth."[10] It was God's force of Faith squeezed into words that saved the day when Jesus was being obliterated by Satan in hell (see chapter 15, "Rebirth in Hell"). From creation to re-creation, according to the proponents of the prosperity message, everything is controlled by words filled with the substance of faith. This is precisely why E.W. Kenyon said, "Faith-filled words brought the universe into being, and faith-filled words are ruling the universe today."[11]

Not only is the Faith movement's concept of faith anti-biblical, but it bears striking similarities to New Thought metaphysics as well. New Age critic Ron Rhodes writes:

> According to New Thought, human beings can experience health, success, and abundant life by using their thoughts to define the condition of their lives. New Thought proponents subscribe to the "law of attraction." This law says that just as like attracts like, so our thoughts can attract the things they want or expect. Negative thoughts are believed to attract dismal circumstances; positive thoughts attract more desirable circumstances. Our thoughts can be either creative or destructive. New Thought sets out to teach people how to use their thoughts creatively.[12]

Parallels to metaphysical cults are by no means a mere coincidence. Kenyon, the real father of the modern-day Faith movement, "majored" in metaphysics. His perversions were embraced and multiplied by Hagin, who presented Kenyon's concepts almost word for word.[13] These distortions have continued to proliferate through men like Frederick Price and Kenneth Copeland. And Price and Copeland have unfortunately gone on to mentor a host of other Faith teachers, including Jerry Savelle and Charles Capps.

Savelle, for example, says that "the raw material or the substance that God used to frame this world was His faith and His Word. . . . The way that He created the world was, first of all, He conceived something on the inside of Him. He conceived, He had an image, He had a picture. God doesn't just sling things into existence without first of all conceiving it first."[14]

When Savelle was asked if a person can change his world through the word of faith, he responded that we can talk our world into existence. "That's how you got the one you're living in now," he says. "You talked it in there. . . . You talked that one in there, the one you're living in right now, brother. You can't blame it on nobody else. Your words got it there. You framed it. Somebody says, 'You mean the world that I'm living in right now originated by the words of my mouth?' They certainly did, because the Bible says you are snared by the words of your mouth, you are taken by your words. Amen?"[15]

Charles Capps repeats the words of his prosperity peers when he says:

> Some think that God made the earth out of nothing, but He didn't. He made it out of something. *The substance God used was faith.* . . . He used His words as a carrier of that faith.[16]

Robert Tilton, who pronounced himself the most anointed prosperity pastor on television, also claims that faith is a force. Says Tilton, "If you have a problem, any kind of need, housing, transportation, situation in a marriage, you can release the creative—see, this all works by faith—the creative force of God into existence."[17] Of course, with Tilton it takes more than just words! In his case, it helps to make a vow of faith sealed with a generous donation. In most cases, a thousand dollars seems to be the magic number.

The Origin of the Faith Teaching

By now you should be asking yourself, "Where on earth do these guys get this stuff?" As hard as it may be to believe, the standard proof text used by the Faith teachers is Hebrews 11:1, which in King James English reads, "Now faith is the substance of things hoped for, the evidence of things not seen."

"There you have it," say the Faith teachers; "faith is a substance!"

Imagine: All the perversions just documented are based primarily on one brief passage, in an old translation, wrenched out of context, and presented as a proof text for the Faith message. Like an elephant tottering on the point of a pen, their entire theology rests on the word "substance" in Hebrews 11:1.

The Faith teachers interpret the word "substance" to mean the "basic stuff" out of which the universe is made. As Copeland puts it, "Faith was the raw material substance that the Spirit of God used to form the universe."[18]

Therefore, according to Faith teaching, the book you're reading is made out of molecules, which in turn are made out of atoms, which are composed of subatomic particles, which are comprised of this thing called "faith." According to Faith theology, virtually everything is made out of faith!

But is this true? Does the word "substance" in Hebrews 11:1 KJV really teach that faith is the tangible stuff out of which the universe is made?

First, remember that *Scripture must always be interpreted in light of Scripture*. That being the case, faith cannot be rightly understood to mean "the building block of the universe," since it is never used in that sense in the book of Hebrews, much less the entire Bible.

Second, the word translated "substance" in the KJV is more accurately rendered "assurance" (see NASB). Far from being a tangible material, faith is a *channel of living trust*—an *assurance*—which stretches from man to God. True biblical faith is only as good as the object in whom it is placed. God is both the object and the origin of our faith. Thus true biblical faith is faith in *God* as opposed to faith in *substance* (or "faith in faith," as Hagin puts it).[19] It is the *object* and the *origin* of faith that renders it effective.

Finally, consulting an interlinear Bible quickly demonstrates that the word translated "substance" in the KJV is the Greek word *hypostasis*, which in the context of Hebrews 11:1 means "an assured impression, a mental realizing."[20] Other translations, in an effort to offer an accurate rendition, translate *hypostasis* variously as "being sure" (NIV) and "assurance" (NASB). Far from meaning "tangible stuff," it specifically refers to the assurance that God's promises never fail, even if sometimes we do not experience their fulfillment in our mortal existence.

As noted theologian Louis Berkhof so eloquently stated, the writer of Hebrews "exhorts the readers to an attitude of faith which will enable them to rise from the seen to the unseen, from the present to the future, from the temporal to the eternal; and [to that] which will enable them to be patient in the midst of sufferings."[21]

True Faith

True biblical faith (*pistis* in the Greek) encapsulates three essential elements. The first entails *knowledge*. The second involves *agreement*. But it is not until we add the third ingredient, or *trust,* that we end up with a full-orbed, biblical perspective on faith.

Imagine that you currently embrace the cultic teachings of Kenneth Copeland. You may *know* about a book titled *Christianity in Crisis*; you may even *agree* that it provides an accurate diagnosis of Copeland's teaching; but it isn't until you stop consuming his poison that you demonstrate "faith" that his disastrous teachings have led you from Christianity into the kingdom of the cults.

Likewise, suppose I told you that a candy bar you were given was laced with cyanide and would poison whoever ate it. Then imagine that you responded, "I know! I agree!" *But then you proceeded to take a great big bite of it!* Your action would prove that you had no faith in what I was telling you. (Incidentally, your good intentions would not change the consequences. In the end you would still convulse and die.)

So what difference does a proper definition of faith really make? It makes all the difference in the world. Just remember the tragedy of Larry and Lucky Parker, who bought the lie and let their son die. And don't forget that for every example of physical death, there are hundreds of unseen examples of spiritual suicide. For every person sitting in a Faith service, there are thousands more who have sown a similar seed of error and who have reaped the deadly whirlwind. Some, like Larry and Lucky, have found their way back to biblical faith. But countless others have been left reeling, not knowing where to turn or who to trust.

I hope by now you agree that the Faith movement has tragically misdefined faith. Next we shall see how it spreads its errors. Let us now turn our attention to the Faith movement's formulas of faith.

The Formula of Faith

*I*n Faith theology, faith is a force. It is the stuff out of which the universe is made and is the force which makes the laws of the spirit world function.[1]

So how do you get the laws of the spirit world to function for you? According to the Faith teachers, it is through the use of formulas. Not only do these formulas of faith cause the laws of the spirit world to function, but they also cause the Holy Spirit to function for you. God is demoted to the status of a mere bellhop who blindly responds to the beck and call of formulas uttered by the faithful.

Faith formulas are the name of the game. This is why the Faith movement has also been called the Positive Confession movement. Faith doctrine teaches that confessions unlock the formula of faith and activate spiritual law. Positive confessions activate the positive side of the force; negative confessions activate the negative side. From a practical perspective, spiritual law is the ultimate force in the universe. In a book titled *Two Kinds of Faith*, E.W. Kenyon insists that "it is our confession that rules us."[2]

Kenneth Hagin once complained that unsaved people were getting better results from their faith formulas than were his church members. And then it dawned on him what the unsaved were doing. As he tells the story in his booklet

Having Faith in Your Faith, these sinners were "cooperating . . . with the law of faith."[3] Ultimately, according to the formula of faith, the wealth of the world is as close as the word on your tongue.

This is why Hagin teaches people to have faith in their faith as opposed to having faith in their God. "It would help you get faith down in your spirit to say out loud: 'Faith in my faith,' " says Hagin. "Keep saying it until it registers on your heart. I know it sounds strange when you first say it; your mind almost rebels against it. But we are not talking about your head; we're talking about faith in your heart."[4]

Hagin then appeals to Mark 11:23 KJV, which reads, "For verily I say unto you that whosoever shall SAY unto this mountain, 'Be thou removed, and be thou cast into the sea,' and shall not doubt in his heart, but shall BELIEVE that those things which he SAITH shall come to pass, he shall have whatsoever he SAITH" [emphasis his]. Says Hagin, "Notice two more things about this 23rd verse: (1) He believes in his *heart*; (2) he believes in his *words*. Another way to say this is: *He has faith in his own faith. . . . Having faith in your words is having faith in your faith.*"[5]

The most basic ingredient in the formula of faith is our words. Words rule! It is through our words that we can learn to activate the force of faith. This is precisely why Faith theology is referred to as "Name it and claim it" or "Blab it and grab it."

Writing Your Own Ticket

Hagin elaborates on this theme in a booklet titled *How to Write Your Own Ticket with God*. (The name itself should shock you.) Here Hagin claims that Jesus Christ Himself appeared to him and personally gave him the formula for faith. In the opening chapter, titled "Jesus Appears to Me," Hagin claims that while he "was in the Spirit"—just like the apostle John on the Isle of Patmos—a white cloud enveloped him and he began to speak in tongues.[6]

"Then the Lord Jesus Himself appeared to me," says Hagin. "He stood within three feet of me."[7] After what sounded like a casual conversation about such things as finances, ministry, and even current affairs, Jesus told Hagin to get a pencil and a piece of paper. He then instructed him to "Write down: 1, 2, 3, 4."[8]

Jesus then allegedly told Hagin that "if anybody, anywhere, will take these four steps or put these four principles into operation, he will always receive whatever he wants from Me or from God the Father."[9] That includes whatever you want financially.[10] The formula is simply: "Say it, Do it, Receive it, and Tell it."

- Step number one is "Say it." "Positive or negative, it is up to the individual. According to what the individual says, that shall he receive."[11]

- Step number two is "Do it." "Your action defeats you or puts you over. According to your action, you receive or you are kept from receiving."[12]

- Step number three is "Receive it."[13] We are to plug into the "powerhose of heaven."[14] *Faith is the plug*, praise God! Just plug in."[15]

- Step number four is "Tell it so others may believe."[16] This final step might be considered the Faith movement's outreach program.

There you have it—the formula of faith, straight from the lips of Hagin's Jesus. According to this Jesus, the formula is to be used by Christians because "it would be a waste of their time to pray for Me [i.e., Jesus] to give them the victory. They have to write their own ticket."[17]

Scripture "Proof"

Despite supposedly having received this dictation straight from Christ Himself, Hagin apparently had some doubts about the veracity of the formula. Therefore he challenged his Christ to "prove it."[18] Without missing a beat, "Jesus" refers Hagin to the account of David and Goliath (1 Samuel 17). "Now wait a minute," protests Hagin. "You're not going to tell me that is what David did?" "Jesus" promptly responds, "Exactly. Those are the four steps he took."[19]

After going over the account of David and Goliath, Hagin agrees that what "Jesus" says is true. Says Hagin, "David knew you can have what you say. He knew *you can write your own ticket*."[20]

Any Christian with an open mind who reads Hagin's booklet must conclude that Jesus Christ of Nazareth did *not* appear to Kenneth Hagin. Nor did He say the things Hagin claims He did. Either Hagin is dreadfully deluded or else he had a conversation with another Jesus who presented him with another gospel (2 Corinthians 11:3,4).

One thing is certain: Hagin's booklet serves up everything but the clear meaning of Scripture. While at times the things Hagin writes are hilarious, all humor quickly vanishes when you consider that vast numbers of people are swallowing his farfetched formulas and are wandering far from the Savior.

In a futile attempt to legitimize his faith formula—especially step number one, "Say it"—Hagin points to Proverbs 6:2, "Thou art snared with the words of thy mouth" (KJV). This, according to Hagin, proves that if you speak positively you will get positive results, but if you speak negatively you will get negative results.

But this verse has nothing to do with any type of "formula of faith." Nor does it even remotely suggest that words per se have power. Solomon in this passage (cf. verse 1) was simply pointing out that whenever you enter into an agreement with someone, you are bound by that agreement. Affirming yourself as a guarantor for another person makes you liable for that person's debt—which you may end up regretting! You are, in short, getting snared (committed) by your own words (pledge or promise). Charles Capps takes this same proof text to an even more illogical conclusion. In warning people that they get exactly what they say, Capps explains that people who utter such expressions as "That just tickled me to death" and "I'm just dying to do that" are "buddying up with death." He then adds that "Adam was smarter than that. It took the devil over 900 years to kill him, but now the devil has programmed his language into the human race, until people can kill themselves in about 70 years or less, by speaking his words."[21]

Such reckless reasoning brings up an interesting question: When God said that He covers us with His wings (Psalm 91:4), does Capps believe the Almighty is in danger of becoming a chicken? And on a more serious note, does Capps believe Jesus would have been "buddying up with death" in the Garden of Gethsemane when He said, "My soul is overwhelmed with sorrow to the point of death" (Matthew 26:38)?

Cultic Copycats

Unfortunately, Capps is not the only Faith teacher who has been influenced by Hagin's formulas. Dad Hagin (as he is sometimes called) has spawned a host of imitators. One of them is named Norvel Hayes. In one of the most irrational interviews I have seen to date on Christian television, Hayes tells Paul and Jan Crouch about a conversation he had with Jesus Christ in which he too received the key to the faith formula.[22]

Like Hagin, Hayes had an out-of-body experience and was transported in a white cloud to the presence of Jesus. No sooner had he arrived than Jesus began to question him about some growths on his daughter's body. Jesus was upset because Hayes had not been able to curse the roots of the growths. Supposedly Jesus said to Hayes, "You belong to me the same way as Hagin does." He then told him, "Whatever Kenneth Hagin can do in Jesus' name, you can do." With that, Jesus gave Hayes the faith formula. Although Hayes's version is more hazy than Hagin's, the gist is similar.

First, he had to command or curse the sickness. As Hayes learned in heaven, you don't talk to Jesus about your trouble; you speak directly to the mountains in your life and they will disappear. Second, Jesus told him to believe and never doubt, regardless of what he saw. As Hayes tells the story, he believed and never doubted for 40 days and 40 nights. After this wilderness experience, Hayes got the breakthrough he was looking for: The growths that had plagued his daughter, Zona, for so long disappeared in an instant.

TBN studios erupted in applause and shrieks of joy as Hayes concluded his story. A little later in the same interview, Hayes told Paul and Jan Crouch a story that Hagin had related to him. In that story, the Lord was said to have healed Hagin's sister of terminal cancer when she was 50 years old. The Lord then supposedly told Hagin's sister that she had five years to build her faith. If she did not, she would die. Five years came and went and Hagin's sister was unable to strengthen her "faith muscle" sufficiently. Thus the cancer came back on her and she died.

Notice the dilemma this creates. On the one hand we are told that we are to claim our healing, even when the physical manifestation has not yet presented itself. On the other hand we are told that when we are healed, disease can appear again if our faith falters. It places you between a rock and a hard place, doesn't it?

I might add that it lets the Faith teacher off the hook every time. If you say to him, "I tried your formula and it didn't work," he can smugly smile at you and say, "If you believe and don't doubt, you can have what you say." But if you are supposedly healed and later lose your healing, you are blamed for your own negative confession. Pretty convenient!

Why Be So Harsh?

At this point you may be thinking, *Well, maybe Hagin, Hinn, Hickey, Hayes, and other Faith teachers are dead wrong. But do you have to judge their words so harshly?* My answer is a resounding "Yes!" When the core of the Christian faith is imperiled, strong measures are necessary. The apostle Paul minced no words in calling Elymas the sorcerer "a child of the devil and an enemy of everything that is right!" (Acts 13:10). And he didn't stop there. He went on to describe Elymas as "full of all kinds of deceit and trickery" and as one who was "perverting the right ways of the Lord."[23]

Jesus Christ Himself blistered the false teachers of His day with this scathing denunciation: "Woe to you, scribes and Pharisees, hypocrites, because you travel about on sea and land to make one proselyte, and when he becomes one, you make him twice as much a son of hell as yourselves. . . . You serpents, you brood of vipers, how shall you escape the sentence of hell?" (Matthew 23:15,33 NASB).[24]

It's time for us to heed the strong words of the Lord Himself, as recorded by Jeremiah the prophet:

> This is what the Lord Almighty says: "Do not listen to what the prophets are prophesying to you; they fill you with false hopes. They speak visions from their own minds, not from the mouth of the Lord" (Jeremiah 23:16).

There can be little doubt that the visions of Hagin, Hinn, Hayes, and other Faith teachers are delusions of their own minds and do not represent words from the Lord.

> "I have heard what the prophets say who prophesy lies in my name. They say, 'I had a dream! I had a dream!' How long will this continue in the hearts of these lying prophets,

who prophesy the delusions of their own minds? ... Therefore," declares the Lord, "I am against the prophets who steal from one another words supposedly from me" (Jeremiah 23:25,26,30).

One of the frightening aspects of my research into Faith theology is that over and over again I have discovered that the Faith teachers, while claiming to be receiving revelation knowledge from God, are in fact simply repeating stories that they have heard from one another.

"Yes," declares the Lord, "I am against the prophets who wag their own tongues and yet declare, 'The Lord declares.' Indeed, I am against those who prophesy false dreams," declares the Lord. "They tell them and lead my people astray with their reckless lies, yet I did not send or appoint them. They do not benefit these people in the least," declares the Lord (Jeremiah 23:31,32).

Tragically, this is precisely what the formulas of the Faith movement do. They "lead my people astray" and "do not benefit these people in the least."

From the Cults to the Occult

As damaging as these faith formulas are, it gets even worse. Kenneth Copeland takes Hagin's formulas from the kingdom of the cults into the world of the occult.

In Copeland's version of the faith formula, words of faith actually penetrate what he calls the Holy of Holies and there create the tangible objects they represent. All it takes is: 1) seeing or visualizing whatever you need, whether physical or financial; 2) staking your claim on Scripture; and 3) speaking it into existence.[25]

How would you like a yacht? Copeland's theology tells the believer first to see his 82-foot yacht; then he must stake his claim on Scripture; and finally he is to speak the word of faith. Carried along on the wings of hope (which he says is an "eternal and living substance" residing in every believer),[26] the word mystically penetrates "that veil in the holiest place that exists in heaven" and hovers there in the Holy of Holies. In time, the word that has pierced the veil undergoes a metamorphosis and becomes the very thing it represents.[27]

This, my friends, is nothing but the New Age technique of creative visualization. Two additional examples confirm such an analysis. First, Copeland discusses a "picture [of a Bible] that came right out of me and went into the Holy of Holies,"[28] and from there developed into an actual physical object. Second, Copeland talks about the application of the same method in the case of physical infirmity:

> When you get to the place where you take the Word of God and build an image on the inside of you of not having crippled legs and not having blind eyes, but when you close your eyes you just see yourself just leap out of that wheelchair, it will picture that in the Holy of Holies and you will come out of there. You will come out.[29]

It is striking how closely Copeland's formula parallels three principal beliefs of an occultic worldview. First, people in the world of the occult are told that the power to create their own reality lies within themselves. Occultists maintain that they have the inherent capacity to supernaturally change, create, or shape the world around them. Second, these people believe that words are imbued with creative power which directly and dramatically affects the real world in which they live. And finally, occultists believe they can use creative visualization to speak things into existence.

Among the other cultic groups which embrace these practices are the metaphysical mind sciences (e.g., Religious Science and Science of Mind), the New Age movement,[30] and various neopagan groups, the most familiar being witchcraft. Copeland is no doubt aware that some people believe he is promoting something which, as he puts it, "sounds like that visualization they do in meditation and metaphysical practices."[31] He therefore immediately attempts to turn the tables: "What they're doing sounds like this. The devil is a counterfeiter. He never came up with anything real. That is the perverted form of the real thing. Where do you think he got it? That sucker doesn't know anything on his own. Amen."[32]

On another occasion, Copeland simply affirms that both positive confession and creative visualization are based on the same principle: "Words create pictures, and pictures in your mind create words. And then the words come back out your mouth. . . . And when that spiritual force comes out it is going to give substance to the image that's on the inside of you. Aw, that's that visualization stuff! Aw, that's that New Age! No, New Age is trying to do this; and they'd get somewhat results out of it because this is spiritual law, brother."[33]

Further Occult Connections

Copeland's occult teachings are widely embraced within Faith circles. Paul Yonggi Cho, for example, a man who accurately lays claim to pastoring the world's largest church (Yoido Full Gospel Church, Seoul, Korea), has codified these same faith formulas under the label of "fourth-dimensional power." In his bestselling book *The Fourth Dimension*,[34] he unveils his departure from historic Christian theology into the world of the occult.

Cho is well aware that pagan religions harness this power. He claims that God told him that Buddhist and Yoga adherents worked miracle cures because they, unlike their Christian counterparts, had more fully developed their fourth-dimensional powers. Referring to the Buddhist version of a "name-it-and-claim-it" cult called Soka Gakkai, Cho says that while they belong to Satan, their fourth-dimensional acumen has provided them with dominion over their bodies and circumstances.[35] By "repeating phrases over and over again...these people are creating something" and performing "miracles," says Cho.[36] "But if the devil could do these things, why should not the Church of Jesus Christ do all the more?"[37]

What is fourth-dimensional thinking? Cho provides the answer in the form of an illustration. Pastor Cho one day coached a 30-year-old woman (who had allegedly been praying for a husband for ten years) into "creating" the man of her dreams. When Cho asked her what kind of husband she wanted, she responded, "Well, that's up to God. God knows all."[38] Cho immediately cautioned her that God does not answer vague prayers and that if she wanted to have a husband she would have to be more specific.[39] Asking her to sit down, he handed her a piece of paper and told her to number it from one to ten.

Number one, Cho asked, "Do you want your husband to be European, Asian, or African?" "European," she answered.[40] Number two, "How tall should he be?" "Six feet," she replied. Number three, "What profession?" "Schoolteacher." (In the first version, question number three asked about desired physical appearance.)[41] Number four, "Hobby?" On they went until she had the ten characteristics of the man of her dreams. Cho then told her to hang the paper by her mirror and to look at it and speak all ten points aloud each day. Cho then triumphantly reports that this spinster had the man of her dreams within a short period of time.[42]

Cho summarizes this "law of incubation"[43] as follows: "First make a clear-cut goal, then draw a mental picture, vivid and graphic,"[44] to "visualize success."[45] Then "incubate" it into reality, and finally "speak" it into existence through "the creative power of the spoken word."[46]

Unfortunately, Copeland and Cho are not the only Faith teachers whose theology can be traced to the world of the occult.[47] Benny Hinn, during one of his appearances on TBN's "Praise the Lord" program, appealed directly to the story of a witch in discussing the "power of the spoken word":

> I had a witch tell me this. . . . She said, "You know that we are taught in witchcraft how to kill birds with words and how to kill people with our mouth. . . . We were taught with words to bring disease on, on, on men . . . by speaking certain words that defeat them." She can actually cause sickness that could very well kill. . . . She said, "With words, I used to kill birds. I used to kill birds." She said she would speak to a bird and the bird would drop dead. . . . I said, "Dear God, I didn't know the Devil has such power." And the Lord spoke to me, and He said, "The Devil can kill with words, then you with your words can bring life." And it just come [sic] and clicked inside of me, brother. . . . And we Christians don't realize the power in our mouths.[48]

It is precisely because their teachings are unbiblical that Faith teachers are forced to appeal to both witchcraft as well as twisted interpretations of Scripture.

Perverting Proverbs

One of the Faith teachers' favorite tactics is the abuse of Proverbs 18:21 ("Death and life are in the power of the tongue, and they that love it shall eat the fruit thereof" [KJV]) to prove that the Bible teaches positive confession.[49] While it is clear from Scripture that our tongue can have a devastating impact on another person, there is no biblical support for the idea that our confessions have the power to create reality.[50] Only God is capable of such a feat.

If God could be controlled through positive confessions, He would be reduced to the status of a cosmic servant subject to the formulas of faith. You would be God and He would be your bellhop! You would sit on the throne of a universe centered around your own ego. And you would wind up with a puny view of God and a bloated view of man.

But Charles Capps claims that God Himself told him, "You are under an attack of the evil one and *I can't do anything about it. You have bound me* by the words of your own mouth."[51]

Frederick Price seemed to be operating on the same wavelength as Capps when he hammered home the false teaching that God is a puppet whose strings are controlled by humanity:

> Now this is a shocker! But God has to be given *permission* to work in this earth realm on behalf of man. . . . Yes! *You are in control!* So, if man has control, who no longer has it? God. . . . When God gave Adam dominion, that meant God no longer had dominion. So, God cannot do anything in this earth unless *we let* Him. And the way we let Him or give Him permission is through prayer.[52]

I hope it is clear by now that the god of the Faith movement is no God at all. He is merely a faith being, bound by the impersonal force of faith. In this strange universe, Faith is king and God is its servant.

The Faith of God

*N*othing is more crucial to our concept of faith than a proper understanding of the nature of God. In fact, the very word "theology" is derived from the Greek words *theos*, which means "God," and *logos*, which means "word" or "discourse." Thus theology is a discourse on God.

In Christian theology God is portrayed as the Sovereign of the universe. He is described as "spirit," perfectly wise, self-sufficient, omnipotent, and omniscient.

Not so in the cultic theology of the Faith movement. In these dreary environs, God is nothing but a "faith being"[1] and man is deemed to be sovereign. God is portrayed as a pathetic puppet at the beck and call of His creation. The faith god has height and weight;[2] he is called a failure;[3] he is bound by the laws of the spirit world and is dependent on the force of faith.[4] This god is impotent rather than omnipotent, limited rather than infinite and omniscient.

In other words, the god of the Faith movement is not the God of the Bible.

How do the Faith teachers strip God of His omnipotence and rob Him of His omniscience? By leading the unsuspecting into thinking that the Bible itself substantiates their flawed theology. Showing little originality, Faith teachers pull the same rabbits out of the same hat. Over and over, they quote Mark 11:22 and Hebrews 11:3.

Mr. Holmes, I Presume?

For just a moment imagine that you are Sherlock Holmes. You have been called upon to solve the mystery of how so many millions of people can be misled into thinking that Mark 11:22 proves that God has faith and is thus a faith being. What will you do?

After carefully considering the options, you decide to begin by paying a visit to Kenneth Copeland, the man dubbed by *Time* magazine as "the chief exponent" of the Faith message.[5] Using all the tools of the trade, you finally succeed in arranging a meeting with Copeland. Upon arrival you get right down to business. You ask him how, in his opinion, Mark 11:22 provides indisputable evidence that God is a faith being. Copeland assures you that it's all really very elementary. Turning to Mark 11:22 in his *Kenneth Copeland Reference Edition of the Holy Bible*, Copeland, in an authoritative tone, begins to read: "And Jesus answering, saith, 'Have faith in God.' " He looks up from the text and triumphantly says, "There you have it—undeniable proof that God has faith."

"But Reverend Copeland," you ask, "I'm not sure I understand. How do you get from 'have faith in God' to 'God has faith'?"

"Well," says Copeland, "all you need to do is look at this little note I've added to the Bible. See, right here it says, 'Or, Have the faith of God.'[6] Get it?"

"Well, I'm not so sure."

"You don't have to take my word for it, either," quips Copeland. "You can check the writings of some of the most anointed men alive today. In fact, let me jot down the titles of a few books that will prove beyond a shadow of a doubt that God has faith."* Feeling much better, you thank Copeland for the list and bid him farewell.

---

* While this conversation with Copeland is imaginary, the substance of everything he is represented as saying is amply documented.

On the way back to the office you stop at your local Christian bookstore to check out your new lead. Hunting down the books on Copeland's list, you sit down in the back of the store and begin to read. Scarcely two pages into a booklet titled *God's Creative Power*, by Charles Capps, you find just what you are looking for. There you read the words "A more literal translation [of Mark 11:22] is 'Have the God kind of faith, or faith of God. . . . God is a *faith* God.'"[7]

The very next book you check—*How Faith Works*, by a Frederick K.C. Price—confirms both Copeland and Capps by appealing to the original Greek text.[8] You think, *maybe Copeland is on to something*. Quickly you open the last book on Copeland's list, *Bible Faith Study Course*, by Kenneth Hagin, and discover that Hagin not only agrees that God has faith but points out that this is precisely what is taught by "Greek scholars."[9]

This is really interesting, you think. Apparently these men have stumbled onto a truth that has escaped the notice of orthodox Christian scholars for the last 2000 years.

While making your way back home, you slowly begin toying with the idea of stopping by the library of a nearby seminary to check out what the Greek scholars have written on the subject. It's only a few blocks away, you reason. But after a brief deliberation, you change your mind.

Surely no one would put his neck on the chopping block by claiming that his position is backed by scholars when it actually isn't. That would be too brazen. Would anyone actually do something as reckless as that?

Just in case, you decide to check it out. Realizing you may be in the library for quite some time, you breathe out a big sigh and roll up your sleeves. It's one thing to pretend you're Sherlock Holmes; it's quite another to assume the role of a Greek grammarian. Nevertheless, you charge ahead.

Finding a Greek-to-English New Testament,[10] you look up Mark 11:22. There you discover that the original text reads *echete pistin theou* (pronounced "eck-ke-te pis-tin thay-u"). You discover that *echete* means "have," *pistin* means "faith," and *theou* means "of God."

Scratching your head, you think, *Well, perhaps the Faith teachers are correct. But why then do all the major English versions of Scripture translate this phrase as "have faith in God" and not "have the faith of God"?*

Now completely perplexed, you decide it's time to call in the experts. Unlike an amateur, you know your limits!

A.T. Robertson to the Rescue

After some investigation, you decide to start by examining the works of a man named A.T. Robertson, who appears to be almost universally accepted as the final word on Greek grammar. Still nervous about trying to understand Greek, you begin by looking at a book with the friendly title *Word Pictures in the New Testament*.

Quickly flipping through it, you arrive at page 361. There it is, halfway down the page! *Echete pistin theou*, says Robertson, "is translated 'have faith in God.'" Robertson explains that this is the correct translation because *theou* is what he calls an "objective genitive."[11]

But now you're really in hot water. You don't have the foggiest idea what an "objective genitive" is.

And so the search continues.

After several hours you end up in one of Robertson's weightier books, *A New Short Grammar of the Greek Testament*. There, on page 227, he explains what he means by subjective and objective genitives. To your great delight, he even uses Mark 11:22 to illustrate his lesson.

In essence, he says an *objective* genitive means that the noun (in this case, *theou*) is the *object* of the action. So, in Mark 11:22, God is the *object* of faith. This requires that the passage be translated "Have faith in God."

You quickly reason that for the Faith teachers to be correct, a *subjective* genitive is needed. In that case God would be the *subject* of faith and the text should read "the faith of God."

But Robertson insists that such a translation is preposterous. "It is *not* the faith that *God has*," he writes, "but the faith of which *God is the object*."[12]

Because you want to be completely fair, you determine that regardless how much A.T. Robertson is revered as a Greek grammarian, you want a second opinion. Thus you spend days looking through the works of other Greek grammarians. You consult H.E. Dana, Julius R. Mantey, William Douglas Chamberlain, Curtis Vaughan, Virtus E. Gideon, James Hope Moulton, and Nigel Turner, among others. To your amazement, the conclusion is always the same: The experts who have given their lives to the study of Greek grammar are unanimous in their opinion that Copeland and his cohorts are in error. Contrary to their assertions, these perversions find no basis in the original Greek![13]

Setting aside our fictitious illustration, the truth is that it doesn't take a detective to determine whether the Faith teachers have been misleading us. In order for their rendering of Mark 11:22 to be accurate, they would have to violate more than one principle of biblical interpretation. A Faith reading of the text dethrones God as Sovereign of the universe and makes Him subject to the impersonal laws of faith.

Hacking Apart Hebrews

The Faith teachers also twist and torture Hebrews 11:3 in their attempts to make God into a faith being. If you've watched Christian television, you have no doubt heard them breezily proclaim that Hebrews 11:3 tells us that God, by His faith, created the world and is thus a faith being.

What do you do when you hear such a thing? You follow the biblical injunction to test everything by the Word of God (see Acts 17:11). When you do so, you discover that the text says nothing of the sort. In fact, rather than saying that God *by His faith created the world*, Hebrews 11:3 says that *we by faith understand that God created the world!*

The Faith teachers have absolutely no excuse for their twisting of Hebrews 11:3. The English rendering of the text is so utterly clear that there is no need to consult the Greek.

Just look at the sentence construction in Hebrews 11. It says:

"By faith Moses . . . chose to be mistreated."

Who chose to be mistreated? Moses chose to be mistreated!

"By faith Isaac blessed Jacob" (verse 20).

Who blessed Jacob by faith? Isaac blessed Jacob by faith!

"By faith Abraham . . . obeyed" (verse 8).

Who obeyed by faith? Abraham obeyed.

"By faith Noah . . . built an ark" (verse 7).

Who built an ark by faith? Noah built an ark by faith.

"By faith Abel offered" (verse 4).

Who offered by faith? Abel offered by faith.

Last, "By faith we understand."

Who understands by faith? We understand by faith.

Far from teaching us that God by His faith created the world, the text clearly states that *we by faith understand that God created the world.* The parallel construction here clearly rules out the spin which the Faith teachers have put on this passage.

Faith disciples believe so strongly that God is a faith being that Zoe College, where such Faith teachers as Drs. Benny Hinn and Ken Copeland got their "degrees," actually teaches course MN204, titled "The God Kind of Faith."[14]

The Bible makes it clear, however, that God could never be a faith being. A being who must exercise faith is limited in both knowledge and power, since faith lies in the region of nonabsolute certainty and control. If God had to have faith, He would be dependent upon something outside of Himself for knowledge or power. And that is clearly unbiblical.

The Bible portrays God as the One who sees all and knows all from all eternity and who wields supreme and absolute authority. He has no need of faith.

You cannot read very far in the Bible without bumping up against statements, such as the one in Psalm 115:3, which blow apart the idea that God is limited in any way: "Our God is in heaven; he does whatever pleases him." All right, you answer, but is His sphere of influence somehow restricted? Better think again: "The Lord does whatever pleases him, in the heavens and on the earth, in the seas and all their depths" (Psalm 135:6).

The fact is that any talk of limiting God is not only antibiblical but it makes God angry! Psalm 50 is one of the strongest statements in Scripture about the self-sufficiency and omnipotence of God—and the Lord Himself makes it clear in that psalm what He thinks about those who would shrink His reign: "You thought I was altogether like you. But I will rebuke you and accuse you to your face. Consider this, you who forget God, or I will tear you to pieces, with none to rescue" (50:21,22).

A Prisoner of Impersonal Laws

Critics of the Faith movement have often referred to its God as the impersonal God of the metaphysical cults. In fact, the Faith teachers present a personal God in principle, but in practice they teach a metaphysical God. This God cannot operate outside the universal laws by which even He is governed. Copeland, for example, insists that "God cannot do anything for you apart or separate from faith."[15] The reason is that *"faith is God's source of power."*[16]

In Copeland's theology, even Jesus Christ was produced as a direct result of the faith of God. In unmistakable terms, he portrays God's positive confession as the force which produced Jesus Christ:

> God began to release His Word into the earth.
> He began to paint a picture of a Redeemer, a
> man who would be the manifestation of His
> Word in the earth.[17]

Sadly, Copeland is not alone in propagating this myth. Charles Capps says, *"It was an act of the God-kind-of-faith that caused the miraculous conception."*[18] Attributing his remarks to the Holy Spirit, he continues, "Mary received the Word sent to her by the angel and conceived *it* in the womb of her spirit. Once *it* was conceived in her spirit [note the repeated use of the word "it"], *it* manifested itself in her physical body."[19] He goes on to say, "The embryo in Mary's womb was nothing but the pure word of God—and it took flesh upon itself."[20] Capps concludes his heretical remarks by saying, "Jesus Christ was born of a virgin through the miraculous conception of faith—the God-kind of faith."[21] With a single stroke of the pen, Capps corrupts the miraculous *conception* of Jesus Christ into a miraculous *confession*.

Friends, if this is not heresy, nothing is.

But the Faith teachers do not stop there. Not only do they teach that Christ was born of the faith of God, but you too are born of this faith! As Copeland puts it, "God is a faith being. You are born of God. You are a faith being. God does not do anything outside of faith. With His faith living in you, you are to operate the same way."[22]

It's all a matter of faith. Faith is the force; words are the containers of the force; faith formulas operate the spiritual laws of the universe. These spiritual laws in turn command and control the pathetic God of the Faith movement.

In Faith theology, it is not the true God who reigns supreme. In Faith theology, the real heroes of the faith are those who learn to work in harmony with the force of faith—and all of this is "sanctified" through the use of the name of Jesus. Jesus is the MasterCard which will allow you to charge to your heart's content. Your only credit limit is the extent of your own faith. As Fred Price puts it, "If you have bicycle faith, all you're gonna get is a bicycle."[23] But if you have Rolls Royce faith, you too, like Price, can drive a Rolls.

Hagin and his imitators loudly proclaim themselves to be the giants of the faith. Hagin actually boasts that he had not "*prayed one prayer in 45 years... without getting an answer. I always got an answer—and the answer was always yes.*"[24]

So what are we to say of those whose prayers go unanswered? What are we to think of someone such as Joni Eareckson Tada, who for years begged God to raise her from her wheelchair—and yet remains a quadriplegic? And how are we to judge a man like Job, who suffered so much and yet was called a righteous man?

As we're about to see, for the Faith fable to have validity, Job has to be vilified. And believe me, he is! According to the Faith teachers, a guy like Job belongs in the "Faith Hall of Shame."

The Faith Hall of Fame

*W*ell, how about it? Who do you think should be inducted into the Faith Hall of Fame? When it's time to cast the ballot, who will you select?

I'd like to suggest that you consider Job. The question you must answer is this: Does Job indeed belong in the Faith Hall of Fame along with such luminaries as Abraham, Isaac and Jacob? Or was Job carnal and faithless, a man whose propensity for negative confessions created his own tragic downfall?

Before you vote, consider what bestselling author Benny Hinn has to say. Hinn claims that Job's troubles came on him because he spoke words of fear and made accusations against God. Hinn describes Job as "carnal," as "bad," and asserts that Job's "mouth was his biggest problem." In essence, Hinn says that Job tapped into the negative side of the force through his voluminous negative confessions.[1]

In order for the Faith message to flourish, Job has to fall. And fall he does—but not through some great moral failure of his own doing. Rather, he is tripped up by a smear campaign, a campaign in which Hinn recklessly caricatures Job as one of the great faith failures of all time.

Of course, Hinn must ignore the clear context of Scripture to deliver his diatribe against Job. When God calls Job upright, Hinn calls him carnal. When God calls Job good,

Hinn calls Job bad. When God says that Job had spoken right, Hinn says Job made a negative confession. Several times in the first two chapters of Job, God makes it clear that Job was blameless and upright, that he feared God and shunned evil (Job 1:1,8; 2:3). In fact, the Lord even declared to Satan that "there is no one on earth like" Job (1:8; 2:3).

Despite this divine commendation, Hinn persists in blasting Job. In one of the most horrifying scenes I have ever witnessed on Christian television, Hinn not only vilifies Job for his lack of faith, but denounces one of the greatest statements of faith ever uttered in the midst of tragedy.

Despite the somber warning of Proverbs 30:6 ("Do not add to his words, or he will rebuke you and prove you a liar."),[2] Hinn *adds* the word "never" to the text in Job 1:21 and thus completely reverses the meaning of the passage. Encouraged by his audience, Hinn sniggers, "You know what? We've said this a million times and it's not even scriptural— all because of Job: 'The Lord giveth and the Lord taketh away. Blessed be the name of the Lord' [Job 1:21]. I have news for you: that is not Bible, that's not Bible. The Lord giveth and *never* taketh away. And just because he said, 'Blessed be the name of the Lord,' don't mean that he's right. When he said, 'Blessed be the name,' he was just being religious. And being religious don't mean you're right."[3]

Hinn's outburst is not unique. Long before Hinn bludgeoned Job, men like Copeland,[4] Capps,[5] Savelle,[6] Crouch,[7] and a host of others had done the same thing.

Not only do these Faith teachers alter the passage to read precisely the opposite of what is recorded in the Bible, but they ignore the fact that the very next verse in Scripture commends Job with the following words: "In all this, Job did not sin by charging God with wrongdoing" (1:22).

Job steadfastly refused to curse his Creator in the midst of some of the most profound pain imaginable. He had been selected as the subject for a stern test of faith because he was indisputably the greatest man of faith alive. God

declared that Job's faith was real faith. Satan claimed that
Job's faith was fickle. Take away Job's possessions, the evil
one suggested, and Job's faith will disappear as well.

As Scripture reveals, Job not only passed the test of
faith with flying colors but also demonstrated the remarkable
depth of his faith when he uttered these unforgettable words:
"Naked I came from my mother's womb, and naked I will
depart. The Lord gave and the Lord has taken away; may the
name of the Lord be praised." Rather than cursing God, as
his wife had goaded him to do (2:9), or blaming his tragedy on
secret sin, as his cruel companions urged him to do, Job
placed his fate in the hands of a God who is both infinitely
just and infinitely merciful.

Job's friends—like their descendants Hinn and the
Faith teachers—declare that Job had sinned and thus de-
served the calamities that befell him. Eliphaz the Temanite,
like Tilton, boasted of having religious authority and mysterious visions; Bildad the Shuhite, like several Faith teachers,
was fond of uttering clever clichés; and Zophar the Naamathite, like the modern-day name-it-claim-it teachers,
believed that Job's calamities were the result of secret sin. All
of these "comforters" clung to the belief that sickness and
suffering were the result of secret sin or negative confessions.
Yet God steadfastly confirmed Job as blameless and upright.

Zophar was the least tactful of those who directly
accused Job. He constantly repeated the refrain, "Job, you
are being punished because of your own sin." Job knew,
however, that his calamities somehow formed a part of God's
sovereign plan. Like the apostle Paul, Job believed that "all
things God works for the good of those who love him, who
have been called according to his purpose" (Romans 8:28).

The book of Job builds an airtight defense for Job's
faith. Who can forget Job's unwavering utterance of faith,
"Though he slay me, yet will I hope in him" (13:15)? This
singular statement proved the depth of his reliance on God.

He cherished his faith above even his life. His eternal perspective is enshrined forever in his words "I know that my Redeemer lives, and that in the end he will stand upon the earth" (19:25).

Indeed, the greatest demonstration of faith is trusting God even when you do not understand. How is it possible for Hinn to miss the central theme of the book of Job? Not only does God make us privy to His conversations with Satan, but He also demonstrates that He permits suffering in the lives of His saints in order to purify and conform them to His will and purpose.

When all is said and done, God commands everyone to cease their ignorant babblings (chapters 38–41). Speaking out of the storm in a speech dripping with divine sarcasm, God asks Job and his friends if they could comprehend the vast expanses of the earth (37:18). His majestic words sweep across the face of the earth and powerfully proclaim His sovereignty over both His creatures and His creation. At the end of His speech, God condemns Job's friends and instructs them to seek out Job's prayer for their forgiveness (42:8,9).[8] Finally, God commends Job because Job has "spoken of Me what is right" (verses 7,8).

Given this evidence, how do you vote? Does Job make it into the Faith Hall of Fame? Or is he a shameful example of negative confession?

The only verdict can be for the induction of Job into the Faith Hall of Fame. Those who besmirch Job's character—including his friends and the Faith teachers—belong in their own Faith Hall of Shame.

The truth is that the characteristics necessary for induction into the Faith Hall of Fame have little or nothing to do with those being touted by the Faith teachers. Faith, far from being a magical force conjured up through pat formulas, is the sort of confidence in God exemplified by Job as he persevered in the midst of affliction, trusting God despite the whirlwind which blew his life into oblivion. True faith is perseverance in the midst of the storm. True faith is the trait most demonstrated in the life of the apostle Paul, who not only fought the good fight but finished the race and kept his faith. Paul's faith, like that of Job, was fixed not on the temporary circumstances of life but on the Author and Finisher of faith, on Christ Himself (Hebrews 12:2).

The Faith Hall of Fame will surely not be bedecked with the glitz and glamour of those who mock the biblical concept of faith. Rather, it will be filled with the men and women who follow in the train of those who willingly gave their lives in service to the King of kings. Those who like Gideon, Barak, Samson, Jephthah, David, Samuel, and the prophets through faith conquered kingdoms; who have been tortured, jeered, and flogged; who have been chained and put in prison; stoned and put to death; destitute; persecuted and mistreated, yet were commended for their faith—because their faith was not fixed on circumstances but on God.

Rest assured that Job was a true hero of faith. In fact, it appears that God did not think it enough to honor Job's faith solely in the book which bears his name. Twice in the book of Ezekiel he is lifted up, along with Noah and Daniel, as a man of uncompromised integrity and faith (Ezekiel 14:14,20). And who can forget the words of James, who commended Job for patience and perseverance in the midst of pain and suffering (James 5:11)?

Ironically, Hinn is snared by his own words when he ends his tirade against Job with this statement: "Every wrong confession comes from Hell. That's what the Bible says. When you say something that disagrees with the Word of God you are literally being controlled by Hell."9 Thus Hinn is hung on the gallows of his own words. For in disagreeing with the clear teaching of Scripture, he is indeed "literally being controlled by Hell."

The biblical Job blazed a trail of faith for all of God's people who would follow—those who, like Joni Eareckson Tada, have learned that true faith does not necessarily equip someone to arise from a wheelchair but rather prepares him or her to use adversity as a means of bringing men and women into the kingdom. The real tragedy is not paraplegia or even dying young. The real tragedy is living a long, robust life and failing to use it for the glory of God. No doubt Joni would rather endure tragedy and pain for a season if, through her suffering, by God's grace she could influence the eternal destiny of millions.

One day soon, health and wealth will matter little. All that will concern you is for the Lord Jesus Christ Himself to turn to you and say, "Well done, good and faithful slave. You were faithful with a few things; I will put you in charge of many things. Enter into the joy of your master" (Matthew 25:21 NASB).

CHRISTIANITY IN CRISIS

PART THREE

Little Gods
or
Little Frauds?

Υears ago I heard the story of a young boy named David who was busily engaged in building the sand castle of his dreams.[1] This was not going to be just an ordinary sand castle; this was going to be the most magnificent sand castle ever built.

David labored long and hard. He worked from the early hours of the morning through the heat of the noonday sun. Gradually his sand castle began to take shape. He crafted a magnificent moat to protect the sand castle from any "invaders." He forged huge fortresses with flying buttresses. And he built tall, stately towers, complete with brightly colored flags that fluttered softly in the gentle ocean breeze.

David became so engrossed in his labor that he failed to notice that the sun was slowly sinking. He was oblivious to the dark clouds forming on the horizon and was blinded to the tide that was moving inexorably closer and closer.

Finally the inevitable occurred. In the growing crescendo of waves there came that mighty torrent of water that crashed over his carefully crafted moat and flattened the castle of his dreams. David stood there, sand and water dripping from his fingers, looking down in utter disbelief as his magnificent sand castle disappeared into the sand around it. The towers had crumbled, the moat had been overwhelmed, and the flags lay muddied in the sand.

A sad story? Perhaps. But not nearly as sad as the fact that this accurately portrays the era in which we live. Like David, we are busily engaged in building our own dream castles. We too seem blithely unaware of the sinking sun, of the dark clouds moving ever closer, and of the inexorable drawing near of the waves.

No doubt the most destructive wave that has crashed upon the already-eroding sands of our culture is the tidal force that has swept America out of the "Piscean Age" (the supposed age of Christianity) and into the so-called "Age of Aquarius." Without a single shot being fired, America has been converted to a new religion, a religion in which humankind has promoted itself to godhood. One can scarcely forget Shirley MacLaine's bold proclamation in the television movie *Out on a Limb*: With arms thrust skyward along the shores of Malibu she shouted, "I am God!"

Over the past few years, Eastern mysticism and the occult, along with multitudes of cultic groups, have gained an alarming level of credibility in the United States. From the mind sciences to the New Age movement, Americans are being constantly bombarded by the idea that "all is one, all is God, and man is God."

One would think that people who profess the name of Christ would be loath to mouth such sentiments. But sadly, this is no longer true, for the airwaves are crowded with a new cluster of religious teachers who take great delight in proclaiming their own deity, all the while naming the name of Christ.

The Faith teachers joyfully promote all this and more. In their topsy-turvy universe, man is promoted to deity while God is demoted to servitude; Satan is boosted to God's orbit while Christ crashes to the bowels of the earth.

The Deification of Man

*E*ver since the dawn of time Satan has tried to peddle the lie that mere men can become gods. His seductive hiss "You will be like God," first heard in Genesis 3, has reverberated across the ages with sensuous frequency. He packages and repackages the lie in whatever size or shape is needed to make it sell.

In *The Road Less Traveled*, M. Scott Peck, a psychologist popular in both New Age and Christian circles, puts words into the mouth of the Creator when he writes:

> God wants us to become Himself (or Herself or
> Itself). We are growing toward godhood. God
> is the goal of evolution.[1]

Well-known witch Margot Adler goes one step further. Quoting the *Whole Earth Catalog*, she says:

> We are as gods and might as well get good at
> it.[2]

Notorious cult leader Rajneesh, who in Poona, India, took on the title Bhagwan Shree (meaning "Sir God"), had the temerity to announce, "When you call Jesus, really you have called me. When you call me, really you have called Jesus."[3]

One would surmise that since Sir God is now dead, he is well aware that the distance between himself and Jesus is the distance of infinity.

Then there is Maharishi Mahesh Yogi, of Transcendental Meditation fame, who sabotaged Scripture when he slipped in the word "you" for "I," and proudly proclaimed, "Be still and know that you are God."[4]

And who can forget the infamous Jim Jones, who personally led almost a thousand men, women, and children to violent deaths? This deluded cult leader screeched: "It is written that ye are gods. I'm a god and you're a god. And I'm a god, and I'm gonna stay a god until you recognize that you're a god. And when you recognize that you're a god, I shall go back into principle and will not appear as a personality. But until I see all of you knowing who you are, I'm gonna be very much what I am—God, almighty God."[5]

It is no surprise that such blasphemy should spew forth from witches, Yogis, and murderous madmen. What is shocking, however, is that similar statements are now being voiced by some of the biggest names in the church.

Move Over, God

Kenneth Hagin asserts, "Man...was created on terms of equality with God, and he could stand in God's presence without any consciousness of inferiority.... God has made us as much like Himself as possible.... He made us the same class of being that He is Himself.... Man lived in the realm of God. He lived on terms equal with God.... *[T]he believer is called Christ.... That's who we are; we're Christ!*"[6]

Kenneth Copeland declares that "God's reason for creating Adam was His desire to reproduce Himself.... He was not a little like God. He was not almost like God. He was not subordinate to God even."[7]

Televangelist John Avanzini claims that the Spirit of God "declared in the earth today what the eternal purpose of

God has been through the ages ... that He is duplicating Himself in the earth."[8]

Morris Cerullo bellows, "Did you know that from the beginning of time the whole purpose of God was to reproduce Himself? ... Who are you? Come on, *who are you?* Come on, say it: 'Sons of God!' Come on, say it! And what does work inside us, brother, is that manifestation of the expression of all that God is and all that God has. And when we stand up here, brother, you're not looking at Morris Cerullo; you're looking at God. You're looking at Jesus."[9]

That's just for openers! The language used by Faith teachers sounds strikingly similar to that of recognized cults. As a case in point, Charles Capps says, "God duplicated *Himself* in kind! ... *Adam was an exact duplication of God's kind!*"[10]

Herbert W. Armstrong, founder of the Worldwide Church of God, mirrored Capps's sentiments when he said:

> As God repeatedly reveals, his purpose is to *reproduce* himself into what may well become billions of God persons.... Why did the Creator God put MAN on the earth? For God's ultimate supreme purpose of *reproducing* himself, of recreating himself.[11]

And this is not an isolated case. The terms "duplicate" and "duplication" constantly appear in the Faith teachers' discourses on humanity (e.g., Avanzini), as do the terms "reproduce" and "reproduction" (e.g., Copeland and Cerullo).

Too Radical for Mormons

The Faith teachings have now become so blasphemous and bizarre that even cultists are denying them. For example, Mormon scholar and author Stephen E. Robinson, referring to the Faith teachers, says:

> Now, in fact, the Latter-day Saints [i.e., the Mormon church] would not agree with the doctrine of deification as understood by most of these evangelists, for in the LDS view we receive the full divine inheritance only through the atonement of Christ and only after a glorious resurrection.[12]

Robinson realizes the absurdity of the Christian church denouncing the Mormon doctrine that men can one day *become* gods while high-profile teachers within the church are consistently proclaiming that we are *already* gods. It is indeed ironic that a scholar from the Mormon cult would find the Faith movement's "little gods" doctrine too rich for his blood.

In any case, the Faith movement's "little gods" doctrine is a classic example of how the biblical view of humankind is oftentimes distorted. Faith teachers take the Scripture's depiction of man made in the image of God and twist it into a monstrosity. When Kenneth Copeland proclaims, "You don't have a god in you, you are one,"[13] and Benny Hinn pronounces, "I am a 'little messiah' walking on earth,"[14] we can only conclude that they are teaching rank heresy.

Before we examine the Scripture-twisting that has led to the Faith movement's "little gods" doctrine, some important clarifications are in order.

What Do They Mean?

First, it should be pointed out that the phrase "little gods" may be unfortunate, but it is not necessarily heretical in and of itself, as long as it is not intended to convey that man is equal with, or a part of, God. The Eastern Orthodox church, for example, teaches that Christians are deified in the sense that they are adopted as sons of God, indwelt by the Spirit of God, and brought into communion with God which ultimately leads to glorification.[15] They do not teach that mere humans are reproductions or exact duplicates of God. Thus their doctrine of deification is consistent with Scripture and in keeping with a monotheistic worldview.

The real issue is the meaning that is poured into the words "little gods." The Faith teachers make it clear that by "little gods" they mean a direct departure from orthodox Christianity, or as they put it, "traditional church."

Next, it is important to draw a clear distinction between the concept of divinity taught by metaphysical cults— such as New Thought, Christian Science, Unity School of Christianity, Mind Science, and Religious Science—and the doctrine of deification taught by the Faith movement. Metaphysics does not teach that we are "little gods running around on the earth," as do Faith teachers such as Benny Hinn. Rather, they believe that an impersonal principle or substance called "the Christ Consciousness" or "Divine Mind" permeates reality, thus making everything divine.[16] In essence, metaphysics is an odd blend of pantheism (all is God) and panentheism (all is part of God). The Faith movement and the metaphysical cults are similar in that they both proclaim the divinity of man. They are distinct in that Faith teachers reject the concept of an impersonal God permeating creation.

Finally, I should clarify that most Faith teachers, like Mormons, hold to a distinct brand of polytheism. While teaching the unbiblical concept of many gods, as we will see later, they reserve worship for only three (God the Father, Jesus Christ, and the Holy Spirit). Thus it is more accurate to classify Faith teachers as henotheistic than polytheistic.[17]

Let us now turn our attention to the Scripture-twisting that has enabled Faith teachers to make their doctrines palatable to tens of thousands of unsuspecting people.

A New Twist of Scripture

The Faith teachers usually cite John 10:31-39 as proof that people are indeed little gods. This passage finds Jesus about to be stoned for claiming He is God. He responds to His opponents by referring to Psalm 82:6. In ironic fashion Jesus asks, "Is it not written in your Law, 'I have said you are gods?'" (verse 34). To this the Faith teachers exclaim, "Jesus said it, I believe it, and that settles it—we are little gods!" Or as TBN president Paul Crouch puts it, "I am a little god! Critics, be gone!"[18]

But before we capitulate to the Faith movement's "little gods" doctrine, let us take a closer look at the Old Testament passage to which Jesus was referring. Should it turn out that the Faith teachers are correct in their interpretation of this passage, then Christians owe an apology to the kingdom of the cults. But, of course, no such apology will be necessary.

Everyone should understand that the notion of Jesus teaching the "little gods" doctrine would carry devastating implications. For starters, it would mean that Christ is confused, since He previously taught there is only one God (Mark 12:29; cf. Deuteronomy 6:4). It would also prove that the Bible is contradictory, because it also teaches only one God (Isaiah 43:10; 44:6). Finally, it would demonstrate that the serpent was correct in telling Eve, "You will be like God" (Genesis 3:5). Any such teaching is nothing but a "doctrine of demons."

So why, in the face of a stoning (John 10:31), does Jesus calmly refer the Jews to Psalm 82? Let's take a look.

A Closer Look at Psalm 82

In Psalm 82 we find God holding court in the great assembly. He is pronouncing sentence on judges who were supposed to be defending the weak but were instead showing partiality to the wicked. In language so clear that it cannot be easily misunderstood, He ridicules human judges who have the audacity to think of themselves as gods. In other words, God's message is this: "So you think you're gods, do you? Well, the grave will prove you are *mere men*! When you die, you will forever know the infinite difference between Myself and the mightiest of mortals."

One thing is certain: A literal interpretation of the term "god" in Psalm 82:6 is clearly ruled out by the context. It is hard to miss that this passage opens with a strong denunciation of the injustices perpetrated by the judges of Israel (verse 2). As representatives of God (cf. Exodus 4:15,16; 6:28–7:2), they should have been just; instead, they were dishonest. How unlike God men are!

God states: "I said, 'You are "gods"; you are all the sons of the Most High.' But you will die like *mere men*; you will fall like every other ruler" (Psalm 82:6,7, emphasis added). These judges are no different from any other men. They are subject to the same weaknesses and frailties. They are indeed very far from being gods—however little—in any literal sense.

To interpret the Hebrew judges' designation as "gods" in a literal fashion is to imply that the nation of Israel believed in the existence of more than one God. But as we have noted above, such notions conflict with what the Bible reveals about God and His people.

But Aren't We Sons of the Most High?

Before we move on, let's take a moment to consider the phrase "sons of the Most High" in verse 6. Isn't it true that offspring take on the nature of their parents? (As Earl Paulk puts it, "Dogs have puppies and cats have kittens, so God has little gods."[19]) And since we are God's "sons," as the verse says, can't we legitimately call ourselves "little gods" who have our Father's nature?

One place we can test this hypothesis is in the book of Job. In few other portions of Scripture does God go to such lengths to compare Himself with mankind. He spends four complete chapters at the end of that book demonstrating for Job, in spellbinding detail, the vast difference between puny men and their awesome Creator. As Frederick Buechner so eloquently states, "God does not explain, He explodes. He asks Job who he thinks he is anyway. Trying to explain the kind of things Job wants explained would be like trying to explain Einstein to a small-necked clam."[20]

This truth is also a recurring theme in the magnificent book of Isaiah. Any number of passages could be cited, but allow me to quote just one:

> "You are my witnesses," declares the Lord, "and my servant whom I have chosen, so that you may know and believe me and understand that I am he. Before me no god was formed, nor will there be one after me. I, even I, am the Lord, and apart from me there is no savior. I have revealed and saved and proclaimed—I, and not some foreign god among you. You are my witnesses," declares the Lord, "that I am God. Yes, and from ancient days I am he. No one can deliver out of my hand. When I act, who can reverse it?"
>
> —Isaiah 43:10-13

Despite all attempts to clarify what should be self-evident to those who set themselves up as the very "anointed of God," the Faith teachers persist in propagating their deadly fantasies. In a conversation with Benny Hinn on the meaning of Psalm 82, Paul Crouch puts those who disagree with him in league with the devil: "So those that would put that teaching down, want us to have a beginning and an end. That's Satan, isn't it?" "Those that put us down are a bunch of morons!" responds Hinn, to which Crouch exults, "Glory to God, Glory to God!"[21]

But if Faith proponents want to take Jesus literally when He makes His ironic statement about men being gods, why not take Him literally when He calls the Pharisees "snakes" (Matthew 23:33)? Clearly, not even evil men are literally snakes—and they most certainly are not little gods. Though we are "sons" of the Most High, we are not sons by *nature* but by *adoption* (Galatians 4:5 8). Only Christ Himself can be said to have the *nature* of God. Christ is the only-begotten, unique, one-of-a-kind (Greek *monogenes*, one generation or nature) Son of God (John 1:14). Only He is truly God by nature (Philippians 2:6; cf. John 1:1; Galatians 4:8).

In Search of Little Gods

It may be helpful to point out that John 10 and Psalm 82 are not the only places in Scripture where men are referred to as gods. Moses, for example, was to function as a godlike judge over Pharaoh in Exodus 4:16. In addition, the Israelite judges were called *elohim*, or gods, in Exodus 21 and 22 because they held the power of life and death over men. But both the immediate and the broader context of Scripture make it clear that neither Moses nor Israel's judges were gods by nature.

Satan is also referred to as a "god" in 2 Corinthians 4:4. But surely no one assumes that this means that Satan is an exact duplicate of God.

Despite the clear teaching of Scripture, the Faith teachers continue to espouse their "little gods" doctrine. In fact, they regularly twist another text in a feeble attempt to support the deity of human beings.

Perverting Peter

Asking the uninitiated to turn to 2 Peter 1:4, the Faith teachers say that the apostle, under the inspiration of the Holy Spirit, here espouses their "little gods" doctrine.

As Copeland puts it, "Now Peter said by exceeding great and precious promises you become partakers of the divine nature. All right, are we gods? We are a class of gods!"[22]

The following verses (5-11), however, show that Peter is not talking about Christians becoming God or gods, but about undergoing a *moral* transformation of our nature from one that emulates the corruption of the world (verse 4) to one that reflects the character of God (verses 5-11). In no way can this text be twisted to mean that believers actually take on the essence or nature of God. While redeemed man may reflect the moral attributes of God, he in no way qualifies as an exact duplicate of God.

Faith teachers surely know that the very first book of the Bible demolishes the myth that mere men are exact duplicates of their Creator. Nevertheless, they continue to perpetuate their blasphemous theories on television, on tape, and in type.

If this Faith doctrine were true, can you imagine what would have happened when Satan tried to seduce Eve? Just picture the scene as Satan slithers up to Adam's partner:

> *"Eat the apple, sweetie pie, and you will become a god!"*
>
> *Eve, looking perplexed, responds, "Become? Become? What in the world do you think I am now? I am a little god! Satan, be gone!"*

Not until the Faith fable is stretched to its illogical conclusion can we catch the full-orbed dimensions of just how flawed and fanciful it really is. Never in Scripture is man declared to be an exact duplicate of God.

Jumbling Genesis

As if assaulting Psalm 82 and twisting 2 Peter 1:4 weren't enough, Faith teachers go on to abuse Genesis 1:26,27 in a pathetic attempt to reposition humanity on a level of equality with God.

In Genesis 1:26 God says, "Let us make man in our image, in our likeness." Charles Capps and Jerry Savelle suggest that the Hebrew word for likeness (*demuth*) literally means "an exact duplication in kind."[23]

But this is simply wrong. Ironically, the very word that Faith teachers abuse to justify their "little gods" doctrine refutes this erroneous teaching. Hebrew scholars point out that the word "likeness" (Hebrew *demuth*) "defines and limits" the other word translated as image (Hebrew *tselem*) in Genesis 1:26,27 *"to avoid the implication that man is a precise copy of God, albeit miniature."*[24]

The Hebrew word for likeness simply means similarity or resemblance, not identity.[25] The assertion that we are *exact duplicates* of God is not only deceptive, but it destroys all distinction between the Creator and His creation.

It is also clear in the broader context of Scripture that humans do not possess the *divine nature* of God.

First, if we are exact duplicates of God—and we, of course, are men—then God must be a man. But the Bible emphatically states that *God is not a man* (Numbers 23:19; 1 Samuel 15:29; Hosea 11:9).

Second, God Himself often makes statements of incomparability. How can there be any exact duplicates of God if, as God states in Exodus 9:14, "there is no one like me in all the earth"?

Third, although we were created in the image of God, we possess none of God's nontransferable or incommunicable attributes—such as self-existence, immutability, eternality, omnipotence, omniscience, omnipresence, and absolute sovereignty. God is *eternal* (Psalm 90:2), but man was *created at a point in time* (Genesis 1:26-31; cf. Job 3; 38:4,21) and has but a brief existence on earth (Job 7).[26] God has *life in Himself* (John 5:26), but man is *dependent on God* to sustain him (Acts 17:28). God is *all-powerful* (Job 42:2),[27] but man is *weak*

(1 Corinthians 1:25).[28] God is *all-knowing* (Isaiah 40:13, 14; Psalm 147:5), but man is *limited in knowledge* (Isaiah 55:8,9).[29] God is *everywhere present* (Jeremiah 23:23,24),[30] but humans are confined to *a single space at a time* (Psalm 139:1-12).[31]

Far from being a *reproduction* of God, humanity is more correctly portrayed as a *reflection* of God. That humans are created in God's image simply means that they share, in a finite and imperfect way, the *communicable attributes* of God. Among these attributes are personality, spirituality (John 4:24), rationality, including knowledge and wisdom (Colossians 3:10), and morality, including goodness, holiness, righteousness, love, justice, and mercy (Ephesians 4:24ff).

These attributes in turn give us the capacity to enjoy fellowship with God and to develop personal relationships with one another. They also equip us "to carry out God's will . . . that man tend and rule the creation in such a way that it would come to realize its full potential."[32] Theologian Millard Erickson summed it up nicely when he wrote that "the image of God in humanity comprises those qualities of God which, reflected in man, make worship, personal interaction, and work possible."[33]

The Dominion Dilemma

We should note at this juncture that Genesis *never* depicts humanity as a some sort of *autonomous sovereign*, but as a *steward* entrusted with the care of his Creator's creation. The cultural mandate makes it crystal clear that while God has given humanity dominion over some of His earthly creation (Genesis 1:26,28), humans are still mere mortals and are therefore held responsible for how they handle all that God has assigned them to do.

Faith teachers replace the biblical view of dominion with their unbiblical concept of deification. Benny Hinn gets particularly absurd at this point. He waxes eloquent on the

THE DEIFICATION OF MAN

Hebrew meaning of the word for dominion. According to Hinn:

> Adam was a super being when God created him. I don't know whether people know this, but he was the first Superman that really ever lived. First of all, the Scriptures declare clearly that he had dominion over the fowls of the air, the fish of the sea—which means he used to fly. Of course, how can he have dominion over the birds and not be able to do what they do? The word "dominion" in the Hebrew clearly declares that if you have dominion over a subject, that you do everything that subject does. In other words, that subject, if it does something you cannot do, you don't have dominion over it. I'll prove it further. Adam not only flew, he flew to space. He was—with one thought he would be on the moon.[34]

Truly, not since Brigham Young of Mormon fame claimed that the sun was inhabited[35] have I heard such bizarre biblical eisegesis. If one were to draw out Hinn's comment to its illogical conclusion, not only would Adam be able to fly like a bird, but he would also be able to spin webs like a spider, hibernate like a bear, and photosynthesize like an eggplant!

Hinn has a grossly mistaken understanding of the concept of dominion. The Hebrew verb translated "have dominion" (*radah*, Genesis 1:26,28) also carries the meanings *rule and reign*.[36] Contrary to Hinn's view, to rule or reign (to have dominion over someone or something) does not mean that the ruler possesses the unique abilities of his subjects. For example, simply because a lion trainer exercises dominion over a lion does not mean that he or she is capable of doing everything the lion does. The point is that the trainer has control (i.e., has dominion) over the lion so that he or she can harness the animal's power and capabilities.

The fact is that the Bible nowhere teaches the "little gods" doctrine. God is infinitely and eternally exalted above humankind. It is the height of arrogance to think that humans can come close to approximating God in His awesome holiness and majesty. Yet this is precisely what the proponents of Faith theology are eager to do.

The Demotion of God

*I*t's one thing to deify man; it is quite another to demote God. Yet that is precisely what the Faith teachers have done. The God of the Faith movement is little more than a cosmic gofer at the beck and call of his creation—a genie waiting for us to rub Aladdin's lamp of faith.

The sad truth is that the Faith teachers have crafted man in the image of God, and God in the image of man.

A Husky Point-Guard

Kenneth Copeland claims that God is "not some creature that stands 28 feet tall, and He's got hands, you know, as big as basketballs. That's not the kind of creature He is. . . . A being that is very uncanny the way He's very much like you and me. A being that stands somewhere around 6'-2", 6'-3", that weighs somewhere in the neighborhood of a couple of hundred pounds, little better, [and] has a [hand] span of nine inches across."[1]

Where in the world does Copeland derive this monstrosity? The answer is that he tortures the words of the prophet Isaiah. When Isaiah, using a common figure of speech, says that God marked off the heavens with His span (40:12), Copeland takes out a ruler, measures the span of his hand, finds it to be 8¾ inches, and speculates that God's hand must be about a quarter of an inch larger than his!

Copeland should know that Isaiah 40:12 cannot be interpreted literally. If it were, it would be reduced to an absurdity: God would not only have body parts, but He would be holding a basket full of dust and would be weighing mountains on a gigantic set of scales.

Bosom Buddies

Copeland is not the only Faith teacher who wrenches Isaiah 40:12 out of context. Jerry Savelle elaborates on his mentor's teaching when he says:

> God is not 437 feet tall, weighing 4000 pounds, and got a fist big around as this room. He's big, but He's not a monster. He measured out heaven with a nine-inch span. . . . The distance between my thumb and my finger is not quite nine inches. So, I know He's bigger than me, thank God. Amen? But He's not some great, big, old thing that couldn't come through the door there and, you know, when He sat down, would fill every seat in the house. I don't serve The Glob. I serve God, and I've been created in His image and in His likeness.[2]

Savelle seems oblivious to the fact that Isaiah is using figurative language (cf. verses 2,5-7,10,11,22,24) to convey the supreme majesty and surpassing greatness of our God (verses 18,25,26,28,29). Rather than reducing God to the dimensions of man, Isaiah goes to great lengths to underscore the difference between the Creator and His creation.

Morris Cerullo, like Copeland and Savelle, also demotes God to the stature of a man. Rather than searching for proof texts, however, he takes a more direct approach. Alluding to one of his out-of-body experiences, Cerullo says:

> As I lay there on the floor in this condition, my spirit was taken out of my body and the next

thing I knew, I was in the heavens.... Suddenly, in front of this tremendous multitude of people, the glory of God appeared. The Form that I saw was about the height of a man six feet tall, maybe a little taller, and twice as broad as a human body with no distinguishing features such as eyes, nose, or mouth.[3]

Benny Hinn takes his stories to an even more fanciful extreme. He not only remakes God in the image of a man, but claims to know what God is wearing. Says Hinn, "I could almost visibly see the Lord, and I could tell you what He was wearing." Jan Crouch, giddy about Hinn's statement, asks, "Was that the Holy Spirit?" Acknowledging that he may get in trouble, Hinn resolutely answers "yes."[4]

Hinn also embraces a heresy known as tritheism—the false belief in the existence of three gods. During a sermon broadcast to a potential listening audience which numbers in the millions, Hinn made the following statement, supposedly via "revelation knowledge":

Man, I feel revelation knowledge already coming on me here. Lift your hands. Something new is going to happen here today. I felt it just as I walked down here. Holy Spirit, take over in the name of Jesus.... God the Father, ladies and gentlemen, is a person; and He is a triune being by Himself separate from the Son and the Holy Ghost. Say, what did you say? Hear it, hear it, hear it. See, God the Father is a person, God the Son is a person, God the Holy Ghost is a person. But *each one* of them is a *triune* being by Himself. If I can shock you—and maybe I should—there's *nine of them*. Huh, what did you say? Let me explain: God the Father, ladies and gentlemen, is a person with his own personal spirit, with his own personal soul, and his own personal spirit-body. You say, Huh, I never heard that. Well you think you're in this church to hear things you've heard for the last 50 years? You can't argue with the Word, can you? It's all in the Word.[5]

When questioned by *Christianity Today* about this heretical statement, Hinn responded, "That was a very dumb statement. . . . I told my church the very next week that the statement was wrong."[6]

I'm glad to see that Hinn admits his statement was dumb, but this raises a serious dilemma: Hinn explicitly claimed that his statement was a revelation from God. Thus, according to Hinn, God would have made a very dumb remark.

After further questioning, Hinn acknowledged that God had nothing to do with his revelation. Rather, says Hinn, it was something he had read somewhere.[7] You might hope that after getting caught red-handed, Hinn would drop this distorted declaration from his repertoire.

Instead, however, two years after his initial "revelation," Hinn once again voiced virtually the same statement. As he puts it, "God the Father, God the Son, and God the Holy Ghost—three separate individuals, one in essence, one in work—and, may I add, each one of them possesses His own spirit-body. You don't like it?"[8]

No, I don't like it because it contradicts the clear teaching of the Bible. The assertion that each member of the Trinity has His own distinct spirit-body implies that there are *three separate and distinct beings*—in other words, *three Gods*. This unbiblical view (tritheism) runs contrary to the whole of Scripture, which affirms *one God revealed in three Persons*.[9]

Truth or Travesty?

At this point you may be tempted to say, "So Hinn, Copeland, and company do say some pretty bizarre things, but let's not make a federal case out of it. After all, we all have our own heresies. Let's allow Jesus to sort it all out in heaven." Sounds pretty tolerant, doesn't it? But just remember that while tolerance in personal relationships may be a virtue, tolerance when it comes to truth is a travesty. In this case, those who believe that God is made in the image of man do not believe in the God of Scripture.[10]

A doctrine that shrinks God to the status of man destroys an essential of the historic Christian faith. No Christian should simply look the other way and pretend it doesn't matter. Once we allow teaching on the nature of God to be twisted to the extent that it has been by the Faith movement, we have departed from the Christian faith and have headed for the kingdom of the cults. The reality is that the Faith God is no God at all. He may, in fact, be more impotent than the god of Mormonism.

If you find this assertion hard to believe, consider this tragic statement by Kenneth Copeland:

> I was shocked when I found out who the biggest failure in the Bible actually is. . . . The biggest one in the whole Bible is God. . . . Now, the reason you don't think of God as a failure is He never said He's a failure. And you're not a failure till you say you're one.[11]

To add insult to injury, he says:

> Adam committed high treason; and at that point, all the dominion and authority God had given to him was handed over to Satan. Suddenly, God was on the outside looking in. . . .

> After Adam's fall, God found Himself in a
> peculiar position. . . . God needed an avenue
> back into the earth. . . . God laid out His prop-
> osition and Abram accepted it. It gave God
> access to the earth and gave man access to
> God. . . . Technically, if God ever broke the
> Covenant, He would have to destroy Him-
> self.[12]

The deity of Faith theology bears little resemblance to
the God of the Bible. The minute God is assigned physical
qualities such as height and weight, He is by definition not the
God of Scripture. As Jesus Himself said, God is spirit (John
4:24; cf. Deuteronomy 4:12).

Of course, to assert that God is a failure is to question
God's own claim to omnipotence. If God is all-powerful, can
any circumstance be beyond His control? Is it ever possible to
frustrate His sovereign will? Clearly, the answer is a resounding NO! Nothing is too hard for the God of all creation
(Jeremiah 32:17,27), with whom all things are possible (Matthew 19:26).

Nebuchadnezzar found this out the hard way. He
dared to exalt himself to the level of God and was treated to a
diet of grass for seven years. But at least he learned his lesson.
This is what he had to say after seven years of hanging out
with the heifers:

> [God's] dominion is an eternal dominion; his
> kingdom endures from generation to gener-
> ation. All the peoples of the earth are
> regarded as nothing.
> He does as he pleases with the powers of
> heaven and the peoples of the earth.
> No one can hold back his hand or say to him:
> What have you done?
> —Daniel 4:34,35

God cannot fail, has not failed, and never will fail. God does not have to negotiate with one of His creatures in order to gain access to His own handiwork. Such an idea is absurd and denies God's unspeakable power. Furthermore, the thought of God losing control implies that He was caught off guard, that He overlooked some vital factor which caused Him to be ejected from the pilot's seat.

But that cannot happen to the God of Scripture. Our God is omniscient (Psalm 147:5; Romans 11:33; Hebrews 4:13) and nothing catches Him by surprise (cf. Isaiah 42:9). The god of Copeland may well be a failure dependent upon the beneficence of His creation, but his god is purely imaginary. The God of Scripture is self-existent, transcendent and invincible; and His knowledge is truly perfect (Job 37:16).

What kind of god cannot even maintain a grip on a changing situation? How can he be taken by surprise and lose control of his own creation? What sort of deity can be evicted from a universe that he himself created, and then rely on mere creatures to reenter that same world? Can any such being be seriously equated with the God of the Bible, whose dominion is an eternal dominion, whose kingdom endures from generation to generation, who does as He pleases with the powers of heaven and the peoples of the earth, and whose hand no one can hold back? There is no comparison. The so-called god of the Faith movement may look like the Faith teachers, but he bears no resemblance to the God of the Bible.

The Deification of Satan

*S*o far we have pointed out that the Faith movement not only deifies man but demotes God. Now it is time to examine a new depth of doctrinal distortion as we examine the Faith teaching regarding the deification of Satan.

According to Faith theology, Satan pulled off the coup of the ages when, in the Garden of Eden, he tricked Adam into committing cosmic treason. For the price of an apple, Adam and Eve sold their godhood to Satan.

Not only did Adam and Eve lose their nature as gods, but they were infused with the very nature of Satan. In one blinding instant, the first man and woman were transformed from the divine to the demonic, and Satan became the god of this world.

In that fateful moment, Adam and Eve were barred from Eden, God was banished from the earth, and Satan acquired the legal rights to all the earth and her inhabitants.

Deadly Dualism

This Faith mythology features an implicit form of dualism: two forces fighting it out for control of the universe, and you never knew who is finally going to win. If God had not caught Satan on a technicality, Jesus would have been doomed, humans would have been eternally lost, and Satan would have won the universe! In fact, as we saw previously (chapter 10), the condition was so dire at one point that God faced the possibility of literally having to "destroy Himself." C.S. Lewis described this type of dualism as "the belief that there are two equal and independent powers at the back of everything, one of them good and the other bad, and that this universe is the battlefield in which they fight out an endless war."[1]

This would be an apt description of what is being taught today in Faith circles, except for an interesting twist: The powers behind both forces—God and Satan—are *activated* by words spoken by humans. As Copeland articulates it, "Fear activates Satan the way faith activates God."[2]

While this concept is foreign to Scripture, it can be found in pagan religions. Although Faith teachers are not as blatantly dualistic as Zoroastrians and ancient Gnostics, by implication they teach that God and Satan are positionally peers.

It is truly difficult to overstate the horrifying implications of this worldview. If embraced, this concept forever destroys the biblical view of God, who is not only omniscient, omnipotent, self-existent, transcendent, eternal, incomprehensible, invisible, immutable, infinite, perfect in wisdom, and holy, but is also the sovereign Being who orders all things according to the counsel of His own will (Ephesians 1:11).

Divine, Demonic or Distinctly Human?

What is particularly strange about Faith theology is that man is portrayed as either divine or demonic. From a practical perspective, there is no such thing as a distinct human nature in Faith theology. Benny Hinn makes this clear in a message broadcast worldwide via the Trinity Broadcasting Network. Says Hinn:

> God came from heaven, became a man, made
> man into little gods, went back to heaven as a

man. He faces the Father as a man. I face
devils as the son of God. ... Quit your nonsense! What else are you? If you say, *I am,*
you're saying I'm a part of Him, right? Is he
God? Are you His offspring? Are you His
children? *You can't be human!* You can't! You
can't! *God didn't give birth to flesh.* ... You
said, "Well, that's heresy." No, that's your
crazy brain saying that.[3]

Incredibly, Hinn prefaced this sermon by saying,
"I'm going to be led by the Holy Ghost today."[4] But the Holy
Ghost could not have been speaking through Hinn because
there is not a shred of biblical evidence that man is anything
but distinctly human. Human beings do not have the nature of
a fallen angel, and as we have seen in the previous chapter,
they most certainly are not little gods.

Adam's fall into a life of sin, terminated by death, did
not transform his nature from divine to demonic, but rather
tarnished it. Even after the fall, the Bible refers to man as
being made in the image of God (Genesis 9:6; 1 Corinthians
11:7; James 3:9). As a result of the fall, human nature was
damaged and distorted, but it was definitely not destroyed.

To borrow Calvin's analogy, the image of God was
shattered within man, but like reflections of one's face in a
broken mirror, distorted images of God's glory can still be
seen within fallen man. While the image of God (*imago Dei*)
makes man like God, it does not make him a god.

Will the Real Sovereign of the Universe Please Stand Up?

The Faith teachers also persist in making both God
and Satan subservient to man in their war for the world. In
their mythological worldview, man was directly responsible
for causing God to became the most colossal failure of all

time. In this regard, remember Kenneth Copeland's assertion that God was the biggest failure of all time.[5] It is almost beyond comprehension that, to the applause of born-again believers, so-called Christian leaders demote God to the status of a failure. Copeland is even willing to give ownership of the earth to Satan:

> God's on the outside looking in. *He doesn't have any legal entrée into the earth. The thing don't belong to Him.* You see how *sassy* the Devil was in the presence of God in the book of Job? God said, Where have you been? *Wasn't any of God's business.* He [Satan] didn't even have to answer if he didn't want to. . . . God didn't argue with him a *bit!* You see, this is the position that God's been in. . . . Might say, "Well, if God's running things He's doing a lousy job of it." *He hadn't been running 'em,* except when He's just got, you know, a little bit of a chance.[6]

How such blasphemy could be tolerated in the Christian community is beyond me. The Bible nowhere deifies Satan. Far from being a sovereign power, Satan is but a created being (cf. Psalm 148:2,5; Colossians 1:16). He is an angel—not a god—and a fallen angel at that. The difference between God and Satan is analogous to the difference between a potter and his clay (cf. Isaiah 29:16; 45:9; 64:8; Jeremiah 18:6). Satan may be described as the prince of *this* (not of *the*) world (John 16:11; 2 Corinthians 4:4), but orthodoxy has always affirmed that Satan is a creature who is subject to the will of his Creator (Psalm 103:20,21).

If God had no legal right to interfere in a world supposedly under the control of Satan, how could He have banished Adam and Eve from Eden or subsequently destroyed the world with the flood? And how could He still have the audacity to claim that "every animal of the forest is mine, and the cattle on a thousand hills. I know every bird in the mountains, and the creatures of the field are mine. . . . The world is mine, and all that is in it" (Psalm 50:10-12)? If we are to take seriously what the Faith teachers say, we must also conclude that God was simply issuing bold but empty proclamations.

The whole notion of Satan gaining ascendancy over the earth is based on the idea that mankind was given ownership of the earth, which he transferred to the devil. But as we already have seen, this is simply untrue. Human beings are caretakers, not owners, of the earth. Everything belongs to God:

> The earth is the Lord's, and everything in it,
> the world, and all who live in it (Psalm 24:1).

Even according to the rules of Faith lore, Satan could never have become the legal owner of the earth. Why? Because the person who allegedly gave it to him, Adam, never owned it in the first place!

The Supreme Court of the Universe

It is astonishing to see how glibly Faith teachers reduce God to a failure and elevate Satan to a sovereign. Today you can browse through many Christian bookstores and find a variety of books which make God accountable to "the Supreme Court of the Universe." Here is just one example from Charles Capps's book, *Authority in Three Worlds*:

> Adam had revelation knowledge that flowed from God, the Father. But when Adam bowed his knee to Satan, he shut God out. God found Himself on the outside looking in. His man, Adam, had lost his authority. Satan . . . had become the god of the world system. . . .

> Satan had gained ascendancy in the earth by gaining Adam's authority, and God was left on the outside. God *couldn't* come here in His divine power and wipe them out. He had to move in an area where it would be *ruled legal* by the *Supreme Court of the Universe*.[7]

Just think of it: "God couldn't"! Here we have Adam taking on the nature of Satan, Satan taking on the nature of God, and God getting banished from His universe! The words "God couldn't" alone should be enough to make us shudder. And just who in heaven's name sits on the so-called "Supreme Court of the Universe"?

The thought of God being accountable to a judicial council is ridiculous in the extreme. Justice itself is a reflection of God's nature (Ezra 9:15; Psalm 119:137; 145:17; Jeremiah 12:1; Daniel 9:14). He delights in exercising kindness, justice, and righteousness (Jeremiah 9:24). If indeed God had to answer to Capps's cosmic committee, He by definition would not really be God.

The God of Scripture is the ultimate Judge of the universe (Genesis 18:25; Psalm 96:13; Ecclesiastes 3:17; Hebrews 12:23; 2 Timothy 4:1); the God of Charles Capps is but the figment of his imagination.

Incredibly, Kenneth Copeland manages to further demote God. In a tape titled "What Happened from the Cross to the Throne" he insists:

> The Bible says that God gave this earth to the sons of men . . . and when [Adam] turned and gave that dominion to Satan, look where it left God. It left Him on the outside looking in. . . . He had no legal right to do anything about it, did He? . . . He had injected Himself illegally into the earth—what Satan had intended for Him to do was to fall for it—pull off an illegal act and turn the light off in God, and

subordinate God to himself. . . . He intended
to get God into such a trap that He couldn't get
out.[8]

   To suggest that God had no legal right, that Satan
might have "turned the light off in God," and that there is a
Supreme Court of the Universe to which God is accountable
is to promote the most extreme form of heresy. If the Faith
teachers do not repent from such blasphemous statements
this side of eternity, they will one day answer to the Supreme
Authority of the universe (cf. Matthew 7:21-23; James 3:1).
And judgment will be meted out not by some mythological
supreme court, but by the self-existent, transcendent, all-
powerful God who rules all things by the edict of His own
will.

The Demotion of Christ

*A*lmost all cults and world religions compromise the deity of Christ, and the Faith movement is no exception.

So far we have seen the Faith teachers re-create man in the image of God, demote God to the status of man, and deify Satan as a god. Now we will see them demote Christ to the level of a mere mortal. Consider this incredible statement by Kenneth Copeland:

> [Adam] was the copy, looked just like [God]. If you stood Adam upside God, they look just exactly alike. If you stood Jesus and Adam side-by-side, they would look and sound exactly alike.[1]

Here a leading Faith teacher claims no difference and no distinction between God and man. But it doesn't stop there. Listen to what Christ supposedly told Copeland in the following prophecy:

> Don't be disturbed when people put you down and speak harshly and roughly of you. They spoke that way of Me, should they not speak that way of you? The more you get to be like Me, the more they're going to think that way of you. They crucified Me for claiming that I was God. But I didn't claim I was God; I just

claimed I walked with Him and that He was in Me. Hallelujah.[2]

Upon being questioned about this blasphemy, Copeland replied, "I didn't say Jesus *wasn't* God, I said He [Jesus] didn't *claim* to be God when He lived on the earth. Search the Gospels for yourself. If you do, you'll find what I say is true."[3]

Searching the Gospels

If Copeland's followers would follow his suggestion to search the Gospels, they would discover how wrong he really is. To begin, consider the Gospel of John. In John 10:30 Jesus says, "I and the Father are one." Modern readers might misunderstand the significance of His statement, but the ancient Jews most certainly did not. They knew precisely what Jesus meant. They didn't even wait for further clarification. Immediately they picked up stones and denounced Christ for blasphemy, because they said, "You, a mere man, claim to be God" (John 10:33). Here Jesus proclaims Himself to be God; but Copeland, like the Jews who wanted to stone Jesus, proclaims Him to be *a mere man.*

Incredibly, the very next verse of the same chapter (John 10:34) is precisely the one used by Faith teachers to prove that *men* are gods! In the space of two verses, Faith theology manages to make Jesus into a little man and man into a little god. Apparently, almost everyone gets to be God . . . except Jesus.

Astonishingly, Copeland deifies man and demotes Jesus Christ. It is mind-boggling to hear Copeland assert:

> What [why] does God have to pay the price for this thing? He has to have a man that is like that first one. It's got to be a man. He's got to be all man. *He cannot be a God* and come storming in here with attributes and dignities that are

not common to man. He *can't* do that. It's not legal.[4]

Not only does Copeland reduce Jesus to a carbon copy of the man who walked through the Garden of Eden—as though Adam were *Theanthropos* (the God-man)—but he clearly divests Christ of every shred of deity.

If John 10:33 is not enough to convince Copeland that Jesus was indeed God in human flesh, how about John 5:18? Here again the Jews try to kill Jesus, not only because He was breaking the Sabbath, but also because "he was even calling God his own father, making himself equal with God" (John 5:18).

Or what about John 8:58, where Jesus says, "I tell you the truth . . . before Abraham was born, I am"? Jesus makes His deity so clear in this text that no one should be able to misunderstand the point. By using the phrase "I am," Jesus unequivocally identifies Himself as the everlasting God (cf. Exodus 3:14; Isaiah 43:10). This is no slip of the pen on John's part, either. On many other occasions the apostle notes Christ using similar terminology to claim deity (cf. John 1:1,14; 3:13; 17:5).[5]

Copeland leaves us on the horns of a dilemma. Either he and Jesus never had the conversation that Copeland claims they had, or Jesus has a flawed memory and merely forgot what had been penned by His beloved disciple, the apostle John.

From Bad to Worse

If possible, Benny Hinn's statements are even more unnerving. In the first edition of the blockbuster *Good Morning, Holy Spirit*, Hinn writes:

> And let me add this: Had the Holy Spirit not been with Jesus, He *would have sinned*. That's right, it was the Holy Spirit that was the power

that kept Him pure. He was not only sent from heaven, but He was called the *Son of Man*—and as such He was capable of sinning.... Without the Holy Ghost, Jesus would have never have made it.... Can you imagine Christ headed for the grave, knowing He would remain there forever, if the Holy Ghost would change His mind about raising Him from the dead?[6]

How is it possible that Benny Hinn, who claims to have frequent communications with God and bills himself as anointed, would not have grasped one of the fundamental principles of Scripture? When Jesus refers to Himself as the Son of Man (no less than 82 times), He is using a title which clearly designates Him as the Divine Messiah (cf. Daniel 7:13,14).[7]

Every orthodox scholar in the 2000-year history of the church has recognized that when Jesus called Himself "the Son of Man" He was indeed claiming to be God. During the incarnation, Jesus was 100 percent God as well as 100 percent man. He did not lay aside His divine attributes. To say that Jesus surrendered even one attribute of divinity is to assert that Jesus Christ is less than God and is therefore not God at all.

While Christ voluntarily veiled His divine *glory* (Philippians 2:5-11), Scripture insists that He did not surrender His divine *attributes*. And as God, Jesus *would not* have sinned.

A Billion Incarnations of God

Just so you don't miss their point about the demotion of Christ, the Faith teachers make it clear by proclaiming that believers are as much incarnations of God as was Jesus. Copeland, in fact, seems to think he is so much like Christ that if he had the knowledge of the Word of God that Jesus did, he himself could have redeemed mankind.[8]

Faith teachers appear to see Christ as little more than

our big brother. Charles Capps even denies the uniqueness of Christ when he asserts that God purposed to make millions and millions of people *exactly like Jesus!*[9]

There is no better word than *blasphemy* for a teaching that demotes Jesus Christ to the level of a man, a mere prototype of millions and millions of others who are exactly like Him.

The Scripture makes it clear that Jesus was not merely *one of many* incarnations of God, but He was *the one and only* incarnation of God. Further, Scripture teaches that He is the unique *monogenes*, the only-begotten Son, the Son of God (John 3:16).

Faith theology not only demotes Jesus but it teaches that the incarnate Christ was spoken into being in the same manner in which God spoke the universe into existence. As Charles Capps puts it, "God spoke it. God transmitted that image to Mary. She received the image inside of her. . . . The embryo that was in Mary's womb was nothing more than the Word of God."[10]

Copeland then stretches this heresy to its most ridiculous extreme. He not only has Jesus spoken into existence by God's Word of faith, but has Him coming together piecemeal. As you may recall, it was Copeland who said:

> The faith it took to make fingers was loosed, the faith it took to make arms was loosed in the earth, and now God had a way to hover over a little woman by the name of Mary. And there was born of that virgin woman a product of God. Once again, something has happened from the insides of God.[11]

In one of the greatest understatements of his career, Copeland promises, "Here's where we're gonna depart from ordinary church":

> Now, you see, God is injecting His Word into
> the earth to produce this Jesus—these faith-
> filled words that framed the image that's in
> Him. . . . He can't just walk onto the earth and
> say, "Let it be!" because *He doesn't have the
> right.* He had to sneak it in here around the god
> of this world that was blockin' every way that
> he possibly could.[12]

Perhaps you are squirming in your seat and thinking,
*If that's what Copeland teaches, I've heard enough! Maybe I
really ought to reevaluate.*

Unfortunately, there's more. Copeland continues by
asserting that "God was making promises to Jesus, and *Jesus
wasn't even there.* But, you see, God deals with things that are
not yet as though they already were. That's the way He gets
them to come to pass."[13]

In what may well be the ultimate demotion, Copeland's reckless statements strip the preincarnate Christ of His
omnipresence and eternal existence—indeed, of His very
Godhood. How can Christ guarantee our salvation if He is not
God?

Clearly, Copeland, Capps, and others who teach this
heresy have a great deal more in common with the cults than
they do with Christianity. With virtually each speaking
engagement, new heresy is brought to the fore. It is indeed
sobering to consider the devastating consequences.

The Difference It Makes

Some people may wonder why it is so important to get
our doctrine in order concerning God and man. Does it really
matter? Even if we were to miss the bull's-eye on this issue,
are the consequences really that serious?

The answer to both questions is YES! Our understanding of God and of ourselves is crucial to our relationship to one
another and, more importantly, to God.

Christianity is first and foremost a relationship. A relationship requires that two or more people have fellowship with one another, spend time together, and establish a personal tie. Suppose someone walks up to you and says: "I have a relationship with God. He appeared to me in my room last night and told me that he had been reincarnated many times, coming into contact with individuals all over the world so that he may share with them the key to life. He also told me that his wisdom has been written for all men to see: It can be found in the Vedas, in the Bible, and in the Koran, to name just a few books. God said that he was once a man, but has now evolved to higher levels of existence. He assured me that I too can achieve that level if I follow his instructions."

I hope you would agree with me that this person's god is not the God of the Bible.

God defines Himself by His character traits. God embodies certain attributes that mark Him off from the rest of creation, including other so-called gods (1 Corinthians 8:5). We can definitively state that the imaginary person we just described could not have a relationship with the one true God. Why? Because the god he spoke about did not match God's own description of Himself in Scripture.

The same is true of the god of the Faith movement. The deity described by the Faith teachers does not match Scripture's revelation about Almighty God. Therefore, the god it concocts is a false god, and its gospel a false gospel (2 Corinthians 11:4,13).

The stakes are high, for countless souls are being led to place their trust in a false deity. And unless a person has a true relationship with the God of the Bible, his eternal well-being hangs in the balance.

Christianity IN CRISIS

PART FOUR

---

*Atonement
Atrocities*

I shall never forget the first time I heard him tell the story. The impact will live on forever in my heart. I can see it all now in my mind's eye as though it were just yesterday. Dr. D. James Kennedy had just mounted the magnificent pulpit of the Coral Ridge Church in Fort Lauderdale, Florida. In moments he was telling the story of a young man named John Griffith.

The time, he said, was the roaring twenties. The place was Oklahoma. John Griffith was in his early twenties— newly married and full of optimism. Along with his lovely wife, he had been blessed with a beautiful, blue-eyed baby. With delight and excitement, John was dreaming the American dream.

He wanted to be a traveler. He imagined what it would be like to visit faraway places with strange-sounding names. He would read about them and research them. His hopes and dreams were so vivid that at times they seemed more real than reality itself. But then came 1929 and the great stock market crash.

With the shattering of the American economy came the devastation of John's dreams. The winds that howled through Oklahoma were strangely symbolic of the gale force that was sweeping away his hopes. Oklahoma was being systematically ravaged by depression and despair.

And so, brokenhearted, John packed up his few possessions and with his wife and little son, Greg, headed east in an old Model-A Ford. They made their way toward Missouri, to the edge of the Mississippi River, and there he found a job tending one of the great railroad bridges that spanned the massive river.

Day after day John would sit in a control room and direct the enormous gears of an immense bridge over the mighty river. He would look out wistfully as bulky barges and splendid ships glided gracefully under his elevated bridge. Then, mechanically, he would lower the massive structure and stare pensively into the distance as great trains roared by and became little more than specks on the horizon. Each day he looked on sadly as they carried with them his shattered dreams and his visions of far-off places and exotic destinations.

It wasn't until 1937 that a new dream began to be birthed in his heart. His young son was now eight years old, and John had begun to catch a vision for a new life, a life in which Greg would work shoulder-to-shoulder with him, a life of intimate fellowship and friendship. The first day of this new life dawned and brought with it new hope and a fresh purpose. Excitedly they packed their lunches and, arm in arm, headed off toward the immense bridge.

Greg looked on in wide-eyed amazement as his dad pressed down the huge lever that raised and lowered the vast bridge. As he watched, he thought that his father must surely be the greatest man alive. He marveled that his dad could single-handedly control the movements of such a stupendous structure.

Before they knew it, noontime had arrived. John had just elevated the bridge and allowed some scheduled ships to pass through. And then, taking his son by the hand, they headed off for lunch. Hand in hand, they inched their way down a narrow catwalk and out onto an observation deck that projected some 50 feet over the majestic Mississippi. There they sat and watched spellbound as the ships passed by below.

As they ate, John told his son, in vivid detail, stories about the marvelous destinations of the ships that glided below them. Enveloped in a world of thought, he related story after story, his son hanging on every word.

Then, suddenly, in the midst of telling a tale about the time the river had overflowed its banks, he and his son were startled back to reality by the shrieking whistle of a distant train. Looking at his watch in disbelief, John saw that it was already 1:07. Immediately he remembered that the bridge was still raised and that the Memphis Express would be by in just minutes.

Not wanting to alarm his son, he suppressed his panic. In the calmest tone he could muster, he instructed his son to stay put. Quickly leaping to his feet, he jumped onto the catwalk. As the precious seconds flew by, he ran at full tilt to the steel ladder leading into the control house.

Once in, he searched the river to make sure that no ships were in sight. And then, as he had been trained to do, he looked straight down beneath the bridge to make certain nothing was below. As his eyes moved downward, he saw something so horrifying that his heart froze in his chest. For there, below him in the massive gearbox that housed the colossal gears that moved the gigantic bridge, was his beloved son.

Apparently Greg had tried to follow his dad but had fallen off the catwalk. Even now he was wedged between the teeth of two main cogs in the gearbox. Although he appeared to be conscious, John could see that his son's leg had already begun to bleed profusely. Immediately an even more horrifying thought flashed through his mind. For in that instant he knew that lowering the bridge meant killing the apple of his eye.

Panicked, his mind probed in every direction, frantically searching for solutions. Suddenly a plan emerged. In his mind's eye he saw himself grabbing a coiled rope, climbing down the ladder, running down the catwalk, securing the rope, sliding down toward his son, and pulling him back up to safety. Then in an instant he would move back down toward the control lever and thrust it down just in time for the oncoming train.

As soon as these thoughts appeared, he realized the futility of his plan. Instantly, he knew that there just wouldn't be enough time. Perspiration began to bead on John's brow, terror written over every inch of his face. His mind darted here and there, vainly searching for yet another solution. What would he do? What *could* he do?

His thoughts rushed in anguish to the oncoming train. In a state of panic, his agonized mind considered the 400 people that were moving inexorably closer toward the bridge. Soon the train would come roaring out of the trees with tremendous speed. But this—this was his son . . . his only child . . . his pride . . . his joy.

His mother—he could see her tearstained face now. This was their child, their beloved son. He was his father and this was his boy.

He knew in a moment there was only one thing he could do. He knew he would have to do it. And so, burying his face under his left arm, he plunged down the lever. The cries of his son were quickly drowned out by the relentless sound of the bridge as it ground slowly into position. With only seconds to spare, the Memphis Express—with its 400 passengers—roared out of the trees and across the mighty bridge.

John Griffith lifted his tearstained face and looked into the windows of the passing train. A businessman was reading the morning newspaper. A uniformed conductor was glancing nonchalantly at his large vest pocket-watch. Ladies were already sipping their afternoon tea in the dining cars. A small boy, looking strangely like his own son, Greg, pushed a long, thin spoon into a large dish of ice cream. Many of the passengers seemed to be engaged in either idle conversation or careless laughter. But no one looked his way. No one even cast a glance at the giant gearbox that housed the mangled remains of his hopes and dreams.

In anguish he pounded the glass in the control room and cried out, "What's the matter with you people? Don't you care? Don't you know I've sacrificed my son for you? What's wrong with you?" No one answered; no one heard. No one even looked. Not one of them seemed to care. And then, as suddenly as it had happened, it was over. The train disappeared, moving rapidly across the bridge and out over the horizon.

Even now as I retell this story, my face is wet with tears. For this illustration is but a faint glimpse of what God the Father did for us in sacrificing His Son, Jesus, to atone for the sins of the world (John 3:16). However, unlike the Memphis Express that caught John Griffith by surprise, God—in His great love and according to His sovereign will and purpose—determined to sacrifice His Son so that we might live (1 Peter 1:19,20). Not only that, but the consummate love of Christ is demonstrated in that He was not accidentally "caught," as was John's son. Rather, He willingly sacrificed His life for the sins of humankind (John 10:18; cf. Matthew 26:53).

In light of this most precious gift of salvation, it is almost inconceivable that anyone—particularly someone within the Christian church—would tamper with the atonement, the central truth of the historic Christian faith. It astounds me that those who set themselves up as the very "anointed of God" are blithely wreaking havoc on the centrality of the atonement. And yet this is precisely what the Faith teachers are doing. They nonchalantly exchange the wonder of God's redeeming sacrifice for the doctrines of demons.

Before we examine the destructive flaws of the Faith doctrines with regard to the atonement, let us take a moment to forge a working definition of the atonement so we are able to note just how seriously this doctrine has been compromised.

Simply put, the atonement means that Christ, in His sacrificial death on the cross, dealt completely with the problem of man's sin. Christ, in His body on the cross, "redeemed [sinners] from the curse of the law by becoming a curse for us" (Galatians 3:13). Christ, the paragon of virtue, became the sacrificial Lamb upon whom the sins of the world were laid. While *practically* He was perfect and sinless, *positionally* He was accounted as sinful in that all of our sin was laid to His account. Conversely, while we are *practically* sinners, all of His righteousness is imputed to those who believe. Thus, through His atoning sacrifice, we are accounted as *positionally* righteous before God.

I cannot emphasize too strongly that the atonement is crucial to the historic Christian faith. Interestingly, the word "crucial" comes from the Latin word *crux* or "cross." So when I say that the atonement is the crux of Christianity, I am in effect saying that just as the cross stands at the center of all history, so also our understanding of the atonement is central to the faith. Tampering with the doctrine of the atonement is the most direct road from Christianity into the kingdom of the cults—and, for some people, into the world of the occult.

The fact is that virtually every cult, in one way or another, denies the doctrine of salvation by grace alone through the sinless sacrifice of Christ on the cross. The Bible plainly states that your eternal salvation rests on what you personally believe about the blood atonement of Jesus Christ. It is *at the cross*—not in hell—that your salvation is either won or lost. And that is precisely the problem with the most notorious of the Faith teachings. These teachings have transferred the saving work of Christ from the cross to the deepest dungeons of hell.

Lest you harbor the illusion that this view is not central to Faith theology, listen to what Kenneth Copeland has to say in one of his taped messages on the atonement:

> The thing that's necessary for the life of a Christian is knowledge of what happened from the cross to the throne. . . . It is the most fascinating thing in the whole Bible. It's very little talked about, almost nonexistent in the traditional church teaching, and I'll never understand why. I guess because it's been covered up and hidden in tradition.[1]

There you have it—not "a" but "the" most fascinating thing in the whole Bible. And, according to Copeland, it has been "covered up and hidden in tradition"! And what is it that has been so cleverly hidden "in the traditional church teaching" that has taken Kenneth Copeland and his compatriots to uncover?

First, many of the Faith teachers contend that Christ was re-created on the cross from divine to demonic. To put it in Faith vernacular, Jesus took on the very nature of Satan himself.

Second, according to Faith theology, your redemption was not secured on the cross, but in hell. In fact, many Faith teachers claim that Christ's torture by all the demons of hell was a "ransom" God paid to Satan so that He could get back into a universe from which He had been banished.[2]

Third, many Faith teachers insist that Jesus was reborn (or born again) in the very pit of hell.

Fourth, Faith theology holds that Christ was reincarnated through His rebirth in hell and that those who (like Christ) are born again can become "incarnated" as well. Thus Faith teachers take Christ, the spotless Lamb, and pervert Him into an unholy sacrifice on the cross.

But if this is true—if Faith theology is right in saying that we have been lied to by the traditional church—then we, by the Bible's own standards, will forever remain in our sins and will one day be subject to eternal torment in hell. Never forget that it is only if Jesus were pure and holy, unblemished and without sin, that He could have fulfilled the Old Testament concept of the sin offering. That offering redeemed man from the curse of the law and was considered most holy even after death.

The stakes here are enormous—no less than salvation itself. Therefore, let us now move from a cursory examination to a more in-depth look at Faith theology with regard to the atonement.

Re-Creation on the Cross

*T*he first flaw in the Faith movement's descent from Christianity into the kingdom of the cults involves Christ's alleged transformation from a divine being into a demoniac.[1] A host of influential celebrities either teach this concept or are willing to defend it. Take, for example, what Benny Hinn once claimed the Holy Ghost personally told him:

> Ladies and gentlemen, the serpent is a symbol of Satan. Jesus Christ knew the only way He would stop Satan is by becoming one in nature with him. You say, "What did you say? What blasphemy is this?" No, you hear this! He did not take my sin; He *became* my sin. Sin is the nature of hell. Sin is what made Satan. . . . It was sin that made Satan. Jesus said, "I'll be sin! I'll go to the lowest place! I'll go to the origin of it! I won't just take part in it, I'll be the totality of it!" When Jesus became sin, sir, He took it from A to Z and said, "No more!" Think about this: He became flesh, that flesh might become like Him. He became death, so dying man can live. He became sin, so sinners can be righteous in Him. He became one with

155

the nature of *Satan*, so all those who had the nature of *Satan* can partake of the nature of God.[2]

Although Hinn claims to have changed his views on certain Faith teachings (see endnote 2), dozens of other such statements can be readily cited by Hinn and others. Kenneth Hagin, for example, also claims that Jesus Christ took on the nature of Satan. He, like Hinn, takes great pains to make us aware of his belief that—

> [s]piritual death means something more than separation from God. *Spiritual death also means having Satan's nature.* . . . Jesus tasted death—spiritual death—for every man.[3]

What is particularly disturbing in Hagin's case is that when I confronted him with this blasphemy, he denied ever having taught it. In a written response addressed to me by his son, Kenneth Hagin, Jr. (who is currently the executive vice-president of Kenneth Hagin Ministries), I was told the following:

> [W]e don't agree with much of the doctrine currently being taught in "word-faith" circles and haven't *ever* taught many of the doctrines now being circulated. . . . It is very frustrating to us to be quoted on the same page with some of these ministers and connected with them as though we believed the same things they are teaching. . . . In many, many cases this is just not true, as I think the enclosed questions and answers will indicate.[4]

In the enclosure referred to, Hagin accuses people like myself of jumping "to their own conclusions" and denies the teaching "that Jesus took on Satan's nature or submitted to his lordship."[5]

It becomes very confusing indeed when someone denies the very thing he affirms. Although I would love to give Hagin the benefit of the doubt, investigation reveals that not only has he *distorted doctrine*, but he has also *distorted his record* in an effort to avoid the criticisms generated by his blasphemous remarks.

Does Hagin really believe that Jesus took on the nature of Satan? Despite all attempts to curb the controversy, I think the evidence speaks clearly for itself.

One of Hagin's foremost disciples, Frederick K.C. Price, moves from the blasphemous to the bizarre. In one instance he alleges that Jesus Christ was re-created spiritually—not on the cross, but rather in the Garden of Gethsemane. As Price puts it:

> Somewhere between the time He [Jesus] was nailed to the cross and when He was in the Garden of Gethsemane—somewhere in there— He died spiritually. Personally, I believe it was while He was in the garden.[6]

The implications of this teaching are horrifying.[7] Ironically, Price, who was "reared in a Jehovah's Witness environment,"[8] here mimics a page right out of the Mormons' playbook! You see, James E. Talmage, who served as an Apostle of the Mormon church, taught precisely the same thing in his book *Jesus the Christ*.[9]

Kenneth Copeland adds his own spin to the discussion through a conversation he allegedly had with God. Copeland says that Jesus became a sign of Satan when He was hanging on the cross:

> The righteousness of God was made to be sin. He accepted the sin nature of Satan in His own spirit. And at the moment that He did so, He cried, "My God, My God, why hast thou

forsaken Me?" You don't know what happened at the cross. Why do you think Moses,
upon instruction of God, raised the serpent
upon that pole instead of a lamb? That used to
bug me. I said, "Why in the world would you
want to put a snake up there—the sign of
Satan? Why didn't you put a lamb on that
pole?" And the Lord said, "Because it was a
sign of Satan that was hanging on the cross."
He said, "I accepted, in My own spirit, spiritual death; and the light was turned off."[10]

Despite Copeland's claim to a private audience with
God, the key question is how such an alleged conversation
compares with Scripture.

In Old Testament days, whenever anyone committed
an offense or sin, a sacrifice called a "sin offering" was
required in order to "cover" the transgression. We learn that
the offering had to be "without defect" (Leviticus 4:3,28;
9:3). Furthermore, animals having any type of serious flaw
were deemed unacceptable for sacrifice (Deuteronomy 15:21).

Since these sacrifices foreshadowed Christ's ultimate
sacrifice on the cross, we know that Christ was offered
without spot or blemish, and that in no way could He have
become one in nature with Satan. In fact, both Hebrews 9:14
and 1 Peter 1:19 make it explicit that Jesus on the cross was
without blemish or defect.

Not only that, but according to Leviticus 6:25-29, the
sin offering was "most holy" to God both before *and* after its
death. In the same way, Jesus as the sin offering remained
holy even after His death on the cross. He was truly the
fulfillment of the Old Testament type of the sin offering.

The troubling question is, How do the Faith teachers
square their view with the Bible? The answer is that, like the
cults, they take biblical texts, words, and phrases out of their
intended contexts. The following are some of the most common examples of their Scripture-twisting.

Scripture Under Siege

Second Corinthians 5:21 tells us that "God made him [Jesus] who had no sin to be sin for us, so that in him we might become the righteousness of God." Here, the Faith teachers say, is indisputable proof that Jesus became sin and thus a satanic being on the cross. But is this true? Must we indeed accept this "revelation knowledge"? Let's take a closer look at the word "sin" in 2 Corinthians 5:21, on which their entire teaching depends.

First, scholars agree that the word "sin" in this passage is used in an abstract sense. They are virtually unanimous in pointing out that the phrase "to become sin" as used here is a *metonym* (a word or phrase substituted for another associated word or phrase) for Christ "bearing the penalty of our sins."[11] Expositor T.J. Crawford maintains that "there can be no doubt that the expression is *metonymical*, since it is impossible that Christ, or any person, could be literally made sin."[12] To interpret this passage as saying that Christ was transformed into sin is to strip the Savior of His personal being and reduce Him to a mere abstraction. Not only is this notion unbiblical, it is utterly absurd!

Scripture does say that man's sin was laid to the account of Christ (see Isaiah 53:4,5). To put it another way, our sins were imputed to Christ and His righteousness is imputed to us. Clearly, the Levitical concepts of substitution and imputation are the background of 2 Corinthians 5:21. Jesus did not literally become sin; sin was *imputed* to Him. The Bible insists that the sacrifice of Christ was a sufficient substitutionary offering *precisely* because it was a sinless sacrifice. One prominent commentator puts it this way:

> But God made Him *sin*: that is to say that God the Father made His innocent, incarnate Son the object of His wrath and judgment, for our sakes, with the result that in Christ on the cross the sin of the world is judged and taken

away. In this truth resides the whole logic of reconciliation. . . . Not for one moment does He cease to be righteous, else the radical exchange envisaged by the Apostle here, whereby our sin is transferred to Him and His righteousness is transferred to us, would be no more than a fiction or an hallucination.[13]

Numbers 21:8,9 and John 3:14 are also often quoted together by Faith adherents to "prove" that Jesus was not the unblemished Lamb on the cross, but rather had taken on the nature of Satan. The argument goes something like this: Since Jesus was "lifted up" on the cross in the manner that Moses "lifted up" the bronze serpent in the desert, so must He have taken on the nature of Satan, who is symbolized by the serpent.

But far from proving that Jesus took on the nature of Satan, these texts refer simply to *the manner* of His death—namely, that *He was lifted up*. This is made particularly clear in John 12:32, where Jesus says, "But I, when I am lifted up from the earth, will draw all men to myself." Verse 33 clarifies the meaning of Christ's words: "He said this to show *the kind of death he was going to die*" (emphasis added). Furthermore, we must ask how Jesus could be a "fragrant offering and sacrifice to God" (Ephesians 5:2) if He truly became as vile as a serpent on the cross.

Those who believe that Jesus became a satanic being on the cross must face other difficult questions as well. For example, why does God in Isaiah 53:11 refer to Jesus as His "righteous servant" during the moment of His suffering on the cross? Such a statement would not make sense if Jesus were truly transformed into a demoniac. It also seems horribly inconsistent for Jesus on the cross—after supposedly taking on the nature of Satan—to pray for His enemies, saying, "*Father*, forgive them, for they do not know what they are doing" (Luke 23:34). If He took on the nature of

Satan at the cross, then who is this "Father"? It is hard to imagine that someone with the nature of Satan would pray to God; but it is harder still to envision anyone asking Satan to show mercy.

Finite individuals cannot fully comprehend the sense in which Jesus was momentarily "forsaken" by the Father (Matthew 27:46). We do know, however, that the Godhead cannot be divided, or else God, as revealed by Scripture, would cease to exist—an impossibility. We must therefore yield to the mystery of the atonement and learn to place our assurance in Jesus, who foretold that while everyone would leave Him, He would not be alone, "for my Father is with me" (John 16:32).

Thus it becomes clear that this doctrine of Faith theology finds no support in the Word of God.

Thorny Questions

Numerous passages in God's Word attest that our sins have been dealt with "through the sacrifice of the body of Jesus Christ once for all" (Hebrews 10:10; cf. Romans 7:4; Colossians 1:22; 1 Peter 2:24; 3:18; 4:1). This poses three difficult questions for the Faith teachers' view of the atonement.

First, why is there no explicit mention of Christ's alleged "spiritual" death, while the Bible is replete with details on the fact and significance of His physical death— especially if it was His spiritual death that did away with the curse?

Second, why does the Bible place so much emphasis on Christ's physical death—to the exclusion of His alleged spiritual death—if His physical death was not *the* factor that eradicated sin?

Third, why is it that Christ Himself told us to remember the sacrifice He made with His body and blood (both of which are essentially physical), while saying nothing about any spiritual sacrifice (cf. Luke 22:19,20; 1 Corinthians 11:24-26)?

All the biblical evidence indicates that Jesus never died spiritually and that His physical death paid the price for humanity's sin.

The Pure Sacrifice of Christ

As we close this section, it seems only appropriate to ponder the precious words echoed each time we take communion:

> "This is My *body* which is broken for you; do this in remembrance of Me. . . . This cup is the new covenant in My *blood*. This do, as often as you drink it, in remembrance of Me." For as often as you eat this bread and drink this cup, you *proclaim the Lord's death* till He comes (1 Corinthians 11:24-26 NKJV, emphasis added).

Truly, it was on the cross that we were pardoned through Christ's broken body and shed blood.

In John 19:30 Jesus said, "It is finished!"[14] He did not say, "It has just begun!" The Greek word used in the original text is *tetelestai*, which means "It is paid; the debt has been paid in full." The finality of Jesus' accomplishment upon the cross is made crystal clear by the tearing of the temple curtain that veiled God's earthly sanctuary, the Holy of Holies, from man, thus signifying that access to God had been restored at that precise moment (Mark 15:38; cf. Hebrews 9:1-14; 10:19-22).

Sadly, the Faith movement has mutilated the truth that your redemption was purchased at Calvary and turned it into the myth that your redemption took place in hell. It is to that myth that we now turn.

Redemption in Hell

$\mathcal{A}$s painful as it is, let us now follow the Faith movement from the cross to the place where it claims that your redemption was secured—the pit of hell itself. As Robert Tilton puts it, "For three days and three nights He [Jesus] was in the pit of hell, breaking the powers of darkness to set us free."[1]

Proponents of Faith theology say it is here that Jesus endured three days and nights of unimaginable abuse at the hands of Satan and his hordes of demons. Let's hear it straight from Frederick K.C. Price:

> Do you think that the punishment for our sin was to die on a cross? If that were the case, the two thieves could have paid your price. No, the punishment was to go into hell itself and to serve time in hell separated from God. . . . Satan and all the demons of hell thought that they had Him bound and they threw a net over Jesus and they dragged Him down to the very pit of hell itself to serve our sentence.[2]

Price then adds, "His [Jesus'] spirit and soul went into hell, or Hades, and served the sentence that you and I should have justly served. He did it for us. He went to hell for us."[3]

Of course, Kenneth Hagin taught this doctrine long before Price was a force within Christianity, and Hagin followed Kenyon, who in turn got his information from the metaphysical cults![4] Let us pause to get Hagin's version of the teaching:

> He [Jesus] tasted spiritual death for every man. And His spirit and inner man went to hell in my place. Can't you see that? Physical death wouldn't remove your sins. He's tasted death for every man. He's talking about tasting spiritual death.[5]

Since Copeland wields such influence in the Faith movement, let's hear his version of this story:

> When Jesus cried, "It is finished!" He was not speaking of the plan of redemption. There were still three days and nights to go through before He went to the throne. . . . Jesus' death on the cross was only the beginning of the complete work of redemption.[6]

As reprehensible as all these quotes are, not one of them can rival that of Paul Billheimer in his book *Destined for the Throne*. Jan Crouch, the wife of TBN president Paul Crouch, approvingly recited the following words from Billheimer's book during a live communion service aired on TBN:

> Because He was "made sin," impregnated with sin, and became the very essence of sin, on the cross He was banished from God's presence as a loathsome thing. He and sin were made synonymous. . . . [I]t was not sufficient for Christ to offer up only His physical life on the cross. *His pure human spirit had to "descend" into hell. . . .* His spirit must not only descend into hell, but into the lowest hell. . . .

The Father turned Him over, not only to the agony and death of Calvary, but to the satanic torturers of His pure spirit as part of the just dessert of the sin of all the race. As long as Christ was "the essence of sin" he was at Satan's mercy in that place of torment. . . . While Christ identified with sin, Satan and the hosts of hell ruled over Him as over any lost sinner. During that seemingly endless age in the nether abyss of death, Satan did with Him as he would, and all hell was "in carnival."[7]

It is a mystery to me how anyone could conclude that Jesus had to complete the work of redemption in hell.[8] Yet some Faith teachers attempt to strengthen their argument by insisting that a number of the ancient Christian creeds—such as the Apostles' Creed and the Athanasian Creed—include the phrase "descended into hell." They seem to be unaware that this phrase did not appear in the creed until the fourth century, that it was not part of the original. It is certain that neither the early church fathers nor the framers of the creeds believed that Christ suffered in hell under Satan.[9] In any event, the Word of God itself must be the court of final appeal.

How can anyone miss what the Lord said to the thief on the cross? Jesus did not say, "Today you will be with me in hell." He said, "I tell you the truth, today you will be with me in paradise" (Luke 23:43). According to the apostle Paul, paradise is in the third heaven (2 Corinthians 12:2). There is simply no way to reconcile this explicit statement made by Christ on the cross with the Faith teaching that Jesus suffered in hell.[10]

Two Key Passages

Faith teachers twist two passages in particular—

Matthew 12:40 and Ephesians 4:9,10—to make their case that Christ did in fact go to hell. Let's take a quick look at these texts.

First, Matthew 12:40 ("the Son of Man will be three days and three nights in the heart of the earth") simply references the time of Jesus' burial in the grave. If the Faith teachers want to use this text to support the idea that Jesus went to hell to be tortured by Satan and his demons, the burden of proof clearly falls on them. And this verse says nothing of the sort.

Second, Ephesians 4:9,10 ("What does 'he ascended' mean except that he also descended to the lower, earthly regions? He who descended is the very one who ascended higher than all the heavens, in order to fill the whole universe") contains an idiomatic expression referring to Christ's incarnation on the earth and not to any incarceration in hell. In fact, David used the same expression ("lower parts" or "depths of the earth") in Psalm 139:15,16 when he said, "My frame was not hidden from you when I was made in the secret place. When I was woven together in the depths of the earth, your eyes saw my unformed body." Surely no one would conclude that David was born in hell! Yet the Faith teachers persist in assigning Jesus to the lowermost regions of that most dreaded place.

To Paradise, Not Hell

It is worth noting that Jesus on the cross cried, "Father, into your hands I commit my spirit" (Luke 23:46; cf. John 19:30). He most certainly did not shout, "Satan, into your clutches I submit my being. Take me, I'm yours. Take me to hell."

If we are to take the Bible seriously, we must conclude that Jesus committed His spirit to the Father, not to Satan. The apostle Paul put it ever so eloquently when he wrote of Christ, "Having disarmed the powers and authorities, he made a public spectacle of them, triumphing over them *by the cross*" (Colossians 2:15, emphasis mine).

Jesus did not suffer horrible torture at the hands of Satan in the bowels of hell. Christ triumphed over the devil at the cross! It was His death on the cross that made possible our salvation. How could the writer of Hebrews have made it any clearer?

> Since the children have flesh and blood, he [Christ] too shared in their humanity so that *by his death he might destroy him who holds the power of death—that is, the devil*—and free those who all their lives were held in slavery by their fear of death (Hebrews 2:14,15).

Rebirth in Hell

Before pressing forward, let's take a moment to retrace our steps. We began this section with Jesus hanging on a cross, where, according to Faith theology, He was recreated from a divine to a demonic being. At this point the Trinity was destroyed and the deity of Christ utterly demolished. According to the Faith teachers, the Lord Jesus' passion on the cross proved insufficient to redeem humankind, and so He had to be trapped and hauled down to the very pit of hell by Satan. It is there, while Jesus is tortured and tormented by a smiling Satan and a host of cackling demons, that we pick up the story.

Little did Satan realize, Faith proponents say, that the last laugh would be on him. For just as Adam had fallen into Satan's trap in the Garden of Eden, now Satan had fallen into God's trap in hell. Copeland explains that—

> [i]n hell He [Jesus] suffered for you and for me. The Bible says hell was made for Satan and his angels (Matthew 25:41). It was not made for men. Satan was holding the Son of God there illegally.... The trap was set for Satan and Jesus was the bait.[1]

Satan blew it on a technicality, according to Faith theology, because Satan had dragged Jesus into hell illegally.

As Copeland puts it, "The Devil forgot to take into consideration that Jesus hadn't sinned Himself but, rather, had merely become sin as a result of the sin of others."[2]

Satan and every demon in hell tortured Christ's allegedly "emaciated, poured out, little, wormy spirit"[3] without legal right. And this was exactly the opening God had been looking for. Seizing the moment, He spoke His faith-filled words into the bowels of the earth, and suddenly—

> [t]hat Word of the living God went down into that pit of destruction and charged the spirit of Jesus with resurrection power! Suddenly His twisted, death-wracked spirit began to fill out and come back to life. He began to look like something the devil had never seen before. He was literally being reborn before the devil's very eyes. He began to flex His spiritual muscles. . . . Jesus was born again—the firstborn from the dead.[4]

That Jesus was in hell *illegally* gave God the break He needed. He spoke His faith-filled words into the bowels of the earth and, as a host of demons looked on, Jesus whipped the devil in his own backyard. He snatched Satan's keys and emerged from hell as a born-again man. With His "can do" attitude, God pulled off the coup of the ages. In fact, according to Charles Capps, it was this pivotal event—namely, Jesus becoming born again—that gave rise to the church:

> Jesus was born again in the pit of hell. He was the firstborn, the firstbegotten, from the dead. *He started the Church of the firstborn in the gates of hell.* . . . He went down to the gates and started His Church there. . . . The Church started when Jesus was born again in the gates of hell.[5]

Kenneth Hagin was one of the early popularizers of the myth that "Jesus is the first person ever to be born again."[6] Despite his occasional protests, this is exactly what he has taught.[7]

Scripture Pretzels

We must ask ourselves, "Where do the Faith teachers find biblical substantiation for all this?"

Many seize upon Colossians 1:18 (especially the phrase "the firstborn from among the dead") to argue for Jesus being born again.[8] As is well-recognized, however, the Greek word translated as "firstborn" (*prototokos*) denotes "primacy," "headship," and "preeminence." All that can be said of this verse is that it points to Christ's supremacy over the whole of creation (cf. verse 15).[9] To say that the reference to "the dead" alludes not to Christ's bodily resurrection but to His spiritual death from which He needed to be reborn is to beg the question, since that is the very issue at hand.[10]

Another text commonly called upon is 1 Peter 3:18, which says that Jesus "was put to death in the body but made alive by the Spirit." To give you an idea of how severely this passage is mauled, consider Billheimer's commentary as read by Jan Crouch on TBN:

> [I]n order to be made alive unto God and restored to fellowship with His Father, He [Jesus] had to be reborn—for He had become the very essence of sin. Since sin had totally alienated Him from the Father, the only way He could be restored to fellowship with the Father was through a new birth to new life.[11]

The Faith teachers reason that the idea of being made alive by the Spirit makes no sense unless one were spiritually dead. But the verse itself rules out this understanding.

First, the verse mentions that Christ was "put to death in the body," indicating that Jesus' sacrifice was *physical* in character. There is no mention of any spiritual death. Christ's lifeless body was left hanging on the cross the moment He gave His spirit over to the Father (Luke 23:46). In other words, it was the parting of His spirit that marked Jesus' "death in the body." In the same fashion, it was the return of His spirit into His body that marked His physical resurrection. To use the language of the text, Christ's body was once again "made alive by the Spirit."[12] There is simply no justification for reading the text the way the Faith teachers do.

Revelation Knowledge

The Faith teachers seem to implicitly recognize that their Scripture-twisting alone will not convince anyone of their claims. That's when they call in a second wave of artillery. It's called "revelation knowledge," which supposedly bypasses the mind and goes directly into the spirit.

Kenneth Copeland called upon such revelation knowledge when he said:

> The Spirit of God spoke to me and He said, "Son, realize this. Now follow me in this and don't let your tradition trip you up." He said, "Think this way—a twice-born man whipped Satan in his own domain." And I threw my Bible down . . . like that. I said, "What?" He said, "A born-again man defeated Satan, the firstborn of many brethren defeated him." He said, "You are the very image, the very copy of that one." I said, "Goodness, gracious sakes alive!" And I began to see what had gone on in there, and I said, "Well now you don't mean, you couldn't dare mean, that I could have done the same thing?" He said, "Oh yeah, if you'd had the knowledge of the Word

of God that He did, you could've done the same thing, 'cause you're a reborn man too."[13]

I cannot overemphasize the significance of this quote. God has supposedly just explained to Copeland not only that Jesus was indeed born again, but that Copeland himself could have done what Christ did if he had simply known the Word of God the way Jesus did. Just think of it: Copeland could have redeemed you from your sins! And remember, Copeland here is claiming that the Holy Spirit is revealing to him this heresy!

Benny Hinn, too, received some "revelation knowledge" on the "rebirth" of Christ in hell:

> My, you know, whoosh! The Holy Ghost is just showing me some stuff. I'm getting dizzy! I'm telling you the truth—it's, it's just heavy right now on me. . . . He's [referring to Jesus] in the underworld now. God isn't there, the Holy Ghost isn't there, and the Bible says He was begotten. Do you know what the word begotten means? It means reborn. Do you want another shocker? Have you been begotten? So was He. Don't let anyone deceive you. Jesus was reborn. You say, "What are you talking about?" . . . He was reborn. He had to be reborn. . . . If He was not reborn, I could not be reborn. Jesus was born again. . . . If He was not reborn, I would never be reborn. How can I face Jesus and say, "Jesus, you went through everything I've gone through, except the new birth?"[14]

After claiming that the Holy Ghost showed him all this, Hinn looked into the camera and said, "I'm telling you the truth." And then he appealed to the audience not to let anyone deceive them into doubting the Faith doctrine of the born-again Jesus!

The Significance of "Begotten"

A crucial question here is, What does the term "begotten" mean? Does it mean "reborn," as Hinn claims? Hardly. The term "begotten" simply means "born." It is in no way synonymous with the word "reborn." Furthermore, the biblical concept of being "reborn" (cf. John 3:3) applies solely to sinful humanity and not to Jesus, the sinless God-man. In fact, John 1:14 (cf. 1:18; 3:16) specifically refers to Christ as "the *only begotten* from the Father" (NASB) or "the *one and only* Son who came from the Father" (NIV), emphasizing the unique nature of the Lord. Jesus alone was fully God and fully man, the unique and eternal Son of the Father. Such a person has no need to be born again, for He is God (John 1:1).

So where did this teaching of a "born-again Jesus" originate? Clearly it came *from below* rather than *from above*. There is zero biblical basis for this despicable doctrine. The only conceivable reason for espousing it is to provide a means by which to restore Jesus' demonic nature to its original sinless state. But, of course, since Jesus never died spiritually to begin with, there was no need for Him to be born again.

To say that Jesus' nature underwent radical corruption which needed complete renewal is to overturn the biblical picture of God. For if Jesus truly became sin (in the sense the Faith teachers mean), then one Person of the Holy Trinity was ripped away from the Godhead. This necessarily implies that the triune God ceased to exist, at least at that point. It also requires the destruction of Christ's deity. For how could God, in the person of Christ, have the nature of Satan? Scripture rejects any such idea, for God is an unchanging Being (Malachi 3:6; Hebrews 13:8) who has "life in himself" (John 5:26).

The picture which Scripture paints of the atonement is infinitely more majestic, breathtaking, and exhilarating than any fiction the Faith teachers might dream up!

And besides all that, the Bible's version is true.

Reincarnation

*A*s the letter "A" is at the center of the acronym F-L-A-W-S, so also the doctrine of the atonement stands at the center of the Christian faith. Yet this central doctrine is the very one the Faith teachers so blithely prostitute.

According to the Faith teachers, Jesus regained His divinity the moment He was reborn in hell. Commenting on Hinn's remarks about Jesus defeating Satan in the underworld, Crouch adds, "That's when His [Jesus'] divinity returned."[1] Of course, to say that Jesus' "divinity returned" presumes there was a point when Christ ceased to be divine— when He was not God. But any such assertion is patently unbiblical (Philippians 2:6; cf. Hebrews 13:8).

It would be depressing enough if the madness stopped there. But it doesn't. Most Faith teachers claim that all Christians, like Jesus, become incarnations of God the moment they are born again. As Hagin states it, "Every man who has been born again is an incarnation and Christianity is a miracle. The believer is as much an incarnation as was Jesus of Nazareth."[2]

One need only recall the uniqueness of the incarnation—God the Son, Second Person of the Trinity, condescending to take upon Himself human form (John 1:14)—to recognize the blasphemy of applying it to every born-again individual. To assert that such an event is a common-day phenomenon is to trivialize the unique person and work of the Savior. Moreover, speaking in this way severely damages the meaning of the word "incarnation" and robs that glorious event of its rich significance.

The word "incarnation" is derived from the Latin word *incarne*, which means "in the flesh." According to Christian theology, Christ, who is the Logos, the Second Person of the Godhead, voluntarily cloaked Himself in human flesh (John 1:18; 14:9,10). Thus we have God in the person of Christ (who is by nature spirit—John 4:24) taking on flesh (1:14) and through His incarnation providing redemption for humankind (1:29).

The concept of incarnation makes sense only if a person existed prior to having a physical body. And while the Bible clearly declares Christ to be preexistent (John 1:1; 8:58; 17:5), nowhere in Scripture do we find the concept of *human* preexistence. In fact, human preexistence remains a concept relegated largely to such cults as Mormonism.[3] The fact that Christians are indwelt by the Father, the Son, and the Holy Spirit (John 14:17,23) in no way implies that the Bible endorses the concept of incarnation for Christians.

Three Difficulties

Three enormous problems are raised by this Faith teaching.

First, if Jesus was reborn in hell, then a form of reincarnation is true. Hagin's insistence that "the believer is as much an incarnation as was Jesus of Nazareth" can only mean one thing: Each time a human being is born again, we have God coming again and again in the flesh, being reincarnated over and over again.

Second, this Faith doctrine would mean that Jesus, who already has a body (Luke 24:39), would take on additional bodies each time someone comes to faith in Christ. The notion is absurd.

And finally, agreeing with the Faith movement means that we end up with a world full of gods. And the Bible utterly rejects polytheism.

In sharp distinction to Faith theology, the Bible and orthodox Christianity teach that every believer is indwelt by God, who inhabits and guides saved humanity. The person who is born again does not lose his or her identity upon spiritual regeneration. In Galatians 2:20 Paul speaks of Christ living within him; yet he goes on to say, "The life *I live* in the body, *I live* by faith in the Son of God."

Genuine Christian theology has always affirmed that a newly regenerated person's relationship with God, which had been severed by sin, becomes restored. Upon coming to faith in Christ, the process known as sanctification begins, whereby the believer is brought to spiritual maturity under the guidance of the Holy Spirit (Galatians 5:13-26).

The truth is that Jesus never died spiritually. He did not take on the nature of a demoniac or the nature of Satan. He did not go to hell to suffer under Satan and his demons. He did not have to be born again, and consequently He was not. And born-again individuals are not incarnations of God! To maintain otherwise is to "fall away from the faith, paying attention to deceitful spirits and doctrines of demons" (1 Timothy 4:1 NASB).

The glorious message of the Christian gospel is that Jesus' work of redemption was completed on the cross at Calvary. All those who place their faith in the finished work of Christ will receive a rich welcome into the eternal kingdom of our Lord and Savior Jesus Christ.

Christianity
IN
CRISIS

PART FIVE

Wealth
and
Want

$\mathcal{T}$he year was 1979. I had only recently committed my life to Jesus Christ. Although exhilarated by my relationship with the Lord of the universe, I was also haunted by all the wasted years—years of living by the dictates of my own will. I desperately wanted to make up for lost time.

More than anything else, I wanted to make my life count. I felt that to make up for lost time I had to free myself from financial constraints and considerations. And so I decided to take some of the financial resources I had accumulated and parlay them into a small fortune.

The silver commodities market seemed to be the quickest route to financial security. I had been watching its rapid ascent and had been hearing about its potential in the financial markets. My research seemed to indicate that silver was grossly undervalued and that it was just a matter of time until it soared to previously unheard-of heights. Even from a biblical standpoint, it seemed to me that the proper ratio between gold and silver should be 10 to 1.

As I continued to consider using silver as the vehicle to achieve financial security, the market began to heat up. I decided to wait for a price correction so I could get into the market at a reasonable entry level.

Meanwhile, I planned a visit to my parents, who lived in the Netherlands. My motive was to map out a strategy for financial security: I wanted to serve God from a position of strength as a prosperous Christian. But, as I would soon discover, God had a radically different plan for my life.

After several days in Holland, I looked for something to read to pass the time. Since reading Dutch had become cumbersome for me, I was delighted to find a book printed in English on the coffee table in my parents' den. It was titled *Evangelism Explosion*. Once I started reading, I just couldn't stop. Within a few hours I encountered a whole new world—a world of spiritual multiplication. As I read on I began to discover how I could become an equipped Christian and how to store up treasure in heaven.

I returned to the States excited about the possibility of spiritual multiplication and immediately enrolled in the evangelism outreach program of my local church. However, my desire for financial security continued to burn brightly.

Silver prices by this time had begun to skyrocket. Anxious to "get on before the train left without me," I jumped into the market at $47.08 per ounce. Often I would look back and kick myself for not having acted sooner. I would calculate exactly how much I lost by not acting when I first began to see silver's meteoric ascent. Leveraged to the hilt, I waited anxiously for silver to continue rising. It did. Within a few days it hit the 50-dollar mark and the predictions were that it wouldn't be long before it would crack the century mark (100 dollars per ounce).

Eagerly I waited, fully believing that God would soon allow me to become financially self-sufficient. But within days I received a call that caused my heart to freeze. The voice on the other end of the line said, "Hank, disaster!" Before I could respond he blurted out the chilling words, "The silver market just crashed." I was told to come over immediately to cover the shortfall (a "margin call") or my position in the market would be liquidated. Over the next few months this would become a recurring scene. The phone call would come and I would have to cover another shortfall, always wondering how far I should chase the rabbit down the hole. With each passing week I was losing more and more of what had taken me years to accumulate. Yet in seeking advice from the experts, I was consistently counseled to hang in there—that they were just "shaking the amateurs out of the market." But something else was happening as well. All the while I was losing financially, I was gaining spiritually. During the on-the-job training portion of Evangelism Explosion I was going into the highways and byways and seeing people come to faith in Christ. On the one hand, I was losing my grip financially. But on the other hand, I was prospering spiritually to a degree I never dreamed possible.

Eventually I lost everything I had worked so long and hard to possess financially. But spiritually, I was gaining an eternal perspective. I was learning to seek first God's kingdom and His righteousness (Matthew 6:33). I was coming to realize that He would take care of my daily needs. Like Agur in Proverbs 30, I was learning to pray, "Give me neither poverty nor riches, but give me only my daily bread. Otherwise, I may have too much and disown you and say, 'Who is the Lord?' Or I may become poor and steal, and so dishonor the name of my God."

While Scripture neither condemns nor commends riches, the goal spiritually is to grow to such an extent in your relationship with Christ that, as the old hymn says, "the things of earth grow strangely dim in the light of His glory and grace." The bottom line is to develop an eternal rather than a temporary perspective—eyes that can look beyond time and space into eternity.

Today I can only manage a wry smile as I think back and read the words of the apostle Paul to young Timothy: "People who want to get rich fall into temptation and a trap and into many foolish and harmful desires that plunge men into ruin and destruction" (1 Timothy 6:9).

In the next four chapters, we will see the devastating results of willfully disregarding Paul's urgent warning.

Cultural Conformity

*A*s though it weren't enough to redefine faith as a force, deify man as a god, and attack Christ's atonement on the cross, the Faith movement has also turned the gospel of grace into a gospel of greed.

Jesus warned, "Watch out! Be on your guard against all kinds of greed; a man's life does not consist in the abundance of his possessions" (Luke 12:15). The Lord then told His disciples the parable of the rich fool who was looking to his possessions for security (verses 16-21). Jesus did not condemn possessions, but instead pointed out the foolishness of a temporary rather than an eternal perspective. Not mincing words, Jesus quoted His Father as saying to the rich man, "You fool! This very night your life will be demanded from you" (verse 20). The Master's command was always the same: Seek first the kingdom of God and His righteousness, and all these things will be added to you as well (Matthew 6:33).

How unlike the message of the Faith teachers! These people relentlessly hawk the idea that prosperity is the divine right of every believer. Such a brand of "Christianity" is little more than a baptized form of greed garbed in a thin veneer of "Christianese." It is a pitiable conformity to the cultural trends of our day. As Quentin Schultze, author of *Televangelism and American Culture*, astutely noted:

Televangelists offer their own personalized expressions of the gospel as adapted from and directed to American culture. To put it more strongly, the faith of some televangelists is more American than Christian, more popular than historic, more personal than collective, and more experiential than biblical. As a result, the faith they preach is highly affluent, selfish, and individualistic.... These three aspects of televangelism's faith system... reflect the American Dream, whereby a self-motivated individual supposedly attains great affluence. They also reflect the impact of modernity on the church.[1]

Christians who are prosperous by the world's standards are considered to be rich spiritually, while the poor are perceived to be spiritual paupers. One Faith teacher even said, "Not only is worrying a sin, but being poor is a sin when God promises prosperity!"[2]

The marketers of this drivel are propped up by the dollars sent in by listeners hoping for easy wealth. When the riches fail to materialize, these followers dejectedly walk away from what they thought was Christianity and look for a new guru in the kingdom of the cults. As the apostle Paul so aptly put it, "There will be terrible times in the last days. People will be...lovers of money...lovers of pleasure rather than lovers of God—having a form of godliness but denying its power" (2 Timothy 3:1-5).

Transformed by the Culture

Far too many Christians are being transformed by our culture rather than by Christ. Seeking the kingdom of God and His righteousness has been perverted into seeking our own kingdom and everything else we can get our hands on.

Nowhere is the prosperity preachers' cultural conformity more apparent than when it comes to the incarnation of Christ. In literature and tape, radio and television, many Faith teachers present a Jesus who looks remarkably like themselves: He is decked out in designer clothes. He lives in a big house. He has a huge donor base and is said to have so much money that He needs a treasurer.[3]

John Avanzini tells his vast television audience that if Jesus was poor, he wants to be poor. If Jesus slept under a bridge, he wants to sleep under a bridge. But if Jesus was rich, it's clear that Avanzini should also be rich! Avanzini reasons that since the followers of Christ in His day were rich, why shouldn't we be rich in our day?[4]

Prosperity preachers are so committed to presenting a Jesus who wears a Rolex that they are willing to do whatever it takes to sell this myth to their parishioners. Oral Roberts, for example, wrote a book titled *How I Learned Jesus Was Not Poor*. Frederick Price says he's trying "to get you out of this malaise of thinking that Jesus and the disciples were poor. . . . The Bible says that He has left us an example that we should follow His steps. That's the reason why I drive a Rolls Royce. I'm following Jesus' steps."[5]

Jesus with a Rolex

Avanzini actually attacks apologists and theologians for teaching that Jesus was poor. In utter disgust he snorts, "I don't know where these goofy traditions creep in at, but one of the goofiest ones is that Jesus and His disciples were poor. Now there's no Bible to substantiate that."[6]

During one TBN broadcast, Avanzini charged theologians with taking Luke 9:57,58 (cf. Matthew 8:18-20) out of context to prove that Jesus was poor. He then presented what he claims to be the true meaning of that passage—a meaning which seems to have escaped the Christian church for nearly 2000 years.

Avanzini's version of the biblical account finds Jesus on His way to conducting a "seminar" in Samaria. But, alas, His "advance team" had not taken care of business properly and the "Jesus seminar" got canceled. In His reply to the man who wanted to follow Him, Jesus was in effect saying, "Foxes have holes *in Samaria*, birds of the air have nests *in Samaria*, but I don't have any place to stay tonight *in Samaria.*" As Avanzini puts it, "In those days there wasn't a Holiday Inn on every corner," so Jesus was forced to go back home to His nice, big house in Jerusalem.[7]

Rather than gleaning from the riches of God's Word, Avanzini uses this text to enrich his ministry.

This is a classic example of a twentieth-century televangelist reading his current lifestyle into a first-century passage dealing with the ministry of Jesus Christ.[8] Not only does Avanzini find himself at odds with every respectable Bible scholar in his interpretation of this passage, but more significantly, his teachings oppose the entire canon of Scripture.

The fact is that if Avanzini were right and everyone else were wrong, we would end up with a schizophrenic Jesus! We would have a Jesus who clearly taught His disciples not to labor for that which perishes (John 6:27), while He wore Himself out doing that very thing.

Disciples with Dough

Not only do Faith teachers such as Crouch, Price, Roberts, Avanzini, and others maintain that Jesus was wealthy, but they assert that His disciples lived in luxury as well. Avanzini, for instance, argues that the apostle Paul was so rich that he had the financial resources to block up the justice system of his day.[9]

But how can anyone read 1 Corinthians 4:9-13 and contend that the apostle Paul and his companions had the kind of money that could block up justice? How could Scripture more clearly articulate their true condition than to claim that "to this very hour, we go hungry and thirsty, we are in rags, we are brutally treated, we are homeless" (verse 11)?

Furthermore, could Paul be anything but a hypocrite if he himself were living in the lap of luxury while teaching Timothy that "people who want to get rich fall into temptation and a trap and into many foolish and harmful desires that plunge men into ruin and destruction" (1 Timothy 6:9)?

Finally, what about Paul's farewell address to the Ephesian elders chronicled in Acts 20? Paul there points out that the Holy Spirit personally warned him of impending imprisonment and hardships (verse 23). Paul put it in perspective when he said, "I consider my life worth nothing to me" (verse 24). In Philippians 3:7-9, Paul once again echoed the same powerful sentiment: "But whatever was to my profit I now consider loss for the sake of Christ. What is more, I consider everything a loss compared to the surpassing greatness of knowing Christ Jesus my Lord, for whose sake I have lost all things. I consider them rubbish, that I may gain Christ and be found in him."

Jesus: An End in Himself

After the resurrection, Jesus' disciples never considered the Master a means to their ends. To them, He *was* the End. Christ's followers had truly internalized the message their Lord preached through both His life and His lips. They rightly understood that their treasure was in another kingdom and that they were simply ambassadors, sojourners, and pilgrims. The disciples knew this was not their final dwelling place. They recognized that their destiny was to be eternity.

Christ did not come to bring financial prosperity; He came to focus our attention on *eternal* prosperity. Even now the words of the Master ring with divine authority: "Do not store up for yourselves treasures on earth, where moth and rust destroy, and where thieves break in and steal. But store up for yourselves treasures in heaven" (Matthew 6:19,20).

How magnificent a sight it must have been to witness the Lord standing on the shore of Galilee, pleading passionately with His followers to labor not for that which perishes but for that which is eternal (John 6:27).

How much Scripture do we need to see the bankruptcy of the Faith movement's teaching on prosperity? Shall we remind ourselves of Christ's account of the rich man and Lazarus in Luke 16:19-31? The rich man, who lived his earthly life in luxury, was not even dignified with a name in eternity. But Lazarus, who lived in poverty, received comfort in the eternal kingdom (verse 25).

Or perhaps we should reread the words of Jesus' own brother, James, who boldly declared to the rich, "Your wealth has rotted. . . . Your silver and gold are corroded. . . . You have hoarded wealth in the last days" (James 5:2,3). The Bible is replete with examples declaring the poverty of the Faith movement's teachings concerning wealth and want. The Faith teachers of our day have not conformed their teachings to the ancient Scriptures. Instead, they have conformed themselves to American society.

American culture is obsessed with upward mobility and crass materialism, which is precisely what the Faith movement panders to. It thrives on the idea that "God's kids" can acquire wealth without work and dollars without discipline. Its watchword is not self-sacrifice but self-aggrandizement. Sadly, a significant portion of contemporary Christianity has bought into the message that we only go around once in this world, so we had better go for all the gusto we can while we're here.[10] We no longer sing "I surrender all." Rather, we say, "I can speak it all into existence through the formula of faith."

We crave "rags-to-riches" stories and frequently cave in to get-rich-quick schemes. T.L. Osborn, for example, promises people that by learning "7 Simple Secrets in Just 60 Seconds a Day" you can "Get the Best Out of Life in Just 7 Days."[11] As proof he cites, among other stories, the tale of a man who was forced to leave his country and found himself in great financial difficulty. But thanks to Osborn's "fast-faith formula," this man was able to buy "a Rolls Royce, and a new home." Predictably, this man goes on to encourage others to "plant $20 or $50" in Osborn's ministry "to see for themselves how God works money MIRACLES."[12]

In sharp distinction, Scripture commands us not to conform to the pattern of this world, but to be transformed by the renewing of our minds. Only then will we be able to "test and approve what God's will is—his good, pleasing and perfect will" (Romans 12:2).

Does Poverty Equal Piety?

Having said all this, let me make it clear that I do *not* associate poverty with piety (although the poor *do* have a special place in God's heart; see Luke 6:20). The issue is not what you have, but what you do with what you have. Our time, talent, and treasure should be used for God's glory rather than our own gain. I am persuaded that the Bible teaches a form of Christian capitalism—in other words, responsibility associated with wealth. It does not promote the possession of money for the sake of money, but instead encourages us to use money for the sake of the kingdom.

While some Faith teachers assert that they have the same concept in mind, the evidence shows otherwise. Not only do most Faith teachers induce their supporters to give by appealing to their greed, but they indulge themselves in the process. As Price boasts, "If the Mafia can ride around in Lincoln Continental town cars, why can't the King's Kids?"[13] Elsewhere he makes the following statement:

> You can talk about me all you want while I'm driving by in my Rolls Royce that's paid for, and I got the pink slip on it. Talk all you want. Bad mouth all you want. Don't hurt me in the

least. Doesn't bother me. It's a whole lot easier to be persecuted when I'm riding in my car and I got the pink slip than it is when I'm riding in a car and owe my soul to the company store.[14]

There can be no denying that primary prosperity proponents teach a lifestyle of self-indulgence and selfishness, as opposed to a lifestyle of self-denial and selflessness. Former leaders in the Faith movement know this firsthand. The ex-wife of televangelist Richard Roberts summed it up memorably when she wrote:

> I know a lot of people were blessed and sincerely ministered to by what we sang on TV, and by what we said—but the overall picture, I'm afraid, seemed to say, "If you follow our formula, you'll be like us," rather than, "If you do what Jesus says, you'll be like Him." It was certainly more exciting to follow us, because to follow us was to identify with success, with glamour, with a theology that made everything good and clean and well-knit together. To identify with Jesus, however, meant to identify with the Cross.[15]

The difference between serving self and serving the Savior is the difference between cultural conformity and conformity to Christ. Jesus said it best when He said, "If anyone would come after me, he must deny himself and take up his cross daily and follow me" (Luke 9:23; cf. Matthew 16:24; Mark 8:34).

A cross may not ride as well as a Rolls, but in the end it will take you a lot farther.

18

Cons and Cover-Ups

*C*ons and cover-ups under the guise of Christianity are certainly nothing new. Nor are charlatans.

During a time of spiritual darkness in the Middle Ages, a crass and carnal monk named Johann Tetzel conned the commoners of his day into buying indulgences (special releases from sin offered by certain Catholic clergy). Tetzel took a complex Catholic creed on purgatory and reduced it to a catchy couplet:

> As soon as the coin in the coffer rings,
> The soul from purgatory springs.

His pitch was simple. According to Tetzel, people could purchase a pardon from God that would purge them from a place called purgatory. Unbelievably, thousands fell for his ruse. In fact, the masses—from monks to magistrates—hailed Tetzel as a messenger from heaven. Capitalizing on their spiritual insecurity and scriptural illiteracy, he fleeced them to fund papal projects and his own extravagant lifestyle.

Although Tetzel's methods for merchandizing the gospel were outrageous, no one seemed willing to expose him. His popularity, backed by the power of Rome, seemed too formidable a foe. That is, until a monk named Martin

Luther came along. Luther could no longer go along with the con. As Philip Schaff so aptly stated: "As a preacher, a pastor, and a professor, he [Luther] felt it to be his duty to protest. . . . To be silent was to betray his theology and his conscience."[1] And so, in 1517, Luther nailed his famous Ninety-Five Theses to the door of the castle church at Wittenberg.

In layman's language, Luther's Ninety-Five Theses protested the pillaging of the poor by the Pope. In Theses 27 and 28, Luther labeled the notion that a soul would fly out of purgatory when money fell into the coffers of the church as a perverted prescription for "avarice and gain."[2]

In Theses 45 and 66, Luther expressed outrage that a person would attempt to purchase God's pardon with money. He called the "treasures of indulgences" nets with which the preachers of pardon fished for the "riches of men."[3] In Theses 50 and 51, Luther stated that the real reason Rome was selling indulgences was not the spiritual well-being of the saints but the financial well-being of the Pope and his pet project—the building of the Basilica of Saint Peter's. He wrote with great passion that the mother Church in Rome would be better "burnt to ashes, than that it should be built up with the skin, flesh, and bones" of the Pope's sheep.[4] Finally, in Thesis 86, Luther put it all in perspective when he asked why a rich Pope, "whose riches are at this day more ample than that of the wealthiest of the wealthy," would not build the Basilica with his own money, rather than taking from the meager resources of the poor.[5]

Rome's reaction was swift and severe. Luther was labeled a "child of the Devil" and a "drunken German who . . . when sober . . . will change his mind."[6] But Luther did not change his mind. Under the ban of the Empire and a bull of excommunication, Luther displayed his raw courage, rare communication skills, and rich convictions. When asked to recant, he responded with the famous words "My conscience is captive to the Word of God. . . . Here I stand. I cannot do otherwise. May God help me."[7]

And help him God did! Luther's courage established a mighty Reformation that exposed the cons and cover-ups of his day.

Today a new Reformation is needed. The pillaging of the poor, sanctified by papal bulls in years gone by, is strikingly similar to the appeals of a new generation of "prosperity popes" today. Tetzel fleeced the poor of his day by promising freedom from purgatory. False teachers today are conning a new generation by promising freedom from poverty and a lifetime of prosperity.

Have a Need, Plant a Seed

In a book titled *Ashes to Gold*, Patti Roberts compares the "seed-faith" tactic of former father-in-law Oral Roberts to Johann Tetzel's practice of selling indulgences. She points out that she had a "very difficult time distinguishing between the selling of indulgences and the concept of seed-faith inflated to the degree to which we had inflated it."[8]

One distinction Patti did observe was that Oral was more subtle than Tetzel. Rather than offering salvation in exchange for money, Oral appealed to such basic instincts as fear and greed. And he is not alone. Oral's tactics have become standard fare among many Faith teachers. While they may not promise their partners heavenly paradise, they do promise them earthly prosperity. Like Tetzel, many of them have become masters at inventing catchy couplets to make their ideas both understandable and memorable. One seed-faith ditty goes something like this:

> Have a need,
> plant a seed.

What exactly is seed-faith? According to Oral Roberts, "The seed of giving is the seed of faith! And the seed has to be planted BEFORE we can speak to our mountain of need to be removed!"[9] Simply stated, "planting a seed" is virtually synonymous with "mail me money." The seed-faith gimmick is little more than a give-to-get gospel of greed.

Oral Roberts has used both television and the mail to raise millions of dollars. His method has been described as "the lowest form of emotional appeal."[10] In his many mailings, Roberts appeals to the sympathies of his partners as well as their greed.

On January 4, 1987, Roberts launched his most notorious campaign to date. Roberts told his followers that if he did not raise a total of 8 million dollars by March, God was going to take his life.[11] In a follow-up direct-mail letter, Roberts announced that the deadline to raise the remaining 1.5 million dollars was set for March 31. To serve as a reminder to his supporters, a caption, printed in handwritten form at the top of the mass mailing's first page, warned, "Just 30 days left!"[12]

Comparing himself to the apostle Paul, Roberts begged people not to let Satan defeat him. "God," he says, "clearly told me he needs me here on earth. And here's why—because of all the ministries, this ministry is the only one God has on this earth that owns a medical school."[13]

Then comes the inevitable punch line: By sending a "seed" of 50 dollars, Oral's partners can spare Roberts's life, save the school, sabotage Satan, and secure lots of money to boot.[14]

Some time later, Oral's son, Richard, took pen in hand to warn of his father's impending doom. Without "the additional $4,500,000," explains Richard, "God will not extend Dad's life." He then pleads, "Partner, we cannot let this man of God die. There is no reason for him to die." And this is no idle threat, Richard claims. As he puts it, "When he [Oral] says God speaks to him, he's not bluffing." And just in case someone should doubt or suspect his motives, Richard offers his stirring assurance: "I feel totally called by God to do this... I'm writing to you as an anointed servant of God—doing what God has called me to do."[15]

After several pages Richard finally gets to the seed-faith solution. Take the enclosed birthday card, slip in a seed-faith gift "check," and "then RUSH IT TO ME TODAY."[16] By the end of the letter, Richard Roberts had done virtually everything to assure his partners that this was a deal they couldn't afford to pass up. Send your seed-faith gift and Richard will be proud of you, Oral will pray for you, and God will prosper you.

So much for the sympathy ploy. But that's just the beginning. His father is not opposed to using fear to threaten his followers.

In one instance, Roberts wrote his partners that he had some good news and some bad news. The bad news was that God supernaturally revealed that 1985 would be a terrible year for Roberts's partners. "Satan is going to bring bad things against you," stated Roberts. "*Worry... Fear...* stress [that] will be a serious threat against your health. Even worse, I see Satan is going to make his biggest effort to surround you with so many problems you will feel a sense of *hopelessness.*"[17]

The good news, however, is that Roberts had already consulted God about "Satan's bad year against you." Supernaturally, "the gift of prophecy came on me," he writes, "and 33 predictions were given to me concerning you."[18] These predictions, Roberts promised, will help you to "avoid TERRIBLE NEW DISEASES" and to "take advantage of the hundredfold return... to receive... PROSPERITY MIRACLES."[19]

After sternly warning, "IF YOU NEGLECT TO PAY ATTENTION... then Satan will take advantage and hit you with bad things and you will wish that 1985 had never come,"[20] Roberts closed his letter with a hard sell. Sending a seed-faith gift will not only enable you to "STOP SATAN IN HIS HATE TO BRING YOU DOWN," it will also "help you get your hundredfold return."[21]

"PROSPERITY MIRACLES . . . are within fingertip reach of your faith," claimed Roberts.[22] Of course, the key was to use your fingertips to send money. Appealing to greed, Roberts held out the prospect of financial gain to those who would send him the green.

Incidentally, don't ever think of sending Roberts money and then later changing your mind. If you do, saving Roberts's life may be the least of your worries. Consider these chilling words Roberts uttered during a recent conference:

> Someone will be watching this ministry on the air, who promised a large sum [of money] to God. And you act like you have given it, but you did not pay it. You are so close to lying to the Holy Ghost, that *within days you will be dead* unless you pay the price God said. And somebody here is getting the message. You're on the edge of lying to the Holy Ghost. Don't lie to the Holy Ghost. *The prophet has spoken.*[23]

While Roberts may try to sanitize his seed-faith tactic by surrounding it with Scripture, his theology remains strikingly similar to that of one well-known metaphysical/prosperity cult—the Unity School of Christianity. In fact, the reasoning Roberts employs directly reflects the reasoning used by Unity's cofounder, Charles Fillmore.[24]

Although Roberts claims that his seed-faith theology came directly from Jesus, at least one of the devotionals from his *Guide to Seed-Faith Living* came from the Unity School of Christianity.[25] The material might be cultic, but at least Roberts had the decency to give credit where credit was due.

The Hundredfold Bandwagon

Years ago, Oral Roberts promised prosperity to those who would "plant a seed." Today a new breed of prosperity teachers champion even bigger promises of financial reward—the so-called "hundredfold" return.

In a book titled *God's Will Is Prosperity*, Gloria Copeland springs the "hundredfold" on her constituents. Expanding on the promise of Jesus to provide a "hundredfold" return to those who leave everything behind for the kingdom, Gloria writes, "Give $10 and receive $1,000; give $1,000 and receive $100,000. I know that you can multiply, but I want you to see in black and white how tremendous the hundredfold return is."[26] And just so you don't miss her point, Gloria explains further:

> Give one house and receive one hundred houses or one house worth one hundred times as much. Give one airplane and receive one hundred times the value of the airplane. Give one car and the return would furnish you a lifetime of cars. In short, Mark 10:30 is a very good deal.[27]

Gloria, of course, is not the only Faith teacher to jump on the "hundredfold" bandwagon. John Avanzini has been used by Faith teachers from Crouch to Cerullo to raise money by using the "hundredfold" tactic. In fact, it was during a Morris Cerullo convention in Abba, Nigeria, that Avanzini came up with his now-famous "hundredfold" concept.[28]

It all began when Cerullo's son, David, joined Avanzini's church in Southern California. Avanzini told David that God "dropped in my heart that the wealth of the wicked was laid up for the just." Avanzini then began to beg him, "Please, I want to go with your daddy [Morris] and I want to speak to the nations of the world."[29]

In time, Avanzini gained an audience with Cerullo. His hopes, however, were dashed when Morris rejected him because he did not have "a breakthrough ministry." As Avanzini was to discover later on, a breakthrough ministry was one characterized by "signs and wonders . . . to prove that there is a move of God going on."[30] After waiting patiently for two years, Avanzini finally got the break he was looking for.

Cerullo summoned Avanzini to Abba, Nigeria. There, in a hotel room, God supposedly appeared to Avanzini and said, "I'm gonna have signs and wonders follow your ministry." After giving Avanzini a wordy discourse on fundraising techniques, God instructed him to take up an offering for Cerullo. As God allegedly put it, "I want you to lay hands on that offering, and I want you to speak hundredfold increase over that offering—that it will be multiplied back to the giver one hundredfold."[31]

Sure enough, the very next day Avanzini had the opportunity to try out the new fund-raising technique. After telling the Nigerian leaders at Cerullo's meeting that they would get a hundred times back whatever they gave in the offering, Avanzini gave the order to pass little collection bowls around the room. Before the bowls had reached the end of the first row, they had already been filled to overflowing. Pillowcases were immediately summoned to take up the rest of the offering. But even that wasn't enough.

By now the crowd was in a frenzy. In fact, as Avanzini put it, "Money was falling out of the balcony." Finally the giving got so out of hand that Cerullo himself had to stand up and shout, "Stop the giving! Stop the giving!"

Eventually order was restored, and once again Avanzini attempted to pray over the offering. But "as I began to pray," says Avanzini, "I felt something hitting me, and I looked up and the people were throwing money. Money was being thrown over the tops of their heads. And I laid hands on that offering and I spoke the hundredfold increase."[32]

According to Avanzini, when Jan Crouch heard about that hundredfold incident, she asked him a dozen times or more to deliver the hundredfold message on TBN. Allegedly, Avanzini answered, "Anything else, but God's just not letting me do it."[33] Nowadays, every time TBN holds a fund-raising drive, God apparently releases John to perform his hundredfold routine.

As in Nigeria, gullible American Christians are now throwing their money to the Faith teachers in the hopes that God will throw back a hundred times as much. Sadly, few seem to notice that the "emperor has no clothes."

If the hundredfold message were fact, prosperity teachers would never again have to ask for money. Instead, they would be in the streets giving it away as fast as they could so they could get more. All poverty would be gone and every believer would live in a mansion. The "wealth of the wicked" would indeed be in the hands of the "King's kids." Instead, it is not uncommon to hear appeals like this one from Paul Crouch:

> If you're broke, if you're at your wit's end, if you're out of a job, out of work, let me tell ya. Not only are we gonna bless the world and preach Christ to millions and multitudes around the world, but you can be saved, yourself, by planting seed in this fertile soil called TBN.[34]

The "Point of Contact" Pitch

Oral Roberts once referred to the "point of contact" as the "greatest discovery" he had ever made.[35] And well he should! In conjunction with the seed-faith strategy, Roberts has used this tactic to raise more money than Tetzel ever dreamed of. Others have also done the same.

Robert Tilton, who describes the point of contact as a link of faith with his partners, has built a financial empire based on this tactic. In mailing after mailing, he claims the Holy Spirit is directing him in the use of this method. In a 1990 mailout to his partners, Tilton says that God told him to send them a green prayer cloth as a point of contact.[36] He then instructs his partners to—

- take the prayer cloth, hold it in their right hand and pray for a release of "POWER to create wealth."

- fill out a "Power to Create Wealth" personal reply sheet.

- send lots of money, or as he puts it, "*Sow your very best seed!*"[37]

Tilton then urges his readers to "seed out of their need." The greater the sacrifice, the greater the return. Tilton goes on to coax people to strike while the iron is hot. As he puts it, "Please respond quickly while the anointing is hot and flowing."[38]

When you return the green prayer cloth with the money, Tilton promises to pray specifically and release his faith for you. The idea is that when you return the cloth with some cash, this "anointed apostle" will add his faith to your faith and you will experience unbelievable results. Tilton's pitch is plain and simple:

> SEND ME YOUR GREEN PRAYER CLOTH AS MY POINT OF CONTACT WITH YOU! . . . WHEN I TOUCH YOUR CLOTH . . . IT WILL BE LIKE TOUCHING YOU! . . . *When you touch this cloth, it will be like taking MY hand and touching me.* I want the anointing that God has put upon my life for miracles of finances and prosperity to come directly from my hand to yours. . . . *You can reign in life like a king!*[39]

To help ensure a positive response, Tilton cites an example of a lady who was down-and-out. When she heard his pitch, she took the plunge, sent in the prayer cloth, and started making payments on a vow of faith. Within months she allegedly received the payoff—286,000 dollars in bonds and 65,000 dollars in cash. As an added bonus her husband was delivered from alcoholism.[40]

Of course, green prayer cloths are not all you can find in the Faith teachers' tactics. Their points of contact come in various shapes and sizes. They include anointed handkerchiefs, hems from their garments, holy oil, and a host of other gimmicks. There is virtually no end to the variations that could be cited. For a suggested donation of $1989 or $890 or $89 (for the year 1989), Marilyn Hickey said she would even slip on a ceremonial breastplate, "press *your* 'Breastplate' prayer requests to my heart" and "place your requests on my shoulders."[41]

The Faith teachers inevitably use the Scriptures to make their tactics seem spiritual. Oral Roberts, for example, derived one of his point-of-contact strategies directly from the book of Acts. When Roberts discovered that people were healed by Peter's passing shadow, he decided that people could have their needs met by his passing shadow as well. As the story goes, at first Oral and Richard could not figure out how to use their shadows as a point of contact for their partners, since it was impossible to walk by all of them personally. So they began to pray in the Spirit, and sure enough God gave them a solution.[42]

God told Roberts to have a photographer take a picture of him and his son praying for the needs of their partners. Then Roberts got some specific instructions "straight from Jesus" to give to his partners.[43]

First, Jesus told the partners to take Oral and Richard seriously as "God's co-evangelists . . . who dream dreams and see visions. . . . Write down what you feel led for us to pray for. . . . This will help us pray SPECIFICALLY when we bring YOUR NAME to the Lord."[44]

Next, Jesus instructed the partners to "place a love gift of Seed-Faith upon the prayer sheet right on top of your needs."[45]

Then Jesus unveiled an ingenious plan! He instructed Roberts's partners to take the picture of Oral and Richard "AND HOLD IT OVER the prayer sheet and your Seed-Faith gift so that the shadow of the picture COVERS THE ENTIRE SHEET." According to Jesus, this "becomes the point of contact for you to loose your faith."[46]

Roberts's Jesus, however, saved His most creative instructions for last. He suggested that the partners fold the prayer sheet and the seed-faith gift together to symbolize their union with Oral and Richard. They were then instructed to "Send it back to Richard and me [Oral] today, if possible, so that he and I can immediately unfold it AND OUR SHADOWS CAN PASS OVER YOUR NAME AND NEEDS ON YOUR PRAYER SHEET."[47]

According to Oral and Richard, Jesus also wanted to make sure that the partners kept "the praying picture" as a "personal reminder that Richard and I [Oral]—co-evangelists of God's healing power—are praying for you daily."[48]

Roberts ends his letter by warning his partners that "skeptics may criticize something scriptural like this."[49] On this point Oral is finally correct.

Seed-Faith in the Light of Scripture

Thousands fall for the tactics of the Faith teachers because they do not test everything by the Word of God. The question ultimately is this: How well do the Faith practices hold up when examined in the light of God's Word? Let's take a closer look.

Despite Roberts's claims that his seed-faith concept came directly from Jesus Christ, it does not fare well in the light of Scripture.

If Roberts were truly a student of Scripture, it should have been obvious there was a problem with his Jesus. Incredibly, this Jesus claims that the core of the Sermon on the Mount is focused on seed-faith giving![50]

This Jesus also claims that Matthew 17:20 KJV ("If ye have faith as a grain of mustard seed, ye shall say unto this mountain, Remove hence to yonder place, and it shall remove; and nothing shall be impossible unto you") teaches the seed-faith principles that would enable people to move mountains.[51]

The problem is that this passage has nothing to say about the seed-faith concept of the Faith movement. Jesus here simply promises His disciples that, if they trust Him to do what He says He will, they will succeed in the mission Jesus gives them. In this case the mission they were given was to heal an epileptic—and they failed due to a lack of faith. Matthew 17:20 is not a blanket promise that God is obliged to give us whatever we demand from Him.

To make matters worse, this Jesus also claims that the New Testament, in its entirety, is based on seed-faith—even trying to use Galatians 6:7 KJV ("whatsoever a man soweth, that shall he also reap") to make his point.[52] But as is obvious from its context, the Galatians passage does not appeal to man's greed by formulating a give-to-get scheme (cf. verse 8). Rather, it appeals to people to crucify their selfishness and serve God (Galatians 5:24,21,26) and one another (6:9,10) selflessly.

Tragically, Roberts goes on to twist the biblical view of the atonement by claiming that Christ's death was a seed that God sowed and His resurrection was the harvest that God reaped. As Roberts's Jesus puts it, "The cross is the seed of My life, the seed I gave which was multiplied back to Me by the Father raising Me from the dead, increasing My life far more than it was when I was a man." This Jesus also declares, "I fulfilled the old law of tithing by paying the full price on the cross." Giving is no longer a debt I owe but a seed I sow.[53]

But our motive for giving must always be based on gratitude, not greed. The seed-faith system is clearly not substantiated by Scripture.

Hundredfold: Too Much of a Good Thing?

The hundredfold teaching fares no better in the light of Scripture. We have seen that Faith teachers like Gloria Copeland frequently point to Mark 10:30 ("receive a hundred times") as the basis for this tactic. But the true meaning of Mark 10 is so plain it can hardly be missed. Simply take the time to read the entire chapter in context. The meaning should jump out at you.

Copeland conveniently skips the part in verse 30 about receiving persecutions. She also neglects what is written five verses earlier, in Mark 10:25, where Jesus warns, "It is easier for a camel to go through the eye of a needle than for a rich man to enter the kingdom of God."

Far from being a chapter focused on investment advice for financial prosperity, Mark 10 is clearly designed to portray the deceitfulness of riches. The multiplication envisioned in Mark 10:30 is spiritual rather than physical, metaphorical rather than literal.

In Mark 10, Jesus is using figurative language when He says we will receive a hundred times what we leave behind. David does the same thing in Psalm 50 when he says God owns the cattle on a thousand hills. Clearly he means that God owns everything, and not that God's ownership of hill-grazing cattle extends to exactly one thousand hills.

To take Jesus literally in Mark 10:30 is to reduce this passage to a logical absurdity. It would be one thing for Christ to promise a 100-to-1 return when it came to houses; it would be quite another to promise a 100-to-1 return on wives and children. I don't know about you, but in my opinion that may be too much of a good thing!

Pointless Contacts

Faith teachers frequently cite Acts 19:11,12 to prove that the apostle Paul used points of contact in the manner that they do. Yet even a cursory examination of the text disproves that assertion.

In Acts 19:11,12 we read that "God did extraordinary miracles through Paul. Handkerchiefs and aprons that had touched him were taken to the sick, and their illnesses were cured and the evil spirits left them."

First, conspicuous by its absence in this text is the mention of finances. Nowhere does Paul ask for money to be sent back to him with the handkerchief as a point of contact. Conversely, the Bible issues a strong warning to all those who would seek to buy God's miracle-working power with money. As Peter said to Simon the sorcerer in Acts 8:20, "May your money perish with you, because you thought you could buy the gift of God with money!"

Next, there is no suggestion in Acts 19 that those being healed had "released" their faith. There is certainly no indication that they sent Paul their points of contact with a seed-faith gift so that Paul could put an "Acts 19 kind of anointing" on them and pray for them in Marilyn Hickey style.[54]

Quite to the contrary, as the text says, God was manifesting *extraordinary* or *unusual* miracles through Paul. Far from being normative, these miracles were proof that Paul had been uniquely chosen by God as the "apostle to the Gentiles" (Romans 11:13; cf. 2 Timothy 1:11).

Finally, a historical perspective proves that God was demonstrating the difference between magical formulas based on the fraud and deception prevalent in Ephesus (Acts 19:13-19) and the genuine power displayed by Paul in the name of the Lord Jesus Christ. In fact, these unprecedented miracles caused "the name of the Lord Jesus [to be] held in high honor" (Acts 19:17; cf. verse 20). Unlike the apostle Paul, today's self-appointed apostles do not bring honor to the name of Jesus. Instead, Christ's name is frequently dragged through the mud.

Twisting Facts

Not only do some Faith teachers victimize the poor and downtrodden by promising what they cannot perform, but they also blame these trusting souls when the results they had expected do not materialize.

In his book *It's Not Working, Brother John!* Avanzini uses every strategy imaginable to lead hapless followers to believe that a failure to receive means that something is wrong with them. He writes, "The problem is, *something is wrong with the saint.* . . . Without fail I find something wrong in their lives."[55]

Avanzini then postulates "25 things that close the windows of heaven."[56] One reason Avanzini cites is double-mindedness.[57] He explains that we have two minds—a conscious mind and a subconscious mind. Our subconscious mind has been conditioned by pastors and teachers to believe that Jesus was poor. Therefore, when our conscious mind is introduced to the prosperity gospel, we reject it because we believe subconsciously that we ought to be poor.

Avanzini's answer to this dilemma is to have our subconscious mind reprogrammed to believe that Jesus was rich, wore designer clothes, and lived in a big house.[58] And Avanzini has just the ticket to reprogram your mind: For a price he will sell you his videotape *Was Jesus Poor?*[59]

Another reason advanced by the Faith teachers to explain why people are not getting rich is improper thinking. As Avanzini puts it, "You Are What You Think. . . . Thoughts Are a Creative Force."[60] Drawing from the false premise that "the way you think in your heart will create what you say,"[61] Avanzini concludes that "Proper Thinking Produces Finances."[62] He sums it up like this: "We can believe and receive, or we can doubt and do without."[63]

Interestingly enough, way back in 1919, Ernest Holmes, the founder of the Church of Religious Science, communicated the same sentiment when he said, "Man is just what he thinks himself to be."[64] Although Avanzini claims that the words in his book were inspired by the Holy Spirit,[65] it is remarkable how closely they mirror the teachings of the metaphysical cults.

Another of Avanzini's explanations for his followers' lack of prosperity is that they do not trust their "man of God." He attempts to use 2 Chronicles 20:20 KJV ("believe his prophets, so shall ye prosper") as a pretext to argue that "if you don't trust God's prophets, *you will not prosper.*"[66] In context, however, this passage does not promise financial prosperity. It is a promise of *military* success to the nation of Israel at a time of great danger from the Moabites and Ammonites.

But Avanzini complains that some people will not even allow their man of God "to have a copy of *[their] complete financial statement.*"[67] In an attempt to drum up a biblical precedent for this outrageous demand, Avanzini refers to the account of the widow's oil in 2 Kings 4:1-7:

> When the widow went to Elisha for help with her back-breaking debt, the first thing the prophet asked for was *a financial statement.* He asked, "What do you have in your house?" Thank God this widow was able to trust her man of God. . . . Her relationship of trust with him set her *free from debt* as well as funded her retirement![68]

Such an irresponsible handling of the sacred text is by no means uncommon. Nor has it been throughout the church age. Just as the Pope used Tetzel to pillage the poor in order to build St. Peter's, so prosperity teachers mislead the flock in order to build their empires.

Covenant-Contract

*I*f you still have lingering doubts as to whether the Faith movement is cultic or Christian, its concept of "covenant-contract" should forever settle the issue in your mind. The Faith teachers' notion that all Christians have a divine right to wealth and prosperity is rooted in the myth that God is a failure.

Not only is the Faith-God prone to making mistakes, but He is also a failure forced into playing a game called "Let's make a deal." That is essentially what the Faith movement's concept of covenant-contract is all about.

Remember that in Faith theology, Adam committed cosmic treason by selling his godhood to Satan for the price of an apple. Satan thereby became the god of this world and God was left on the outside, desperately searching for a way back in.

But give the Faith-God some credit. He may have been a failure, but he was certainly not a quitter. Rather than throw in the towel, he began to devise a clever comeback—which is precisely where the Faith movement's concept of the covenant enters the picture. Here is how Kenneth Copeland explains it:

> After Adam's fall in the Garden, God needed
> an avenue back into the earth. . . . Since man
> was the key figure in the Fall, man had to be

the key figure in the redemption, so God approached a man named Abram. He reenacted with Abram what Satan had done with Adam, except that God did not sneak in and use deception to get what He wanted as Satan had. God offered Abram a proposition and Abram bought it.[1]

According to Benny Hinn, God told Abram He "could not touch this earth till a man gave it back to Him."[2] Or as Copeland commented, "I'm making a proposition to you. You can tell me to bug off if you don't like it."[3] Presumably, the proposition was much too posh for Abram to pass up. So rather than telling God to bug off, he took the deal. In exchange for unlimited wealth and prosperity, Abram gave God an avenue back into the earth. Abram and God sealed their deal in blood and became "blood brothers."[4]

Covenant Confusion

Right from the outset, the problem with this doctrine should be apparent. The God of Scripture does not negotiate deals; He issues declarations. God's covenant with Abraham was not a bilateral proposition (i.e., arising from the mutual agreement of two equal parties), but a unilateral promise (initiated by the superior party, who sets nonnegotiable stipulations). Far from having the option to tell God to "bug off," Abraham could only bow humbly before the grace and goodness of his Creator (Genesis 17:3).

The difference between the Faith concept of covenant and the Christian concept of covenant is not a peripheral issue; it makes all the difference in the world.[5] At stake is nothing less than the sovereignty of God. Speaking of the Abrahamic Covenant, Kenneth Copeland essentially says God was the lesser party and Abraham was the greater.[6]

Abraham lived under tremendous pressure because, as Charles Capps put it, "*if Abraham failed, the Covenant would be void.*"7 Fortunately, Abraham did not fail. As agreed upon, he became the first in a long line of prophets that would act as God's mouthpiece in the earth. Copeland picks up the story by saying, "Through the mouths of His prophets, He kept sending His Word and sending His Word. Finally, the great moment came when that Word was brought forth in human form. . . . His name was Jesus."8

By now you know the rest of the story. Jesus was wealthy and prosperous just like his forefather Abraham. For 33 years He lived the high life. Like Abraham, Jesus appropriated all His rights under the covenant.

The "good news" of Faith theology is that we, like Jesus, are Abraham's seed and therefore heirs to the covenant. "Since God's Covenant has been established and prosperity is a provision of this Covenant," reasons Copeland, "you need to realize that prosperity belongs to you *now*!"9 Fred Price offers the following point:

> Christ has redeemed us from the curse of the Law, that the blessing of Abraham might come upon us. . . . How did God bless Abraham? With *cattle, gold, manservants, maidservants, camels, and asses. Abraham was blessed materially.*10

How foreign to Scripture is all of this! The Bible is not a mere contract we can use to command God. Jesus is not a magic mantra we can use to open Fort Knox. God's covenant with Abraham is the proclamation of His sovereign plan to redeem humanity from its sin (Romans 4; Galatians 3:6-9). The overarching message of Scripture is God's redemption of mankind. The covenant is not a simple contract that guarantees us wealth.

Heads You Win, Tails You Want

According to the Faith teachers, there are two sides to the covenant coin: Heads you *win*, tails you *want*. In other words, you can either live beneath the umbrella of prosperity or under the curse of poverty. "We have seen that prosperity is a blessing of Abraham and that poverty is under the curse of the law," maintains Copeland. "Jesus bore the curse of the law in our behalf. He beat Satan and took away his power. Consequently, there is no reason for you to live under the curse of the law, no reason for you to live in poverty of any kind."[11]

The Faith teachers insist that prosperity signifies spiritual favor while poverty is a sign of spiritual failure. Robert Tilton summed up the sentiments of the Faith movement when he said, "Being poor is a sin."[12]

Another famous prosperity teacher once preached the same message. And then something happened: He lost it all. The glitz, the glamour, and the gold all vanished. So did the cheering crowds. Almost overnight his riches were replaced with rags. Stripped of his star status, he found himself alone with Scripture. And so he began to read:

> I spent months reading every word Jesus spoke. I wrote them out over and over, and I read them over and over again. There is no way, if you take the whole counsel of God's Word, that you can equate riches or material things as a sign of God's blessing. . . . I have asked God to forgive me . . . for preaching earthly prosperity.[13]

Contritely, he confessed that "many today believe that the evidence of God's blessing on them is a new car, a house, a good job, and riches."[14] That, he said, would be far from the truth. "Jesus did not teach riches were a sign of God's blessing. . . . Jesus said 'Narrow is the way that leads to life and few there be that find it.' "[15]

Jim Bakker, who in 1989 was convicted of 24 counts of fraud, continued with these stirring words: "It's time the call from the pulpit be changed from 'Who wants a life of

pleasure and good things, new homes, cars, material possessions, etc.?' to 'Who will come forward to accept Jesus
Christ and the fellowship of his suffering.'"[16]

"I believe," concludes Bakker, "the heart of God is
grieved when we cannot delay self-gratification for earthly
things in exchange for life in eternity with Him."[17]

Perhaps Bakker has discovered the true meaning of
prosperity. Perhaps he has truly internalized the words of
Spurgeon, who summed it up eloquently: "The old covenant
was a covenant of prosperity. The new covenant is a covenant
of adversity whereby we are being weaned from this present
world and made meet for the world to come."[18]

If Bakker has truly been weaned from the Faith movement's commitment to earthly prosperity, then his following
words from prison say it all: "I wouldn't want to trade places
with anyone."

Context, Context, Context

lot of backslapping and Faith promoting goes on during the big conferences held by the leaders of the Faith movement. Every host and speaker has that one tale of faith at work, that one story of how he or she has spoken some financial miracle into existence or stopped some mighty calamity from touching his person or family. The audiences cheer and stomp their feet. You have probably seen them on TV, sharing insights to their godly powers of speaking to the things that are not as though they were.

But one need only walk through the parking lot of a Faith rally or Sunday service to answer the question "Does this teaching really work?" I did so recently at the world headquarters and church of one of the leading Faith teachers and got my answer. There *were* Cadillacs, Mercedes, and a few shining Lexus sedans sitting there—but they were in the slots reserved for the pastors and their staff.

By and large, however, the lot looked like any other parking lot in town, with its wide array of cars, pickups, and vans. Listen carefully to that: *Just like any other lot in town.* Now, how can that be?

There were at least a thousand cars out there, probably representing more than 3000 people. These folks were sitting under the teaching of one of the world's most powerful and successful Faith teachers and TV evangelists. They were feeding on a steady diet of messages proclaiming man's own godhood and the creative power of faith at work in their confessions.

And yet most of them arrived at the meeting in a ten-year-old used Ford, and left the same way. Why?

What I discovered in the parking lot that day was that this "Say it, do it, receive it, and tell it" gospel really doesn't work. Somehow, except for a select few, the message never gets past the joyous exultation of the meeting and into the physical realm. If it did, the lot would be full of gleaming examples of prosperity such as those parked in the spots reserved for the pastors.

What is the reason for this failure? It's simple. *The promise is false.* The people present at that service will eventually wear out. They will tire of jumping up and down in expectation. Their shouts of confession for health and wealth will fade away. Eventually they will despair and drift off. Some will be angry with their Faith teacher. Others will rail against God. Too many will accept another lie from the pulpit and believe that the weak link was their own faith. They will think of themselves as a failure and may never recover from the blow.

But none of this will bother the preacher. More initiates will rush in to fill the empty seats with joy and offerings. No one will go after the missing ones. Oh, if circumstances open up, someone might tell the lost one that it was his own fault that things didn't work out, but that's about the extent of it.

Attack the Critics!

So what happens when somebody speaks out against the hurtful doctrines of the Faith movement? You don't have to guess. Just turn on your television.

TBN founder and president Paul Crouch has made it clear that, in his opinion, it is acceptable to judge a man's heart but unacceptable to judge his heresy. In unmistakable terms he judged those who speak out against the Faith movement as being "damned and on their way to hell." He goes on to say, "I don't think there's any redemption for them."[1]

Only a few weeks after I spoke out against the deadly doctrines of Faith theology on Crouch's internationally syndicated televison broadcast, he responded to his critics with these ominous words: "To hell with you! Get out of my life! Get out of the way! . . . I say get out of God's way! Quit blocking God's bridges or God's going to shoot you if I don't. . . . I don't even want to even talk to you or hear you! I don't want to see your ugly face!"[2] Ironically, while fervently condemning "heresy hunters" to the fire of hell, Crouch consigned reincarnationist General George Patton to a future in heaven.[3]

What did Crouch have to say about judging heresy? His advice was simply to let God "sort out all this doctrinal doo-doo."[4] Elaborating further, he complained, " 'We can't have faith preaching.' 'You can't have confession stuff.' 'You can't do this, you can do that.' Who cares? Who cares? Let Jesus sort that all out at the judgment seat of Christ. We'll find out who was right and wrong doctrinally."[5]

Jesus, however, had a totally different perspective. He made it clear that as mere mortals we are incapable of infallibly judging another man's heart (cf. Jeremiah 17:9,10). When it comes to judging heresy, however, we are to *test all things in the light of Scripture* (1 Thessalonians 5:21; Acts 17:11; 2 Timothy 3:16).

The question immediately arises, "How can I determine whether someone is correctly interpreting God's Word?" Fortunately, with a little help from the acronym L-I-G-H-T-S, you will be equipped to discern between wheat and chaff.

The best antidote to heretical teaching is good hermeneutical training. Hermeneutics is the science and art of biblical interpretation. Hermeneutics is a science in that it is regulated by rules and an art in that it involves intuitive and analytical acumen. The rules can be remembered easily with the help of the acronym L-I-G-H-T-S. Hermeneutics "lights your path" as you walk through the Word. The acronym L-I-G-H-T-S will serve to remind you of the following elements involved in biblical interpretation:

> **L** = Literal Interpretation
> **I** = Illumination by Holy Spirit
> **G** = Grammatical Principle
> **H** = Historical Context
> **T** = Teaching Ministry
> **S** = Scriptural Harmony

Literal Principle

The "**L**" in **L-I-G-H-T-S** will remind you of what is known as the *literal principle* of biblical interpretation.

This means that we should interpret the Word of God in its most normal and natural sense. When the Bible uses a metaphor or a figure of speech, it should be instantly apparent and you should interpret it accordingly. Thus when Jesus says that He is "the door" (John 10:7 KJV), it's clear He isn't talking about wood and hinges.

In a similar sense, when Jesus says that those who leave their families for Him and the gospel will receive a "hundredfold" return, the natural assumption is that He is speaking metaphorically. Any other interpretation leads to a logical absurdity.

Faith teachers are masters of attributing esoteric or mystical meanings to biblical passages,[6] thereby spawning doctrinal monstrosities. When the *literal principle* of biblical interpretation is compromised or contradicted, truth becomes clouded and the totality of Scripture is confused.

Illumination Principle

The "**I**" in **L-I-G-H-T-S** will remind you of the *illumination* of Scripture that can only come from the Spirit of

God. As 1 Corinthians 2:12 puts it, "We have not received the spirit of the world but the Spirit who is from God, that we may understand what God has freely given us." Because the author of Scripture, the Holy Spirit (2 Peter 1:21), resides within each child of God (1 Corinthians 3:16), he or she is in a unique position to receive God's illumination (1 Corinthians 2:9-11). The Spirit of truth not only provides insights that permeate the head, but also provides illumination that penetrates the heart.

Clearly, however, the Holy Spirit does not supplant the scrupulous study of Scripture. Rather, He provides us with insights that can only be spiritually discerned. In this way the Holy Spirit helps us to exegete (draw out of) rather than eisegete (read into) Scripture. He only illumines what is *in* the text; illumination does *not* go *beyond* the text.

This is precisely where virtually all the Faith teachers falter. They claim that the Holy Spirit has given them special illumination and then proceed to read their individual bias into the Scriptures.

The acid test for any doctrine is the text of Scripture. Illumination must always be tested by the Word. Remember, Satan wants us to encounter him and think we are in touch with the living God. Whenever a teaching runs counter to God's revealed truth, you can be sure the Holy Spirit is not behind it (John 16:13).

Grammatical Principle

The "G" in L-I-G-H-T-S will remind you that Scripture is to be interpreted in accordance with typical rules of grammar, including syntax and style. For this reason, it is important that the student of Scripture have a basic understanding of grammatical principles. It is also helpful to have a basic grasp of the Greek and Hebrew languages.

If you do not know Greek or Hebrew, however, don't panic. Today there are a host of eminently usable tools to aid you in gaining insights from the original languages of

Scripture. Besides commentaries, there are "interlinear" translations that provide the Hebrew and Greek text of the Bible in parallel with the English text. In addition, there are dictionaries of Old and New Testament words that are keyed to *Strong's* concordance. Tools such as these make it easy for the layperson to obtain insights on the original Hebrew or Greek of the Bible without being fluent in these languages.[7] Using tools such as these, along with some common sense, will keep you from being fooled by people who claim a mastery of the biblical languages while undermining the grammatical principles of biblical interpretation. For example, one passage that John Avanzini often misuses is Mark 12:44, where Jesus, speaking of the poor widow, states, "They all gave out of their wealth; but she, out of her poverty, put in everything—all she had to live on." Avanzini takes the word "poverty" and changes it to "want," the word used in the King James Version. So far so good.

But then, during a TBN fund-raising drive, Avanzini smiles and tells his audience that this widow did not give out of her poverty, but out of her want. In other words, Avanzini claims that the widow gave "because she wanted something from her God."[8] In other words, she gave to get. Avanzini then explains that the church throughout the ages has missed the true meaning of this passage and that he has now presented the world with the deeper meaning of the text.

It's true that the English word "want" can mean "to desire or wish for something." However, the same word can also refer to a state of poverty, lack, or destitution. In order to determine which meaning of "want" is applicable to Mark 12:44, the reader need simply look at the context and construction of the text. Closer inspection makes it clear that Christ was contrasting the giving of the "poor widow" (verses 42,43) with those who were "rich" (verse 41) and had an "abundance" (verse 44). Therefore the word "want" points to the poverty-stricken state of the widow, not her personal desires.

It should also be noted that the parallel account of the poor widow in Luke 21:4 employs the word "penury" in place of "want." All Avanzini had to do was consult any nearby dictionary to see that "penury" is simply a fifteenth-century word for extreme poverty. Furthermore, had Avanzini bothered to check a Greek lexicon, he would have realized that the word translated "want" in Mark 12:44 is derived from the Greek word *husteresis*, which means "poverty."[9] Hence Avanzini's so-called exposition of the verse is bogus and lacks true biblical insight.

Historical Principle

The "H" in L-I-G-**H**-T-S will remind you that the Christian faith is *historical* and evidential (Luke 1:1-4). The biblical text is best understood when one is familiar with the customs, culture, and historical context of biblical times. Such background information is extremely helpful in drawing out the full meaning of any given text.

Unfortunately, the Faith teachers seem to have neglected this crucial dimension of hermeneutics. Often they end up misquoting and misinterpreting a passage as a result of their failure to observe its historical context. A classic example is their handling of 3 John 2.

The King James version of this text reads, "Beloved, I wish above all things that thou mayest prosper and be in health, even as thy soul prospereth." When Oral Roberts first came across this text he excitedly told his wife, "Evelyn, now this means that we're supposed to prosper." Roberts then went on to recount how, after discovering this verse, God gave him a brand-new Buick. According to Roberts, "Everything that has happened to us since that day started with that verse of Scripture." Evelyn enthusiastically agreed with Oral that to prosper "is God's highest wish for us."[10]

Do Oral and Evelyn have an accurate handle on this passage? The answer is an emphatic NO! Remember, we must take into consideration the passage's historical context. This opening remark in John's letter to his friend Gaius is, as Bible scholar Gordon Fee puts it, "the *standard* form of greeting in a personal letter in antiquity."[11] Fee concludes that "to extend John's wish for Gaius to refer to financial and material prosperity for all Christians of all times is *totally foreign* to the text. John neither intended that, nor could Gaius have so understood it. Thus it cannot be the 'plain meaning' of the text."[12] It may also be instructive to note that, as Fee points out, "the Greek word translated 'prosper' means 'to go well with someone.'"[13]

When it comes to the context and customs of antiquity, there is no need to be led astray. Thankfully, there are a host of excellent handbooks and commentaries to aid you in understanding the people and places of the Bible.

Teaching Principle

The "T" in L-I-G-H-T-S will remind you that even though the ultimate illumination of Scripture comes through the ministry of the Holy Spirit, God has also provided the church with uniquely gifted human *teachers* as well (Ephesians 4:11). Indeed, there exists a wide chasm between those who are skilled in biblical interpretation and those who claim the "anointing" but clearly make up their theology as they go.

James no doubt had such dubious teachers in mind when he solemnly warned, "Not many of you should presume to be teachers, my brothers, because you know that we who teach will be judged more strictly" (James 3:1). Paul echoed the same warning when he exorted Timothy to "do your best to present yourself to God as one approved, a workman who does not need to be ashamed and who correctly handles the word of truth" (2 Timothy 2:15). Scripture makes it abundantly clear that the task of teaching should never be undertaken in a cavalier fashion.

Following the example of the Bereans (Acts 17:11), we should make sure that what human teachers say is in line with Scripture (cf. 1 Thessalonians 5:21). When it comes to understanding the Word of God, we ought to seek reliable sources for assistance. As we seek to rightly interpret God's Word (2 Timothy 2:15), we would do well to consult those whom God has uniquely gifted as teachers in the church (cf. Titus 2:1-15) and who guard against wolves in sheep's clothing that will not spare the flock (Acts 20:29).

Scriptural Harmony Principle

Finally, the "S" in L-I-G-H-T-S will remind you of the principle of *scriptural harmony*. Simply stated, this means that individual passages of Scripture must always harmonize with Scripture as a whole. One text can never be interpreted in such a way as to conflict with other passages. In other words, if a particular passage can be interpreted in several ways, the only choice is that interpretation which harmonizes with the rest of Scripture. The biblical interpreter must keep in mind that all of Scripture, though communicated through various human instruments, has a single Author: God. And God does not contradict Himself.

This principle in and of itself rules out the Faith teachers' misinterpretation of John 10:34. There is no possibility that Scripture is here teaching that the believer is a god, because this would result in the Bible contradicting itself. The Faith view of this verse slanders the Holy Spirit, who reveals that there is only one God (Deuteronomy 6:4; Isaiah 43:10; 44:6).

The Bible was written over a period of 1600 years by 40 authors on different continents, in three languages and on hundreds of subjects—yet without contradiction and with such flawless harmony that all other literature pales by comparison. This principle alone invalidates the Faith message.

A Biblical View of Wealth

With the principles of L-I-G-H-T-S fresh in your mind, let us conclude this section with a biblical view of wealth. It is one thing to rail against the darkness; it is another to light a candle and illuminate the landscape.

The place to begin is Psalm 24:1. Without understanding who owns everything, we are liable to believe all sorts of nonsense. Listen to what David has to say:

> The earth is the Lord's, and everything in it,
> the world, and all who live in it.

It is crucial that we understand this text. God is the landlord; we are just tenants. The Lord of Glory has title to the universe; we are simply stewards. All the things we acquire in this life are only on loan. We didn't arrive with them and we won't take them with us; they all belong to God, and He will do with them just as He pleases. Just remembering this basic fact will save us a world of trouble.

It is good for us to periodically answer the apostle Paul's question in 1 Corinthians 4:7: "What do you have that you did not receive?" The answer, of course, is *nothing*. Everything that you have, God gave you. As Paul told the Athenians, "He himself gives all men life and breath and everything else" (Acts 17:25). If you ever start deceiving yourself into believing that by your own strength or godliness you have been able to accumulate great wealth, remember Paul's question.

Second, remember that the accumulation of wealth is not the purpose or the calling of any of God's children. Yes, God prospers some; but He places others in more humble circumstances. Poverty does not equal piety, but neither do riches equal righteousness. If there were a one-to-one ratio between godliness and prosperity, then the godliest people in the world would also be the wealthiest. But any check of the Forbes 500 will quickly dash that illusion.

Third, our attitude toward wealth should mirror the apostle Paul's outlook in the book of Philippians. Several nuggets in that book form almost a primer for a biblical view of wealth. We might begin by looking at Philippians 4:12,13:

> I know what it is to be in need, and I know what it is to have plenty. I have learned the secret of being content in any and every situation, whether well fed or hungry, whether living in plenty or in want. I can do everything through him who gives me strength.

Then we might consider the apostle's words two chapters earlier, where he instructs his friends on the godly use of the resources God entrusts to them:

> Do nothing out of selfish ambition or vain conceit, but in humility consider others better than yourselves. Each of you should look not only to your own interests, but also to the interests of others (2:3,4).

Next we might recall the example that Paul uses to illustrate what happens when God's people use their resources in a way that honors and glorifies their Creator:

> It was good of you to share in my troubles. Moreover, as you Philippians know, in the early days of your acquaintance with the gospel . . . not one church shared with me in the matter of giving and receiving, except you only; for even when I was in Thessalonica, you sent me aid again and again when I was in need. Not that I am looking for a gift, but I am looking for what may be credited to your account. . . . And my God will meet all your needs according to his glorious riches in Christ Jesus (4:14,17,19).

We need to remind ourselves that while we have been promised an *eternal* inheritance far beyond our wildest dreams, God's promise for us *on this earth* sometimes takes on a darker hue:

> It has been granted to you on behalf of Christ not only to believe on him, but also to suffer for him (1:29).

Finally, we need to consider both the warning and the glorious hope that the apostle joyfully lays out for us in Philippians 3:18–4:1:

> I have often told you before and now say again even with tears, many live as enemies of the cross of Christ. Their destiny is destruction, their god is their stomach, and their glory is in their shame. Their mind is on earthly things. But our citizenship is in heaven. And we eagerly await a Savior from there, the Lord Jesus Christ, who, by the power that enables him to bring everything under his control, will transform our lowly bodies so that they will be like his glorious body. Therefore, my brothers, you whom I love and long for, my joy and crown, that is how you should stand firm in the Lord, dear friends!

Wealth comes from the Lord, says Paul. But don't get too attached to it. What you have, use for the furtherance of the gospel and for the betterment of those around you. Expect that hardship will come your way. And never forget that one day Jesus will roll up this earth like a ball of yarn and will bestow upon us a body that will never decay, never hurt, never be in need of food or gold or earthly riches. In other words, lead your life here below as a responsible steward so that one day, at the judgment, God Himself will richly reward you (Matthew 25:21).

I am strongly tempted at this point to quote several passages from the chapter on money in John Piper's book *Desiring God*, but I will content myself with one quotation only. In my opinion, Piper's words in that chapter are among the best I have ever read on the issue of the Christian's use of money. See if you don't agree:

A wealth-and-prosperity doctrine is afoot today, shaped by the half-truth that says, "We glorify God with our money by enjoying thankfully all the things he enables us to buy. Why should a son of the King live like a pauper?" And so on. The true half of this is that we should give thanks for every good thing God enables us to have. That does glorify him. The false half is the subtle implication that God can be glorified in this way by all kinds of luxurious purchases.

If this were true, Jesus would not have said, "Sell your possessions and give alms" (Luke 12:33). He would not have said, "Do not seek what you are to eat and what you are to drink" (Luke 12:29). John the Baptist would not have said, "He who has two coats, let him share with him who has none" (Luke 3:11). The Son of Man would not have walked around with no place to lay his head (Luke 9:58). And Zacchaeus would not have given half his goods to the poor (Luke 19:8).

God is not glorified when we keep for ourselves (no matter how thankfully) what we ought to be using to alleviate the misery of unevangelized, uneducated, unmedicated, and unfed millions. The evidence that many professing Christians have been deceived by this doctrine is how little they give and how much they own. God *has* prospered them. And by an almost irresistible law of consumer culture (baptized by a doctrine of health, wealth, and prosperity) they have bought bigger (and more) houses, newer (and more) cars, fancier (and more) clothes, better (and more) meat, and all manner of trinkets and gadgets and containers and devices and equipment to make life more fun.

They will object: Does not the Old Testament promise that God will prosper his people? Indeed! God increases our yield so that by giving we can prove our yield is not our god. God does not prosper a man's business so that he can move from a Ford to a Cadillac. God prospers a business so that 17,000 unreached peoples can be reached with the gospel. He prospers a business so that twelve percent of the world's population can move a step back from the precipice of starvation. . . .

The issue is not how much a person makes. Big industry and big salaries are a fact of our times, and they are not necessarily evil. The evil is in being deceived into thinking a $100,000 salary must be accompanied by a $100,000 lifestyle. God has made us to be conduits of his grace. The danger is in thinking the conduit should be lined with gold. It shouldn't. Copper will do.[14]

Folks, it's your choice. You can swallow the Faith preachers' nonsense about your right to wallow in self-indulgence, or you can set your heart on the deep satisfaction that can only come through using your resources generously to further the gospel and improve the lot of those around you. You can live responsibly as a steward of God's resources and expect to hear Him say, "Well done, good and faithful servant," or you can squander His gifts and let these words fall with full force upon your foolish soul: "I tell you the truth, you have your reward in full."

I aim to lay up for myself "a good foundation for the future, so that [I] may take hold of that which is life indeed" (see 1 Timothy 6:17-19 NASB). But I do not intend to lay up for myself "treasures upon earth, where moth and rust destroy and where thieves break in and steal" (see Matthew 6:19-21 NASB).

Friends, it's your bank statement in *heaven* that counts.

If your hope is fixed on the one you have down here, you're bankrupt no matter how many digits you count next to your name.

Christianity
IN
CRISIS

PART SIX

*Sickness
and
Suffering*

I truly did not think I could ever be happy again. In one blinding instant my whole world fell apart. One moment, excitement; the next moment, excruciating pain. If only I could turn back time! Please God, this can't happen. How could You let this happen? Please help me!

With my mind spinning, I gathered up my critically injured son and sped off toward the nearest hospital. I felt as though a knife had been plunged into my heart.

Only hours earlier I had arrived home from a long week of ministry. My son David had slipped quietly into our bedroom in the early morning hours. "Dad," he whispered, "will you help me put my new bike together?" Quietly, so as not to wake anyone in the house, we tiptoed down the stairs. Together we brought the carton containing his new bike into the kitchen and began to undo the packing.

The rest of what happened is still a blur in my mind. David pulled a sharp knife out of the kitchen drawer. Impulsively he jabbed the knife into the cardboard box and pulled up with all his might. Unexpectedly, the packing gave way with little resistance. The knife gathered speed as it moved up through the box, and the unimpeded motion of his arm carried the blade upward toward his face. With lightning speed the sharp point of the knife entered through the center of his cornea, pierced deep into the inner chamber, and split open my son's eye.

As I paced the halls of the hospital that morning, I was sure I could never be happy again. I had lost all perspective. My world plunged into deep darkness and despair. Pain and sorrow had thrust their unwelcome presence into the midst of my family.

But I am not alone. Sooner or later every person experiences sadness and sorrow. It is precisely during those times that each of us, like Job, is put to the test. Job, in fact, was faced with the ultimate test of faith. Even though God acknowledged Job as "blameless and upright," Job suffered unspeakable tragedy. First he lost his financial base; then he lost his family. Finally even his health failed.

Questions and doubts must surely have raced through Job's mind. Was this just a bad dream? Was the sickness but an illusion and the symptoms a satanic ploy to rob him of his faith? Had he indeed given Satan an avenue of attack because he had uttered words of fear rather than words of faith? Were Job's friends correct in suggesting that tragedy had befallen him because he had indulged himself in some secret sin? Or was a sovereign God working all things together for good in the life of a man who loved God and was called according to His purpose?

Job and those closest to him were left in the dark, for Scripture reveals that what was happening in the heavenlies was hidden from them.

Job's wife impugned the Sovereign of the universe. "Curse God and die," she said (Job 2:9).

Job's "friends" impugned Job. Unanimously they accused him of suffering for some secret sin. "Surely God does not reject a blameless man," they cried.[1]

Job, however, impugned neither himself nor God. Emotionally he was on a roller coaster as his mind searched for answers, but in the end he uttered the ultimate words of faith: "Though he slay me, yet will I hope in him" (Job 13:15).

Today, as each one of us journeys down the road of life, we, like Job, will face the specter of sickness, suffering, and ultimately death. How will you respond? Will you follow in the direction of Job's wife and friends, or will you follow in the footsteps of Job? Job's wife and friends had an excuse. They were not privy to what was taking place in the heavenlies. But we are! Scripture reveals that all the while Job suffered, God was in control.

As we proceed though this section on sickness and suffering, we will draw a clear line between the cultic concepts of the Faith movement and those of the historic Christian faith. As this line becomes blurred, tragedy inevitably ensues.

Sickness and suffering are indeed the common denominator of a fallen world. We all get sick and eventually we all die—including every single person committed to the Faith movement. As much as the Faith teachers would have you believe otherwise, there are no exceptions to the rule.

Fred Price may proudly proclaim, "We don't allow sickness in our home,"[2] but the reality is that his wife has been stricken with cancer and has profusely thanked her doctors for the painful radiation and chemotherapy she has received from them.[3] Kenneth Hagin may brag that he has not had a headache, the flu, or even "one sick day" in nearly 60 years,[4] yet he has suffered at least four cardiovascular crises, including one full-scale heart stoppage and another episode persisting for six weeks.[5] Although Hagin claims his "rights" and literally stands on his Bible[6] when illness comes, his six-week bout with heart trouble defies his "positive confession."

Hagin may boast that his confessions of divine healing get results "within just a few seconds," but some of his followers admit it is better "not to insist on seeing a *spectacular* manifestation of healing, but . . . a *progressive* healing," as one cancer victim said who wisely underwent chemotherapy during "the many months" when "we saw no 'spectacular' manifestation [of healing]" during two separate bouts with the disease.[7] Faith teacher Hobart Freeman may have blamed the death of his grandson on the lack of faith of his son-in-law, but the truth is that a routine medical procedure could have easily saved the boy's life. Ironically, Freeman's own disdain for science and medicine, along with his flawed Faith formulas, led to his apparently premature death in 1984.[8]

Most ironic of all, veteran faith healer Oral Roberts suffered a heart attack just hours after supposedly being healed of chest pains by Paul Crouch on TBN's live television show on October 6, 1992—just a few months after Crouch himself suffered from two days of "heart pains," flutters, and "stops."[9]

Sadly, the tragedies of yesterday go unheeded by multitudes of Faith followers today. Recently, after a Sunday morning service where I had spoken on the biblical meaning of faith, a woman came to me and tearfully pleaded for help. Her sister in the Lord had tuned into the Trinity Broadcasting Network and had begun to follow the teachings of Marilyn Hickey, Kenneth Copeland, and Benny Hinn. As a result she had decided to forgo surgery for ovarian cancer. In a letter she wrote, "I'm laying my life on the line of God's Word. He said by his stripes I was healed, am healed, past, present and future. Jesus is real. His Word is real and it is for me to accept and know, trust as though my very breath depended on it." She concluded her letter with the words, "Believe it and receive it."[10]

I wrote this dear but deceived lady a lengthy letter refuting the fatally flawed teachings of the Faith teachers in hopes it would reach her before it was too late.[11] For some, however, it is already too late!

Not long ago I received a letter from another woman whose brother-in-law had enrolled in Kenneth Hagin's Rhema

Bible Training Center. While there, his wife contracted ovarian cancer. Rather than seeking medical attention, they denied the symptoms of cancer. Predictably, she died.[12]

Unfortunately, however, Faith follies do not die as quickly as did this dear lady. Not only did these folks attempt to raise her from the dead, but when life did not return, they confessed that she would come back in another body. In the end, they resorted to regurgitating the standard line of the Faith movement: The woman had not been healed due to lack of faith.

Who knows what untold tragedies testify to the devastation that has followed in the wake of the false teachings of the Faith movement. Yet these perversions continue to expand. The time has come to demonstrate the utter falsity of these deadly deceptions.

21

Symptoms and Sickness

*A*ccording to Faith mythology, Adam's sin not only got God thrown off planet Earth but also resulted in a satanic nature for Adam. Ever since then, mankind has been susceptible to sin, sickness, suffering, and death.

Fortunately, as we have seen, God had a plan. He got a man by the name of Abraham to strike a deal with him. As part of the deal, Abraham and his seed were promised both tremendous wealth and total health. As Copeland puts it, "The basic principle of the Christian life is to know that God put our sin, sickness, disease, sorrow, grief, and poverty on Jesus at Calvary. For Him to put any of this on us now would be a miscarriage of justice. Jesus was made a curse for us so that we can receive the blessing of Abraham."[1]

The Faith teachers hold that those who believe in Christ are Abraham's seed and thus heirs to the Covenant. Says Copeland, "You have a covenant with Almighty God, and one of your covenant rights is the right to a healthy body."[2] Just so you don't miss his point Copeland says:

> The first step to spiritual maturity is to realize your position before God. You are a child of God and a joint-heir with Jesus. Consequently, you are entitled to all the rights and privileges in

the kingdom of God, and one of these rights is health and healing. You will never fully realize or understand healing until you know beyond any doubt that . . . God wants *you* healed. . . . Whether or not you accept that and purpose to walk in the reality of the truth is your own decision to make.[3]

Benny Hinn cuts directly to the heart of the matter when he writes, "The Bible declares that the work was done 2,000 years ago. God is not going to heal you now—He healed you 2,000 years ago. All you have to do today is receive your healing by faith."[4]

Hinn believes that Moses should be our example. Moses lived 120 years without his eye growing dim and his natural force abating; therefore we should as well. Says Hinn, "Sickness does not belong to you. It has no part in the Body of Christ. Sickness does not belong to any of us. The Bible declares if the Word of God is in our life, there will be health, there will be healing—divine health and divine healing. There will be no sickness for the saint of God. If Moses could live such a healthy life, so can you."[5]

By the way, when Hinn says "Sickness does not belong to any of us" he really means it. Several pages later he writes, "He promises to heal *all*—every one, any, any whatsoever, everything—all our diseases! That means not even a headache, sinus problem, not even a toothache—nothing! No sickness should come your way."[6]

Don't think for a moment that this is merely a peripheral doctrine for Hinn. He continues by boldly asserting that "God's greatest desire for the church of Jesus Christ . . . is that we be in total and perfect health."[7]

Like Hinn, Jerry Savelle believes that "divine health is something we already possess. When symptoms come, it is nothing more than the thief trying to steal the health which is ours. In other words, divine health is not something we are trying to get from God; it is something the Devil is trying to take away from us!"[8]

The Subterfuge of Symptoms

Says Savelle, "When the Devil tries to put a symptom of sickness or disease on my body, I absolutely refuse to accept it. A short time ago he tried to put symptoms of the flu on me. My nose and eyes started to run. I began to sneeze and ache all over. I haven't had the flu since 1969, and I'm not going to have it now. I'm redeemed from the flu! Immediately I began to confess God's Word that I'm healed by the stripes of Jesus. I rebuked Satan and refused his lying symptoms. I wasn't trying to *get* something I don't have; I was *keeping* something I already have. I *am* healed."[9]

Savelle does not seem troubled by the absurdity of being "healed" of the flu yet continuing to suffer just as badly from the symptoms. And neither does Kenneth Hagin.[10] Fred Price has his own twist to the idea. He tells the story of how Satan attacked him with symptoms that were so severe that he literally thought he might die. As Price tells the story:

> . . . the devil wanted to scare me into thinking that the pain would kill me. Well, I just let the pain come. My wife can tell you; I crawled around on my bedroom floor, shouting and hollering at the top of my voice. I was in such pain I couldn't stand on my feet. . . . I was under attack to that extent. But I refused to give in to it. . . . I wanted my faith to work for me. I didn't want to have to call you up and have you pray for me.[11]

Like Savelle and other Faith teachers, Price is convinced that symptoms are nothing more than the tricks of Satan which he uses to steal what is rightfully yours. Savelle explains it this way:

Suppose a stranger walked into your kitchen, loaded your refrigerator on a dolly, and started wheeling it out the door. What would you do? You would probably stop him. . . . No one in his right mind would open the door for a thief, stand there and watch his refrigerator being rolled away. . . . He is going to step in front of that thief and say . . . "Where do you think you're going with my refrigerator? Get your hands off my property and get out of here!" He wouldn't be trying to *get* a refrigerator; he would be *keeping* the one he has. So it is with healing. I *am* healed. When symptoms come, I just brace myself and tell the Devil, "Hold it right there, bud!"[12]

Deadly Doctrine

Such pronouncements might sound merely silly, but they have a darker side. Perhaps Kenneth Copeland does not recognize that ignoring symptoms may well be lethal: "I refuse to consider my body, I refuse to be moved by what I see and what I feel. . . . I'm going to choose His Word, instead of what my body's trying to say. . . . *I've had people die, and me standing there saying, 'Bless God, you ain't going to die!' And they did anyway.* And I'm glad I stood. I ain't never stood for anything in my own life that didn't come to pass. I can only use my faith so far with you."[13]

From the following quotation, it appears that Kenneth Hagin believes the same thing:

Real faith in God—heart faith—believes the Word of God regardless of what the physical evidences may be. . . . A person seeking healing should look to God's Word, not to his symptoms. He should say, "I know that I am healed because the Word says that by His stripes I am healed."[14]

In his bestselling book *Right and Wrong Thinking*, Kenneth Hagin tells how during a Full Gospel convention he began to experience "sharp pains" around his heart. Says Hagin, "It seemed to quiver and stop. It even felt as if my breath were being cut off."[15]

Hagin then recounts how the devil came to him and suggested that he be prayed for, to which Hagin responded:

> "Why you foul devil, what is the matter with you? Why in the world would I want to be prayed for? God healed me five years ago, and I am still healed." Suddenly, Satan had camouflaged a few symptoms and was trying to make me believe that I was not healed. . . . All he could do was to try to get me to believe the symptoms and go by my senses. Nevertheless, I stood my ground. I maintained that God had healed me, and I would not accept anything else. I would not even permit a doubtful thought to enter my mind. The symptoms left me.[16]

The danger of denying symptoms or pawning them off as devilish decoys can hardly be overstated. With diseases like cancer, early detection and diagnosis are crucial to effective treatment and recovery. Far from being the devilish decoys they are claimed to be by Faith teachers, symptoms provide testimony to the powerful healing potential that God has designed into our bodies.

Physician Paul Brand summed it up best when he wrote, "The *symptoms that cause patients alarm* are usually spectacular demonstrations of the *body's healing mechanisms* at work."[17] Not only can symptoms serve as signals that alert us to impending physical peril, but they can also be signs that point to the body's healing processes themselves. Thus symptoms are often a divine demonstration of *God's sovereign healing power* in progress. Dr. Brand points out that in the case of an infected wound that is red and swollen with pus:

> The redness comes from an emergency blood supply rushing white cells and agents of repair to the scene, and the pus, composed of lymph fluids and dead cells, gives stark and beautiful evidence of cellular warfare being fought. Similarly, a fever represents the body's effort to circulate blood more quickly and also create a hostile environment for some bacteria.[18]

Despite these well-documented medical facts, Faith teachers continue to convince their followers that symptoms are tricks of the devil designed to rob them of divine health and healing. And with each passing day the toll of those who have been victimized by the Faith message continues to grow. All the while thinking they are following the teachings of Christ, Faith followers are actually being lured into the kingdom of the cults.

Cultic Faith Healing

When it comes to symptoms and sickness, the cultic teachings of the Faith movement are in practice indistinguishable from such metaphysical cults as Christian Science, Religious Science, and the Unity School of Christianity. Cult leader Mary Baker Eddy, like Hagin, taught adherents to ignore their senses as well as the physical symptoms of sickness. In *Science and Health*, the textbook of Christian Science, she writes, "When the first symptoms of disease appear, dispute the testimony of the material senses with divine Science. . . . 'Agree to disagree' with approaching symptoms of chronic or acute disease, whether it is cancer, consumption, or smallpox."[19]

Hagin's teachings and those of New Thought guru Phineas Quimby are also strikingly similar. Quimby, for example, says, "If I believe I am sick, I am sick, for my feelings are my sickness, and my sickness is my belief, and my belief is my mind. Therefore all disease is in the mind or belief."[20] Hagin echoes Quimby's sentiments when he writes:

> It makes a great deal of difference what one thinks. I believe that is why many people are sick. . . . The reason they are not getting healed is that they are thinking wrong. . . . They simply kept thinking, believing, and talking wrong. . . . The thing that makes a believer a success is right thinking, right believing, and right confession.[21]

Actually, the cultic concepts of New Thought are even more in line with the Faith movement than Christian Science. Unlike Christian Science, New Thought does not deny the reality of physical matter. Rather, New Thought teachers—like Faith teachers—claim that mental confessions can control physical conditions.

Devotees of the Faith movement are so committed to the cultic concept of denying symptoms that they seldom, if ever, admit they are sick. They are convinced that any acknowledgment of sickness opens the door to satanic control. According to Kenneth Copeland:

> When you say, "Every time the flu comes to town, I get it," you are not licensing the angels of God; you are licensing Satan and his agency. Then your actions support your words and give him continuous access to your affairs. When the flu season comes, you go to the drugstore and buy nine boxes of pills and all the cold medicine you can get. Your actions have supported your words.[22]

Price depicts medicine as a crutch for the immature believer: "If you need a crutch or something to help you along, then praise God, hobble along until you get your faith moving to the point where you don't need the crutch."[23] Mature believers, according to Price, can do without this crutch. "When you have developed your faith to such an extent that you can stand on the promises of God, then you won't need medicine. That's the reason I don't take medicine."[24]

As in New Thought metaphysics, Faith followers are taught that mature believers can dispense with disease, doctors, and drugs. As Hagin puts it, "I believe that it is the plan of God our Father that no believer should ever be sick. . . . It is not—I state boldly—it is not the will of God my Father that we should suffer with cancer and other dread diseases which bring pain and anguish. No! It is God's will that we be healed."[25]

Warping the Word

In much the same manner as their Mind Science counterparts, the Faith teachers use the Bible to snag the unsuspecting. In some cases their interpretation of Scripture seems reasonable; in others it is downright ridiculous and easy to reject.

In the latter category is Benny Hinn's outrageous argument to "prove" his doctrine of perfect health and healing. In his book *"Rise & Be Healed!"* Hinn writes that "the Bible says in Ephesians 5:23 that Jesus Christ is the savior of the body. . . . If Jesus Christ is the savior of the body, then your body ought to be made whole." Next appears a quotation apparently meant to represent Ephesians 5:23: "You are the savior of my body, Lord Jesus, you are the savior of my soul." A quick check of Ephesians 5:23, however, reveals that Hinn has altered the text to fit his doctrine.[26] The actual Bible text has nothing to do with the physical body.

Rather, the "body" referred to in Ephesians 5:23 is clearly identified as "the church." This is so obvious that it simply cannot be missed. Here is what Ephesians 5:23 says:

"For the husband is the head of the wife as Christ is head of *the church, his body, of which he is the Savior.*" People often fall for Hinn's misinterpretations because they fail to test what he says in the light of Scripture. In some cases they blindly trust him because he says he is God's anointed. In other cases they accept his teachings because high-profile Christian leaders assure them that what he preaches is in line with "the Word of God."

Recently, for example, Paul Crouch sent a financial supporter a letter in which he wrote:

> Leaders at CRI know very well that the people you have mentioned such as Benny Hinn, Dwight Thompson, and others are *not in any sense preaching error.*[27]

Sadly, TBN's viewers often believe such assurances as do Faith followers in general.

Think back to the two ladies I wrote about at the beginning of this section. One of them has already died. The other tuned in to TBN and subsequently staked her life on the teachings of Hinn, Hickey, and Copeland.

Kenneth Copeland may say that those who do not accept his teaching have fallen for "a lie straight from the pit of hell!"[28] but the Scriptures say otherwise. He may proclaim that putting "sickness on you after it was put on Jesus would be a miscarriage of justice" and that "any time a believer has a problem receiving healing, he usually suffers from ignorance of God's Word,"[29] but the truth is that the false teachers of healing are the ones in error.

By His Wounds We Are Healed

One of the Faith movement's favorite proof texts is the wonderfully true Isaiah 53:5, which says, "He was pierced for our transgressions, he was crushed for our iniquities; the punishment that brought us peace was upon him, and by his wounds we are healed." Contrary to Faith teachings, it is common knowledge that the Hebrew word *raphah* often refers to spiritual rather than physical healing. For example, when the prophet Jeremiah says, "Return, O faithless sons; I will heal [*raphah*] your faithlessness," he is obviously not referring to physical healing (Jeremiah 3:22 NASB).[30]

Isaiah could hardly make it more clear that he has spiritual healing in mind when he writes that the Messiah (Christ) was to be pierced for our *transgressions* and crushed for our *iniquities* (Isaiah 53:5).

Peter builds on this understanding when he writes, "He himself bore our *sins* in his body on the tree, so that we might die to *sins* and live for righteousness; by his wounds you have been healed. For you were like sheep going *astray*, but now you have returned to the Shepherd and Overseer of your souls" (1 Peter 2:24,25, emphasis added). Peter's theme here could not be more clearly stated. He says that Christ "bore our *sins*," *not* "our sicknesses." Peter makes it plain that the healing referred to in Isaiah 53:5 is spiritual, not physical.

But let us suppose, for the sake of argument, that Isaiah 53:5 *did* refer to physical healing. Even so, it wouldn't teach the panacea the Faith teachers claim it does, for such an interpretation carries an unwelcome corollary.

If healing is in the atonement and is accessed by faith, then those who die due to lack of faith must remain in their sins. They die without hope. Why? Because if both healing and salvation are included in this passage, they must be accessed in the same way. And if one does not have enough faith to make oneself well, it follows that he cannot have enough faith to be saved. Therefore those who die physically due to lack of faith must also wind up in hell for the same reason. But I doubt you will hear the Faith teachers proclaim this point any time soon, since relatives and friends of the deceased are not likely to applaud teachers of such a melancholy doctrine.

No, it is clear that Isaiah 53:5 does not have physical healing in view. Interestingly, however, the verse immediately preceding it *does* speak of healing for the body. Here Isaiah writes, "Surely he took up our infirmities and carried our sorrows, yet we considered him stricken by God, smitten by him, and afflicted." Physical healing here is not only crystal clear in context, but it is also affirmed by the Gospels, where it is given an important qualification. Matthew writes, "When evening came, many who were demon-possessed were brought to him, and he drove out the spirits with a word and healed all the sick. This was to *fulfill what was spoken through the prophet Isaiah*: 'He took up our infirmities and carried our diseases'" (Matthew 8:16,17, emphasis added). Thus the healing mentioned in Isaiah 53:4 was fulfilled *during the healing ministry of Christ*—before His atonement on the cross!—and consequently does not guarantee our healing today.

The Curse of the Law

Isaiah 53:5 may be the main text the Faith teachers use on the subject of healing, but it is not the only one. Another example of text abuse is found in their correlation of Galatians 3:13 with Deuteronomy 28. Their argument goes something like this. Galatians 3 says that Christ redeemed us from the "curse" of the law. Deuteronomy 28 is part of the "law" and it lists sickness and disease as a "curse." Therefore Jesus died so that believers would not have to suffer from sickness or disease.

This argument can be dispensed with quickly. When Paul refers to being redeemed from the "curse" of the law, there is not even the slightest possibility that he is referring to the "curses" described in Deuteronomy 28. The context demonstrates conclusively that the "curse" referred to by Paul is the "curse" of having to live up to God's requirements in our own strength. As Paul points out, "All who rely on observing the law are under a curse, for it is written: 'Cursed is everyone who does not continue to do everything written in the Book of the Law' " (Galatians 3:10). Paul is obviously referring to man's *moral* curse—his inability to observe the requirements of the law apart from Christ—and not to the *physical* curse of sickness and disease. While it can be argued that Christ's atonement upon the cross extends to redeeming the physical realm (Romans 8), we will continue to suffer the effects of the fall (such as sickness and disease) until God establishes a new heaven and a new earth wherein dwells righteousness. Paul made this ever so clear when he wrote:

> The creation itself will be liberated from its bondage to decay. . . . Not only so, but we ourselves, who have the firstfruits of the Spirit, groan inwardly as we wait eagerly for our adoption as sons, the redemption of our bodies. . . . We hope for what we do *not yet have, we wait for it* patiently (Romans 8:21,23,25, emphasis added).

The Bible is replete with a long list of godly men who suffered sickness and disease:

- Job, who is affirmed by Scripture as a great man of faith, was covered with painful sores from the soles of his feet to the top of his head (Job 2:7).

- The great apostle Paul "confessed" to the Galatians that because of a "bodily illness" he preached the gospel to them for the first time (Galatians 4:13).

- Timothy was called Paul's "son in the faith," yet suffered from frequent stomach problems. Instead of telling him to "positively confess" his healing, Paul gave him some practical advice: "Stop drinking only water, and use a little wine" (1 Timothy 5:23).

- Elisha was blessed with a "double-portion anointing," yet he suffered and died a sick man (2 Kings 13:14; cf. 2:9).

Many other biblical examples could be cited: Paul left Trophimus sick in Miletus (2 Timothy 4:20); Epaphroditus fell ill and nearly died (Philippians 2:25-30); King Hezekiah became sick and was at the point of death (2 Kings 20:1). Even Faith teachers, in their more honest moments, have to confess that they themselves have experienced the ravages of sickness and disease. And despite their protests, they will in the end be stung by the ultimate sickness: death. As Walter Martin used to say, "The death rate is still one per person and we're all going to make it!"

Satan and Sickness

*T*he cruelty displayed by the Faith movement when it comes to the sick is almost beyond comprehension. Those who are sick have only themselves to blame, they are told. By speaking words of fear instead of words of faith, they have given Satan the authority to wreak havoc in their lives. Kenneth Copeland puts it this way: *"Your tongue is the deciding factor in your life...."* [1] *"You can control Satan by learning to control your own tongue."* [2] He then says:

> You have been trained since birth to speak negative, death-dealing words. Unconsciously in your everyday conversation, you use the words of death, sickness, lack, fear, doubt, and unbelief: *That scared me to death. That tickled me to death. I laughed until I thought I would die. I'm just dying to go. That makes me sick. I'm sick and tired of this mess. I believe I'm taking the flu. We just can't afford it. I doubt it....* You say these things without even realizing it. When you do, you set in motion negative forces in your life and the fire blazes.... Your words loosed the powers of Satan.... [3]

Finis Dake, who has had a profound influence on many of the Faith healers, even said:

255

Disease germs, which are so closely allied to the work of demons . . . are really material agents of Satan corrupting the bodies of his victims. No remedy has ever been found that can cure diseases outside of the blood of Jesus Christ. No drug can cure a single disease. Any honest physician will admit that there is no healing power in medicines.[4]

As Easy As 1-2-3

It's as simple as one, two, three. First, if you are sick, it's your own fault. Second, your answer is not in medicine. Even Faith teachers more circumspect than Finis Dake will still tell you basically the same thing: "Medicine is not God's highest or best," says Fred Price. "Use your faith, and then you won't need the medication."[5] As Price elaborates elsewhere, "Doctors are fighting the same enemies that we are; the only difference is they're using *tooth-picks* and we are using *atomic bombs!*"[6] Third, if you don't think you have enough faith, God has raised up a special class of anointed faith healers who can do the job for you.

Kenneth Hagin claims to be one of those anointed healers. In his book *I Believe in Visions*, he tells story after story of how he has been miraculously used to heal people of their sicknesses. In each case, the problem was demonic. On one occasion, scarcely a month after Jesus appeared to him, Hagin healed a young girl of cancer of the left lung.

It all happened one day while he was in the midst of a healing service. "Suddenly" he says, "the Spirit of God enveloped me like a cloud. . . . This young girl and I were standing in the midst of the white cloud. As I looked at her I saw fastened to the outside of her body, over her left lung, an evil spirit, or an imp. He looked very similar to a small monkey."[7]

Hagin healed the girl by casting out the evil spirit. According to Hagin, the demon fell to the floor, then ran down the aisle of the church and out the door.

Hagin also tells the story of how on another occasion God permitted him to see into the realm of the spirit. This time he saw an evil spirit sitting on a man's shoulder. "The spirit's arms," he said, "were around the man's head in an armlock."[8] Immediately Hagin sprang into action. He commanded the spirit to leave in the name of Jesus, and the man was miraculously healed.

These stories should make it clear that in Faith lore, demons are not only behind every bush, they are behind every disease. That is why you can tune in "Christian television" on virtually any given day and hear Faith healers screaming at demons. The following is a transcript of Robert Tilton raging at what he believes to be the demonic forces attacking his followers in TV land:

> Satan, you demonic spirits of AIDS, and AIDS virus—I bind you! You demon-spirits of cancer, arthritis, infection, migraine headaches, pain—come out of that body! Come out of that child! Come out of that man. . . . Satan, I bind you! You foul demon-spirits of sickness and disease. Infirmities in the inner ear and the lungs and the back. You demon-spirits of arthritis, sickness, and disease. You tormenting infirm-spirits in the stomach. Satan, I bind you! You nicotine spirits—I bind you! In the name of Jesus![9]

What Is Binding and Loosing?

We need to note that the concept of "binding and loosing" found in Matthew 18:18 has nothing to do with demons. The context of this passage involves *church discipline*.[10] Not only that, but many of the demons that Tilton binds are clearly described by Scripture as "the desires of the sinful flesh." (Just what did the demon of nicotine do before the invention of cigarettes?) Sadly, because such human vices as lust, selfish ambition, and gluttony are pawned off as demons, believers are prone to pass them off as satanic attacks. When a married man commits adultery, he can conveniently rationalize away his sin, be exorcised of the "demon" of lust, and go his way without ever dealing with his root spiritual problem and its true solution—repentance.

Believers with barf bags in hand are herded into "deliverance sessions" to be "exorcised" of demons ranging from alcoholism to zymosis. All the while they seem ignorant of the vast difference between Satan's temptations and satanic possession.

It is deeply troubling that thousands of people standing before their Faith gurus believe they are being healed "from the tops of their heads to the soles of their feet." In many cases they are even warned that to acknowledge their sickness in any way is tantamount to giving Satan the authority to afflict them all over again. As Fred Price puts it, "I don't look at cancer. I don't look at the tumor. . . . I can't look at the natural and . . . say . . . 'I'm sick.' Because when I say that, I've signed for the package. I have taken authority for it, and it belongs to me legally. Satan can enforce it upon my body. And he will kill me with it."[11]

Hagin develops a similar idea this way: "Jesus plainly taught that sickness is of the devil, and not of God. . . . *Since Satan is the author of sickness, I ought to walk free from it.* . . . *Divine health is my covenant right!* . . . Everybody healed under the ministry of Jesus was oppressed of the devil. . . . The devil is behind all sickness. . . . There is no such thing as the separation of sickness and disease from Satan. . . ."[12]

We must examine what the Faith teachers say in the light of Scripture. Is it true that the author of sickness is always Satan and never God? Despite Gloria Copeland's sarcastic assurance that even her three-year-olds were smart enough to figure out that Satan is the author of sickness, pure and simple,[13] the biblical evidence leads to another conclusion.

God and Sickness

We live in a cursed creation, with aging the primary sickness of humanity. As we get older we all get wrinkles, some of us need glasses, our muscles get shorter, and eventually we all die.

While Scripture makes it clear that Satan is often the agent of sickness, he is certainly not always its author. For example, in Exodus 4:11 God Himself asks the rhetorical question "Who gave man his mouth? Who makes him deaf or dumb? Who gives him sight or makes him blind? Is it not I, the Lord?"

This is no isolated instance. In 2 Kings 15:5 we read the well-known story of the Lord striking King Azariah with a skin disease (presumably leprosy) from which he suffered till the day he died. In Luke we read that the angel of the Lord came directly from God's presence to strike Zacharias with an affliction because he had doubted God's word regarding the birth of John the Baptist (Luke 1:19,20).

You're to Blame

When Faith teachers bind the devils of disease and the diseases do not depart, rather than test their experience by the Word of God, they resort to the cruelest tactic of all: They say that the sick among them must surely be suffering because of some dark and secret sin.

Imagine the cruelty of telling a quadriplegic or a blind person that his or her condition tarnishes his relationship with God! Imagine hearing Fred Price say:

> ...how can you glorify God in your body, when it doesn't function right? How can you

glorify God? How can He get glory when your body doesn't even work? ... What makes you think the Holy Ghost wants to live inside a body where He can't see out through the windows and He can't hear with the ears? *What makes you think the Holy Spirit wants to live inside of a physical body where the limbs and the organs and the cells do not function right?* ... And what makes you think He wants to live in a temple where He can't see out of the eyes, and He can't walk with the feet, and He can't move with the hand? ... The only eyes that He has that are in the earth realm are the eyes that are in the body. If He can't see out of them then God's gonna be limited. ...[14]

How I pray that thousands of unfortunate souls caught up in the Faith movement will somehow catch a glimpse of the true God, the majestic God, the awe-inspiring God who in His infinite glory, power, and holiness fills the heavens and the earth! For if they glimpse but an instant of His splendor, they will never again be content to spend even a moment more with the pitiable god of the Faith movement.

Sin and Sickness

Over the past few years I have received hundreds of letters from people who have fled the Faith movement. In many cases these letters tell heartrending stories of sick people who were told that their sickness is a direct result of sin.

One of these letters is a personal testimony from a woman who had been blind from birth. After coming to faith in Christ, she joined a church that had been infiltrated by the Faith movement. It wasn't long before they were instructing her to confess perfect sight and commanding God to honor His Word.

When nothing happened, they began to denounce this woman for her lack of faith. They told her that there was "something in my life that hindered God's will," she wrote. "God," they said, "was held up because of some point of sin or disobedience that He just couldn't get around until I straightened up."[1]

This dear lady writes, "I spent hours, sleepless nights, agonizing over the issue. I became depressed and began to lose my joy. I even quit praying. Some Sundays I simply couldn't stand church because I felt like an outsider in God's family, watching His pet children get 'blessed' because of their 'Faith.' . . . If I was doing or not doing something that

hindered God, I was at a loss trying to discern what it was. 'God!' I said in utter dispair, 'What do you want me to do?'"
In time she discovered that God had never forsaken her. Her blindness was not a result of her sin, and the real problem was not her lack of faith but the Faith followers' lack of understanding. She felt like a "different person." "I finally recognized that in Jesus' eyes I was whole and that I was still as important to Him as I had been at the beginning of our relationship. I determined that no one was ever again going to take His joy away from me."

She makes some astute observations about some of the real motivations behind the Faith movement: "I've discovered that many people want to see me healed (or pretend to be) because my blindness upsets their theological applecart. It's hard to believe in their beliefs when a disabled person who thanks God for her disability comes along. It's as if their 'faith' won't stand if I don't go along with their agenda. I believe that they want my healing for their own sake, not mine. It might sound harsh, but I don't think they have a thumbnail of faith."

She closes her letter with these words: "I want the staff there at CRI to know that I heartily support your stand concerning this issue. It's a killer, spiritual cancer. . . . It grieves me that so few in the body of Christ are willing to listen to the truth that you have so diligently exposed. . . . I pray that God will continually encourage you and direct your path through the criticism and denouncements. . . . I almost didn't hear the truth in time. . . ."

Another letter chronicles the story of a lady with incurable lupus and fibrosis. Her best friend began listening to Kenneth Copeland, Fred Price, and John Avanzini, and immediately started telling the lady her ailments were a result of sin and lack of faith. She closes her letter by saying that she sometimes wishes she could suffer without being punished by her friends, too.[2]

These stories are not the exception; they are the rule. In case after case, Christians with such diseases as cancer or congenital birth defects are condemned for suffering as a result of some unknown sin. The day I wrote these lines, I received a letter which told of a couple who had a stillborn baby. When this grieving couple needed comfort most, they were told their baby died as a result of sin—not the baby's, but the couple's. They were told they had sinned by allowing "fear to set in and . . . did not have enough faith to believe the baby could be risen from the dead."[3]

Back to the Whipping Boy

These people do not suffer alone. Remember Job? He was declared by God to be a great man of faith, but when the Faith teachers get done with him, he is accused of bringing disaster upon himself. Kenneth Copeland says, "When are we *all* going to wake up and learn God didn't allow the Devil to get on Job. *Job* allowed the Devil to get on Job. . . . All God did was maintain His confession of faith about that man. He said 'that man is upright in the earth.' But Job, himself, said he was *not* upright in the earth. He said 'I'm miserable. My tongue is disobedient.' "[4]

When forced to see that no less an authority than God Almighty says Job is upright and blameless, Copeland claims God was simply making a positive confession. If this were true, God would not only be a deceiver, but He would also be self-deluded. Other Faith teachers such as Hinn and Price attack Job even more viciously. Hinn even calls Job a "carnal bad boy" (see chapter 8). Price calls Job a "Big Mouth."[5]

And Job is not the only man of faith the false teachers go after. The apostle Paul is also said to be responsible for his own sickness. In Paul's case, the sin is said to be a propensity for boasting. Says Fred Price: "Paul was saying in essence, that he interpreted this situation [sickness] to be a part of the plan of Satan, to keep him humble. . . . If you read his writings, you will know that there was a peculiarity about the

Apostle Paul, and that was that he was a man very prone to brag. . . . But that was his opinion. That was his opinion."[6]

This is a classic example of how the Faith teachers misinterpret Scripture. Athough the text does not explicitly identify Paul's "thorn in the flesh" (2 Corinthians 12:7), it is clear the "thorn" was not a result of a sinful propensity to boast. The text plainly tells us the thorn was given to Paul to *keep him from boasting*, not *because* he boasted.[7]

And consider what this thorn produced in Paul's life. It certainly does not sound like something Satan would be happy to generate:

> Therefore I will boast all the more gladly about my weaknesses, so that Christ's power may rest on me. That is why, for Christ's sake, I delight in weaknesses, in insults, in hardships, in persecutions, in difficulties. For when I am weak, then I am strong (2 Corinthians 12:9b,10).

Before we leave Paul, note one last thing: Paul claims that God's power rested on him *precisely because of his affliction*. That is poles apart from what you hear from Faith teachers who boast that it is *because they are strong in body* that God blesses them. Paul maintains that it is only when he is weak that Christ's power rests on him; who do you think is closer to the truth?

Charismatic scholar Gordon Fee, in brilliant prose, puts the Faith issue into perspective:[8]

❏ ❏ ❏

This false theology lay at the very heart of the Corinthian rejection of Paul. His bodily weaknesses did not commend him to their view of apostleship. An apostle should be "spiritual," . . . living in glory and perfect health. They rejected Paul and his theology of the cross (with its ongoing suffering in the present age), because they saw themselves as "spiritual" redeemed from such weakness. . . .

Paul tries everything in his power to get them back to his gospel. In 1 Corinthians 1:18-25, he reminds them that the gospel has as its very base a "crucified Messiah." For the Corinthians that's like saying "fried ice." Messiah means power, glory, miracles; crucifixion means weakness, shame, suffering. Thus they gladly accepted the false apostles, who preached a "different Gospel" with "another Jesus" (2 Corinthians 11:4), and condemned Paul for his bodily weakness (10:10).

In 1 Corinthians 4:8-13 he tried irony. "Already you have all you want! Already you have come into your kingdom— and without us!" he tells them. Then, with absolutely brilliant strokes, he annihilates them with the stark contrasts between himself and them, with himself as the example of what it means to live out the future in the present age.

In 2 Corinthians 3–6, he tries to explain the true nature of apostleship, which has a glorious message but is proclaimed by a less-than-glorious messenger. "We have this treasure in jars of clay to show that this all-surpassing power is from God and not from us" he explains (4:7).

Finally in 2 Corinthians 10–13, he attacks their false teachers head-on. To do so he plays the role of the "fool" as in the ancient dramas. Paul is forced to boast (because of his opponents), so in what does he boast? In all the very things the Corinthians are against—Paul's weaknesses. In total irony he finally sets himself alongside the boasts of the false apostles, with their great visions and the miracle-stories. . . . God's strength is perfected *not* in His delivering His Messiah *from* crucifixion, nor in delivering His apostle *from* physical suffering, but is seen *in* the crucifixion *itself*, and *in* the apostle's weaknesses.

❑ ❑ ❑

Again and again throughout his writings, Paul paints a precise picture of human weakness and suffering. He goes to great lengths to keep us from repeating the error of the Corinthian church. Like the Faith teachers of our day, they were convinced that because God heals, every believer should experience perfect health. That was the very reason they shunned the apostle Paul.

But Faith teachers continue to propagate this Corinthian error today. They fail to realize that death is the universal sickness of mankind. For example, Benny Hinn callously asserts, "If your body belongs to God, it does not and cannot belong to sickness."[9] Such a statement fails to recognize that some of God's choicest saints endure sickness and die young, while some of the most ruthless sinners enjoy soundness of body and live long, robust lives.

Sickness to the Glory of God

Charles Haddon Spurgeon, well-known as the Prince of Preachers, was severely afflicted with gout, a condition which sometimes brings on excruciating pain. In a sermon published in 1881 he wrote, "Were you ever in the melting pot, dear friends? I have been there, and my sermons with me. . . . The result of melting is that we arrive at a true valuation of things [and] we are poured out into a new and better fashion. And, oh, we may almost wish for the melting-pot if we may but get rid of the dross, if we may but be pure, if we may but be fashioned more completely like unto our Lord!"[10]

Spurgeon did not live a long, robust life. In fact, it may well be said that he had everything except his health. At age 57 he died. Yet while he lived, he made his life count for time and for eternity. Spurgeon today is history's most widely read preacher. His sermon series stand as the largest set of books by a single author in the history of the Christian church. Spurgeon's life bears eloquent testimony that the tragedy is not in dying young, but in living long and never using your life for what is of eternal significance.

Kenneth Copeland says, "The religious idea that God chastises His own with sickness and disease and poverty is the very thing that has caused the church to go 1500 years without the knowledge of the Holy Spirit."[11] Spurgeon, however, said, "I am certain that I never did grow in grace one-half so much anywhere as I have upon the bed of pain."[12]

Three thousand years ago, King David gave proof positive that Copeland and the Faith teachers are dead wrong. God does indeed chastise His own. David was a man after God's own heart, yet he wrote, "It was *good* for me to be afflicted so that I might learn your decrees. . . . I know, O Lord, that your laws are righteous, and in faithfulness *you* have afflicted me" (Psalm 119:71,75, emphasis added).

Reasons for Sickness

It is tragic indeed that Faith teachers have resorted to accusing sick followers of some secret sin. While the Bible does teach that some Christians are sick as a result of sin (see 1 Corinthians 11:29,30), Jesus made it clear that this is not always the case.

Consider the man born blind mentioned in John 9. Jesus' disciples asked Him, " 'Master, who did sin, this man, or his parents, that he was born blind?' Jesus answered, 'Neither hath this man sinned nor his parents, but that the works of God should be made manifest in him' " (John 9:2,3 KJV).

Christ's statement here should be impossible to misinterpret. This man was not born blind due to his own sin nor due to the sin of his parents. Instead, his blindness was a sovereign act to display the work of God in his life. This is so obvious that Faith teachers have gone to great lengths to explain away the plain meaning of the text.

Fred Price tries to argue that the phrase "but that the works of God should be made manifest in him" doesn't have anything to do with the blind man, but is actually the beginning of another sentence going on to verse 4.[13] Price has to change the punctuation in order to alter the text. When the Bible doesn't agree with certain Faith teachers, they rewrite it!

Price's teaching here directly mirrors George Lamsa's cultic translation of the New Testament.[14] Despite the well-known fact that Lamsa promotes wildly esoteric interpretations of Scripture—such as that Jesus and Christ are two different people[15]—Price favorably characterizes Lamsa's remarks as "an eye opener."[16] They are, but not for the reasons Price thinks.

Kenneth Copeland, like Price, is vehemently opposed to biblical passages that point to God as the author of sickness. He denies the effects of the curse on all of creation, asserting instead that we control the universe with our tongue: "Every circumstance—the entire course of nature," says Copeland, "is started with the tongue."[17] Then, like other Faith teachers, he is content to put the blame for sickness squarely on the shoulders of the believer. Copeland writes, *"God intends for every believer to live completely free from sickness and disease. It is up to you to decide whether or not you will."*[18] Thus, when the believer continues to suffer with physical ailments, he has only himself to blame.

But the Bible makes it plain that sickness and suffering are not always the result of personal sin. Since the fall of mankind, both the righteous and the unrighteous have been subject to disease and decay. In the book of Romans we read that "the whole creation has been groaning as in the pains of childbirth. . . . Not only so, but we ourselves . . . groan inwardly as we wait eagerly for . . . the redemption of our bodies" (Romans 8:22,23).

Paul summed up the ultimate truth when he wrote, "The body that is sown is perishable, it is raised imperishable; it is sown in dishonor, it is raised in glory; it is sown in weakness, it is raised in power; it is sown a natural body, it is raised a spiritual body" (1 Corinthians 15:42-44). He makes it clear that our frail and fragile bodies will not be changed now, but rather when we are resurrected from the dead. "*Then*," says Paul, "the saying that is written will come true: 'Death has been swallowed up in victory'" (1 Corinthians 15:54, emphasis added).

And for that day we must wait. Whether we want to or not.

Sovereignty and Sickness

*I*n his book *"Rise & Be Healed!"* Benny Hinn exhorts his followers to "never, ever, ever go to the Lord and say, 'If it be thy will. . . .' Don't allow such faith-destroying words to be spoken from your mouth. When you pray 'if it be your will, Lord,' faith will be destroyed. Doubt will billow up and flood your being. Be on guard against words like this which will rob you of your faith and drag you down in despair."[1]

In this Hinn simply agrees with other Faith teachers. Frederick Price, for example, instructed his followers that praying for the Lord's will to be done is "really stupidity." He calls such prayers a "farce" and "an insult to God's intelligence." In fact, says Price, "If you have to say, 'If it be Thy will,' or 'Thy will be done,' . . . then you're calling God a fool."[2]

In the real world, however, Jesus Christ contradicts these statements in the strongest terms possible. In what is perhaps the greatest literary masterpiece of all time, the majestic Sermon on the Mount, Jesus taught us to pray, *"Thy will be done"* (Matthew 6:10 KJV, emphasis added). If Price is right, Jesus Himself would be "stupid," because in His passionate prayer in the Garden of Gethsemane He prayed, "My Father, if it is possible, may this cup be taken from me. Yet *not as I will, but as you will"* (Matthew 26:39, emphasis added).

Of course, while Jesus may be our greatest example, He is certainly not our only example. His half-brother James also warns those who are prone to "boast and brag" that they ought to pray instead, "*If it is the Lord's will*, we will live and do this or that" (James 4:15, emphasis added). Christ's closest friend during His earthly ministry, the "beloved" apostle John, echoes the words of the Master when he writes, "This is the confidence we have in approaching God: that if we ask anything *according to his will*, he hears us" (1 John 5:14, emphasis added).

It is sad beyond words that in the face of this and other overwhelming biblical evidence (check the 11 additional verses in the endnote),[3] prosperity teachers such as Price can look into the lens of a television camera and assert that it is "stupidity" to pray "Thy will be done." Does Price think the apostle Paul was "stupid" when he earnestly prayed that "*by God's will*" he might have the opportunity to visit the believers in Rome (Romans 1:10, emphasis added)? Can Price seriously suggest that the believers in Rome were "being robbed of their faith" when Paul encouraged them to pray that "*by God's will*" he might join them in Rome (Romans 15:32, emphasis added)?

God in Control

The sovereignty of God is an overarching principle of Scripture, and we ought to be thankful that this world is under His control and not ours. We would be in deep trouble if God gave us everything we asked for! The truth is that we often don't know what is best for us. A noted Pentecostal scholar has well said, "Our asking is based on our own limited knowledge, and all too often it is colored by our self-interest. We can only praise God that He does not answer every prayer 'prayed in faith.' Hezekiah, after all, had his prayer answered and was granted fifteen more years, but it was during those years that Manasseh was born!"[4]

Had Hezekiah known, as God did, that in those 15 additional years he would father the most wicked king in the history of Judah, position his kingdom for plunder by the Babylonians, and end up dying with his heart lifted up in pride, he might well have added these words to his prayer: "Nevertheless not my will but *Thy will be done*."

Walter Martin drove the point home with humor when he told the story of the girl he wanted to marry in high school. He said that he pounded on the gates of heaven until his hands were bloody stumps, but in the end God said "No!" Twenty years later at his class reunion he saw this girl again. He quickly took two aspirin and thanked God that the Lord had not paid the slightest bit of attention to his prayers. Billy Graham's wife, Ruth Bell Graham, has a similar story. "If God had answered every prayer of mine," she says, "I would have married the wrong man seven times."

One of the most comforting thoughts to a human mind yielded to the will of God is that He who has created us also knows what is best for us. If we walk according to His will rather than trying to command Him according to our own, we will enjoy not a counterfeit panacea, but what He promised: peace in the midst of the storm.

There is great peace in knowing that the One who created us also has every detail of our lives under control. Not only is He the object of our faith, but He is also the originator of our faith. Indeed, He is the originator of our salvation and even the originator of our prayers. When we pray the prayer of faith for healing and our will is in harmony with His will, healing will indeed take place—every time, 100 percent of the time.

But when we pray earnestly as Christ did, "Nevertheless not my will but thy will be done," we can rest assured that even in sickness and tragedy all things work together for good to those who love God and are called according to His purpose (Romans 8:28).

Living Trust Versus Imaginary Force

Far from being a force through which we can confess into existence divine health and healing, *faith is a channel of living trust between a creature and his Creator*. Think of Job once more. In his case, all Job wanted was to hear from God. He just wanted to know why! Job got half his wish, for God revealed Himself majestically. But He did not answer the question *why*. Instead, He asked Job a question: Where were you when the foundations of the earth were laid? (See Job 38:4.)

In essence, He asked if Job would like to try his hand at running things for awhile. "Say, Job—try creating a lightning bolt. How about producing even a tiny drop of dew?" (See Job 38:25,28.)

When you reach the end of this ancient literary masterpiece, you finally understand. Like a refreshing drink of water on a dry, dusty day, your thirst for answers is quenched: God is sovereign, and you are not. In this world you will have trouble (John 16:33). Disease, decay, disorder, discouragement, and even death are the natural consequences of a fallen world. In fact, it is the very uncertainty of life that prepares some people to consider their eternal destiny. This explains why Jesus talks the way He does about human suffering:

> Now there were some present at that time who told Jesus about the Galileans whose blood Pilate had mixed with their sacrifices. Jesus answered, "Do you think that these Galileans were *worse sinners* than all the other Galileans because they suffered this way? I tell you, no! But unless you repent, you too will perish. Or those eighteen who died when the tower in Siloam fell on them—do you think they were *more guilty* than all the others living in Jerusalem? I tell you, no! But unless you repent, you

too will all perish" (Luke 13:1-5, emphasis added).

Yes, death comes to all of us in this world. Heartache and suffering naturally accompany a world sunk in sin. But as the Master so eloquently put it in John 16:33, "Take heart! I have overcome the world." For the child of God, the hope is not perfect health in this lifetime, but a resurrected body in the life to come. As John the apostle so beautifully put it, "No more death or mourning or crying or pain, for the old order of things has passed away. . . . I am making everything new!" (Revelation 21:4,5). True faith does not consist in always understanding why, but in trusting the Sovereign of our souls even when we do not understand.

Up Is the Best Place to Look

When my son David suffered his serious eye injury, the only place I could look was up. All of the positive confession in the world would not put his eye back together again. Truly this was a problem far above my limited human resources. In anguish I cried out to God for help. And almost immediately a friend was there to comfort me rather than condemn me for a lack of faith. Scriptures memorized years earlier began to flood my mind, bringing peace, not perplexity. In that moment I felt closer to the Lord than ever before.

I now look back and see how God has used even this tragedy for His glory. Yet I must confess that I do not have all the answers. I do know from Scripture that sickness and suffering can be the result of a satanic attack. I also know that it can be the direct result of sin. Above all, however, I know that God is sovereign and that "All things . . . work together for good to those who love God, to those who are called according to His purpose" (Romans 8:28 NASB).

In God's providence, David did not lose his eyesight, though he might have. With the use of a contact lens he can see past the scar that has formed on the surface of his eye. In the meantime, God has provided for all our needs, including a marvelous physician. Someday in eternity I will finally understand. Better yet, in that day David's eye will be completely whole.

In the epilogue to Job's spellbinding story, God commands Job's friends to humbly ask Job for forgiveness and to pray that God will not judge them according to their folly. Job prayed for his friends and God accepted Job's prayer.

May those in the Faith movement, by God's grace, one day soon turn from their foolish notions and place their lives, their fortunes, and their sacred honor into the hands of a sovereign God. And when they do, may those whom they have harmed welcome them back with open arms and forgive them—as they too have been forgiven.

PART SEVEN

Back
to
Basics

*W*hen I first heard the news I was stunned. Only days before we had been scrunched together in the backseat of a compact car. "Hank," Glenn had said urgently, "don't ever forget! You only have one life. Soon it will be past. Only what you do for Christ will last."

The words had not meant much to me then. But now, with the news that Glenn was dead, they hit me with hurricane force. I just could not believe it. In a flash he had been changed from mortality to immortality.

I met Glenn just days before going into full-time Christian work. He immediately became a role model. Not only was he an equipped Christian who could articulately share his faith, but he was committed to train others to do so as well.

One day he urged me to make my life count; the next his life came to an abrupt end. The newspaper headline that read "TRAGEDY IN THE AIR OVER FORT LAUDER-DALE" seemed to say it all.[1] The story behind the story, however, provided a completely different perspective.

Glenn's wife, Gail, gave him an early Christmas surprise. It was something he had long dreamed of—the exhilaration of a hot-air balloon ride. And now, early one Saturday morning, he and two of his friends were poised for the thrill of a lifetime.

Glenn and his friends had a zest for living. But they loved the Lord even more than they loved life itself. Before taking off, they told their wives and loved ones they were looking forward to sharing their faith with the pilot of the balloon.

Their families were thrilled as they watched the brightly colored balloon rise magnificently into the air. With great excitement they followed its pristine path through the blue skies over Fort Lauderdale.

Suddenly their ecstasy turned to agony. The gondola struck a high-tension wire and was instantly engulfed in flames. The added heat shot the balloon upward. Then the inevitable occurred. In full view of their loved ones, the men and their pilot plunged from the sky to their deaths on the ground below.

If ever there was a time to test the truth of the verse "Death has been swallowed up in victory" (1 Corinthians 15:54), that time was at hand. The three courageous women who watched their loved ones fall stood fast in the midst of heartrending pain—not because of their own strength, but because God's strength had been made perfect in their weakness.

These women turned tragedy into a tremendous testimony for Christ. Gail, who like Glenn was an equipped Christian, shared her faith with an unbeliever who was badly shaken in the face of death. Not only did she personify the peace that Christ brings in the midst of the tempest, but she also displayed the assurance that her husband leaped from the heat of the flames into the arms of his heavenly Father.

Lois, who like her husband, Jack, had committed herself to Christ's Great Commission, shared her faith with reporters from around the globe. To a reporter from the *Miami Herald* she said, "Write this down! We know that our loved ones are in heaven, not because of their own good works, but because of their faith in the finished work of Jesus

Christ." She then spoke of the peace and joy and life that only the Lord can bring to the human heart.

Kathy's faith moved us all. Her fiancé, Rick, died before her eyes. Yet she bore eloquent testimony to the triumph that only Christ can bring out of tragedy.

But the testimony of her life that day was not nearly as meaningful to me as the testimony of her lips months earlier. Back then, she had been simply a frightened evangelism trainee who desperately wanted to know how to share her faith effectively. Along with two others, she had knocked on my door while I was still a hardened skeptic. That night I saw the reality of Christ in her life in a way I had never seen. The seeds she planted not only led to my conversion, but also to what I am doing today.[2]

You see, although I had grown up in a Christian home and was the product of a godly heritage, I had never been willing to become a disciple of Christ. Deep down inside I knew that to surrender to Christ meant to submit to His lordship. And that I was not willing to do. I did not want to be deprived of the pleasures this world had to offer. And so for 29 years I chose rebellion rather than repentance.

Yes, you could find me in church from time to time. But I was not there because I wanted to extend God's kingdom; rather, my goal was to extend my own. My eyes were not fixed on things above but focused on things below. I strove for happiness, for moving from one "happening" to another, for grabbing for all the gusto. But I always came up empty. Regardless of my outward successes, I was never inwardly satisfied.

The night Kathy called on me I was exposed to what it truly means to be a disciple of Christ. While I was padding my life with passing earthly pleasures, Kathy was pursuing eternal heavenly treasures. It wasn't until I caught her eternal perspective that my life was radically transformed.

Jesus warned His followers that He was not merely a means to their ends but that He was the end itself. "Do not work for food that spoils," He said, "but for food that endures to eternal life" (John 6:27). Paul echoed the warning when he said, "We brought nothing into the world, and we can take nothing out of it." We would do well, said Paul, to lay up treasure for the coming age and in this way take hold of life that is truly life (1 Timothy 6:7,19).

Are you looking for the real thing? Setting your heart on things above is where you'll find true contentment! This earth is not your dwelling place; you're on your way to another kingdom. Suddenly there will be that crushing pain in your pericardium or the crashing of glass and you will be translated from the temporary to the eternal. In a microsecond everything will change. The prosperity message will have lost its luster and some of us will no doubt wonder why we did not spend more time pursuing the eternal.

When tragedy struck, Kathy's faith did not fail. Why not? Because her heart had been set on things above. That's what getting back to basics is all about.

Back to Basics

I happen to love the game of golf. Although it has brought me great satisfaction over the years, it has been extremely frustrating as well. At times I felt I was on the verge of setting new course records. In other instances I wondered why I ever took up the game in the first place.

After many years of practice and playing, however, I have finally stumbled upon a secret: When things go wrong, it is usually not because I am failing to follow some newfangled faddish formula, but because I have compromised one of the basic fundamentals of the game. I never cease to be amazed at how quickly things fall back into place when I get back to basics.

What's true in the game of golf is also applicable to Christianity in crisis. People today run frantically from church to church, looking for a quick fix and getting more and more confused with each passing fancy. From "Miracle Invasion" rallies to "revelation knowledge," hype and sensationalism have become the name of the game. Doctrinal fads proliferate at such breakneck speed that people have become disoriented. Over and over again I hear their frantic cry: "I just don't know what to believe anymore!"

The good news is that everything can come back quickly into focus by getting back to basics. That's where the real excitement is!

We have covered the five basic flaws that led the Faith movement out of the kingdom of Christ and into the kingdom of the cults. They are memorable through the use of the acronym "F-L-A-W-S." To get back from the counterfeit to the reality of victorious Christian living, we need to follow five basic steps. Fortunately, they are as easy to remember as A-B-C-D-E.

25

$\mathcal{A} = \mathcal{A}men$

$\mathcal{N}$o relationship can flourish without constant, heart-felt communication. This is true not only in human relationships, but also in our relationship with God. If we are to nurture a strong walk with our Savior, we must be in constant touch with Him. The way to do that is through prayer.

"A" represents the word "Amen." Amen traditionally comes at the end of every prayer, and prayer is our primary way of communicating with God.

Amen is a universally recognized word that is far more significant than simply signing off or saying, "That's all." With the word "Amen" we are in effect saying, "May it be so in accordance with the will of God." It is significant that the apostle John saw Jesus as the very personification of the word "Amen": "These are the words of the Amen," he wrote, "the faithful and true witness, the ruler of God's creation" (Revelation 3:14).

The word "Amen" is a marvelous reminder that any discussion on prayer must begin with the understanding that prayer is a means of bringing us into conformity with God's will, not a magic mantra that ensures God's conformity to our will.

This is a radical point of departure between true biblical faith and the Faith movement. As we have seen,

Faith teachers such as Benny Hinn, Kenneth Copeland, and Frederick Price are vehemently opposed to praying, "Thy will be done." Price, you may recall, said, "If you have to say, 'If it be Thy will' or 'Thy will be done'—if you have to say that then you're calling God a fool."[1]

In one of his pamphlets on prayer, Price boasts that at one time he thought it was a mark of humility to end his prayers with the words "Lord, if it be Thy will." He claims he has since come to a true knowledge of the things of God, and thus no longer ends his petition prayers that way.[2] Says Price, " 'If it be Thy will' is a badge of *doubt*."[3] Elsewhere he adds, "If you put, 'If it be,' on the end of a petition prayer, it will not be answered."[4] Price even has the temerity to write, "I believe the 'Lord's Prayer' is not for Christians today."[5]

Moreover, Price claims that "there are different kinds of prayers, just like there are different sports, and each kind of prayer, like each sport, has SPECIFIC and DEFINITE rules that govern and control it. If you misapply the rule for a particular kind of prayer, that prayer will not work."[6]

To clarify his point, Price writes: "If I believe I receive at 10:39 A.M., I cannot pray that prayer again at 10:40. If I pray the exact same prayer at 10:40, I am saying I DID NOT receive what I asked for at 10:39. I will CANCEL OUT the prayer I prayed at 10:39."[7]

But if this were true, it is hard to see what Jesus was driving at in Luke 18:1-8, a passage that is sometimes referred to as the parable of the "persistent widow." Jesus here tells a story about a widow who hounds an unjust judge for a favorable judgment, even though the judge would rather she just go away. The point of the story is not that God is like the judge, but that we should be like the widow. Our persistence in prayer reveals how serious we are. That is exactly the point Luke says Jesus intended to convey: "Then Jesus told his disciples a parable to show them *that they should always pray and not give up*" (Luke 18:1, emphasis added).

Price does not stop with such comments, however; even worse are his remarks concerning silent prayer: "To pray, you have to SAY something. Some people say, 'Well, I'm praying a silent prayer'—then their 'silent prayers' never get answered! *THERE IS NO SUCH THING AS A SILENT PRAYER. GOD TOLD YOU TO ASK.* . . . God has to have permission to operate in this earth realm."[8]

But if silent prayer is unbiblical (Price's statement about God needing "permission" contradicts Daniel 4:35), what did Paul mean in 1 Thessalonians 5:17, where he wrote, "Pray continually"? If he meant "Be in a constant attitude of prayer," as most interpreters think, there is no problem. One can be in an attitude of prayer while remaining silent. But if true prayer is only verbal, Paul either constantly broke his own direction or he must have been an extremely annoying neighbor and a horribly messy eater.

And what are we to think of Nehemiah? He tells us he found himself in a terrible dilemma one day as he was attending to the needs of King Artaxerxes. Chapter 2 of his book explains his predicament. There's a prayer of his between verses 4 and 5, but you'll look in vain for the words he spoke. Not only was his prayer silent, but it was enormously effectual, for it both saved his life and led to the rebuilding of a devastated Jerusalem.

And let's not forget Hannah, the mother of the great prophet Samuel. You can read her full story in 1 Samuel 1:9-20, but for now note especially verse 13: "Hannah was praying in her heart, and her lips were moving but her voice was not heard." You cannot get any more explicitly *silent* than that. Yet her prayer was answered; the proof was the birth of her son Samuel.

So much for the Faith movement's fiction! Now let's take a moment to examine the facts. Better yet, let's use the word "F-A-C-T-S" to remind us of the truth concerning prayer.

Faith

For prayer to be truly meaningful, it must be founded on faith. Since we have previously devoted an entire section to the subject of faith (see Part Two), I will not belabor the point here. I simply want to reemphasize that it is the *object of faith* that renders faith effective. Faith must always be directed upward rather than inward—not faith in *faith* but faith in *God.*

Since God is awesomely revealed in Scripture, the prayer of faith must always be rooted in the Word of God. As R.A. Torrey so wonderfully expressed it:

> *To pray the prayer of faith we must,* first of all, *study the Word of God, especially the promises of God, and find out what the will of God is.* . . . We cannot believe by just trying to make ourselves believe. Such belief as that is not faith but credulity; it is "make believe." *The great warrant for intelligent faith is God's Word.* As Paul puts it in Romans 10:17, "Faith cometh by hearing, and hearing by the word of God."[9]

Jesus summed up the prayer of faith with these words: "If you remain in me and my words remain in you, ask whatever you wish, and it will be given you" (John 15:7).

Adoration

Faith in God naturally leads to adoration. Through adoration we express our genuine, heartfelt love and longing for God. Adoration inevitably leads to praise and worship, as our thoughts are focused on God's surpassing greatness. The Scriptures are a vast treasury overflowing with descriptions of God's grandeur and glory. The Psalms in particular can be transformed into passionate prayers of adoration. As you commit them to memory, such passages as Psalms 96, 104, and 150 will become marvelous ways to express your adoration to the King of kings and the Lord of lords.

> Come, let us worship and bow down;
> Let us kneel before the Lord our Maker.
> For He is our God,
> and we are the people of His pasture,
> And the sheep of His hand.
>
> —Psalm 95:6,7 NASB

Confession

Not only do the Psalms abound with illustrations of adoration, but they are replete with exclamations of confession as well. In Psalm 51, for example, King David contritely confesses his sin:

> Against you, you only, have I sinned
> and done what is evil in your sight,
> so that you are proved right when you speak
> and justified when you judge.
>
> —Psalm 51:4

The concept of confession carries the acknowledgment that we stand guilty before God's bar of justice. There is no place for self-righteousness before God. We can only develop intimacy with the Lord through prayer when we confess our need for forgiveness and contritely seek His pardon. The apostle John sums it up beautifully when he writes, "If we confess our sins, he is faithful and just and will forgive us our sins and purify us from all unrighteousness" (1 John 1:9).

Thanksgiving

Nothing is more basic to prayer than thanksgiving. Scripture teaches us to "enter His gates with thanksgiving and His courts with praise" (Psalm 100:4). Giving thanks is a function of faith rather than feelings. It is an action that flows from the sure knowledge that our heavenly Father knows exactly what we need and will supply it. The apostle Paul encourages us to "be joyful always; pray continually; give thanks in all circumstances, for this is God's will for you in Christ Jesus" (1 Thessalonians 5:16-18).

Supplication

Supplication is no doubt the dominant focus of our daily prayers. Indeed, it is God's desire for His children to bring their requests before Him with praise and thanksgiving. Jesus Himself taught us to pray, "Give us this day our daily bread." Yet despite His provision, we must never forget that the purpose of prayer is not to pressure God into providing us with pleasures, but rather to conform us to His purposes. As we read in 1 John 5:14,15, "This is the assurance we have in approaching God: that if we ask anything according to his will, he hears us. And if we know that he hears us—whatever we ask—we know that we have what we asked of him."

So there you have it—the F-A-C-T-S on prayer: Faith, Adoration, Confession, Thanksgiving, Supplication. Don't just memorize these facts, but put them to personal use. The *power* of prayer will become a living reality only as we participate in the *practice* of prayer!

𝑩 = 𝑩𝑖𝑏𝑙𝑒

𝑩 stands for Bible. The Bible not only forms the foundation of an effective prayer life, but it is foundational to every other aspect of Christian living. While prayer is our primary way of communicating with God, the Bible is God's primary way of communicating with us. Nothing should take precedence over getting into the Word and getting the Word into us.

If we fail to eat well-balanced meals on a regular basis, we will eventually suffer the physical consequences. What is true of the outer man is also true of the inner man. If we do not regularly feed on the Word of God, we will suffer spiritual consequences.

Jesus said, "Man does not live on bread alone, but on every word that comes from the mouth of God" (Matthew 4:4). Great physical meals are one thing; great spiritual meals are quite another. In fact, the acronym M-E-A-L-S will serve us well as we get back to basics with regard to the Bible.

Memorize

One of the best things that happened to me as a new believer was being told that all Christians memorize Scripture. By the time I found out that not all of them did, I was already hooked. Now, as I look back, I can say truthfully that nothing compares with the excitement of memorizing Scripture. Charles Swindoll summed it up nicely when he wrote:

> I know of no other single practice in the Christian life more rewarding, practically speaking, than memorizing Scripture. That's right. No other single discipline is more useful and rewarding than this. No other single exercise pays greater spiritual dividends! Your *prayer life* will be strengthened. Your *witnessing* will be sharper and much more effective. Your *counseling* will be in demand. Your *attitudes* and *outlook* will begin to change. Your *mind* will become alert and observant. Your *confidence* and *assurance* will be enhanced. Your *faith* will be solidified.[1]

Despite these marvelous benefits, far too few Christians have made Scripture memorization a lifestyle. For the most part, it is not because they don't *want* to, but because they have never been taught *how* to. While they may think they have bad memories, the reality is that they simply have *untrained* memories.

I am convinced that anyone, regardless of age or acumen, can memorize Scripture. God has called us to write His Word on the tablet of our hearts (Proverbs 7:1-3; cf. Deuteronomy 6:6), and with the call He has also provided the ability to do so. Your mind is like a muscle. If you exercise it, you will increase its capacity to remember and recall information. If you don't, like a muscle, it will atrophy. Here are a few practical tips to get you started:

- Set goals. He who aims at nothing invariably hits it.

- Make goals attainable. If your goals are unrealistic, you will undoubtedly become discouraged and give up.

▪ Memorize with a family member or friend. One of my treasured experiences was swinging back and forth on a hammock, memorizing Proverbs 2 with my daughter, Michelle. Memorizing with someone else is enjoyable and will also make you accountable.

▪ Use normally unproductive time to review what you have memorized, such as while waiting in lines, or falling asleep.

Remember, there's no time like the present to get started! A good place to begin is Psalm 119. In fact, committing verse 11 of that passage to memory—"I have hidden your word in my heart that I might not sin against you"—may well encourage you to make Scripture memorization part of your lifestyle.

While you're at it, you may also wish to consider memorizing Joshua 1:8. The wonderful words of that passage remind us that knowing portions of the Bible helps us meditate upon them. The text reads: "Do not let this Book of the Law depart from your mouth; meditate on it day and night, so that you may be careful to do everything written in it. Then you will be prosperous and successful." If you want true prosperity, there it is![2]

Examine

In Acts 17:11 we read that the Bereans *examined* the Scriptures daily to see if what Paul was teaching was true. For that they were commended as being noble in character.

There is an extremely important lesson to be learned here. The Bereans were not *condemned* for examining what Paul said in light of Scripture. Rather, they were *commended*. Ultimate authority was not placed in the revelation of a man, but in the revelation of the Word.

I cannot overemphasize the importance of examining the Word of God. Examination requires the use of our minds, and the Bible exhorts believers to use their minds to honor God and examine the teachings of men in the light of Scripture. Jesus taught that the first and greatest commandment is to love God with all our heart, soul, and mind (Matthew 22:37). Peter beckoned believers to prepare their minds for action (1 Peter 1:13). Paul urged Christians to test all things (1 Thessalonians 5:21) and to be transformed by the renewing of their minds in order to discern the will of God (Romans 12:2).

Examining the Scriptures may take discipline and dedication, but the dividends are dramatic. The Bereans examined the Bible daily, and so should we. Here's how you can get going:

- Pray that Jesus Christ will become ever more real to you through the reading of God's Word.

- Read a chapter a day. You may wish to start with the Gospel of John. It is divided into 21 chapters, and experts tell us that if we repeat the same action for 21 days in a row, it may well become a habit for life.

- Read thoughtfully. Ask the Holy Spirit to give you understanding as you carefully reflect upon the meaning of God's words (2 Timothy 2:7). Buried in the texts are all sorts of precious gems. It is up to you to mine their wealth.

- Read Scripture systematically rather than using the "scatter-gun" approach. The Bible is one book comprised of 66 individual books. To fully understand the big picture presented by God, we must read not merely those individual books or sections of books that we find interesting. Rather, we need to read and carefully consider the entire Word of God in an intelligent and organized manner.

- Understanding the science of biblical interpretation will greatly enhance your ability to examine the Scriptures daily. The acronym L-I-G-H-T-S discussed in Chapter 20 should prove extremely helpful.

Apply

As wonderful and worthwhile as it is to memorize and examine Scripture, that's simply not enough! We also must take the knowledge we have gleaned from the Word of God and *apply* it to every aspect of our daily lives. Wisdom is the *application* of knowledge.

When Jesus got to the end of His Sermon on the Mount, He concluded with the following words:

> Therefore everyone who hears these words of mine and puts them into practice [or *applies* them] is like a wise man who built his house on the rock. The rain came down, the streams rose, and the winds blew and beat against that house; yet it did not fall, because it had its foundation on the rock. But everyone who hears these words of mine and does not put them into practice [or does not *apply* them] is like a foolish man who built his house on sand. The rain came down, the streams rose, and the winds blew and beat against that house, and it fell with a great crash (Matthew 7:24-27).

James used irony to drive home the same point. In essence, he said that anyone who hears the Word and does not apply it is like a man who looks in a mirror and sees that his face is dirty, but doesn't wash it (James 1:23,24).

In God's view, obedience is better than sacrifice (1 Samuel 15:22). As James so aptly put it, "Be ye doers of the Word and not hearers only" (James 1:22 KJV).

Listen

In order for us to apply God's directions to our everyday lives, we must first *listen* carefully as God speaks to us personally through His Word. Like Samuel, we should say, "Speak, [Lord,] for your servant is *listening*" (1 Samuel 3:10, emphasis added).

One of the most amazing aspects of Scripture is that it is alive and active, not dead and dull. Indeed, God still speaks today through the mystery of His Word. The Holy Spirit illumines our minds to what is revealed in Scripture. The Holy Spirit makes us "wise up to what is written, not beyond it."[3]

While we *listen*, we must also "test the spirits." As John, the apostle of love, warns, "Do not believe every spirit, but test the spirits to see whether they are from God, because many false prophets have gone out into the world" (1 John 4:1). It is particularly important to "test the spirits" because Satan's foremost strategy of spiritual seduction is to disguise himself as an angel of light (cf. 2 Corinthians 11:14). His slickest slogan is "Feel, don't think."

God's Spirit, on the other hand, illumines our minds so that we may understand what He has freely given us (1 Corinthians 2:12). Before I became a Christian, reading the Bible was like reading someone else's mail. Now, however, the Scriptures have become 66 love letters from God, addressed specifically to me. As Jesus so wonderfully stated, "My sheep *listen* to my voice; I know them, and they follow me" (John 10:27, emphasis added).

Study

Scripture exhorts us to study to show ourselves approved to God, workmen who do not need to blush with embarrassment, correctly handling the word of truth (2 Timothy 2:15).

In *examining* Scripture, it is typically best to start with one good translation and then to stick with it. This will provide you with consistency as well as help you in the process of memorizing Scripture. In *studying*, however, it is best to use a number of good Bible translations. Since there are so many translations available today, let me point out some of the more notable differences.

An example of a good word-for-word translation is the New American Standard Bible. Although it is sometimes stilted, it is excellent for the purpose of study. A great thought-for-thought translation is the New International Version. It is extremely reliable as well as extraordinarily readable. To preserve the majesty of the English language, there is no better translation than the King James Version.

It should be noted, however, that due to recent manuscript discoveries, the Greek text from which the KJV was translated (the so-called "Textus Receptus" or Received Text) doesn't take into account some of the texts on which the NASB and NIV are based. There are also a number of paraphrases on the market today, such as the J.B. Phillips paraphrase and The Living Bible. While these are both readable, I do not recommend them for close study.

A number of Bible translations should be avoided at all costs. Among them are the New World Translation, which reflects the cultic concepts of the Jehovah's Witnesses,[4] and the Lamsa translation, which is doctrinally biased and highly esoteric.[5]

To aid in your study of Scripture, here are some other practical tools I recommend.

1. *Study Bibles.* There are some excellent study Bibles on the market today, including the *Student Bible*, the *NIV Study Bible*, and *The International Inductive Study Bible*. There are also some terrible study Bibles. Notable examples include the *Word Study Bible*, with contributions by 13 leading Faith teachers; the *Holy Bible: Kenneth Copeland Reference Edition Bible*; and the *Dake's Annotated Reference Bible*.

Perhaps the worst collection of false teachings is found in the popular *Dake's Annotated Reference Bible*. "God . . . goes from place to place in a body like all other persons," says Dake, and He is just "an ordinary sized being." "He *wears clothes* . . . *eats* . . . *rests* . . . dwells in a *mansion* and *in a city* located *on a material planet* called Heaven."[6]

On the very first page of the New Testament, Dake writes that Jesus "became the Christ or the 'Anointed One' 30 years after He was born of Mary."[7] Even a biblically illiterate person who has watched the "Charlie Brown Christmas Special" (1965) or has sung Christmas carols should be familiar with Luke 2:11, which says, "For unto you is *born this day* in the city of David a Savior, which is *Christ the Lord*" (KJV, emphasis added).

2. *Study tools.* The toolbox of every serious student of Scripture should include:

Chain-reference Bible

- This is one of the most powerful, compact tools around. A good chain-reference Bible such as Thompson's will help you find every parallel passage on the same topic or even the same word or phrase every time it is used. A large topical numbered section in the back, plus a selective concordance, maps, and charts help round out this excellent reference work. A word of caution about both chain-reference Bibles and concordances: Always study the full context of passages and don't get steered into a narrow interpretation; a good commentary, Bible dictionary, or systematic theology can help you avoid such problems.

Commentary

- A Bible commentary serves as a system of checks and balances through which you can evaluate your insights by the the insights of others. There are a variety of good commentaries available today, such as the *International Bible Commentary*, edited by F.F. Bruce and based on the NIV translation.

Exhaustive concordance

- An exhaustive or complete concordance is an indispensable tool. With it you can find every citation of every word used in the Bible, along with a half-sentence excerpt to help you recognize the verse. With most editions, such as *Strong's*, you can also compare English words with the original Hebrew, Aramaic, and Greek.

Interlinear translation

- An interlinear translation will provide you with the Greek text and its word-by-word English equivalent. Some interlinears such as Green's (look for the inexpensive paperback edition) will also give you the *Strong's* reference number to each Hebrew or Greek word. That way you can look up each word easily in lexicons keyed to *Strong's* numbering system. A good interlinear with the appropriate lexicons can help give you direct access to the Word of God in the original languages even if you have no training in Hebrew or Greek.

Bible dictionary

- A good Bible dictionary will give you access to information about the history, culture, people, places, and events in Scripture. One of the best conservative volumes is the *New Bible Dictionary*, edited by J.D. Douglas.

Systematic theology

- Systematic theology simply refers to systematizing Scripture to provide a clear understanding of the foundational doctrines of the historic Christian faith. A grasp of systematic theology will enable you to understand, defend, and mature in the faith. Bruce Milne's *Know the Truth* is a good

300

introduction to theology and recommends several more comprehensive systematic theologies.

Additional tools

▪ Some worth considering include: a handbook on Bible difficulties, such as *When Critics Ask*, by Norman Geisler and Thomas Howe; language aids such as *An Expository Dictionary of Biblical Words*, by W.E. Vine; and introductions to the science and art of biblical interpretation, such as R.C. Sproul's *Knowing Scripture* or James Sire's *Scripture Twisting*.

Jesus said, "I am the bread of life. He who comes to me will never go hungry, and he who believes in me will never be thirsty" (John 6:35). It is my passionate prayer that the acronym M-E-A-L-S will remind you daily to nourish yourself with the Bread of life.

C = Church

C stands for Church. In Scripture, the church is referred to as the body of Christ. Just as our body is one and yet has many parts, so the body of Christ is one but is composed of many members. Those who have received Christ as the Savior and Lord of their lives are already a part of the church universal. It is crucial, however, that we become vital, reproducing members of a healthy, well-balanced local body of believers as well.

Scripture exhorts us not to neglect the gathering of ourselves together, as is the custom of some (Hebrews 10:25). Sadly, multitudes today turn from the church and tune into television.

The impact of televangelism on the church has been massive. But by and large, instead of conforming us to Christ, televangelism has conformed us to our culture. Worship has been replaced with entertainment, fellowship has been transformed into individualism, and the biblical concept of "every believer a witness" (Acts 8:1) has been replaced by the dubious witness of the televangelist. Indeed, the very form and function of the church has been dramatically altered.

Getting back to basics means returning our focus to the church as the God-ordained vehicle through which *God* is worshiped, *oneness* is demonstrated, and through which we are equipped to make *disciples*. Let's use the "G" in God, the

"O" in Oneness, and the "D" in Disciple to form the acronym G-O-D, which will help us remember the basic aspects of a healthy, well-balanced church.

God

The first sign of a healthy, well-balanced church is a pastor who is committed to leading his community of believers in the worship of God through prayer, praise, and the proclamation of the Word.

1. Prayer

Prayer is so inextricably woven together with worship that it would be unthinkable to have a church service without it. From the very inception of the early Christian church, prayer has been a primary means of worshiping God. Jesus Himself set the pattern when He taught His disciples to pray:

> Our Father in heaven, hallowed be your name.
> Your kingdom come, your will be done on
> earth as it is in heaven.
> Give us today our daily bread.
> Forgive us our debts, as we also have forgiven
> our debtors.
> And lead us not into temptation, but deliver us
> from the evil one.
> For yours is the kingdom and the power and
> the glory forever.
> Amen.

2. Praise

Praise is another way through which a body of believers worships God. Paul urged the church at Ephesus to "sing to one another with psalms, hymns and spiritual songs" (Ephesians 5:19). In the Psalms, no doubt the hymnbook of the early church, we see a stunning portrayal of a God who is worthy of our praise and adoration. As the psalmist wrote:

> Praise the Lord.
> Praise God in his sanctuary; praise him in his
>   mighty heavens.
> Praise him for his acts of power; praise him for
>   his surpassing greatness.
> Praise him with the sounding of the trumpet,
>   praise him with the harp and lyre, praise
>   him with the tambourine and dancing,
>   praise him with the strings and flute, praise
>   him with the clash of cymbals, praise him
>   with resounding cymbals.
> Let everything that has breath praise the Lord.
> Praise the Lord!
>   —Psalm 150

3. Proclamation

In addition to prayer and praise, the proclamation of the Word is a vital aspect of worshiping God. In 1 Timothy 4:13 Paul exhorts Timothy, "Devote yourself to the public reading of Scripture, to preaching and to teaching" and in 2 Timothy 4:2 he writes, "Preach the Word; be prepared in season and out of season; correct, rebuke and encourage—with great patience and careful instruction." Through proclaiming God's Word, believers are edified, educated, and equipped for evangelism.

It is through prayer, praise, and proclamation that we are "being built into a spiritual house to be a holy priesthood, offering spiritual sacrifices acceptable to God through Jesus Christ" (1 Peter 2:5).

Oneness

The second sign of a healthy, well-balanced church is its oneness. Jesus Christ breaks the barriers of sex, race, and background that divide us and makes us into one body under the banner of love. Communism claimed to turn men into comrades, but Christ turns us into brothers and sisters. The oneness we share as the body of Christ is tangibly manifested through community, confession, and contribution.

1. Community

Baptism symbolizes our entrance into a community of believers who are one in Christ. It is a sign and seal that we have been buried to our old life and raised to newness of life through His resurrection power. Holy communion is the chief expression of the oneness we share as a community of believers, for as we all partake of the same elements, we also partake of that which the elements symbolize: Christ, who binds us together. Our fellowship on earth, celebrated through communion, is a foretaste of the heavenly fellowship we will share when the symbol gives way to what it represents.

2. Confession

The confession of our oneness in Christ is based on a core set of beliefs which Walter Martin referred to as "essential Christianity." These beliefs, which have been codified in the creeds of the Christian church, form the basis of our unity as the body of Christ. Augustine's words bear repeating: "In essentials, unity; in nonessentials, liberty; and in all things, charity."

3. Contribution

The contribution of our time, talent, and treasure also tangibly demonstrates our oneness in Christ. The pastor is not called to do the work of the ministry. Rather, the pastor is called to "prepare God's people for works of service, so that the body of Christ may be built up" (Ephesians 4:12). God has given the individual members of the church spiritual gifts to be used "for the common good" (1 Corinthians 12:7).

Christ has called individuals from every tongue and tribe and nation to oneness as the family of God. Remember: No man is an island! God has called each member to the body for a purpose. Many logs burning together burn brightly, but when a log falls to the side, its embers quickly die.

Disciples

In the Great Commission, Christ called us not only to make *converts* but to make *disciples* (Matthew 28:19). A disciple is a learner or follower of the Lord Jesus Christ. We are called to the task of making disciples through the testimony of our love, the testimony of our lips, and the testimony of our lives.

1. Love

One of the secrets of growth in the early church was the testimony of its love. The love of Christ not only compelled early Christians to be ambassadors (2 Corinthians 5:20), but constrained the world to take notice of them as well. The love of Christ was so contagious that it swept through the Roman Empire like wildfire. Jesus said, "All men will know that you are my disciples if you love one another" (John 13:35).

2. Lips

The early Christian church not only transformed the Roman Empire through the testimony of its love but also through the testimony of its lips. The book of Acts tells us that on the day Stephen was martyred, a great persecution arose against the church in Jerusalem, and all except the apostles were scattered throughout Judea and Samaria. Those who were scattered preached the Word wherever they went.

Therein lies the second secret of growth in the early church: Every believer was a witness for Christ. While it is true that not everyone is called to be an *evangelist*, everyone is called to *evangelize*. This is why the church must take seriously the task of equipping believers: For the rest of their lives, as God provides opportunities, believers are to be prepared to make disciples.

Jesus said, "This is to my Father's glory, that you bear much fruit, showing yourselves to be my disciples" (John 15:8).

3. Life

Closely related to the testimony of our lips is the testimony of our life. The story is told[1] of a man who was working in a factory in the north of England. While standing on a ladder, he lost his balance and was skewered on a red-hot metal disk. His workmates were frantically scurrying about, looking for a doctor, when the man called out, "Forget the doctor! I'm dying! Can anyone tell me how to get right with God?"

Of the more than 300 men in the factory, not one stepped forward. Later one of the men confessed that he could have stepped forward, but the testimony of his life had long ago refuted the testimony of his lips.

If we testify only by our life, we are in danger of testifying only to ourselves. On the other hand, if our lives belie the testimony of our lips, we may well be dragging the name of Christ through the mud. We must testify through both our life and our lips.

May we, like the early Christian church, come to understand more fully the biblical concept of the priesthood of all believers. Clearly it is not the pastor's calling to do the work of the ministry single-handedly. Rather, the pastor is called to "prepare God's people for works of service, so that the body of Christ may be built up until we all reach unity in the faith and in the knowledge of the Son of God and become mature" (Ephesians 4:12,13).

It is my prayer that the acronym G-O-D will remind you of your privilege to be vitally connected to a healthy, well-balanced local church: a church in which *God* is worshiped, in which you enjoy *oneness* in fellowship, and from which you go out to make *disciples* of all nations. Indeed, you are "a chosen people, a royal priesthood, a holy nation, a people belonging to God, that you may declare the praises of him who called you out of darkness into his wonderful light" (1 Peter 2:9).

$\mathcal{D}$ = $\mathcal{D}efense$

$\mathcal{D}$ stands for Defense. Getting back to basics means equipping yourself for the defense of the faith. The Cold War may be over, but the need to defend the Christian faith is just beginning to heat up. As we move into what has been described as post-Christian America, it is increasingly important for Christians to know *what* they believe as well as *why* they believe it. And that is what the defense of the faith (apologetics) is all about.

The apostle Peter put it this way: "*Always* be prepared to give an answer [*apologia*] to everyone who asks you to give the reason for the hope that you have. But do this with gentleness and respect" (1 Peter 3:15). It is significant to note that apologetics has a dual purpose.

First, the defense of the faith involves *pre-evangelism*. In post-Christian America, few people are aware that Christianity is not a blind leap into the dark, but faith founded on fact. It is historic and evidential. Whenever you are asked "to give the reason for the hope that you have," you have an opportunity to use your well-reasoned answer as a springboard to present the good news of the gospel. Apologetics is not an end in itself, but a means to an end. It is not merely an opportunity to demonstrate your mental acumen, but an opportunity to present the claims of Christ. That is precisely why Walter Martin referred to apologetics as "the hand-maiden of evangelism."

Second, the defense of the faith involves *post-evangelism*. During an age in which Christianity is in crisis, apologetics serves to strengthen our faith. In a time when Christian leaders are falling all around us, it encourages us to know that our faith is not based on the reliability of men but on the revelation of God.

In light of the strategic significance of apologetics, it is tragic that apologetics is being vilified and mischaracterized by the Faith movement. Paul Crouch, for example, describes apologetics as "apologizing for Scripture,"[1] while John Avanzini asserts that God has forgiven him for being an apologist and promises never to engage in apologetics again.[2]

Too many people believe that the task of apologetics is the exclusive domain of scholars and theologians. Not so! The defense of the faith is not optional; it is basic training for *every Christian*. And that means *you*!

Thankfully, learning to defend our faith is not nearly as difficult as one might think. In fact, it all boils down to being able to answer three basic issues. We need to be prepared to demonstrate:

1. That the universe was intelligently designed by a Creator and thus did not evolve by random chance.

2. That Jesus Christ is God and proved it through the undeniable fact of His resurrection.

3. That the Bible is God-given rather than human in origin.

Now let's look briefly at all three areas. For those who would like a fuller treatment of this material, Appendix B features three easy-to-remember acronyms—F-A-C-E, F-E-A-T, and M-A-P-S—to give you a solid basis for further practice in this critical area of apologetics.

A Designed Universe

First, we must be prepared to demonstrate that the universe was created by God and did not evolve by random chance. In dealing with the creation/evolution issue, you should know that:

- The fossil record is an embarrassment to evolutionists. Darwin said that the fossil record would bear him out, yet more than 100 years after his death there is no evidence for transitions from one species to another (macroevolution).[3]

- Ape-men frauds and blunders abound. Perhaps the most notable is *Pithecanthropus erectus* (Java man).[4] You may remember him staring back at you from the pages of your school textbook. You know—the one with the eyes of a philosopher. More than 60 years after he was thoroughly discredited, he still appears in some textbooks!

- The idea that the organized complexity of the universe came about through chance is a statistical impossibility. Even forming something as basic as a protein molecule by random processes is unthinkable.

- The basic laws of science refute the theory of evolution. The second law of thermodynamics—entropy—in particular contradicts the theory of evolution. Evolution postulates that everything goes from randomness to complexity and from disorder to order. Entropy demonstrates that everything is going in exactly the opposite direction—toward randomness and disorder. It should also be noted that evolution is an unproved hypothesis, while entropy is a well-documented law of science.

Jesus, the Incarnate Son of God

Second, we must be equipped to demonstrate that Jesus Christ is God and proved it through the undeniable fact of His resurrection. The resurrection of Jesus Christ is the greatest feat in the annals of recorded history. Through the resurrection, Jesus demonstrated that He does not stand in a line of peers with Buddha, Mohammed, or any other founder of a world religion. They died and are still dead, but Christ is risen!

The resurrection is the capstone in the arch of Christianity; if it is removed, all else crumbles. It is the singular doctrine which elevated Christianity above all the pagan religions of the ancient Mediterranean world. As Paul put it, "If Christ has not been raised, your faith is futile; you are still in your sins. . . . If only for this life we have hope in Christ, we are to be pitied more than all men" (1 Corinthians 15:17,19). It is precisely because of its strategic importance to the Christian faith that each person who takes the sacred name *Christian* must be prepared to demonstrate that:

- The resurrection of Jesus Christ is a well-attested fact of history. It is neither myth, legend, nor hoax.

- The first major fact supporting the resurrection of Christ is the empty tomb. Even the enemies of Christ admitted that the tomb was empty and could not produce the body.

- The second major fact supporting the resurrection is the appearances of Christ. After the resurrection He appeared to over 500 eyewitnesses at a single time (1 Corinthians 15:6). He also appeared to numerous other people, providing "many convincing proofs" of His resurrection (Acts 1:3).

- The third great apologetic for the resurrection is the radical transformation which took place in the lives of Christ's disciples. After the *crucifixion* they were scattered, disappointed, and without hope. After the *resurrection*, however, they united to change the world, confident and secure in the fact of the resurrection. From them emerged the greatest movement in history.

313

Indeed, the evidence for Christ's resurrection is so overwhelming that no one can examine it with an open mind, desiring to know the truth, without becoming convinced that it really happened.

The Bible Is God's Word

Third, we must be prepared to demonstrate that the Bible is divine rather than human in origin. In fact, if you can demonstrate that the Bible was inspired by God rather than conspired by men, you can answer a host of other objections by referring directly to Scripture. It is crucial that every believer can demonstrate that:

- The manuscript evidence for the preservation of the biblical text is stronger than for any other manuscript of classical literature—including Homer, Plato, Aristotle, Caesar, and Tacitus. The reliability of Scripture is also confirmed through the eyewitness credentials of the authors. We can be confident that the text we possess today accurately represents the original text of Scripture.

- Archaeology affirms the historical reliability of the Bible. In order to be intellectually responsible, secular scholars must revise their biblical criticism in the light of solid archaeological evidence. Truly, with every turn of the archaeological spade we see even more evidence for the trustworthiness of Scripture.

- The Bible records predictions of events that could not have been anticipated by chance, common sense, or collusion. Careful research *affirms* the predictive accuracy of the Bible. Predictive prophecy is a principle of biblical reliability that often reaches even the hard-boiled skeptic!

- It is statistically impossible that the Bible's very specific, detailed prophecies could have been fulfilled through chance, good guessing, or deliberate deceit. The Bible was written over a span of 1600 years by 40 authors in three languages

(Hebrew, Aramaic, and Greek) on hundreds of subjects. And yet there is one consistent, noncontradictory prophetic theme that runs through it all: God's redemption of humankind. Clearly, statistical probability concerning biblical prophecy is a powerful indicator of the trustworthiness of Scripture.

That, in a nutshell, is what apologetics is all about. And remember—if you're looking for a real experience, try becoming a defender of the faith. Not only will you experience the power and presence of the Holy Spirit working through you, but you may just find yourself in the middle of an angelic praise gathering when a lost son or daughter of Adam finds his or her way into the kingdom of God.

29

E = $Essentials$

$\mathcal{M}$uch today is said about unity within the body. But unity at what cost? Paul Crouch seems to believe in unity at all cost, even if that cost entails compromising essential Christian doctrine. Not only does Crouch promote the cultic theology of the Faith movement, but he has gone out of his way to affirm a cult which openly denies the biblical doctrine of the trinity.

On a worldwide broadcast of "Praise the Lord," he said he agreed "a million billion percent" with a former United Pentecostal Church member that to divide over such a doctrine "is a trick of the devil."[1]

The truth, however, is that unity cannot exist apart from the essentials for which the martyrs spilled their blood.

Christ warned us to beware of false prophets, and the history of the church age has borne eloquent testimony to the necessity of the warning. The Bible throughout warns of false apostles and deceitful workmen who masquerade as apostles of Christ. Paul concludes that if Satan himself "masquerades as an angel of light," it should not surprise us that his disciples "masquerade as servants of righteousness" (2 Corinthians 11:13-15).

As the storm clouds gather, these warnings must be heeded as never before. We must become so familiar with genuine Christianity that when counterfeits loom on the horizon, we recognize them immediately. The American Banking Association had a training program which beautifully illustrates the point.

Each year the association sent hundreds of bank tellers to Washington to learn how to detect counterfeit money. At no time during the entire two-week training program, however, were the tellers ever brought into contact with counterfeit currency. Instead, the training project focused completely on handling the real thing. Why? The American Banking Association was convinced that if someone became familiar with the genuine article, he could not be deceived by its counterfeit, no matter how much like the real thing it appeared.[2]

That is precisely why we now turn our attention to the essentials on which the faith is founded. These essentials have served the church well through many perilous times.

Sailors in days gone by fixed their course by the North Star. That star provided an unchanging reference point which guided their ships safely toward their destinations. The essentials have likewise guided Christ's body through the doctrinal storms that have sought to sink it. While shooting stars may light the sky for a moment, following them only leads to shipwreck.

Many people today claim that a tidal wave is sweeping us out of the age of the church into a New Age of Aquarius. But this is impossible, for Christ promised that the gates of hell would not prevail against the church. In His final commission He said, "Surely I will be with you always, to the very end of the *age*" (Matthew 28:20). Jesus' promise suggests the acronym A-G-E, which serves as a point of reference in getting back to basics.

A = *Athanasian Creed*

The Athanasian Creed,[3] widely used throughout the church, is one of the classic creeds of Christianity. It has been said that no other statement of the early church sets forth so incisively and with such clarity the profound theology implicit in the scriptural affirmation that God was in Christ reconciling the world to Himself. Its primary purpose— along with that of the other universally accepted creeds— was to refute heresies that had arisen in the church. One of the obvious functions of the Athanasian Creed was to counter deviant views of the trinity, including tritheism. The Athanasian Creed is especially meaningful in view of the fact that tritheistic teachings peddled by heretics in the medieval church have resurfaced through the teachings of men such as Benny Hinn and Bibles like Dake's.

Other major creeds of the church were used to combat heresy as well. The Nicene Creed was written to combat the dangerous Arian heresy, which denied Christ's full and unqualified deity. The Creed of Chalcedon refuted heresies which challenged the biblical teaching concerning Christ's nature and person. *They all did so by pointing people back to the essentials of historic Christianity.* The Athanasian Creed not only codifies the truth concerning the trinity, but also affirms Christ's incarnation, resurrection, ascension, second coming, and final judgment.

Another important aspect of the creeds is that they help us separate essential from secondary doctrines. The creeds do not discuss disputable areas in eschatology (the study of last things) such as the rapture, the tribulation, or the millennium. Instead, they simply state the central issue, which is that "He [Christ] shall come again, with glory, to judge the living and the dead."

It is important to note that the creeds find their basis in Scripture. The Israelites in the Old Testament used the *Shema* (Hear, O Israel: the Lord our God, the Lord is one) as a creedal expression for the unity and uniqueness of Yahweh. The New Testament contains several passages first used as protocredal statements during apostolic times. The most commonly used is found in 1 Corinthians 15:3,4: "For what I received I passed on to you as of first importance: that Christ died for our sins according to the Scriptures, that he was buried, that he was raised on the third day according to the Scriptures."

Because the creeds are a concise expression of biblical truth, they are helpful in affirming doctrinal truth, refuting error, and encouraging doctrinal instruction. However, like all statements written by imperfect men, they are subject to the supreme authority of the written Word of God.

G = Gospel

The gospel is at the heart of the Christian faith. If Christians do not know how to share their faith, they have probably never been to "boot camp."* The gospel should be so much a part of you that presenting it becomes second nature.

The first step in communicating the gospel involves learning to develop a *relationship* with an unbeliever. In part, that involves using your personal testimony as a bridge into the presentation of the Good News. This is precisely the reverse of grabbing somebody by the lapels and saying, "Brother, are you saved?"

After a relationship is established, you should be equipped to move naturally into a presentation of the *gospel*. In short, that involves:

- Communicating the difference between religion (man's attempt to reach up and become acceptable to God by his own goodness) and a relationship (God reaching down and providing a way for us to know Him through the person and work of Jesus Christ).

---

* A program designed to teach you how to communicate your faith called *Personal Witness Training: Your Handle on the Great Commission* by Hendrik Hanegraaff can be ordered through Memory Dynamics, Box 667, San Juan Capistrano, CA 92693-0667.

- Demonstrating the problem of sin. If people do not realize they are sinners, they will not realize their need for a Savior.

- Pointing out that God is not only a perfect Father who has loved us with an everlasting love, but is also a perfect Judge whose eyes are too pure to look upon iniquity.

- Communicating that Christ died to be our Savior and lives to be our Lord.

- Explaining what it means to repent and receive Jesus Christ as Savior and Lord.

Once you have presented the gospel, you also need to know how to be used by the Holy Spirit to lead people in *response* to the Good News and to the assurance of their salvation.

Finally, since we are not called to make converts, but rather to make disciples, we need to know how to lead people through the basic steps of discipleship and growth as new believers.

Consider what would happen if every evangelical Christian led just one person to faith in Christ each year. If we began with only 12 committed Christians and each of them led one person to Christ and discipled that person, next year there would be 24 believers. If each of them in turn led one person to Christ and discipled that person, the third year there would be 48 believers. If this process continued,[4] it would take less than 30 years to evangelize the five billion or more people alive today on planet Earth! If in the same time frame the population doubled, it would take only one additional year.

If we re-created this scenario, but instead of beginning with 12 disciples began with approximately 174 million,[5] in six years we would run out of people to evangelize!

Many people today run from church to church in search of the ultimate experience. No experience, however, can compare with that of the Holy Spirit working through you in the process of bringing someone to a saving knowledge of the Lord Jesus Christ.

E = Essential Christian Doctrine

The gospel is rendered meaningless if it does not rest on the firm foundation of essential Christian doctrine. The Mormons, for example, proclaim a "gospel," and even acknowledge Jesus as "Lord." But their Jesus is vastly different from the Jesus of Scripture. Far from being the One who spoke and caused the universe to leap into being, He is said to be the spirit brother of Lucifer. The New Age movement also has a gospel. It's called the Aquarian gospel. In this gospel Jesus is reduced to the status of an avatar or a divine messenger. The Faith movement, too, has a gospel—but its Jesus was defeated by Lucifer upon the cross and has been relegated to the status of a cosmic gofer.

All three of these movements have something in common: They have completely redefined essential Christian doctrine. In fact, it is precisely because these essentials have been redefined that millions of people today have a distorted view of what it means to be a Christian.

The Faith movement may use Christian terminology when it comes to essentials, *but the meaning it pours into the words is decidedly unbiblical.* As we have seen, Faith teachers have redefined faith as a force and God as a faith being, and they have completely redefined Christ's substitutionary death upon the cross. They have transformed the Christian message from a gospel of grace into a gospel of greed.

While the importance of essential Christian doctrine has been trivialized by Faith teaching, it is as important today as ever. Without the essentials there is no basis for unity within the body of Christ.

Thankfully, there are many inviting and easy-to-understand resources available on essential Christian doctrine or what C.S. Lewis termed *Mere Christianity.* Two of my favorites are *Know What You Believe*, by Paul Little, and *Does It Matter What I Believe?* by Millard Erickson. Typically, they present the essentials in the following basic categories: the authority of Scripture; the nature of God; the trinity; the creation; humanity; sin; Jesus Christ; Holy Spirit; salvation; angels, Satan, and demons; the church; and things to come. Essential Christian doctrine provides the key to successful Christian living. It provides the framework through which we properly relate to God in *prayer*, accurately understand the *Bible*, and actively involve ourselves in vital *church* membership. It is also the way in which we ably defend our faith. *What we believe is demonstrated inevitably in how we live.* That is why the apostle Paul instructed Timothy, "Watch your life and doctrine closely. Persevere in them, because if you do, you will save both yourself and your hearers" (1 Timothy 4:16).

Epilogue

*P*art Seven began with the tragic story of "Fire in the Sky over Fort Lauderdale." I'm convinced, however, that the real tragedy is not that three men died in the prime of their lives; the real tragedy is to live a long and prosperous life without ever using it to serve the Master.

That is essentially the problem with Faith theology. In compromising, confusing, and contradicting the crux of Christianity, the Faith teachers have focused men's hearts on the temporary rather than on the eternal. Benny Hinn summed up the sentiments of the Faith movement during a TBN fund-raiser when he said, "Years ago they used to preach, 'O we are going to walk on streets of gold.' I would say, 'I don't need the gold up there. I've got to have it down here.'"[1] Jerry Savelle echoed his remarks by exclaiming, "Dear God, I can't wait until I get to heaven to be free from sickness and disease and grief and sorrow. I found out I don't have to have any more of that stuff down here."[2]

How unlike the teachings of Jesus! He never promised my friends who lost their loved ones a paradise on earth. Rather, He promised them *Himself*. He promised them *a relationship with Him now and forever*.

Truly Jesus Christ is not a mere means to our ends; He is the End! Long before this tragedy took place in the sky over Fort Lauderdale, these men and their loved ones had developed an eternal perspective. They knew that life was but a vapor, here today and gone tomorrow. They had indeed internalized the words I heard from Glenn in the cramped quarters of that compact car: "You have only one life. Soon it will be past. Only what you do for Christ will last."

This is the real message of hope. When tragedy strikes, those seduced by the cultic theology of the Faith movement suffer guilt. True faith, on the other hand, brings grace.

In the book of Ephesians the apostle Paul urged Christians to become mature in the faith, attaining to the whole measure of the fullness of Christ. "Then," he said, "we will no longer be infants, tossed back and forth by the waves, and blown here and there by every wind of teaching and by the cunning and craftiness of men in their deceitful scheming. Instead, speaking the truth in love, we will in all things grow up into him who is the Head, that is, Christ" (Ephesians 4:14,15).

It is high time for the church to grow up and mature. Christianity is in crisis because Christians have fixed their eyes on passing earthly fancies rather than eternal heavenly treasures. This is not our dwelling place; we are merely pilgrims on our way to another kingdom. The solution for a Christianity in crisis is to turn from the fables of the Faith movement back to the basics of the faith once for all delivered to the saints.

Here is a portion of a letter written in prison by a former prosperity celebrity who in his heyday raised as much as 170 million dollars in a single year. We heard from Jim Bakker in chapter 19, and while I do not pretend to know his heart, his letters have the ring of authenticity. I have read this second letter several times now, and each time I have been moved. Jim writes:

❏ ❏ ❏

It is easy to praise God at Heritage U.S.A. with the orchestra playing and the singers and thousands of Christians worshiping God, but those times are not a test of our love for God. It's when everything is going wrong and we still praise

God... that is the real test.... True worship has nothing to do with where we are or what is happening. It is who God is and our attitude toward Him.

Job 1:2 tells us of Job's seven sons and three daughters. Job 1:3 tells us what he owned. Then he was totally bankrupt and bereaved of all ten children in one day. The chapter ends by telling us that Job fell down on the ground and *WORSHIPED*....

Yes, in the world's eyes I have lost everything. I have lost Heritage U.S.A., the television network, the daily program, my reputation, our family home, our car, our life savings.... All is gone, and my wife of 31 years has divorced me, and I am in prison. Some would say to me like Job's wife, "Why don't you curse God and die?" But like Job, I cry out, "Though God slay me, yet will I trust Him." I pray my life will be *WORSHIP* to God with all self-pity gone. I have learned that happiness is not in things or circumstances, but in knowing God.

Dietrich Bonhoeffer, a Christian theologian who died a martyr's death in a Nazi death camp, in his last letter to his dearest friend said, "What is happiness and unhappiness? It depends so little on the circumstances; it depends really only on that which happens inside a person.... When Christ calls a man, He bids him, come and die."

I too have learned that happiness is not in things or circumstances, but in knowing God.... The call to accept Christ should be "Who will come to Christ and be willing to die for Him?" Not "who wants all the good things of life, come to Christ."

We love to read about God's honor roll of faith in Hebrews 11, the great faith chapter. But many stop reading at verse 35. Let me give you the last part of this great faith chapter from The Living Bible. "But others trusted God and were beaten to death, preferring to die rather than turn from God and be free—trusting that they would rise to a better life afterwards. Some were laughed at and their backs cut open with whips, and others were chained in dungeons. Some died by stoning and some by being sawed in two; others were promised freedom if they would renounce their faith, then were killed with the sword. Some went about in skins of sheep and goats, wandering over deserts and mountains, hiding in dens and caves, they were hungry and sick and ill-treated— too good for this world. And these men of faith, though they trusted God and won His approval, none of them received all that God had promised them; for God wanted them to wait and share the even better rewards that were prepared for us."

After reading these verses, I'm more convinced than ever that what God wants is blind faith—the Job-kind-of-faith, that still stands when material blessings are gone. Even though the Hollywood screen image would somehow make us believe that there are some people who lead a charmed life with no pain or loneliness that the rest of us face, it is simply not true. No one has their lives in total control and pain free. Everyone you meet is fighting their own battles. We need each other.

I can almost hear you ask, "What would you do if you had to do it over?" Oh, there is so much. It would take volumes. But one of the most important things is, I would not emphasize the physical structure, but would work with all my heart to point people to the eternal—helping them to fall in love with our Lord and Savior, Jesus Christ. . . . If, by some miracle, I was transported back seven years to P.T.L., I would plead with people to get, and keep, their eyes off the physical and onto Jesus Christ and things eternal. God can still use the buildings at Heritage, or a cathedral, or a cow shed, or people gathered in an open field. Don't fall in love with the gift wrapping, fall in love with Jesus Christ, the Gift of eternal life.

It is time for sackcloth and ashes—it is time to do what God says, "If my people who are called by My Name will humble themselves and pray and seek My Face and turn from their wicked ways, then will I hear from heaven and forgive their sin and heal their land . . ." (2 Chronicles 7:14).

Let me leave you with the words of Jesus found in Mark 8: "What shall it profit a man if he shall gain the whole world and lose his own soul? Or what shall a man give in exchange for his soul?" Keep your eyes on the prize!—on Heaven, on Christ, on things above, "For it has not entered the hearts of men, the things God has prepared for them that love Him." THE BEST IS YET TO COME!

❏❏❏

I earnestly hope these words of Jim Bakker's are genuine, for if so they reveal a man who has exchanged his love of what is on the Master's table for love of the Master Himself.

It is my deepest hope that this book will enable thousands of readers to follow Bakker's footsteps and return with all their hearts to the God of the Bible—the omnipotent, omniscient, infinitely holy and eternally wise King of the universe. It is only that kind of return that will avert the current crisis in Christianity.

Christianity
IN
CRISIS

Kenyon and the Leading Proponents of a Different Gospel

Appendixes
Notes
Bibliography
Indexes

Kenyon and the
Leading Proponents
of a Different Gospel

*W*hile the ranks of the Faith teachers are legion (and growing every day), this movement, like any other, has its stars and leading lights. This special section highlights some of the best-known and most influential of today's Faith teachers, plus a brief sketch of the movement's spiritual founder. Others could be mentioned, but by getting to know these men and women, you will gain a good overview of the nature of the Faith movement.

Essek William Kenyon

Ask almost anyone embracing Faith theology who the father of the Faith movement is, and he will invariably point to "Dad" Hagin. Ask him where it originated, and he will most likely say that its roots can be found in the Pentecostal-charismatic movement. The truth, however, is that Essek William Kenyon is the real father of the modern-day Faith movement and that "Dad" Hagin merely popularized his material.

Born on April 24, 1867, E.W. Kenyon began his public ministry in the Methodist Church. In the early 1900's Kenyon established the Bethel Bible Institute, but subsequently resigned from his position as the school's superintendent in 1923 under a cloud of controversy. A true pioneer of religious broadcasting, Kenyon started a radio program in 1931 called "Kenyon's Church of the Air." The taped transcripts of this broadcast eventually became the basis for many of his writings, which have proven to be his most lasting legacy. Many of the phrases popularized by present-day prosperity preachers, such as "What I confess, I possess,"[1] were coined by Kenyon himself.

There is little doubt that New Thought metaphysics had an enormous impact on Kenyon. The evidence from his works, from eyewitnesses, and from external sources provide ample testimony to his cultic connections. Since a number of individuals have already established the cultic origins of the Faith movement via Kenyon, I will not belabor the point here.[2] However, I think it is worth mentioning that Kenyon attended Emerson College of Oratory, which was a virtual hotbed of New Thought metaphysics.[3]

Kenyon's reach of influence within Pentecostal circles was not confined to Kenneth Hagin. He was apparently widely-read and quoted by the post-World-War-II healing revivalists, including William Branham and T.L. Osborn.[4] Kenyon is also said to have visited the meetings of Pentecostal leaders such as F.F. Bosworth and Aimee Semple McPherson.[5]

Although Kenyon was mild in comparison to some of the more outrageous Faith teachers today, he did communicate both the bizarre and the blasphemous throughout his lifetime. For example, Kenyon said that if Jesus' physical death was sufficient to pay for sin, then every Christian should be able to pay the penalty for their sin with their own deaths. In fact, he even said that the physical death of our Lord did not touch the sin issue at all:

> If Jesus' physical death could pay the penalty of Sin as some contend, then why is it necessary that a Christian die? If a Christian dies physically, does he not pay the penalty of his own sin? If physical death is the penalty for sin, then why do not the whole human race pay their own penalty and save themselves, for all die? But we hold that the physical death of Jesus did not touch the sin issue at all.[6]

As blasphemous as that quote is, Kenyon was constantly outdoing himself. For example, in a book titled *The Father and His Family*, Kenyon states that "every man who has been 'born again' is an Incarnation, and Christianity is a miracle. The believer is as much an Incarnation as was Jesus of Nazareth."[7]

That quote should sound very familiar to you by now, for Hagin used this quotation as well as multitudes of others from Kenyon, who was the real father of the Faith movement.

Kenneth Hagin

To a large degree, Kenneth Hagin merely popularized and proliferated Kenyon's publications. Hagin has responded "by claiming that the Holy Spirit gave him the same words as Kenyon without his having prior knowledge of the sources."[8] Despite solid evidence to the contrary, Hagin insists:

> Kenyon's influence on my ministry has been minute. Only his teachings on the name of Jesus have much to do with my theology. I absolutely deny any metaphysical influences from Kenyon. I teach not Christian Science, but Christian sense.[9]

One of Hagin's more notorious "visionary" tales involves a "demon monkey."[10] The story opens with Jesus and Hagin having a conversation on casting out demons, when suddenly a "demon monkey"[11] jumps between them and begins to drown out Jesus' words by yelling, "Yackety, yack, yack, yack" in a shrill voice.

Finally, after some time had passed, Hagin takes control of the situation by telling the demon to "shut up in the name of Jesus." Jesus, no doubt relieved, tells Hagin that "if you hadn't done something about that, I couldn't have."[12] Shocked by Jesus' statement, Hagin immediately suggests to Jesus that perhaps He stumbled over His own words and that, rather than saying He "couldn't have," He meant to say He "wouldn't have."[13] Jesus calmly assures Hagin that He had not misspoken. Hagin, however, was not convinced. He tells the Lord he cannot accept that and presses Christ to prove His claim with two or three proof texts. After telling Hagin that "sometimes your theology needs upending,"[14] Jesus smiles sweetly and proceeds to accommodate him with four proof texts instead of three.

What is particularly ironic about this so-called vision is that, according to Hagin, Jesus was instructing him personally on some of the finer points of spiritual warfare and yet was Himself unable to practice what He was preaching. In fact, without Hagin, Christ was impotent in the presence of the alleged demonic monkey.

Despite Hagin's record—including his own admission that he was "excommunicated" by the Southern Baptists in 1937[15]—his span of influence has been nothing short of phenomenal. Virtually every major Faith teacher today has been impacted by Hagin in some significant manner. Hagin's disciples include such men as Kenneth Copeland, Charles Capps, and Frederick K.C. Price. Ken Hagin, Jr., writes:

> Other people have gotten started because of my Dad's ministry. They'll even admit it. They have preached his sermons *almost verbatim* from his tapes. Ken Copeland did.[16]

Ken Copeland gave "Dad" Hagin a ministry airplane worth about 160,000 to 170,000 dollars, and Hagin later gave it to Jerry Savelle.[17] Hagin also helped his son-in-law, Doyle "Buddy" Harrison, organize an International Convention of Faith Churches and Ministers, which has ordained such men as Charles Capps and Benny Hinn.[18]

Hagin's syndicated radio show is currently carried by some 249 radio stations,[19] and his Rhema Bible Training Center (located near Tulsa, Oklahoma) continues to produce graduates at a hefty rate. In 1992 alone, Hagin's *Word of Faith* magazine recorded 777 enthusiastic Rhema graduates, making a total of more than 12,000 graduates since the school opened in 1974. Two of these, Paul and Nikki, were specially featured because they were the first Russians to graduate from Rhema and appear to be set to spread Hagin's heresies in their homeland.[20] In addition to on-site training, Rhema offers correspondence courses which boasted 16,000 students during its first dozen years of existence.[21]

Hagin's *Word of Faith* magazine now reaches close to 400,000 homes,[22] and as of 1992 the ministry had sold more than 47 million copies of the various books and publications, with translations of many into 26 foreign languages.[23] More than 100 books, pamphlets, and tapes are listed in Hagin's most recent catalog.[24] Hagin's ministry reported a total of 290 full- and part-time employees, and his annual camp meetings boast an attendance of upwards of 20,000 participants.[25]

Hagin's popularity can be attributed, at least in part, to his claim to be an authority on spiritual matters. In turn, Hagin's "authority" appears to be derived largely from his alleged personal contacts with Jesus via visions. During one of these many visits, chronicled in *I Believe in Visions*, Jesus takes Hagin on a whirlwind tour of heaven and hell. Hagin devotes page after page to the details of his apocalyptic journeys to the place of the "damned."[26]

Not only does Hagin boast about his alleged visits to heaven and hell, but in his writings he recounts numerous out-of-body experiences (OBE's) in vivid detail.[27] During his conversion in 1933, Hagin reports he had a near-death out-of-body experience: "I slipped back into my body as a man slips into his trousers in the morning, the same way in which I had gone out—through my mouth."[28]

Hagin, on one memorable occasion, was in the middle of a sermon when instantly he was transported back in time to a little town 15 miles from the church where he was preaching. Leaning up against a building, he watched a woman walking down the street. Suddenly a car pulled up to the curb and honked the horn, and she got in. Just as suddenly Hagin found himself in the backseat. Upon reaching a spot away from the town, the driver committed adultery with the woman under Hagin's watchful eyes. The entire experience lasted about 15 minutes, after which Hagin abruptly found himself back in church summoning his parishioners to prayer.[29] This, by the way, was not an isolated experience.

A few paragraphs later in the same booklet, Hagin recalls walking home from the church he was pastoring at the time. He was taking a shortcut through an alley overgrown with trees. Suddenly he noticed a car backed into the shadows. Instantly the inside of the car was illuminated with supernatural light so that he could see everything. And there in the car he saw another woman that someone had tried to get him interested in sitting in another man's lap. Fortunately, Hagin spared his readers the detailed documentation of what he observed taking place. As Hagin puts it, "He had his arm around her and that's not all they were doing, but that's as much as I'll describe."[30]

Hagin claims that Jesus appeared to him in 1950 and gave him a special anointing to minister to the sick. As Hagin puts it, Jesus—

> went on to instruct me that when I would pray and lay hands upon the sick I was to lay one hand on each side of the body. If I felt the fire jump from hand to hand, an evil spirit or demon was present in the body causing the affliction. . . . If the fire, or anointing, in my hand does not jump from hand to hand, it is a case of healing only. I should pray for the person in His name, and if he will believe and accept it, the anointing will leave my hands and go into his body, driving out the disease and bringing healing. When the fire, or the anointing, leaves my hands and goes into his body, I will know he is healed.[31]

During this incredible encounter, Christ, in King James English, tells Hagin to "stretch forth thine hand." Jesus then stretches out His own hands so that Hagin can look into them. "For some reason," remarks Hagin, "I expected to see a scar where the nail had pierced His flesh and had since grown together. I should have known better, but many times we get ideas that are not really Scriptural, yet they are accepted beliefs. I saw in the palms of His hands the wounds of the crucifixion—three-cornered, jagged holes. Each hole was large enough so that I could put my finger in it. I could see light on the other side of the hole."[32]

What is noteworthy about this story is that after criticizing "ideas that are not really Scriptural," Hagin himself proceeds to narrate a story that has no basis in reality. You see, Jesus could never have shown Hagin the alleged holes in His palms. As any student of Scripture and history knows, the nails were driven through Christ's *wrists* as opposed to His palms. The Greek word used in the text (*cheir*) actually refers to the entire forearm, including the hand.[33]

In addition to Scripture, archaeology and medicine provide strong evidence that crucified individuals could not have been nailed through the palms of their hands: The weight of the body would have ripped the nails right through the fingers of the hands.[34] Hagin's fanciful story conclusively demonstrates that the Jesus who supposedly anointed him "to minister to the sick" could not have been the Jesus of the Bible (cf. 2 Corinthians 11:4).

Despite glaring distortions in his stories, Hagin still has the temerity to pronounce divine judgment on those who dare to question his so-called prophetic ministry. He has even sneered at fellow prophets, saying, "I've drawn back from the prophet's ministry because I don't want to be classed with all those idiots and half wits."[35]

Hagin ominously claims that God Himself told him that if individuals, churches, and pastors do not accept his message, they may well pay the ultimate price. Speaking of his prophetic pronouncements, Hagin states, "There will be ministers who don't accept it and will fall dead in the pulpit."[36] Continuing on, Hagin relates an incident in which he predicted the untimely death of a pastor who doubted his message. According to Hagin, "The pastor fell dead in the pulpit . . . because he didn't accept the message that God gave me to give him from the Holy Spirit."[37]

Hagin's own wife, Oretha, experienced the devastating impact of divine judgment firsthand. During one of Hagin's meetings, a woman levitated from an altar and "stood in mid-air dancing."[38] Several people, including Hagin's wife, questioned whether this was of God. As a direct result of her doubt, she was supposedly "slain" by the Spirit of God. Reeling backward, as though struck with a "ball bat," Oretha was knocked flat and, as it were, "glued to the floor."[39] It wasn't until she acknowledged that what was going on in the meeting was of God that God permitted Hagin to release her. With a touch of Hagin's finger, Oretha was restored.

It is indeed tragic that many of today's Faith teachers have taken Hagin's sinister pronouncements to new extremes. Benny Hinn, for example, boldly declared on national television that he wished he could blow the heads off his "stink[ing]" enemies with a "Holy Ghost machine gun."[40] After apologizing for this remark, Hinn came back a year later with a vengeance.[41] During a rally (which I personally attended) of some 17,000 people, Hinn made the following chilling pronouncement:

> The Holy Ghost is upon me. . . . The day is coming when those that attack us will drop dead. You say, "What did you say?" I speak this under the anointing of the Spirit. Can I tell you something? Don't touch God's servants; it's deadly. . . . Woe to you that touch God's servants. You're going to pay. "And the day will come," the Lord said that to me. He said, "The day will come when I will punish instantly. Woe to those who touch my chosen." They will fear us. Hear this: today they mock us; tomorrow they will fear us.[42]

Hinn's warning mirrored John Avanzini's claim that CRI founder Walter Martin was struck dead because he dared to speak out against God's anointed.[43] On a similar note, Paul Crouch stated that if God did not shoot his enemies, he would.[44] But Kenneth Copeland, to whom we will now turn our attention, not only claimed that "Faith critics" would go to an early grave, but would also experience the dreaded disease of cancer.[45] Lest you think these men are just blowing off steam, let me underscore what has already been documented—namely, that the Faith teachers are convinced that their words can literally bring death into the life of their critics.

Kenneth Copeland

While Kenneth Hagin, Jr., will no doubt lead his father's Faith empire into the future, Kenneth Copeland will likely carry the torch for the movement as a whole. Copeland got his start in ministry as a direct result of memorizing his mentor Hagin's messages.[46]

Although he once worked as a pilot for Oral Roberts's ministry, it was Kenneth Hagin who ultimately revolutionized Copeland's life.[47] Hagin's impact was first felt in 1967, when former Hagin manager (now son-in-law) Doyle "Buddy" Harrison took pity on young Copeland and gave him a selection of Hagin's tapes, which Copeland at the time was too poor to purchase.[48]

Within a year of this acquisition, the husband-and-wife team of Kenneth and Gloria Copeland felt they had learned enough from Hagin's tapes to establish their own evangelistic association. So, in 1968, in the city of Fort Worth, Texas, a brand-new cult was born. The small home Bible studies held by the Copelands were soon transformed into mass revivals conducted in internationally famous arenas.[49] This was only the beginning.

In 1973 Copeland began publishing a newsletter called the *Believer's Voice of Victory*; three years later he launched his "Believer's Voice of Victory" radio program.[50] Copeland says God "spoke" to him on March 23, 1979, giving him a "broadcasting . . . commission" to expand into television."[51] From there he advanced into the high-tech world of satellite communications in 1981. In August of the following year, the ministry says it "made history by initiating the first *global* religious broadcast," linking a reported "two hundred cities across the United States and over twenty countries around the world . . . by satellite."[52]

With offices in such distant locations as England, the Philippines, South Africa, Australia, Canada, and Hong Kong, Copeland's organization today truly can be regarded as international in scope and significance. In fact, I recently experienced firsthand Copeland's far-reaching influence. I had the privilege of delivering the keynote address at the National Day of Prayer in the Kingdom of Tonga, located in the South Pacific. During my stay I learned there was only one Christian bookstore on the island. Thinking it might be interesting to see what items were available, I decided to pay the store a visit, and quickly discovered that the store was selling Copeland's materials. Since Tonga can be described as being the "last place in time" (when it is midday in Jerusalem, it is midnight in Tonga), it may well be said that Copeland's destructive doctrines have now reached the uttermost parts of the earth.

Not only does Copeland espouse concepts common to cultists, but he often throws reckless remarks that make even the deviant doctrine of the cults seem tame. Consider for a moment the striking similarity between Copeland's assertion that "Adam, in the Garden of Eden, was God manifested in the flesh"[53] and Mormon prophet Brigham Young's teaching that "Adam is our father and our God."[54]

Or compare Copeland's teaching that God is 6'-2" to 6'-3", weighs around 200 pounds, and has a handspan of about nine inches[55] with Mormon founder Joseph Smith's statement that if you were to see God today "you would see him like a man in form—like yourselves in all the person, image, and very form as a man."[56] Now if that doesn't shock you, consider how Copeland's claim—that Adam was an exact duplicate of God, and not even subordinate to Him[57]—parallels Joseph Smith's statement that "God himself was once as we are now, and is an exalted man."[58] Not only does Copeland teach that Adam and God were exact duplicates, but he also perpetuates the myth that earth is an exact replica of the Mother Planet on which God lives.[59]

All this, however, is but the tip of the iceberg. As we have seen, Copeland also brashly pronounces God to be the greatest failure of all time,[60] boldly proclaims that "Satan *conquered* Jesus on the Cross,"[61] and describes Christ in hell as an "emaciated, poured out, little, wormy spirit."[62]

Copeland is as at home in the world of the occult as he is in the kingdom of the cults. As a case in point, Copeland is clearly committed to the magical concept that intangible words, imbued with the force of faith, can take on tangible reality. Remember his insistence that a believer can command an 82-foot yacht into existence.[63]

That Copeland advocates a method of occult visualization is incontrovertible. As Copeland himself clarifies, "Any image that you get down on the inside of you that is so vivid when you close your eyes you see it, it'll come to pass."[64] He knows that cultists do similar things, for he says, "The visualization they do in meditation and metaphysical practices . . . is the perverted form of the real thing."[65] Referring to creative visualization and positive confession, Copeland claims that "New Age is trying to do this; and they'd get somewhat results out of it because this is spiritual law, brother."[66]

In addition to tantalizing his converts with the possibility of creating wealth through occultism, Copeland also tempts them with the dangerous doctrine that they can create their own health as well. As we have seen, he suggests to scores of suffering saints that when "you get to the place where you take the Word of God and build an image on the inside of you of not having crippled legs and not having blind eyes, but when you close your eyes you just see yourself just leap out of that wheelchair, it will picture that in the Holy of Holies and you will come out of there. You will come out."[67]

As though it weren't bad enough to devastate the lives of multitudes of physically handicapped people, Copeland's wife, Gloria, attacks the reputation of the man who was perhaps the greatest apostle of all time. With shrill voice she claims that the apostle Paul did not receive his healing because he asked God when he should have done it himself![68]

Volumes could be devoted to the dangerous doctrines espoused by Kenneth and Gloria Copeland. Only from the perspective of eternity will we comprehend fully the human suffering that has followed in their wake. Yet despite the unassailable evidence that Copeland is a cultist, Benny Hinn, whom we will now consider, ominously warned an international audience that "those who attack Kenneth Copeland are attacking the very presence of God."[69]

Benny Hinn

"The very presence of God" is exactly what thousands of people clamor for when they attend one of Benny Hinn's "Miracle Crusades." They hope to see God move in a mighty way through an outpouring of miraculous healing power.

After personally attending one of Hinn's crusades, however, I can say from experience that the likelihood of being hurt during such an occasion is vastly greater than that of being helped or healed. I observed with great anguish scores of men, women, and children who could not even get near the stage to be healed by Hinn. The scenario can be best described as a vulgar display of "survival of the fittest," with people stampeding madly to get on stage so they can experience falling at Hinn's feet.

Tragically, those who attended the meeting in wheelchairs ended up leaving in the same physical condition. Some departed in tears. Others told me they left feeling that God neither cared for them nor had the time to consider their needs.

You might wonder how Hinn got into the traveling miracle business in the first place. It happened in 1990, when Hinn claims the Lord directed him to begin monthly crusades around the country.[70] According to Hinn:

> At these crusades I immediately began to receive power to drive out devils of sickness and affliction and to receive specific direction as to what the Holy Spirit was doing among the crowds of twelve to fifteen thousand that attended each night. Hundreds of verified healings and thousands of conversions have occurred, including people rising from wheelchairs and leaving crutches. Several blind eyes and deaf ears have been opened and verified.[71]

Not only does Hinn claim to have raised people out of wheelchairs, given blind eyes sight, and opened the ears of the deaf, but he also claims he has healed at least four people of AIDS.[72] However, when pressed for verification, Susan Smith, who apparently helps document such healings for Hinn, becomes strangely elusive.[73]

When it comes to the AIDS case, her response was that the final tests are not yet in. When queried about an Orlando woman who was allegedly cured of blindness due to diabetes, Susan would not divulge the name of the woman. She subsequently stated that the woman's vision may still be cloudy and that she still has diabetes, which ironically enough precipitated the problem in the first place. "I wish she would get off insulin," says Susan. "That's what makes them blind."[74]

In Part 2 I told the story of Wesley Parker, a diabetic boy who died a ghastly death when his parents heeded the suggestions of a faith healer. As prescribed by the healer, they "claimed" a healing and then proceeded to throw away their son's insulin. One can only hope that the Orlando woman does not make the same deadly miscalculation.

Make no mistake: I personally believe in God's healing power. But if God is in fact healing through Hinn, the evidence is conspicuous by its absence. Where, for example, are those whose missing eyes or legs have been restored? If God has indeed used Hinn to heal multiple hundreds as Hinn boasts, then why hasn't even one quadriplegic stepped forward to show the world that Hinn represents the real power of the Holy Spirit?

Benny Hinn has provided CRI with "3 healing testimonies that have doctors' records and documentation"[75] out of the many hundreds he claims. Presumably, this is the best evidence Hinn can supply, his strongest case. But according to CRI's medical consultant, Dr. Preston Simpson, M.D., all three cases are poorly documented and confused.[76]

Case 1: Colon cancer. A careful examination of the partial medical records supplied by Hinn indicates that the malignant tumor had apparently been surgically removed (prior to an appendectomy), rather than miraculously healed.[77]

Case 2: Lupus and related disorders. This is a particularly interesting case in that lupus is well-known to go into remission spontaneously for years at a time. This naturally makes miraculous healing difficult to verify. What can be verified are the *effects* of lupus—in this case damage to the sacroiliac joint—which was definitely *not* healed.[78]

Case 3: Spinal tumor and various cancers. This case really has problems.[79] To begin with, the tapes of the CAT scan of the spine were "erased before the bones could be evaluated."[80] Next, the records reveal that the spinal tumor began shrinking some three months *prior* to Hinn's Miracle Invasion Rally. And finally, the tumor was still present—not healed—months after the alleged "healing."[81]

Hinn claims that there are "hundreds" of authenticated healings and that he will document them in a new book due to be published in 1993.[82] But it is clear that if evidence like this is the best Hinn can muster after years of "miracle rallies"—with a staff working at each rally to document cases of healing—then there is no credible evidence that he has ever been involved in a bona fide healing.

The illusion that Hinn's miracle-working power comes from God is one thing, but the delusion that much of his theology is given to him via the Holy Spirit is quite another. While claiming to be "under the anointing," Hinn has uttered some of the most off-the-wall statements imaginable. For instance, Hinn claims the Holy Spirit revealed to him that women were originally designed to give birth out of their sides.[83]

Hinn also attributes to the Holy Spirit such sacrilegious statements as that man is a "little god" (see chapter 9). Hinn also admits he frequents the gravesites of both Kathryn Kuhlman and Aimee Semple McPherson to get the "anointing" from their bones.[84] On one occasion Hinn got more than he could reasonably handle. Said Hinn, "Oh, I was drunk, still drunk."[85] In this instance, Hinn was so "intoxicated" that he could not even remember the prophecy he had just uttered. Sadly, he had to ask his audience to tell him what he had just been saying under the "anointing."

Despite all this and more, Hinn has managed to gain wide acceptance through his visibility on television as well as his promotion by a major publisher. Still, Hinn's books may be long on looks but short on substance. For if one examines Hinn from a theological perspective truth too often turns into mythology.

Just who is Benny Hinn? He is the pastor of the Orlando Christian Center in Florida, where more than 7000 people attend services each week.[86] Hinn reaches a potential viewing audience of some 16 million households over TBN's cable system alone.[87] Hinn tells his story in the blockbuster bestseller *Good Morning, Holy Spirit*, which reportedly has sold more than a million copies to date. His second bestseller, *The Anointing*, allegedly has sold some 700,000 copies.[88]

Hinn is a master at creating the illusion of credibility. For example, he points to his years in Israel (where he was born and reared) to lead people into thinking he is an expert in the Hebrew Scriptures. But no one who has heard his rhetoric on the Trinity Broadcasting Network could accept that story (see chapter 9, "The Deification of Man," for Hinn's exegesis on the Hebrew word for "dominion" and how it supposedly proves Adam could fly to the moon).

Hinn does the same thing when it comes to the Holy Spirit. In his books and tapes he creates the illusion that he has special, mystical powers. In *Good Morning, Holy Spirit*, for example, Hinn recalls a scene where his mother was cleaning the hallway outside his room while he was inside having one of his customary chats with the Holy Spirit. (By the way, if Hinn is to be believed, these chats were so meaningful that the Spirit of God begged Benny for " 'five more minutes. Just five more minutes.' The Holy Spirit longed for my fellowship.")[89]

When Hinn stepped out into the hallway, the presence of the Lord emanating from him was so strong that his mother was thrown back against the wall. So that no one can miss the point of the story, Hinn adds that his "brothers will tell you of the times they came near me and didn't know what was happening—but they felt something unusual."[90]

Scores of examples could be cited to document Hinn's methods for creating the illusion of a special anointing from God. Here is one example.

The date was December 7, 1974. The place was Oshawa, Ontario. The occasion was the very first time Hinn had ever stood behind a pulpit.[91] After preaching a message replete with insights that continue to amaze him even to this day, Hinn lifted his hands and summoned the Holy Spirit. "Instantly the power of God hit the place," Hinn writes. "People began to cry and many fell to the floor." The power was reportedly so incredible that Hinn ended up crying, "Oh, dear God, what do I do now?"

At that point Hinn tried to turn the service over to "the fellow who was leading the meeting, hoping he would come and take the service out of my hands. But as I turned and pointed toward him, he fell backward several feet. I was trying to get him to come close and suddenly he was farther away."[92] The raw power emanating from young Hinn was allegedly so potent that each time the leader would struggle to get near him, he would be hurled against the wall.

Hinn then tells the reader that this was but the beginning of a ministry characterized by Holy Ghost anointing and powerful preaching. Says Hinn, "Miraculously my ministry began and instantly mushroomed."[93]

The Anointing might best be characterized as overpromising and underperforming.[94] His message to charismatic Christians in particular is that if all you have experienced to date is "the baptism of the Holy Spirit" and speaking in tongues, then you haven't had much. As Hinn himself puts it, "If this is all there is, I'm not sure there's much to it."[95] His solution, of course, is "the anointing."

So what is the anointing? Answer: It is power! Hinn tells story after story of how that power (allegedly from God) is displayed through him, all the while reinforcing the theme that without it you have nothing. "I am not overstating the case," says Hinn. "The anointing is mandatory if you are called to serve the Lord. Without it there will be no growth, no blessing, no victory in your ministry."[96] Notice that Hinn does not qualify his statement. He does not say, for example, "Without it your growth will be limited." No, he says, "Without it there will be *no* growth."

But just buy Benny Hinn's book and he will explain how you too can grow to experience the real thing. In fact, Hinn claims he has experienced so much of the real thing that he has reached that state of perfection whereby he has not lost *some* but *all* worldly desires. "In my case," Hinn states, "I know I have lost complete desire for anything to do with the world. My worldly desires are gone. . . . I no longer have any rebellion in me."[97] If that were true, then Hinn, like Christ, would indeed be sinless. But of one thing I am certain: Hinn is no more sinless than the rest of us mere mortals.

Despite this fact, I was cautiously optimistic that Hinn would reject some of his erroneous doctrines after I met with him for the first time on December 5, 1990. There appeared to be some real glimmers of hope. Hinn agreed to remove some of the more egregious doctrinal errors from his book, *Good Morning, Holy Spirit.* Although there were some unannounced changes in the subsequent printings of the book, the problem was never completely resolved. Still, it appeared to be a step in the right direction.

Hinn, in an interview with *Christianity Today* in 1991, admitted his mistakes and vowed to make changes.[98] He said the revelation from the Holy Spirit that there were "nine of them" in the Trinity (because the Father, the Son, and the Holy Spirit each had His own personal spirit, soul, and body) was "a very dumb statement."[99]

Hinn also said he would no longer attack his critics, expressing regret over his previous statement that he wished God would give him "a Holy Ghost machine gun" so he could blow off the heads of his critics.[100] The icing on the cake, however, was Hinn's comment on Faith theology: "I really no longer believe the faith message. I don't think it adds up."[101]

Was Hinn sincere, or was this just damage control? The answer appears to be the latter. Within weeks, Hinn was back to his old ways.

Hinn's supposed revelation from the Holy Spirit that each member of the Trinity possessed a separate spirit, soul, and body poses a dilemma: If that declaration was truly divinely revealed, how could Hinn dare to issue a retraction—even calling the statement "dumb"—of an allegedly "God-given truth"? The inescapable conclusion is that Hinn's revelations could not have come from God. The sincerity of Hinn's retraction is placed in further doubt by the fact that, barely a week after the interview with *Christianity Today*, he was back teaching that both the Father and the Holy Spirit have "bodies."[102]

Today Hinn laughs at the notion that he ever claimed there were "nine of them" in the Godhead, but he still maintains that each member of the Trinity—the Father, Son, and Holy Spirit—"possesses his own spirit body."[103]

Hinn has likewise lost no time getting back into one of his favorite pastimes—uttering ominous threats against his critics. As quoted earlier, Hinn chose November 22, 1991, the anniversary of President John F. Kennedy's assassination, to launch a new series of threats.[104]

Then Hinn unleashed his most chilling threat to date, this time directly against CRI (as he admitted to *Christianity Today*). At the World Charismatic Conference on August 7, 1992—meeting in Anaheim, California, not far from CRI headquarters—he let loose his threats. Hinn told the camera crew to stop taping, but we have his recorded warnings against us and our children, complete with eerie background music:

> Now I'm pointing my finger with the mighty *power of God on me*. . . . You hear this: There are men and women in Southern California attacking me. *I will tell you under the anointing now*, you'll reap it in your children unless you stop. . . . And *your children will suffer*.

> You're attacking me on the radio every night—you'll pay and *your children will*. Hear this from the lips of God's servant. *You are in danger*. Repent! Or God Almighty will move His hand. Touch not my Anointed. . . .[105]

When confronted by *Christianity Today* with this latest threat, Hinn claimed it was in self-defense, that he felt under attack personally, that he was afraid someone might physically harm him.[106] He admitted he made the threat against staff members of CRI and their families.[107]

And Hinn continues to issue dire threats. In a TBN-sponsored marathon of televised attacks on "heresy hunters" (obviously alluding to CRI) on October 23, 1992, Hinn warned, "You have attacked me, *your children will pay for it.*"

As for Hinn giving up his Faith teaching, that too can be discounted. Hinn has completely flip-flopped. Not only has he continued teaching his own brand of Faith theology, but he has gone out of his way to defend such Faith teachers as Hagin and Copeland—whose International Convention of Faith Churches and Ministers ordained Hinn.[108] Within months, Hinn warned, "Those who attack confession are on the devil's side."[109] Soon after that, Hinn dogmatically stated that "words create reality."[110] Then Hinn came completely out of the closet, boldly proclaiming, "Faith is released when I speak the word of faith."[111]

In listening to Hinn over a long period of time, I have come to the sad conclusion that what he attributes to revelations from the Holy Spirit are usually little more than repetitions from the mouths of other Faith teachers.

Frederick K.C. Price

We now turn our attention to another in a long line of men who were influenced by Kenneth E. Hagin. His name is Frederick K.C. Price. In fact, Price has said that "Kenneth Hagin has had the greatest influence upon my life of any living man."[112]

Price is by far the most prominent of a growing number of black Faith preachers today. His Crenshaw Christian Center in south-central Los Angeles claims more than 16,000 members.[113] He launched a national television ministry in 1978, and is today a frequent guest on TBN's "Praise the Lord" program.

Price's first brush with the theology of the cults came as a result of being reared in a Jehovah's Witness family.[114] After his conversion Price experimented with a wide range of denominations, including Baptist, African Methodist Episcopal, Presbyterian, and Christian and Missionary Alliance.[115] As his wife puts it, he and she were "in all kinds of trouble going nowhere!"[116] That is, until a friend gave him a booklet titled *The Authority of the Believer*, by Kenneth Hagin.[117]

Since becoming a Faith teacher, Price has called himself the "chief exponent of NAME IT AND CLAIM IT."[118] He has also referred to his organization as a "Star Wars program for the Lord" and as a "Stealth bomber for Jesus."[119] Referring to his own wealth, Price once said, "That's the reason why I drive a Rolls Royce—I'm following Jesus' steps."[120]

Price's teachings have come home to visit even his own family. Price boldly asserts, "We don't allow sickness in our home."[121] Price also discourages the use of medication, saying, "When you have developed your faith to such an extent that you can stand on the promises of God, then you won't need medicine."[122] However, after publicly announcing in October 1990 that she had developed cancer—an "inoperable malignant tumor in her pelvic area"—Price's wife, Betty, underwent an "ordeal of pain, chemotherapy, and radiation treatments."[123] Price now claims she is free of cancer, medication, and pain (but only "95 percent free of a limp"[124]). One can only hope Price will learn the difference between biblical faith and presumption before it is too late for his followers.

Not only has Price become an able communicator of the Faith teachings he learned from Hagin, but he has also added his own personal stamp. For example, Price made the following remark concerning praying in accordance with God's will: "If you have to say, 'If it be thy will' or 'Thy will be done'—if you have to say that, then you're calling God a fool."[125] This, of course, directly contradicts such passages as James 4:15 and Matthew 6:9,10. The implications of Price's comment pose serious problems for the biblical doctrine of God's sovereignty (Psalm 115:3; 135:6; Daniel 4:35; Romans 9:20).

Unfortunately, Price's rhetoric does not end there. Like Hinn, Price misdefines the biblical concept of dominion and sneers at those who believe that God has dominion over this earth. Commenting on Genesis 1:20, Price has this to say:

> If them animals belonged to, if those animals belonged to God, how come God didn't give them their names? Why did he leave it up to a puny man to give them the names to the animal kingdom, the plant kingdom, and the vegetable kingdom? Because they belonged under the control of Adam and not of God. . . . Why? He had dominion. Not God, Adam.[126]

Price has made a habit of calling into question God's overarching authority. His theological errors, however, touch on other equally crucial areas as well. For example, Price believes that Jesus died spiritually, thereby taking on the nature of Satan before His crucifixion. Referring to Christ, Price states, "Somewhere between the time He was nailed to the cross and when He was in the Garden of Gethsemane—somewhere in there—He died spiritually. Personally, I believe it was while he was in the Garden."[127] On an equally sobering note, Price mocks the sufficiency of Christ's atonement at Calvary. The following is a transcript of what he says in this regard:

> Do you think that the punishment for our sin was [for Jesus] to die on a cross? If that were the case, the two thieves could have paid your price. No, the punishment was [for Jesus] to go to hell itself and to serve time in hell separated from God.[128]

Tragically, Price is not content to wreak havoc upon the centrality of Christ's work upon the cross. He also portrays a completely different Christ during His earthly ministry. Consider, for example, Price's argument that Jesus "must have had a whole lot" of money.[129] Here's how he puts it:

> The Bible says that He [Jesus] had a treasurer . . . named Judas Iscariot; and the rascal was stealing out of the bag for three-and-a-half years and nobody knew that he was stealing. You know why? Because there was so much in it. . . . If He had three oranges in the bottom of the bag and he stole two of them, don't tell me He wouldn't know that some was missing. Beside that, if Jesus didn't have anything, what do you need a treasury for?[130]

Upon such a flawed foundation rests a fundamental Faith fantasy—namely, that Jesus was wealthy, that He wore expensive clothing, and that His disciples lived in luxury.

John Avanzini

Dr. John Avanzini bills himself as a noted Bible teacher and recognized authority on biblical economics. "Brother John," as he likes to call himself, claims to have studied the life of Christ to the extent that he is now prepared to dispel the popular misconception that our Lord was poor. Contrary to "tradition," Avanzini asserts Jesus was so wealthy that He wore custom-made designer clothes.[131]

Avanzini uses John 19:23 in an attempt to make his point. What Avanzini doesn't seem to realize is that what he describes as a seamless custom-made designer coat is considered by competent Bible scholars to refer to an undergarment.[132] Thus, if we are to take Avanzini seriously, he has built the case that Jesus wore custom-made designer underwear!

Avanzini continues his attempt to demonstrate that Christ was wealthy by pointing out that, contrary to what people have been taught, "Jesus had a nice house, a big house."[133] Anticipating a rebuttal, Avanzini offered this response to Matthew 8:20:

> "Foxes have holes and the birds in the air have nests, but the Son of man hath nowhere to lay His head" is not a declaration that Jesus didn't have a house. . . . It meant that [the] Samaritans canceled the meeting that He was going to, if you remember the account. And in those days, there wasn't a Holiday Inn on every corner. . . . If your advance men got canceled, then you walked to the next meeting and take up there. It's very clear that He had a house. . . . The Bible states he had a house.[134]

This is no mere academic point, for, according to Avanzini, until you know that Jesus was prosperous, you won't be either. Elsewhere he says, "If Jesus was poor, I want to be poor, if Jesus slept under a bridge, I want to sleep under the bridge, but if Jesus was rich, I too want to be rich."[135]

Armed with a bundle of biblical texts which he takes out of context, Avanzini teaches people that they should give to get. Avanzini has even suggested that "a greater than a lottery has come. His name is Jesus!"[136] For those who have failed to get what they paid for, Avanzini has written a book titled *It's Not Working, Brother John*.[137] Avanzini lists no less than 25 reasons why his techniques for personal prosperity may not be working for some people. He puts the blame on virtually everyone and everything—not tithing, no faith, no patience, not trusting God's man, hidden sin, tradition, etc.—but not himself.

What is particularly noteworthy is that Avanzini begins virtually all of his arguments by mounting a diatribe against theologians and apologists. Claiming that he once was an apologist himself, Avanzini said, "I'm not impressed with the apologists any longer, and I may as well get it out—I used to be one, and God forgave me, and I promised not to ever do it again."[138]

Avanzini is quick to point out that "theologians don't get their prayers answered" and that "they deal with an impersonal God."[139] He also has lodged the following criticism against "heresy hunters":

> You know what the problem is with all those heresy hunters? They do not believe in a personal God. They

believe in a general God that laid down some rules, then went on vacation and said, "You operate by these rules."[140]

What makes Avanzini's remark so interesting is that the God he erroneously ascribes to theologians and heresy hunters sounds remarkably like the false god of the Faith movement—a god who himself is caught up in a universe governed by spiritual laws. Perhaps that is why Avanzini has now exchanged his former "apologetic" role for that of a self-proclaimed prophet.[141] Avanzini has made full use of his newfound office. He misquotes and misapplies to himself the words contained in 2 Chronicles 20:20: You say, "Brother John, can I believe you?" He answers, "Believe the prophet and you will prosper."[142]

Perhaps the saddest fact of all is that Avanzini takes the Word of God—which was designed to bring men light—and reduces it to a means to bring in funds. In the words of Benny Hinn, "The wicked are piling up the funds and I love the way John teaches on this. He's the best there is when it comes to teaching you on how to get the wealth of the wicked. Man, I like it!"[143]

Robert Tilton

Just as McDonald's has popularized "fast food," Robert Tilton's ministry has propagated "fast faith." Boiled down to its irreducible minimum, Tilton's message is simple: God wants you to flourish financially and physically. But you need faith. To prove your faith you need to make a vow of faith, and all vows should be sent in care of Brother Bob. Typical vows begin at 1000 dollars, but the sky's the limit.

Although the material that Tilton uses for his sermons has been adapted largely from Hagin and Kenyon, the marketing techniques appear to have been adapted directly from a real-estate marketer named Dave Del Dotto.[144] As Tilton tells the story, the successful current format of his show—the "infomercial"—emerged from his heartache over repeated failures with his television show.[145] So he went into the wilderness to hear from God. (When Tilton says "wilderness," he doesn't mean self-denial and deprivation. What he means is Hawaii. As Tilton puts it, "If I'm going to go to the cross, I'm going to go in a pretty place. Not some dusty place like Jerusalem. That's gravel is all that place is.")[146]

After his wilderness experience, Tilton turned to TV and found Dave Del Dotto.[147] Inspired by Del Dotto's real-estate "infomercials," Tilton came up with a religious infomercial called "Success-N-Life."[148] Tilton has used 84 percent of his air time for fund-raising and promotion, compared to 5 percent for Billy Graham's broadcasts or the 22 percent average for commercial television.[149]

Tilton's program has been ranked as high as twelfth in the national religious Arbitron ratings. Before scandal sapped his audience share, it was viewed by an estimated six million households over 212 stations.[150] Add to that his cable television audience, his mailing list of 880,000, and his full-time staff of more than 850 employees,[151] and Tilton truly has been a megastar in the Faith movement's constellation of prosperity preachers. According to his wife Marte's testimony during a recent federal court hearing, their 8000-member Word of Faith Family Church & World Outreach Center in the north Dallas suburb of Farmers Branch takes in an amazing 65 million dollars per year.[152]

Network television is sounding its own warnings about Tilton. The prayer requests that Tilton promises he will personally pray over all too often end up in garbage dumpsters, as ABC-TV "PrimeTime Live" cameras showed on November 21, 1991, and July 9, 1992, and as Tilton's former employees have testified.[153] First the requests are routed to a bank and the money is removed. Then they proceed to a mail processing facility. Finally they are transferred to a recycling center.[154]

At least two widows are now suing Tilton's ministry for sending letters seeking donations and promising to heal their already-dead husbands.[155] Altogether, at least ten civil suits have been filed for claims totaling more than 500 million dollars.[156]

Regrettably, after his financial indiscretions were aired on the first ABC "PrimeTime Live" broadcast, Tilton merely regrouped.[157] Tilton went on the offensive with an attack video titled *PrimeTime Lies*, which attempted to investigate the investigators, complete with a newscast-type studio set and a reporter who looked like ABC's Diane Sawyer.[158]

Tilton tells his followers he is being persecuted for the cause of Christ.[159] Assuring them that ABC was wrong and that he personally prayed over each of the thousands of prayer requests that came into his ministry daily, Tilton provided the following incredible rebuttal:

> Those prayer request forms have ink on them and all kinds of chemicals. I laid on top of those prayer requests so much that the chemicals actually got into my bloodstream and began to swell my capillaries. . . . It got into my immune system and I had two small strokes in my brain that brought about some numbness in my body.[160]

As a result, Tilton said he had to undergo plastic surgery to remove the bags from under his eyes.[161]

Marilyn Hickey

Marilyn Hickey, much like Tilton, uses a wide range of gimmicks to get her followers to send money. Among her many tactics are anointed prayer cloths, ceremonial breastplates, and ropes that can be used as "points of contact" for miracles.

In one letter,[162] Hickey promised to send a special anointing if the enclosed prayer cloth, along with money, was sent back to her immediately. Hickey promised that if it was returned "right now," she would have it "anointed with an Acts 19 kind of anointing for 'special,' 'unusual' and 'extraordinary' miracles." Hickey assured the reader that the Holy Spirit had been dealing with her about the entire matter and that she was excited about it.

Hickey then suggested that the prayer cloth was the perfect remedy for those who are sick, those who need to sell something, and those who need to break a spirit of rebellion. So that the point would not be missed, Hickey explained that the prayer cloth is so powerful that when a mother slipped it under the pillow of a rebellious child, the spirit of rebellion was broken. Not only that, but with a mere touch of the prayer cloth, a tumor the size of a small grapefruit vanished in just five days.

Hickey then promised that anyone suffering from an extreme financial crisis need only carry the prayer cloth in a purse, wallet, or checkbook to receive a financial breakthrough. There was one small catch: Before the cloth could work, it had to be sent back to Hickey. The prayercloth, according to Hickey, presently "does not carry or contain any special anointing or qualities. It is just a simple piece of plain cloth . . . but in a few days (if you act in faith RIGHT NOW) it can become a MIRACLE PRAYER CLOTH."

But Hickey had one more suggestion: When you return the cloth, be sure to send money. As Hickey puts it, *"Receiving follows giving."*

In another of her appeal letters, Hickey promised that she would slip into a ceremonial breastplate, "press your prayer request to [her] heart" and "place your requests on [her] shoulders" (donation suggested).[163]

Hickey also teaches people to speak to their wallets and checkbooks. Says Hickey:

> What do you need? Start creating it. Start speaking about it. Start speaking it into being. Speak to your billfold. Say, "You big, thick billfold full of money." Speak to your checkbook. Say, "You, checkbook, you. You've never been so prosperous since I owned you. You're just jammed full of money."[164]

So that you too can experience big miracles, Hickey will send you tiny mustard seeds to remind you to sow a seed in her ministry. Sowing a seed, of course, is another way of saying, "Please send money." When you send the seed, Hickey promises to send you her booklet titled *God's Seven Keys to Make You Rich*, and assures you that "God will bless and multiply your gift."[165]

In response to a critic who said that Faith teachers were "always following after prosperity" Hickey retorted, "No, we're not. It's following after us."[166] While prosperity may not be following all of Hickey's followers, success is certainly following Hickey. If you can't see her in person, you can see Hickey on scores of television stations and hear her via radio. Her *Outpouring* magazine boasts a circulation of approximately 200,000.[167] She is also the chairman of the Board of Regents of Oral Roberts University in Tulsa, Oklahoma.[168]

Hickey's teachings are for the most part a blend of the theologies of Tilton, Hagin, Copeland, and a host of other "prosperity personalities." Her message is peppered with such Faith jargon as "the God-kind of faith"[169] and "confession brings possession."[170] Hickey's theology has not only been influenced by the kingdom of the cults, but the world of the occult as well. In fact, her most direct exposure to occultism may well have come from serving on the board of Paul Yonggi Cho.[171]

Paul Yonggi Cho (David Yonggi Cho)

Paul Yonggi Cho serves as the pastor of the world's largest church. Located in South Korea, Cho's Full Gospel Yoido Church boasts some 700,000 members.[172] But lest you confuse size and success with spiritual truth, consider that the Buddhist cult of Soka Gakkai (the Buddhist version of "name it and claim it") is larger than Cho's church.[173] Cho rejected his Buddhist background shortly after he was reportedly diagnosed as "having advanced and terminal tuberculosis."[174] Jesus later allegedly appeared to Cho dressed as a fireman and called him to preach.[175]

Strangely, Cho rejected his own name, Paul Yonggi, and replaced it with the name "David" in April 1992. Cho felt it was necessary to change his name in order to reunify the Assemblies of God churches in Korea (Cho had set up a rival Assemblies denomination). Let Cho explain it himself:

> In prayer, God showed me that Paul Cho had to die. I needed to change my name and become a different person. . . . It was one of my greatest sacrifices. Paul Cho was the pastor of the world's largest church.

People around the world knew Paul Cho. Paul Cho's name was on the cover of numerous books. But Paul Cho had to die. So I put Paul Cho to death, and last Easter Sunday it was David Cho who was resurrected. God Himself chose the name David.[176]

Cho's message is essentially a blend of positive thinking and positive confession formulas.[177] The evidence of Cho's allegiance to Faith theology is voluminous. For example, Cho says, "You create the presence of Jesus with your mouth. . . . He is bound by your lips and by your words. . . . Remember that Christ is depending upon you and your spoken word to release His presence."[178]

Cho's distinctive is a concept called the "fourth dimension." Therein lies the fundamental flaw in his theology. According to Cho, the material world makes up the first three dimensions and is under the control of the fourth dimension—the spirit.[179] Cho claims the Holy Spirit revealed this truth to him, along with the means to put it to practical use. He contends that, as spiritual beings, believers and unbelievers alike can alter and create reality "through the development of concentrated visions and dreams in their imaginations."[180] He calls the process "incubation."

Cho's concept of fourth-dimensional thinking is nothing short of occultism. In his bestselling book *The Fourth Dimension*, Cho unveils his departure from historic Christian theology and his entry into the world of the occult. Cho lists four steps in his incubation formula: 1) Visualize a clear-cut goal or idea in your mind; 2) have a burning desire for your objective; 3) pray until you get the guarantee or assurance from God that what you desire is already yours; 4) speak or confess the end result into existence.[181]

You create tangible reality in the third dimension by means of visualization in the fourth dimension. In Cho's own words, "Through visualizing and dreaming you can incubate your future and hatch the results,"[182] much "like a hen sitting on her eggs, incubating them and hatching chickens."[183]

Cho is well aware of his concept's link to occultism, alleging that a number of occult-based religions utilize the power of the fourth dimension.[184] "Sokagakkai [Soka Gakkai] has applied the law of the fourth dimension," says Cho, "and has performed miracles."[185] Likewise, "many people involved in yoga," according to Cho, "are healing the sick by yoga meditation"; and "in Buddhism monks also have performed fantastic miracles."[186] Cho maintains that if non-Christians are able to accomplish incredible feats via the fourth dimension, then Christians, using the same means, ought to be able to do all that and much more.[187]

Charles Capps

Some of the concepts that Charles Capps claims were given to him by God are just plain ridiculous. For example, Capps claims that if someone says, "I'm just dying to do that" or "That just tickled me to death," he is "buddying up with death"; that is, his words could literally come true. According to Capps, these are forms of "perverse speech" that are "contrary to the Word of God." Says Capps, "Adam was smarter than that. It took the Devil over 900 years to kill him, but now the Devil has programmed his language into the human race until people can kill themselves in about seventy years or less by speaking his words."[188]

On the other hand, some of Capps's concepts are outright blasphemous. His statements regarding the virgin birth, for example, convey the heretical notion that Jesus was the final product of God's spoken words or positive confession:

> This is *the* key to understanding the virgin birth. God's
> Word is full of faith and Spirit power. God spoke it. God
> transmitted that image to Mary. She received the image
> inside of her. . . . The embryo that was in Mary's womb
> was nothing more than the Word of God. . . . She con-
> ceived the Word of God.[189]

Here Capps takes the concept of visualization and confession to its most heretical extreme. In his book *Authority in Three Worlds*, Capps even says that the "pure Word of God" he refers to with the impersonal pronoun "it" literally "took flesh upon *itself*."[190] Capps's statement, drawn to its logical conclusion, denies the very personality of the preincarnate Christ, who is the Word made flesh (John 1:1,14).

Ironically, in the same chapter Capps states, "If you continually sit under teaching that is wrong, the spirit of error will be transmitted to you."[191] He makes no doubt about the transmission source of his own peculiar doctrine: "Most of my teaching came from Brother Kenneth Hagin."[192] So with those kind of credentials, it should come as no surprise that Capps was ordained in 1980 by Kenneth Copeland as a minister in the International Convention of Faith Churches and Ministries.[193]

The spirit of error conveyed in the teachings of Capps has been transmitted to millions of people. At last count his books have sold an incredible three million-plus copies.[194] And many more individuals have been impacted by his national radio show.[195]

Let me leave you with Capps's "coon-dog" story. Remember that when Capps tells this story he is dead serious. The point he is trying to make is that confession must always precede possession:

> I'm going to put in my coon-dog story to make this next point clear. There was a guy who was bragging about having the best coon dog in the country.
>
> "He's the fastest thing on a coon you ever saw. And one thing about this dog, he never lies. When he trees, you'll get a coon."
>
> His friend said, "I want to see that dog hunt."
>
> So they went hunting and, sure enough, that dog treed a coon in ten minutes. But after a while the dog treed up a little sapling that didn't have a leaf on it.
>
> The sapling was 20 feet high, not a hole in it, and there was no coon to be found in that tree.
>
> The friend said, "I thought you said this dog didn't lie."
>
> The guy said, "Well, I forgot to tell you one thing. Not very often but once in a while this dog is so fast that sometimes he gets here before the coon does. Just sit down. That coon will be along any minute!"[196]

Charles caps off the story by pointing out that this is precisely how our faith should work. "If your house payment is due January 1, don't start December 29 confessing that you have abundance," advises Capps. "Start confessing a year before the payment is due."[197]

Capps has plowed under Scripture and uprooted the faith of many an ungrounded Christian.

Jerry Savelle

Jerry Savelle's greatest claim to fame may well be his ability to mimic his mentor, Kenneth Copeland. Here is Copeland's description of God compared with Savelle's version.

Copeland's
Description of God

The Bible said He measures the heavens with a 9-inch span. Now the span is the difference between the end of the thumb and the end of the little finger. And that Bible said, in fact—the Amplified translation translates the Hebrew text that way—that He measured out the heavens with a 9-inch span. Well, I got a ruler and measured mine, and my span is 8¾ inches long. So now, God's span is a quarter of an inch longer than mine.

So you see, that faith didn't come billowing out of some giant monster somewhere. It came out of the heart of a being that is very uncanny the way he's very much like you and me. A being that stands somewhere around 6'-2", 6'-3", that weighs somewhere in the neighborhood of a couple of hundred pounds or a little better, has a span of 9 inches across. Glory to God! Hallelujah![198]

Savelle's
Description of God

He measured out heaven with a span. A span is an old English unit of measure that's the distance between the tip of the finger and the tip of the thumb—a span. In fact, the literal Hebrew says that God measured out the heavens with a 9-inch span. See, God is not 437 feet tall, weighing 4000 pounds, and got a fist big around as this room.

He's big, but He's not a monster. He measured out heaven with a 9-inch span. In fact, the Bible says that Jesus was the express image of God. So, I'm convinced that Jesus was—you know—had to look quite a lot like God looked. And He measured out the heavens with a 9-inch span. Now, I don't—my fingers is not quite 9 inches. The distance between my thumb and my finger is not quite 9 inches. So, I know He's bigger than me, thank God. Amen? But He's not some great, big, old thing that couldn't come through the door there, and you know, when He sat down, would fill every seat in the house. I don't serve the Glob.[199]

Savelle repeats virtually every heresy in the Faith movement. When it comes to health, he contradicts Revelation 21 by repeating the standard Faith line—namely, that through the force of faith we can enjoy perfect health here and now:

> Dear God, I can't wait until I get to heaven to be free
> from sickness and disease and grief and sorrow. I found
> out I don't have to have any more of that stuff down

here, in this world that I'm living in, praise God. Sickness and disease cannot come into my world.[200]

When it comes to wealth, Savelle merely repeats the well-worn Faith phrase "You can speak your world into existence." His rendition is as follows:

> Your world, first of all, starts on the inside of you, praise God. And then as you begin to, begin to speak that world into existence. Now I'm not talking about that you're gonna be talking a car into existence, necessarily. The car is already out there somewhere, praise God. But what it will do is come into your world. The house is already out there somewhere, but thank God it will come into your world. The clothes you need is already out there somewhere and they'll come into your world, praise God. The finances you need—God's not gonna rain 20-dollar bills out of heaven, probably. If He wants to, He can. I'll welcome that, but probably that's not the way it will come. They're already in here somewhere. They'll just come into my world, praise God. Amen?[201]

Although Savelle is clearly a Copeland clone, he also mimics many of the other Faith teachers. In the fashion of Price and Capps, Savelle portrays Job as both faithless and foolish—who was to be blamed for all of his own troubles. As Savelle puts it, "Job talked his world into destruction."[202]

Prior to becoming a prosperity preacher, Savelle was an auto body repairman.[203] He has gone from what he himself has characterized as a "fender bender"[204] to what might best be described as a Scripture twister. The transition has proven lucrative. From humble beginnings in 1969, Savelle's World Outreach Center in Fort Worth, Texas, now peddles his material to 36 countries. In addition, his books and tapes reportedly sell at the rate of some 300,000 per year.

Morris' Cerullo

Morris Cerullo claims he first met God when he was eight years old. He was allegedly standing on a ledge getting ready to end it all when God miraculously intervened, filling the room behind Morris with His presence and speaking words of assurance to the young Cerullo.[205] As

Cerullo tells the story, his life from that point on has been a mind-blowing miracle marathon.

At age 14, after being schooled by "the leading rabbis" of a New Jersey town,[206] Cerullo was led out of a Jewish orphanage[207] "by two angelic beings to a refuge that had been prepared for him."[208] Less than a year later Cerullo was transported to heaven, where he had a face-to-face meeting with God.[209] According to the tale, "As Moses beheld the glory of God in the burning bush, Cerullo was taken in the spirit into the heavenlies where he beheld the Presence of God and his life's ministry was clearly detailed before him."[210]

God, who was described by Cerullo as about six feet tall and twice as broad as a human body,[211] took as it were "the lid off Hell and allowed me to see from heaven down into the portals of the underworld."[212] Then, says Cerullo, the Lord spoke to him for the first time. Although Cerullo claims he had never heard these words, it turns out that God told him exactly what He had previously told the prophet Isaiah—namely, "Arise and shine, for My light is come upon thee, and the glory of the Lord shall surround thee, for the multitude of the sea of the Gentiles shall be converted unto thee."[213]

Thus, according to Cerullo, he became a mouthpiece for God, capable of "revealing things which had not yet come to pass, precisely communicating direct 'Thus saith the Lord' words from God."[214] That's why Cerullo gave up his "driving ambition to one day become governor of my state of New Jersey" to become "a minister of the Gospel."[215] Cerullo tells and retells this tale as indisputable proof that he is in fact "a chosen vessel of God."[216]

But is he? His teachings give him away. Ask Cerullo who Jesus was during the incarnation and he'll tell you that when "Jesus came to this world, He came not in His divinity, not as Deity (God)."[217] As for his view of God, Cerullo had this to say:

> Did you know that from the beginning of time the whole purpose of God was to reproduce Himself? . . . Who are you? Come on, *who are you?* Come on, say it: "Sons of God!" Come on, say it! . . . And when we stand up here, brother, you're not looking at Morris Cerullo; you're looking at God. You're looking at Jesus.[218]

In a promotional piece Cerullo acknowledges that "the true test of a prophet is—what he speaks will come to pass."[219] Yet even a cursory examination of his predictions demonstrates that Cerullo's batting average when it comes to prophecy is little better than that of the Watchtower organization. In 1972, for example, Cerullo claims God told him "the U.S. is about to witness a great revival."[220] It is now more than 20 years later and that "great revival" has not yet appeared.

In September 1991 the Holy Spirit allegedly spoke to Cerullo and said, "Son, the world *will* be reached with the gospel by the year 2000!"[221] According to Cerullo, this means that there are only 2921 days left to reach one billion souls. (God has supposedly supplied Cerullo with the Global Solution: Just send him money.)

If Cerullo is to be believed, it would seem that God channels some of the most manipulative fund-raising appeals imaginable through the mouth of his prophet. Here, for example, is one of God's alleged pitches:

> Would you surrender your pocketbooks unto me, saith
> God, and let me be the Lord of your pocketbooks.
> . . . Yea, so be thou obedient unto my voice, saith God.[222]

Paul Crouch

To say that Paul and Jan Crouch are influential in Christian circles may well be the understatement of the year. With an estimated net worth of half a billion dollars,[223] Crouch's Trinity Broadcasting Network owns or carries more than 300 stations, with 150 more in the works.[224] In addition, TBN is "carried on over 1,315 Cable Systems, reaching 16 million households."[225] As Crouch himself puts it, "God has, indeed, given us the MOST POWERFUL VOICE in the history of the WORLD."[226] Unfortunately, that voice is now being used to promote the false doctrines and teachers of the Faith movement.[227]

As a case in point, Avanzini has become a major force in Christian broadcasting as a direct result of TBN's sponsorship. According to Avanzini, when Jan Crouch heard about the "hundredfold" hoax she began to beg him to use it during TBN fund-raisers. "Jan Crouch has asked me a dozen times to speak the hundredfold message," says Avanzini, "and I have to say, 'Jan, anything else, but God is just not letting me do it.' "[228] Eventually, however, Jan's persistence paid off.

Now, during virtually every one of TBN's "Praise-a-Thons," Avanzini prays the hundredfold, and thousands are led to believe that what they give will be multiplied back to them one hundred times. During one "Praise-a-Thon" alone, Avanzini's hundredfold helped TBN to raise millions of dollars.

What many of the people who support TBN do not realize is that much of this money is being used to support doctrines that come out of the kingdom of the cults. Crouch, for example, pays for and promotes people like Roy Blizzard[229] and Joseph Good, both of whom openly deny the trinity.[230] Crouch also gives his staunch support to the United Pentecostal Church (UPC),[231] a cult which claims that the trinity is a pagan doctrine. Truly, it is hard to think of a greater irony than that a broadcasting network named "Trinity" should promote antitrinitarian doctrine!

To those who would speak out against this promotion of cultic doctrine, Crouch issues this ominous warning: "Get out of God's way. Quit blocking God's bridges, or God's *gonna shoot* you if I don't!"[232] So that there can be no ambiguity about his opinion of "heresy hunters," Crouch declares, "I think they're damned and on their way to hell; and I don't think there's any redemption for them."[233]

Despite such violent outbursts, Crouch maintains that he would never compromise the cardinal truths by which we are saved. He even says, "If you don't believe those [cardinal truths], you are not a Christian."[234] Still, the vast majority of the Faith teachers that Crouch promotes overtly deny these cardinal truths. I have personally given Crouch ample evidence to prove that Faith teachers such as Hagin, Copeland, and a host of others compromise the very crux of Christianity: the atonement of Christ upon the cross.[235]

During my personal interactions with Crouch, I have found him to be both reasonable and gracious. Publicly, however, he has made remarks that have caused me to shudder. On one occasion, for instance, Crouch angrily declared, "If you want to criticize Ken Copeland for his preaching on faith, or Dad Hagin, get out of my life! I don't even want to talk to you or hear you. I don't want to see your ugly face. Get out of my face, in Jesus' name."[236]

In a January 1992 letter to one of his financial partners, Crouch wrote that "CRI people . . . should return to their original reason for being, under Dr. Walter Martin, and that was to expose the heresies of the cults, those who depart from the divinity of Christ and His atonement."[237]

But the Faith teachers do in fact "depart from the divinity of Christ and His atonement." Not only have I provided Crouch with solid proof of the fact, but so did Dr. Martin before me. As Dr. Martin said before he went home to be with the Lord, "For ten years I have warned—and I'm on tape and in print on this—that we were heading into the kingdom of the cults with the Faith teachers. You are no longer heading there, baby, you are there!"[238]

Sadly, Paul Crouch is now so entrenched in his position that he has publicly proclaimed, "Those who oppose the Faith message have reached me too late."[239] Crouch calls the Faith message a "revival of truth that comes along in the Word of God," restored by "a few precious men" like Kenyon, Hagin, Copeland, and Savelle.[240]

Lesser Lights

Numerous other proponents also could be cited in the Faith constellation.[241] Examples range from Casey Treat, who says that "God created man and woman an exact *duplicate* of Himself,"[242] to John Osteen, who believes that "faith, created by the Word of God, enables you to reach out into the dimension of the invisible and activate the creative power of God,"[243] to T.L. Osborn, who maintains that "HEALTH, SUCCESS, HAPPINESS and PROSPERITY are God's Will for YOU when you believe His Word enough to ACT ON IT."[244]

Almost every day a new Faith figure seems to emerge out of nowhere. However, they all have one thing in common: The consequences of their teachings are deadly. In some cases the damage is physical; in others, spiritual; and tragically in yet others, both.

We can only pray that the Christian church will finally recognize the Faith proponents for what they are: false teachers who are leading their followers out of the true faith and into the kingdom of the cults.

Appendix A

Are "God's Anointed" Beyond Criticism?

During His Sermon on the Mount, Jesus Christ exhorted His followers not to judge self-righteously or hypocritically. Is this necessarily what Christians do when they question the teachings of "God's anointed" preachers and evangelists? Many teachers who claim such anointing would say so, and many more of their followers commonly reply to all manner of criticism: "Touch not God's anointed."

Some of these teachers even add that such actions carry literally grave consequences. Consider what prominent Faith teacher Kenneth Copeland affirmed in his taped message "Why All Are Not Healed" (#0I-4001):

> There are people attempting to sit in judgment right today over the ministry that I'm responsible for, and the ministry that Kenneth E. Hagin is responsible for. . . . Several people that I know had criticized and called that faith bunch out of Tulsa a cult. And some of 'em are dead right today in an early grave because of it, and there's more than one of them got cancer.

In addition to certain Faith teachers, such sentiments may be found among various groups involved with *shepherding* and other forms of authoritarian rule (from diverse "fivefold" ministries to a host of large and small "fringe churches"). The leaders of these groups are commonly regarded by their followers as having a unique gift and calling that entitles them to unconditional authority—sort of a heavenly carte blanche. To dispute any of their teachings or practices is not distinguished from questioning God Himself.

Advocates of such unquestionable authority assume that Scripture supports their view. Their key biblical proof text is Psalm 105:15: "Touch not mine anointed, and do my prophets no harm" (KJV). But a close examination of this passage reveals that it has nothing to do with challenging the teachings and practices of church leaders.

First, it needs to be noted that the Old Testament phrase "the Lord's anointed" is typically used to refer to the *kings of Israel* (1 Samuel 12:3,5; 24:6,10; 26:9,11,16,23; 2 Samuel 1:14,16; 19:21; Psalm 20:6; Lamentations 4:20), at times specifically to the royal line descended from David (Psalm 2:2; 18:50; 89:38,51), and *not* to especially mighty prophets and teachers. While the text does also mention prophets, in the context of

363

Psalm 105 the reference is undoubtedly to the *patriarchs* in general (verses 8-15; cf. 1 Chronicles 16:15-22), and to Abraham (whom God called a prophet) in particular (Genesis 20:7). It is therefore debatable whether this passage can be applied to select leaders within the body of Christ. Even if the text *can* be applied to certain church leaders today, in the context of this passage the words "touch" and "do harm" have to do with inflicting *physical* harm upon someone. Psalm 105:15 is therefore wholly irrelevant to the issue of *questioning* the teachings of any self-proclaimed man or woman of God.

Moreover, even if we accepted this misinterpretation of Psalm 105:15, how are we to know who not to "touch"—that is, who God's anointed and prophets are? *Because they and their followers say they are?* On such a basis we would have to accept the claims of Sun Myung Moon, Elizabeth Clare Prophet, and virtually all cult leaders to be prophets. *Because they reputedly perform miracles?* The Antichrist and False Prophet will possess that credential (Revelation 13:13-15; 2 Thessalonians 2:9)! No, God's representatives are known above all by their purity of character *and* doctrine (Titus 1:7-9; 2:7,8; 2 Corinthians 4:2; cf. 1 Timothy 6:3,4). If a would-be spokesperson for God cannot pass the biblical tests of character and doctrine, we have no basis for accepting his or her claim, and no reason to fear that in criticizing his or her teaching we might also be rejecting God.

Finally, if any individual Christian is to be considered anointed, then every single Christian must be considered anointed as well. For this is the *only* sense in which the term is used (apart from Christ) in the New Testament: "You [referring to *all* believers] have an anointing from the Holy One" (1 John 2:20). Thus no believer can justifiably claim any sort of *special* status as God's "untouchable anointed" over other believers. With this in mind, it is significant that the apostle John does not use this term with reference to inspired or dynamic preaching or teaching, but to the ability and responsibility of each believer to discern between true and false teachers (verses 18-24).

Nobody's teachings or practices are beyond biblical evaluation—especially influential leaders. According to the Bible, authority and accountability go hand in hand (e.g., Luke 12:48). The greater the responsibility one holds, the greater the accountability one has before God and His people.

Teachers and other leaders of the Christian community should be extremely careful not to mislead any believer, for their calling carries with it a strict judgment (James 3:1). *They should therefore be grateful* when sincere Christians take the time and effort to correct whatever erroneous doctrine they may be holding and preaching to the masses. And if the criticisms are unfounded or unbiblical, they should respond in the manner prescribed by Scripture, which tells them to correct misguided doctrinal opposition with gentle instruction (2 Timothy 2:25).

There is, of course, another side to this issue: Criticism often can be sinful, leading to rebellion and unnecessary division. Christians should respect the leaders that God has given them (Hebrews 13:17). Theirs is the task of assisting the church in its spiritual growth and doctrinal understanding (Ephesians 4:11-16). At the same time, believers should be aware that *false teachers will arise among the Christian fold* (Acts 20:29; 2 Peter 2:1). This makes it imperative for us to test *all* things by Scripture, as the Bereans were commended for doing when they examined the words of even the apostle Paul (Acts 17:11).

Not only is the Bible useful for preaching, teaching, and encouragement, but it is equally valuable for correcting and rebuking (2 Timothy 4:2). In fact, we as Christians are held accountable for proclaiming the whole will of God and warning others of false teachings and those responsible for them (Acts 20:26-28; cf. Ezekiel 33:7-9; 34:1-10).

We need to heed Scripture's repeated warnings to be on guard for false teachings (e.g., Romans 16:17,18; cf. 1 Timothy 1:3,4; 4:16; 2 Timothy 1:13,14; Titus 1:9; 2:1), and to point them out to brothers and sisters in Christ (1 Timothy 4:6). With so much scriptural support, such actions can hardly be considered unbiblical.

Appendix B

Apologetics: The Defense of the Faith

There are three major questions all Christians must be prepared to answer in defending the Christian faith. To help make the process of learning these questions more enjoyable, I have developed three easy-to-remember acronyms. From now on, the words F A C E, F E A T, and M-A-P-S may well take on a whole new meaning for you. Let's look at them one by one.

F-A-C-E*

We begin with the FACE that demonstrates the farce of evolution. Anyone who has gone to school in America has no doubt seen the "face" of *Pithecanthropus erectus*, the Java man. This is the ape-man you may remember staring at you from the pages of your science textbook. You know—the one with the eyes of a philosopher. His slightly perplexed and preoccupied gaze was no doubt designed to give the illusion of intelligence in the making. The truth is, however, that *Pithecanthropus* is little more than the figment of an artist's imagination. But more on that later. Let's begin by looking at the first letter in the acronym F-A-C-E.

F = Fossils. In dealing with the creation/evolution issue, the first thing you should know is that the fossil record is an embarrassment to the evolutionist. Darwin said that the fossil record would bear him out, yet 100 or more years after his death there is no evidence for transitions from one species to another (macroevolution). As Harvard evolutionist Stephen Jay Gould says, the fossil record is an "embarrassment" because of "the extreme rarity of transitional forms in the fossil record [which] persists as the trade secret of paleontology."[1]

A = Ape-men. Next, you should know that ape-men frauds abound. Not only is *Pithecanthropus erectus* a gross mistake (it has since been proved that he was only a gibbon), but so are such notable ape-men as Piltdown man and Peking man. Nebraska man was based on a single tooth found in 1922 by Harold Cook on a farm in Nebraska. With a little creativity, the tooth was imagined to belong to a human skull (it was later proven to belong to a rare pig), the skull was imagined to belong to a

---

* A more in-depth booklet and tape titled *The F-A-C-E that Demonstrates the Farce of Evolution*, by Hendrik Hanegraaff, can be ordered through Memory Dynamics, Box 667, San Juan Capistrano, CA 92693-0667.

skeleton, and the skeleton was drawn to perfection with flesh and features. By the time he hit the London newspapers, Nebraska man was being pictured with Nebraska mom. Imagine that: two people from just one tooth! At the time of the famous Scopes monkey trial in 1925, Nebraska man was presented as evidence to prove that evolution was a fact. But to say that man evolved from apes because they both have bones is as ridiculous as supposing that a bird and a plane are closely related because they both have wings. The chasm between the smartest ape and the dumbest man simply cannot be bridged.

C = Chance. The idea that the complexity of our universe came about through chance is a statistical impossibility. Even forming something as basic as a protein molecule by random processes is unthinkable. Despite the evidence, many people seem convinced that, given enough time, even improbable events become probable. This argument, however, only seems reasonable when specifics are not considered. We can put it into perspective with the "million monkeys" illustration.[2]

If a million monkeys continually typed on a million typewriters, one of them might eventually pound out a Shakespearean play. Now assume a million monkeys typed 24 hours a day at 100 words a minute on typewriters that had 40 keys. Suppose each word of the play contained four letters. How long would it take to get the first four words? About 800 billion years! No one could imagine the amount of time required to produce the first scene.

E = Entropy. The second law of thermodynamics—entropy—militates against the theory of evolution. Evolution postulates that everything goes from randomness to complexity and from disorder to order. Entropy demonstrates that everything is going in exactly the opposite direction—toward randomness and disorder.[3] It should also be noted that evolution is a low-grade hypothesis, while entropy is a well-documented law of science. Entropy will serve to remind you of many other scientific laws that could be cited to refute the theory of evolution. Among the others are the law of conservation and the law of cause-and-effect.

While a great deal more could be said, I trust that this brief overview will motivate you to become equipped to defend the faith when it comes to the issue of origins. Remember: If Adam did not eat the forbidden fruit, if he did not fall into a life of constant sin terminating in death, what need is there for redemption? What all this means is that if you cannot defend your faith when it comes to the Genesis account of creation, the rest of the Bible becomes irrelevant.

F-E-A-T*

The resurrection of Jesus Christ is the greatest F-E-A-T in the annals of history. Through the resurrection, Jesus demonstrated that He does not stand in a line of peers with Buddha, Mohammed, or any other founders of a world religion. They died and are still dead, but Christ is risen. As someone has well said, the resurrection is the very capstone in the arch of Christianity; if it is removed, all else crumbles. It is the singular doctrine which elevated Christianity above all the pagan religions of the ancient Mediterranean world. As Paul put it, "If Christ has not been raised, your faith is futile; you are still in your sins. . . . If only for this life we have hope in Christ, we are to be pitied more than all men" (1 Corinthians 15:17,19). It is precisely because of the resurrection's strategic importance that each Christian must be prepared to defend its historicity. Let's use the acronym F-E-A-T to help us do just that.

F = Fact. The resurrection of Jesus Christ is an undeniable *fact* of history. And that's not just anyone's opinion. That was the opinion of Dr. Simon Greenleaf, the greatest authority on legal evidence of the nineteenth century. In fact, he was the famous Royall Professor of Law at Harvard and was directly responsible for the school's rise to eminence among American law schools. After being goaded by his students into examining the evidence for the resurrection, Greenleaf suggested that any cross-examination of the eyewitness testimonies recorded in Scripture would result in "an undoubting conviction of their integrity, ability and truth." Dr. Greenleaf not only became a Christian, but in 1846 wrote a defense for the resurrection titled: *An Examination of the Testimony of the Four Evangelists by the Rules of Evidence Administered in the Court of Justice.*

E = Empty Tomb. The first major fact supporting the resurrection of Christ is the empty tomb. Even the enemies of Christ admitted that the tomb was empty. The record shows that they even attempted to bribe the guards to say the body had been stolen (Matthew 28:11-15). If the Jewish leaders had stolen the body, they could have later openly displayed it to prove that Jesus had not risen from the dead. Although many flawed theories have been concocted over the years, the fact of the empty tomb has never been refuted.

---

* A more in-depth booklet and tape titled *The F-E-A-T that Demonstrates the Fact of the Resurrection,* by Hendrik Hanegraaff, can be ordered through Memory Dynamics, Box 667, San Juan Capistrano, CA 92693-0667.

A = Appearances. The second major fact supporting the resurrection is the appearances of Christ after the resurrection. He appeared to over 500 eyewitnesses at a single time (1 Corinthians 15:6). He also appeared to many other people as well, providing "many convincing proofs" of His resurrection (Acts 1:3). Christ in His resurrection body was even touched on two occasions (Matthew 28:9; John 20:17), and challenged the disciples (Luke 24:39) and Thomas (John 20:27) to feel His wounds.

T = Transformation. The third great apologetic for the resurrection is the radical transformation which took place in the lives of Christ's disciples. Before the resurrection, they might best have been characterized as cowards. After the resurrection, they were transformed into lions of the faith. Despite intense persecution and even cruel deaths they testified to the truth of the resurrection.

While it is conceivable that some people might die for what they believed to be the truth, it is inconceivable that so many would die for what they knew to be false. As Greenleaf puts it, "If it were morally possible for them to have been deceived in this matter, every human motive operated to lead them to discover and avow their error. . . . If then their testimony was not true, there was no possible motive for this fabrication."[4]

Not only did the resurrection of Christ transform the disciples from cowards to lions of the faith, but His resurrection continues to transform lives today. Because Christ lives, the Scripture says, we will live also. In an instant, in the twinkling of an eye, our bodies shall be transformed into resurrected bodies like unto His resurrected body. Indeed, the evidence for Christ's resurrection is so overwhelming that no one can examine it with an open mind without becoming convinced of its truth.

M-A-P-S*

Finally, to defend the faith we must be equipped to demonstrate that the Bible is divine rather than human in origin. If we can successfully accomplish this, we can answer a host of other objections simply by appealing to Scripture. To chart the course we will use the acronym M-A-P-S. Since most Bibles have maps in the back, this should prove to be a memorable association.

---

* A more in-depth booklet and tape titled *MAPS to Chart Our Course to Biblical Reliability*, by Hank Hanegraaff, can be ordered through Memory Dynamics, Box 667, San Juan Capistrano, CA 92693-0667.

M = *Manuscripts*. Since we don't have the original biblical manuscripts, the question is, "How good are the copies?" The answer is that the Bible has stronger manuscript support than any other work of classical literature—including Homer, Plato, Aristotle, Caesar, and Tacitus. The reliability of Scripture is also confirmed through the eyewitness credentials of the authors. Moses, for example, participated in and was an eyewitness to the remarkable events of the Egyptian captivity, the Exodus, the 40 years in the desert, and Israel's final encampment before entering the Promised Land, all of which are accurately chronicled in the Old Testament.

The New Testament has the same kind of eyewitness authenticity. Luke says that he gathered the eyewitness testimony and "carefully investigated everything" (Luke 1:1-3). Peter reminded his readers that the disciples "did not follow cleverly invented stories" but "were eyewitness of [Jesus'] majesty" (2 Peter 1:16).

Secular historians confirm the many events, people, places, and customs chronicled in the New Testament. Secular historians like Josephus (before A.D. 100), the Roman Tacitus (around A.D. 120), the Roman Suetonius (A.D. 110), and the Roman governor Pliny the Younger (A.D. 110) all affirm historical New Testament references. Early church leaders such as Irenaeus, Tertullian, Julius Africanus, and Clement of Rome—all writing before A.D. 250—also shed light on New Testament historical accuracy. Even skeptical historians agree that the New Testament is a remarkable historical document.

A = *Archaeology*. Over and over again, comprehensive field work (archaeology) and careful biblical interpretation affirms the reliability of the Bible. It is telling when a secular scholar must revise his biblical criticism in light of solid archaeological evidence.

For years, critics dismissed the book of Daniel, partly because there was no evidence that a king named Belshazzar ruled in Babylon during that period. Later archaeological research, however, confirmed that the reigning monarch, Nabonidus, appointed Belshazzar as his co-regent while he was waging war away from Babylon.

One of the most well-known New Testament examples concerns the books of Luke and Acts. A biblical skeptic, Sir William Ramsay, was trained as an archaeologist and then set out to disprove the historical reliability of this portion of the New Testament. But through his painstaking Mediterranean archaeological trips, he became converted as, one after another, the historical allusions of Luke were proved accurate. Truly, with every turn of the archaeologist's spade we continue to see evidence for the trustworthiness of Scripture.

P = Prophecy. The Bible records predictions of events that could not be known or predicted by chance or common sense. Surprisingly, the predictive nature of many Bible passages was once a popular argument (by liberals) *against* the reliability of the Bible. Critics argued that various passages were written *later* than the biblical texts indicated, because they recounted events that happened sometimes hundreds of years later than when they supposedly were written. They concluded that, subsequent to the events, literary editors went back and "doctored" the original, non-predictive texts.

But this is simply wrong. Careful research *affirms* the predictive accuracy of the Bible. For example, the book of Daniel (written before 530 B.C.) accurately predicts the progression of kingdoms from Babylon through the Medo-Persian Empire, the Greek Empire, and then the Roman Empire, culminating in the persecution and suffering of the Jews under Antiochus IV Epiphanes, his desecration of the temple, his untimely death, and freedom for the Jews under Judas Maccabeus (165 B.C.).

Old Testament prophecies concerning the Phoenician city of *Tyre* were fulfilled in ancient times, including prophecies that the city would be opposed by many nations (Ezekiel 26:3); its walls would be destroyed and towers broken down (26:4); and its stones, timbers, and debris would be thrown into the water (26:12). Similar prophecies were fulfilled concerning *Sidon* (Ezekiel 28:23; Isaiah 23; Jeremiah 27:3-6; 47:4) and *Babylon* (Jeremiah 50:13,39; 51:26,42,43,58; Isaiah 13:20,21).

Since Christ is the culminating theme of the Old Testament and the Living Word of the New Testament, it should not surprise us that prophecies regarding Him outnumber all others. Many of these prophecies would have been impossible for Jesus to deliberately conspire to fulfill—such as His descent from Abraham, Isaac, and Jacob (Genesis 12:3; 17:19); His birth in Bethlehem (Micah 5:2); His crucifixion with criminals (Isaiah 53:12); the piercing of His hands and feet on the cross (Psalm 22:16); the soldiers' gambling for His clothes (Psalm 22:18); the piercing of His side and the fact that His bones were not broken at His death (Zechariah 12:10; Psalm 34:20); and His burial among the rich (Isaiah 53:9). Jesus also predicted His own death and resurrection (John 2:19-22). *Predictive prophecy* is a principle of Bible reliability that often reaches even the hard-boiled skeptic!

S = Statistics. It is statistically preposterous that any or all of the Bible's specific, detailed prophecies could have been fulfilled through chance, good guessing, or deliberate deceit. When you look at some of the improbable prophecies of the Old and New Testaments, it seems incredible that skeptics—knowing the authenticity and historicity of the texts—could reject the statistical verdict: The Bible is the Word of God, and Jesus is the Divine Messiah, just as Scripture predicted many times and in many ways.

The Bible was written over a span of 1600 years by 40 authors in three languages (Hebrew, Aramaic, and Greek), on hundreds of subjects. And yet there is one consistent, noncontradictory theme that runs through it all: *God's redemption of humankind.* Clearly, *statistical probability* concerning biblical prophecy is a powerful indicator of the trustworthiness of Scripture.

The next time someone denies the reliability of Scripture, just remember the acronym M-A-P-S, and you will be equipped to give an answer and a reason for the hope that lies within you. *M*anuscripts, *A*rchaeology, *P*rophecy, and *S*tatistics not only chart a secure course through the turnpikes of skepticism but also demonstrate conclusively that the Bible is indeed divine rather than human in origin.

Appendix C

The Three
Universal Creeds

The Apostles' Creed

I believe in God the Father Almighty, Maker of heaven and earth.

And in Jesus Christ, His only Son, our Lord; who was conceived by the Holy Ghost, born of the Virgin Mary; suffered under Pontius Pilate, was crucified, dead, and buried; He descended into hell; the third day He rose again from the dead; He ascended into heaven, and sitteth on the right hand of God the Father Almighty; from thence He shall come to judge the quick and the dead.

I believe in the Holy Ghost; the holy Catholic Church, the communion of saints; the forgiveness of sins; the resurrection of the body; and the life everlasting. Amen.

The Nicene Creed

I believe in one God, the Father Almighty, Maker of heaven and earth, and of all things visible and invisible.

And in one Lord Jesus Christ, the only-begotten Son of God, begotten of the Father before all worlds, God of God, Light of Light, very God of very God, begotten, not made, being of one substance with the Father; by whom all things were made; who for us men, and for our salvation, came down from heaven, and was incarnate by the Holy Ghost of the Virgin Mary, and was made man, and was crucified also for us under Pontius Pilate; He suffered and was buried; and the third day He rose again according to the Scriptures; and ascended into heaven, and sitteth on the right hand of the Father; and He shall come again with glory to judge the quick and the dead; whose kingdom shall have no end.

And I believe in the Holy Ghost, the Lord and Giver of life, who proceedeth from the Father and the Son; who with the Father and the Son together is worshiped and glorified; who spoke by the Prophets.

And I believe in one holy Catholic and Apostolic Church.

I acknowledge one Baptism for the remission of sins; and I look for the resurrection of the dead, and the life of the world to come. Amen.

The Creed of Athanasius,
Written Against the Arians

Whosoever will be saved, before all things it is necessary that he hold the Catholic faith.

Which faith except every one do keep whole and undefiled, without doubt he shall perish everlastingly.

[Concordia Triglotta, p. 33]

And the Catholic faith is this, that we worship one God in Trinity, and Trinity in Unity;

Neither confounding the Persons, nor dividing the Substance.

For there is one Person of the Father, another of the Son, and another of the Holy Ghost.

But the Godhead of the Father, of the Son, and of the Holy Ghost is all one: the glory equal, the majesty coeternal.

Such as the Father is, such is the Son, and such is the Holy Ghost.

The Father uncreate, the Son uncreate, and the Holy Ghost uncreate.

The Father incomprehensible, the Son incomprehensible, and the Holy Ghost incomprehensible.

The Father eternal, the Son eternal, and the Holy Ghost eternal.

And yet they are not three Eternals, but one Eternal.

As there are not three Uncreated nor three Incomprehensibles, but one Uncreated and one Incomprehensible.

So likewise the Father is almighty, the Son almighty, and the Holy Ghost almighty.

And yet they are not three Almighties, but one Almighty.

So the Father is God, the Son is God, and the Holy Ghost is God.

And yet they are not three Gods, but one God.

So likewise the Father is Lord, the Son Lord, and the Holy Ghost Lord.

And yet not three Lords, but one Lord.

For like as we are compelled by the Christian verity to acknowledge every Person by Himself to be God and Lord,

So are we forbidden by the catholic religion to say, There be three Gods, or three Lords.

The Father is made of none; neither created nor begotten.

The Son is of the Father alone: not made, nor created, but begotten.

The Holy Ghost is of the Father and of the Son: neither made, nor created, nor begotten, but proceeding.

So there is one Father, not three Fathers; one Son, not three Sons; one Holy Ghost, not three Holy Ghosts.

And in this Trinity none is before or after other; none is greater or less than another;

But the whole three Persons are coeternal together, and coequal: so that in all things, as is aforesaid, the Unity in Trinity and the Trinity in Unity is to be worshiped.

He, therefore, that will be saved must thus think of the Trinity.

Furthermore, it is necessary to everlasting salvation that he also believe faithfully the incarnation of our Lord Jesus Christ.

For the right faith is, that we believe and confess that our Lord Jesus Christ, the Son of God, is God and Man.

[Concordia Triglotta, p. 35]

God of the Substance of the Father, begotten before the worlds; and Man of the substance of His mother, born in the world;

Perfect God and perfect Man, of a reasonable soul and human flesh subsisting.

Equal to the Father as touching His Godhead, and inferior to the Father as touching His manhood;

Who, although He be God and Man, yet He is not two, but one Christ:

One, not by conversion of the Godhead into flesh, but by taking the manhood into God;

One altogether; not by confusion of Substance, but by unity of Person.

For as the reasonable soul and flesh is one man, so God and Man is one Christ;

Who suffered for our salvation; descended into hell, rose again the third day from the dead;

He ascended into heaven; He sitteth on the right hand of the Father, God Almighty; from whence He shall come to judge the quick and the dead.

At whose coming all men shall rise again with their bodies, and shall give an account of their own works.

And they that have done good shall go into life everlasting; and they that have done evil, into everlasting fire.

This is the catholic faith; which except a man believe faithfully and firmly, he cannot be saved.

Before We Begin
1. I adapted this illustration from one provided by Stephen Covey, *The 7 Habits of Highly Effective People* (New York: Simon & Schuster, 1990), 30-31. Although I disagree with a number of the concepts presented by Covey, it is a good read for those who are equipped to discern wheat from chaff.

Part 1—Turning the Truth into Mythology
1. Kenneth Copeland: "Heaven has a north and a south and an east and a west. Consequently, it must be a planet." ("Spirit, Soul and Body I" [Fort Worth, TX: Kenneth Copeland Ministries, 1985] audiotape #01-0601, side 1.)
2. Kenneth Copeland: See chapter 10, page 121.
3. Charles Capps: "God filled His words with faith to cause the things He said to come into manifestation. There was an image inside Him. He expressed it in words." (*The Substance of Things* [Tulsa, OK: Harrison House, 1990], 19.)
4. Kenneth Copeland: "Faith is a power force. It is a tangible force. It is a conductive force." (*The Force of Faith* [Fort Worth, TX: KCP Publications, 1989], 10.)
5. Charles Capps: "Faith is the substance, the raw material.... Faith is the substance that God used to create the universe, and He transported that faith with His words.... Faith is the substance of things, but you can't see faith. Faith is a spiritual force." (*Changing the Seen & Shaping the Unseen* [Tulsa, OK: Harrison House, 1980], 14-15.)
6. Jerry Savelle: See chapter 5, page 68.
7. Kenneth Copeland: "You don't think earth was first, do you? Huh? Well, you don't think that God made man in His image, and then made earth in some other image? There is not anything under this whole sun that's new. Are you hearing what I'm saying? This is all a copy. It's a copy of home. It's a copy of the Mother Planet. Where God lives, He made a little one just like His and put us on it." ("Following the Faith of Abraham I" [Fort Worth, TX: Kenneth Copeland Ministries, 1989], audiotape #01-3001, side 1.)
8. Charles Capps: "He framed the world with His words. You can't build without substance. He took words—faith-filled words were God's substance. Here, essentially, is what God did. God filled His words with faith. He used His words as containers to hold His faith and contain that spiritual force and transport it out there into the vast darkness by saying '*Light be!*' That's the way God transported His faith causing creation and transformation." (*Dynamics of Faith & Confession* [Tulsa, OK: Harrison House, 1987], 28-29, emphasis in original.)
9. Charles Capps: "God said, *Let us make man in our image after our likeness.* The word *likeness* in the original Hebrew means "an exact duplication in kind." ...*Adam was an exact duplication of God's kind!*" (*Authority in Three Worlds* [Tulsa, OK: Harrison House, 1982], 15-16, emphasis in original.)
10. Paul Crouch, speaking to Kenneth Copeland, said: "Somebody said—I don't know who said it—but they claim that you Faith teachers declare that we are gods. You're a god. I'm a god. Small 'g' now, but we are the gods of this world.... Well, are you a god—small 'g'?" To this, Jan Crouch, referring to Copeland, enthusiastically exclaimed: "He's gonna say, 'Yes.' I love it." ("Praise the Lord" program on TBN [5 February 1986].)
11. Paul Crouch: "He [God] doesn't even draw a distinction between Himself and us.... You know what else that's settled, then, tonight? This hue and cry and controversy that has been spawned by the Devil to try and bring dissension within the body of Christ that we are gods. I am a little god!... I have His name. I'm one with Him. I'm in covenant relation. I am a little god! Critics, be gone!" ("Praise the Lord" program on TBN [7 July 1986].)
12. Kenneth Copeland: "God *spoke* Adam into existence in authority with words (Gen. 1:26,28). These words struck Adam's body in the face. His body and God were exactly the same size." (*Holy Bible: Kenneth Copeland Reference Edition* [Fort Worth, TX: Kenneth Copeland Ministries, 1991], 45, emphasis in original.)
13. Kenneth Copeland: "God's reason for creating Adam was His desire to reproduce Himself. I mean a reproduction of Himself, and in the Garden of Eden He did just that. He was not a little like God. He was not almost like God. He was not subordinate to God even.... Adam is as much like God as you could get, just the same as Jesus.... Adam, in the Garden of Eden, was God manifested in the flesh." ("Following the Faith of Abraham I," side 1.)
14. Kenneth E. Hagin: "Originally, God made the earth and the fullness thereof, giving Adam dominion over all the works of His hands. In other words, Adam was the god of this world." (*The Believer's Authority*, 2d ed. [Tulsa, OK: Kenneth Hagin Ministries, 1991], 19.)

15. Frederick K.C. Price: "God can't do anything in this earth realm except what we, the body of Christ, allow Him to do. Now that statement is so—that's so—that's so foreign and so contrary to tradition that, like I said, if they could get their hands on me right now most evangelicals would burn me at the stake and dismember me and feed me to the crocodiles, because they'll consider that statement to be just heresy." ("Ever Increasing Faith" program on TBN [1 May 1992], audiotape #PR11.) Cf. chapter 6, 85.

16. Benny Hinn: "Adam was a super-being when God created him. I don't know whether people know this, but he was the first superman that really ever lived. First of all, the Scriptures declare clearly that he had dominion over the fowls of the air, the fish of the sea—which means he used to fly. Of course, how can he have dominion over the birds and not be able to do what they do? The word 'dominion' in the Hebrew clearly declares that if you have dominion over a subject, that you do everything that subject does. In other words, that subject, if it does something you cannot do, you don't have dominion over it. I'll prove it further. Adam not only flew, he flew to space. He was—with one thought he would be on the moon." ("Praise the Lord" program on TBN [26 December 1991].)

17. Kenneth Copeland: "Adam was made in the image of God. He was as much female as he was male. He was exactly like God. Then God separated him and removed the female part. Woman means 'man with the womb.' Eve had as much authority as Adam did as long as they stayed together." (*Sensitivity of Heart* [Fort Worth, TX: KCP Publications, 1984], 23.)

18. Kenneth Copeland: "He [Lucifer or Satan] tried to use the power of words against God.... At that point, their words clashed and God's Word—the Word of a free Spirit, a Spirit with authority—reigned in victory over the word of an angelic power." (*The Power of the Tongue* [Fort Worth, TX: KCP Publications, 1980], 6-7.)

19. Kenneth E. Hagin: "Adam committed high treason and sold out to Satan, and Satan, through Adam, became the god of this world. Adam didn't have the moral right to commit treason, but he had the legal right to do so." (*The Believer's Authority*, 19.)

20. Kenneth E. Hagin: "God came down in the cool of the day in the Garden of Eden to commune and fellowship with him [Adam], as he had in the past. And he couldn't find him. He called out to him, 'Adam, where art thou?' And he said, 'I hid myself.' Why? Because of sin. Because, first, sin separates you from God. Secondly, by sinning, by listening to the Devil, he took upon himself the nature of the Devil into his spirit being." ("How Jesus Obtained His Name" [Tulsa, OK: Kenneth Hagin Ministries, n.d.], audiotape #44H01, side 2.)

21. E.W. Kenyon: "Man [i.e., Adam] was actually Born Again when he sinned. That is, he was born of the Devil. He became a partaker of Satanic Nature." (*The Father and His Family*, 17th ed. [Lynnwood, WA: Kenyon's Gospel Publishing Society, 1964], 48.)

22. Benny Hinn: "He [the Holy Spirit] says, 'God's original plan is that the woman was to bring forth children out of her side.'... Adam gave birth to his wife out of his side. It was sin that turned the thing around.... And it was sin that transformed her flesh and her body. When God took the woman out of man, He closed up his rib. But she was created identically as him. In other words, she was created with an opening in her side, and children were supposed to be born. And I get that from the very fact that you'll never see birth spiritually, except from the side." ("Our Position In Christ #5—An Heir of God" [Orlando, FL: Orlando Christian Center, 1990], audiotape #A031190-5, side 2.)

23. E.W. Kenyon: "Adam evidently had a legal right to transfer this dominion and authority into the hands of the enemy. God has been obliged through the long period of human history to recognize Satan's legal standing, and legal right and authority, and on this ground, and this only, can we understand the legal side of the Plan of Redemption.... Adam had legally transferred to him [Satan] the Authority with which God had invested him." (*The Father and His Family*, 38-39.)

24. Kenneth Copeland: "God had no avenue of lasting faith or moving in the earth. He had to have covenant with somebody.... He had to be invited in, in other words, or He couldn't come.... God is on the outside looking in. In order to have any say so in the earth, He's gonna have to be in agreement with a man here." ("God's Covenants With Man II" [Fort Worth, TX: Kenneth Copeland Ministries, 1985], audiotape #01-4404, side 1.)

25. Kenneth Copeland: "I was shocked when I found out who the biggest failure in the Bible actually is.... The biggest one is God.... I mean, He lost His top-ranking, most anointed angel; the first man He ever created; the first woman He ever created; the whole earth and all the fullness therein; a third of the angels, at least—that's a big loss, man.... Now, the reason you don't think of God as a failure is He never said He's a failure. And you're not a failure till you say you're one." ("Praise-a-Thon" program on TBN [April 1988].)

26. Frederick K.C. Price: "Adam, as I said, gave it [the earth] away to the serpent, to the Devil. As a result of it, he got his behind kicked out of the garden. He went out of Eden, out of the garden. He began to wander around, and he has troubles from day one. Now God was out of the business. God was out of the earth realm. God had no more stock in this earth realm. No more. None at all. Nothing He could do. Not a thing in the world He could do.... The only way God could get back into this earth realm, He had to have an invitation. Ha-hah! He had to have an invitation. And so, God looked around—saw different men, saw Noah, saw different ones. He gave them a few instructions. They did what He said. So and so and so and so. But, finally, He got to a point where He had His plan ready for operation. And He saw a man named Abraham." ("Ever Increasing Faith" program on TBN [1 May 1992], audiotape #PR11.)

27. Kenneth Copeland: See chapter 19, 212.

28. E.W. Kenyon: "[A]s soon as they [the parties of the covenant] cut the covenant, they are recognized as blood brothers by others, and they are called the blood brothers.... God and Abraham had entered the Covenant.... God cut the Covenant with Abraham." (*The Blood Covenant* [Lynnwood, WA: Kenyon's Gospel Publishing Society, 1969], 14, 16.)

29. Charles Capps: "In this [the Abrahamic Covenant], God is establishing some legal entry into the earth, and He is giving Abraham access to Himself.... This Covenant gave God legal entry into the earth through Abraham.... Until that time God was, to a certain extent, still on the outside looking in. He needed a legal entry through man so that He could destroy the works of the Devil who was running rampant on earth.... Abraham was God's avenue of entry into the earth." (*Authority in Three Worlds*, 60-61.)

30. Kenneth Copeland: "Once that [Abrahamic] covenant was established, God began to release His Word into the earth. He began to paint a picture of a Redeemer, a man who would be the manifestation of His Word in the earth." (*The Power of the Tongue*, 9.)

31. Kenneth Copeland: "So before Jesus came to the earth, God spoke His Word and then spoke His Word again. How many times did He say the Messiah was coming? It was prophesied over hundreds, even thousands, of years. He kept saying, 'He is coming. He is coming.' The circumstances in the earth made it look as if there was no way He could accomplish it; but He just kept saying it. He would not be moved by what He saw.... God would not relent." (Ibid., 9-10.)

32. Kenneth Copeland: "The angels spoke the words of the covenant to her [Mary]. She pondered them in her heart, and those words became the seed. And the Spirit of God hovered over her and generated that seed, which was the Word that the angel spoke to her. And there was conceived in her, the Bible says, a holy thing. The Word literally became flesh." ("The Abrahamic Covenant" [Fort Worth, TX: Kenneth Copeland Ministries, 1985], audiotape #01-4405, side 2.)

33. Benny Hinn: "The Bible says the prophets spoke the Word not knowing what they were saying. But 4000 years passed when the *Word* became a human being and walked and talked and moved. The spoken Word became a human being. The spoken Word became flesh. The spoken Word got legs on, arms, eyes, hair, a body. And He was no longer saying, 'Thus sayeth the Lord.' He was saying, 'I say unto you.' The Word that was spoken through the lip [sic] of prophets was now walking on the seashore of Galilee. ("Benny Hinn" program on TBN [15 December 1990, emphasis in original]. This message, titled "The Person of Jesus" [delivered during Orlando Christian Center's Sunday morning service on 2 December 1991], comprises Part Four of Hinn's six-part series on "The Revelation of Jesus" [Orlando Christian Center, 1991], videotape #TV-292.)

34. John Avanzini: "Jesus had a nice house, a big house—big enough to have company stay the night with Him at the house. Let me show you His house. Go over to John the first chapter and I'll show you His house.... Now, child of God, that's a house big enough to have company stay the night in. There's His house." ("Believer's Voice of Victory" program on TBN [20 January 1991].)

35. John Avanzini: "Jesus was handling big money because that treasurer He had was a thief. Now you can't tell me that a ministry with a treasurer that's a thief can operate on a few pennies. It took big money to operate that ministry because Judas was stealing out of that bag." ("Praise the Lord" program on TBN [15 September 1988].)

36. John Avanzini: "John 19 tells us that Jesus wore designer clothes. Well, what else you gonna call it? Designer clothes—that's blasphemy. No, that's what we call them today. I mean, you didn't get the stuff He wore off the rack. It wasn't a one-size-fits-all deal. No, this was custom stuff. It was the kind of a garment that kings and rich merchants wore. Kings and rich merchants wore that garment." ("Believer's Voice of Victory" program on TBN [20 January 1991].)

37. Frederick K.C. Price: "The Bible says that He [Jesus] had a treasurer—a treasury (they called it "the bag"); that they had one man who was the treasurer, named Judas Iscariot; and the rascal was stealing out of the bag for three-and-a-half years and nobody knew that he was stealing. You know why? Because there was so much in it, He couldn't tell. Nobody could tell that anything was missing. If He had three oranges in the bottom of the bag and he stole two of them, don't tell me He wouldn't know that some was missing. Beside that, if Jesus didn't have anything, what do you need a treasury for? A treasury is for surplus. It's not for that which you're spending. It's only for surplus—to hold it until you need to spend it. Therefore, He must have had a whole lot that needed to be held in advance that He wasn't spending. So He must have had more than He was living on." ("Ever Increasing Faith" program on TBN [23 November 1990].)

38. Charles Capps: "Notice that when Jesus said, 'I have finished the work' [John 17:4], we know that He had *not* finished the work. But I want you to catch something in the way He prayed and the way He talked—*He spoke the end results.* He never spoke what *was.* He never admitted death or defeat.... Jesus was speaking the end results in His prayer to the Father." (*Authority in Three Worlds*, 258-59, emphasis in original.)

39. Kenneth Hagin: "Jesus used the fig tree to demonstrate that He had that God-kind of faith, then He said to the disciples—and to us—'*You* have that kind of faith.'... Jesus said He had the God-kind of faith; He encouraged His disciples to exercise that kind of faith; and He said that 'whosoever' could do it.... That is why Jesus said, '*whosoever shall say... and shall not doubt IN HIS HEART.*'" (*Having Faith in Your Faith* [Tulsa, OK: Kenneth Hagin Ministries, 1988], 3, emphasis in original.)

40. John Avanzini: "You don't think these Apostles didn't walk around with money? I mean, they had money. I just thank God that I saw this and gave up the denominational line and got on God's line before I starved me and all my family to death. Go to Acts 24. I mean, you don't think there wasn't money in this Paul's life?... Paul had the kind of money that people, that government officials, would, would block up justice to try to get a bribe out of old Paul." ("Believer's Voice of Victory" program on TBN [20 January 1991].)

41. Kenneth Copeland (through whom Jesus allegedly delivered the following prophecy): "They crucified Me [Jesus] for claiming that I was God. But I didn't claim I was God; I just claimed I walked with Him [the Father] and that He was in Me." ("Take Time to Pray," *Believer's Voice of Victory* 15, 2 [February 1987]:9.)

42. E.W. Kenyon: "Jesus was conceived without sin. His body was not mortal. His body did not become mortal until the Father laid our sin nature upon Him when He hung on the cross. The moment that He became sin, His body became mortal, only then could He die. When this happened, spiritual death, the nature of Satan, took possession of His Spirit.... He was to partake of Spiritual Death, the nature of the Adversary.... Jesus knew that the moment had come, and He was to be made Sin. He must partake of that dread nature of the Adversary. His body would become mortal. Satan would become His master.... He [Jesus] had been lifted up as a serpent. Serpent is Satan. Jesus knew He was going to be lifted up, united with the Adversary." (*What Happened from the Cross to the Throne* [Lynnwood, WA: Kenyon's Gospel Publishing Society, 1969], 20, 33, 44-45.)

43. Benny Hinn: "I'm going to be led by the Holy Ghost today. Is that all right with you?... God came from heaven, became a man, made man into little gods, went back to heaven as a man. He faces the Father as a man. I face devils as the son of God. Do you see what I'm talking about? You say, 'Benny, am I a little God?' You're a son of God, aren't you? You're a child of God, aren't you? You're a daughter of God, aren't you? What else are you? Quit your nonsense! What else are you? If you say, 'I am,' you're saying I'm a part of Him, right? Is He God? Are you His offspring? Are you His children? You can't be human! You can't! You can't! God didn't give birth to flesh. He gave birth to a new creation. And the new creation is not flesh and blood and bone, for no flesh and blood would inherit heaven. Did you hear what I said? Some of you didn't really hear what I said. You said, 'Well, that's heresy.' No, that's your crazy brain saying that." ("Our Position in Christ #2—The Word Made Flesh" [Orlando, FL: Orlando Christian Center, 1991], audiotape #A031190-2, side 2.)

44. Benny Hinn: "When you were born again the Word was made flesh in you. And you became flesh of His flesh and bone of His bone. Don't tell me you have Jesus. You *are* everything He was and everything He is and ever He shall be.... It [the new man] says, 'I am as He is.' That's what it says. As He is, so are we in this world. Jesus said, 'Go in my name, go in my stead.' Don't say, 'I have.' Say, 'I am, I am, I am, I am, I am.' That's why you never ever, ever, ever

ought to say, 'I'm sick.' How can you be sick if you're the new creation? Say, 'I'm healed!' Don't say, 'I'm a sinner.' The new creature is no sinner. I'm the righteousness of God in Christ." (Ibid.)

45. Frederick K.C. Price: "Do you think that the punishment for our sin was to die on a cross? If that were the case, the two thieves could have paid our price. No, the punishment was to go into hell itself and to serve time in hell separated from God.... Satan and all the demons of hell thought that they had Him bound. And they threw a net over Jesus and they dragged Him down to the very pit of hell itself to serve our sentence." (*Ever Increasing Faith Messenger* [June 1980], 7; quoted in D.R. McConnell, *A Different Gospel* [Peabody, MA: Hendrickson Publishers, 1988], 120.)

46. Charles Capps: "The sinless son of God became as a serpent that He might swallow up all evil.... If you will behold what happened when the sin offering was made and the fact that Jesus became a serpent upon the pole, it will change your life.... Jesus died spiritually, not for any of His own sin! He became the serpent on the pole, the snake on the ground, in the Old Testament type." (*Authority in Three Worlds*, 177, 166-67.)

47. Paul E. Billheimer: "The Father turned Him over, not only to the agony and death of Calvary, but to the satanic torturers of His pure spirit as part of the just dessert of the sin of all the race. As long as Christ was 'the essence of sin' he was at Satan's mercy in that place of torment.... While Christ identified with sin, Satan and the hosts of hell ruled over Him as over any lost sinner. During that seemingly endless age in the nether abyss of death, Satan did with Him as he would, and all hell was 'in carnival.' " (*Destined for the Throne*, special edition for TBN [Fort Washington, PA: Christian Literature Crusade, 1988 (orig. 1975)], 84.)

48. Charles Capps: "If there's any part of hell Jesus did not suffer, you'll have to suffer it. But, thank God, Jesus suffered it *all*, for *you!* In the place of the wicked dead, all the demons of hell and Satan rejoiced over the prize. The corridors of hell were filled with joy. 'We've done it! We've captured the Son of God! We'll no longer be in the pit of the damned! The earth and all that is therein is ours! Forever it will be ours!' Rejoicing in hell had never been so great as it was that day. But it was short-lived." (*Authority in Three Worlds*, 143, emphasis in original.)

49. Kenneth Copeland: "Satan didn't realize He [Jesus] is in there [hell] illegally.... This man had not sinned. This man has not fallen out of the covenant of God, and He had the promise of God for deliverance. And Satan fell into the trap. He took Him into hell illegally. He carried Him in there [when] He did not sin." ("What Happened from the Cross to the Throne" [Fort Worth, TX: Kenneth Copeland Ministries, 1990], audiotape #02-0017, side 2.)

50. Charles Capps: "When Jesus was in the pit of hell, in that terrible torment, no doubt the Devil and his emissaries gathered around to see the annihilation of God's Son. But in the corridors of hell, there came a great voice from heaven: '*Turn Him Loose! He's there illegally!*' And all of hell became paralyzed." (*Authority in Three Worlds*, 143, emphasis in original.)

51. Kenneth Copeland: "He [Jesus] is suffering all that there is to suffer. There is no suffering left apart from Him. His emaciated, poured out, little, wormy spirit is down in the bottom of that thing [hell]. And the Devil thinks he's got Him destroyed." ("Believer's Voice of Victory" program [21 April 1991]. This message was originally delivered at the Full Gospel Motorcycle Rally Association 1990 Rally at Eagle Mountain Lake, Texas.)

52. Kenneth Copeland: "That Word of the living God went down into that pit of destruction and charged the spirit of Jesus with resurrection power! Suddenly His twisted, death-wracked spirit began to fill out and come back to life. He began to look like something the devil had never seen before." ("The Price of it All," *Believer's Voice of Victory* 19, 9 [September 1991]:4.)

53. Kenneth Copeland: "He [Jesus] was literally being reborn before the devil's very eyes. He began to flex His spiritual muscles.... Jesus was born again—the firstborn from the dead the Word calls Him—and He whipped the devil in his own backyard. He took everything he had away from him. He took his keys and his authority away from him." (Ibid., 4-6.)

54. Kenneth E. Hagin: "Every man who has been born again is an incarnation and Christianity is a miracle. The believer is as much an incarnation as was Jesus of Nazareth." ("The Incarnation," *The Word of Faith* 13, 12 [December 1980]:14; cf. E.W. Kenyon, *The Father and His Family*, 100.)

55. Frederick K.C. Price: "The whole point is I'm trying to get you to see—to get you out of this malaise of thinking that Jesus and the disciples were poor and then relating that to you—thinking that you, as a child of God, have to follow Jesus. The Bible says that He has left us an example that we should follow His steps. That's the reason why I drive a Rolls Royce. I'm following Jesus' steps." ("Ever Increasing Faith" program on TBN [9 December 1990].)

56. Benny Hinn: "When you say, 'I am a Christian,' you are saying, 'I am mashiach' in the Hebrew. I am a little messiah walking on earth, in other words. That is a shocking revelation.... May I say it like this? You are a little god on earth running around." ("Praise-a-Thon" program on TBN [6 November 1990].)
57. Frederick K.C. Price: "When I first got saved they didn't tell me I could do anything. What they told me to do was that whenever I prayed I should always say, 'The will of the Lord be done.' Now, doesn't that sound humble? It does. Sounds like humility, it's really stupidity. I mean, you know, really, we insult God. I mean, we really do insult our Heavenly Father. We do; we really insult Him without even realizing it. If you have to say, 'If it be thy will' or 'Thy will be done'—if you have to say that, then you're calling God a fool because He's the One that told us to ask.... If God's gonna give me what He wants me to have, then it doesn't matter what I ask. I'm only gonna get what God wants me to have. So that's an insult to God's intelligence." ("Ever Increasing Faith" program on TBN [16 November 1990].)
58. Kenneth Copeland: "As a believer, you have a right to make commands in the name of Jesus. Each time you stand on the Word, you are commanding God to a certain extent because it is His Word." (*Our Covenant with God* [Fort Worth, TX: KCP Publications, 1987], 32.)
59. Jerry Savelle: See chapter 5, 68.

Chapter 1—The Cast of Characters
1. See, for example, Phineas P. Quimby, quoted in *The Quimby Manuscripts*, ed. by Horatio W. Dresser (New Hyde Park, NY: University Books, Inc. 1969 [orig. 1921]), 32-35, 61, 165, 186, 279, 295. Quimby's writings in this book were taken from his manuscripts dating between 1846 and 1865. Note the striking parallel in Kenneth Hagin's remark: "It makes a great deal of difference what one thinks. I believe that is why many people are sick, even though they are prayed for by everyone in the country. They get in every healing line and still never receive healing. The reason they are not getting healed is that they are thinking wrong." (Kenneth E. Hagin, *Right and Wrong Thinking* [Tulsa, OK: Kenneth Hagin Ministries, 1978], 19.)
2. New Thought writer Warren Felt Evans (1817-1889) is one such example. See Charles S. Braden, *Spirits in Rebellion* (Dallas: Southern Methodist University Press, 1970), 121-23.
3. See, for example, Claude Bristol, *The Magic of Believing* (New York: Prentice-Hall, Inc., 1948), 122; H. Emilie Cady, *Lessons in Truth* (Unity Village, MO: Unity Books, n.d.), 41:9; 43:17; 45:25; 46:31; 48:40-42; 51:6; 52:9; 53:11; 55:22; 57:32; Mary Baker Eddy, *Science and Health with Key to the Scriptures* (Boston: The First Church of Christ, Scientist, 1971 [orig. 1875]), 376:21-27; Charles Fillmore, *Prosperity* (Lee's Summit, MO: Unity Books, 1967), 103-4; and Ernest Holmes, *How to Use the Science of Mind* (New York: Dodd, Mead and Co., 1950), 39-45.
4. Warren Felt Evans, *Mental Medicine: A Treatise on Medical Psychology*, 15th ed. (Boston: H.H. Carter & Co., 1885 [orig. 1873]), 152; quoted in Braden, *Spirits in Rebellion*, 121.
5. Warren Felt Evans, *Esoteric Christianity and Mental Therapeutics* (Boston: H.H. Carter & Karrick, 1886), 152, emphasis in original; quoted in Braden, *Spirits in Rebellion*, 122-23.
6. Cady, *Lessons in Truth*, 56:30; cf. Holmes, *How to Use the Science of Mind*, 72, 78.
7. Cady, ibid., 52:8.
8. For a fine historical treatment of the healing revivalists, see David Edwin Harrell, Jr., *All Things Are Possible: The Healing and Charismatic Revivals in Modern America* (Bloomington, IN: Indiana University Press, 1975). It should be pointed out that a number of the healing revivalists' unsound teachings and practices were previously spread by their predecessors—most notably John Alexander Dowie, Maria B. Woodworth-Etter, Smith Wigglesworth, F.F. Bosworth, and Thomas Wyatt.
9. Osborn's indebtedness to both Kenyon and faith healer F.F. Bosworth (another "Kenyonite") is mentioned in T.L. Osborn, *Healing the Sick*, 23d ed. (Tulsa, OK: Osborn Foundation, 1959), 6, 203, 205. Cf. Richard M. Riss, "Kenyon, Essek William," *Dictionary of Pentecostal and Charismatic Movements*, ed. by Stanley Burges, Gary B. McGee, and Patrick H. Alexander (Grand Rapids, MI: Regency/Zondervan, 1988), 517; and Don Gossett and E.W. Kenyon, *The Power of the Positive Confession of God's Word*, 2d pr. (Blaine, WA: Don & Joyce Gossett, 1979), 3. On Osborn's teaching regarding the "little gods" doctrine, see T.L. Osborn, *You Are God's Best!* special TBN edition (Santa Ana, CA: Trinity Broadcasting Network, n.d.), 30-31, 93-94, 122. Osborn has also stated, "He [referring to God] came down in human flesh, and we call him William Branham." (Tommy L. Osborn, *A Tribute to William Marrion Branham* [Bartow, FL: Spoken Word Outreach Center, Inc., n.d.], 18; cf. 11, 13, 17; also see "Praise the Lord" program on TBN [19 June 1989].)

10. William Marrion Branham, "Revelation Chapter Four #3 (Throne of Mercy and Judgment)" (Jeffersonville, IN: Voice of God Recordings, Inc., 1961), audiotape #61-0108, side 2; cf. William Marrion Branham, *Footprints on the Sands of Time: The Autobiography of William Marrion Branham, Part Two* (Jeffersonville, IN: Spoken Word Publications, 1975), 606-7.
11. Benny Hinn, "Praise the Lord" program on TBN (12 April 1991).
12. Benny Hinn, "Double Portion Anointing, Part #3" (Orlando Christian Center, n.d.), audiotape #A031791-3, sides 1 and 2. This sermon was also aired on TBN (7 April 1991).
13. Benny Hinn, "Praise the Lord" program on TBN (16 April 1992).
14. Quoted in Russell Chandler, "Talked with Jesus, Evangelist Says," *The Los Angeles Times* (3 February 1983), 3, 16.
15. Clark Morphew, "What's to become of Oral Roberts' City of Faith?" *St. Paul Pioneer Press* (27 June 1992); reprinted in *The Christian News* (20 July 1992), 2.
16. A.A. Allen, *The Secret to Scriptural Financial Success* (Miracle Valley, AZ: A.A. Allen Publications, 1953); quoted in Harrell, *All Things Are Possible*, 75.
17. A.A. Allen, "Miracle Oil Flows at Camp Meeting," *Miracle Magazine* (June 1967):6-7; quoted in Harrell, *All Things Are Possible*, 200.
18. Reported in "New Revival Tent Dedicated in Philadelphia," *Miracle Magazine* (September 1967):15; quoted in Harrell, *All Things Are Possible*, 200.
19. See Harrell, ibid., 199.
20. Ibid., 70-71.
21. Ibid., 202. One writer describes Allen's cause of death as "cirrhosis" of the liver. See Gary L. Ward, "Allen, Asa Alonzo," in J. Gordon Melton, *Religious Leaders of America* (Detroit, MI: Gale Research, 1991), 9.

Chapter 2—Cult or Cultic?

1. J. Milton Yinger, *Religion, Society and the Individual* (New York: The Macmillan Company, 1962 [orig. 1957]), 154. Most modern sociological studies involved with the classification of religious groups have built on Ernst Troeltsch, *The Social Teaching of the Christian Churches,* trans. by Olive Wyon (London: George Allen and Unwin, 1931), 2 vols. Troeltsch, in turn, "acknowledged the stimulation of [sociologist Max] Weber in developing his concepts" (David O. Moberg, *The Church As a Social Institution* [Englewood Cliffs, NJ: Prentice-Hall, Inc., 1962), 76 n. 4.

   Another sociologist, John Lofland, comments that "cults are 'little groups' which break off from the 'conventional consensus and espouse very different views of the real, the possible, and the moral.' " (Quoted in Ronald Enroth, "What Is a Cult?" in *A Guide to Cults and New Religions* [Downers Grove, IL: InterVarsity Press, 1983], 14.) James T. Richardson, meanwhile, defines a cult as " 'a group that has beliefs and/or practices that are counter to those of the dominant culture,' adding that these 'beliefs and practices may also be in opposition to those of a subculture.' " (Quoted in Irving Hexham and Karla Poewe, *Understanding Cults and New Religions* [Grand Rapids, MI: Wm. B. Eerdmans Publishing Co., 1986], 6.) See also James T. Richardson, *The Brainwashing/Deprogramming Controversy: Sociological, Psychological, Legal and Historical Perspectives* (Toronto: Edwin Mellen Press, 1983); and Bryan Wilson, *Religious Sects*, World University Library Series (Englewood, NJ: McGraw-Hill, 1970), cited in Hexham and Poewe, ibid.
2. J. Gordon Melton, *Encyclopedic Handbook of Cults in America* (New York: Garland Publishing, Inc., 1986), 5.
3. An interesting discussion in this area can be found in Ronald M. Enroth and J. Gordon Melton, *Why Cults Succeed Where the Church Fails* (Elgin, IL: Brethren Press, 1985), 11-19.
4. Gordon R. Lewis, *Confronting the Cults* (Grand Rapids, MI: Baker Book House, 1975), 4.
5. Walter Martin, *The Kingdom of the Cults*, rev. ed. (Minneapolis, MN: Bethany House Publishers, 1985), 11.
6. For an excellent corrective, see James W. Sire, *Scripture Twisting* (InterVarsity Press, 1980).
7. See Martin, *The Kingdom of the Cults*, 18-24.
8. Referring to the International Convention of Faith Churches and Ministers (ICFCM), some have pointed out that there is an active move to form a distinct Faith denomination. However, as of late, the enterprise seems to have lost its momentum. See D.R. McConnell, *A Different Gospel* (Peabody, MA: Hendrickson Publishers, 1988) 84-87; cf. J. Gordon Melton, *The Encyclopedia of American Religions*, 3d ed. (Detroit: Gale Research Inc., 1989), 377-78.

9. A discussion of essential Christian doctrine can be found in chapter 29 of this book.
10. For a fuller treatment of this subject, see Robert M. Bowman, "A Biblical Guide to Orthodoxy and Heresy," Parts 1 and 2, *Christian Research Journal* 13, 1 (Summer 1990):28-32; 13, 2 (Fall 1990):14-19; expanded into *Orthodoxy and Heresy* (Grand Rapids, MI: Baker Book House, 1992).

Chapter 3—Charismatic or Cultic?

1. For the purposes of this book, I will not draw the distinction commonly made between Pentecostals and charismatics. I believe that to do so in this setting would be to invite confusion, since my goal at this point is to clarify the controversy between those who hold to the perpetuity of spiritual gifts ("charismatics") and those who do not ("noncharismatics"), with reference to the Faith movement.
2. Walter Martin, "The Health and Wealth Cult" (San Juan Capistrano, CA: Christian Research Institute, n.d.), audiotape #C-152; "The Errors of Positive Confession" (Christian Research Institute, n.d.), audiotape #C-100; "Healing: Does God Always Heal?" (Christian Research Institute, n.d.), audiotape #C-95.
3. Gordon Fee, *The Disease of the Health and Wealth Gospels* (Beverly, MA: Frontline Publishing, 1985).
4. D.R. McConnell, *A Different Gospel* (Peabody, MA: Hendrickson Publishers, 1988).
5. Charles Farah, *From the Pinnacle of the Temple* (Plainfield, NJ: Logos, 1978); and "A Critical Analysis: The 'Roots' and 'Fruits' of Faith-Formula Theology" (paper presented at the Society for Pentecostal Studies, November 1980).
6. Elliot Miller, *Healing: Does God Always Heal?* (San Juan Capistrano, CA: Christian Research Institute, 1979).
7. H. Terris Neuman, *An Analysis of the Sources of the Charismatic Teaching of "Positive Confession"* (unpublished paper, Wheaton Graduate School, 1980); and "Cultic Origins of Word Faith Theology Within the Charismatic Movement," *PNEUMA: The Journal of the Society for Pentecostal Studies* 12, 1 (Spring 1990):32-55. Neuman also lists a number of articles and papers by members of the Assembly of God which critique the Faith movement (p. 52, n. 154).
8. Dale H. Simmons, *A Theological and Historical Analysis of Kenneth E. Hagin's Claim to Be a Prophet* (master's thesis, Oral Roberts University, 1985).
9. See Bruce Barron, *The Health and Wealth Gospel* (Downers Grove, IL: InterVarsity Press, 1987), 23.

Part 2—Faith in Faith

1. Marilyn Hickey, "Claim Your Miracles" (Denver: Marilyn Hickey Ministries, n.d.), audiotape #186, side 2.

Chapter 5—The Force of Faith

1. Kenneth Copeland, *The Force of Faith* (Fort Worth, TX: KCP Publications, 1989), 10.
2. Kenneth Copeland, *The Laws of Prosperity* (Fort Worth, TX: Kenneth Copeland Publications, 1974), 19.
3. *Forces of the Recreated Human Spirit* (Fort Worth, TX: Kenneth Copeland Ministries, 1982), 8.
4. Kenneth Copeland, "Spirit, Soul and Body I" (Fort Worth, TX: Kenneth Copeland Ministries, 1985), audiotape #01-0601, side 1.
5. Kenneth Copeland, *Freedom from Fear* (Fort Worth, TX: Kenneth Copeland Ministries, 1980), 11-12.
6. Ibid.; cf. Copeland, *The Force of Faith*, 11.
7. Charles Capps, *The Tongue—A Creative Force* (Tulsa, OK: Harrison House, 1976), 92.
8. *Forces of the Recreated Human Spirit*, 15; cf. 14.
9. Kenneth Copeland, *The Power of the Tongue* (Fort Worth, TX: KCP Publications, 1980), 4.
10. Ibid.
11. E.W. Kenyon, *Two Kinds of Faith*, 14th ed. (Lynnwood, WA: Kenyon's Gospel Publishing Society, 1969), 20.
12. Ron Rhodes, *The Counterfeit Christ of the New Age Movement* (Grand Rapids, MI: Baker Book House, 1990), 149.
13. See D.R. McConnell, *A Different Gospel* (Peabody, MA: Hendrickson Publishers, 1988), 3-12.

14. Jerry Savelle, "Framing Your World with the Word of God, Part 2" (Fort Worth, TX: Jerry Savelle Evangelistic Assn., n.d.), audiotape #SS-36, side 1.
15. Jerry Savelle, "Framing Your World with the Word of God, Part 1" (Fort Worth, TX: Jerry Savelle Evangelistic Assn., Inc., n.d.), audiotape #SS-36, side 1.
16. Charles Capps, *Authority in Three Worlds* (Tulsa, OK: Harrison House, 1982), 24, emphasis in original.
17. Robert Tilton, "Success-N-Life" program (18 October 1990).
18. Kenneth Copeland, "Authority of the Believer II" (Fort Worth, TX: Kenneth Copeland Ministries, 1987), audiotape #01-0302, side 1.
19. See, for example, Kenneth E. Hagin, *Having Faith in Your Faith* (Tulsa, OK: Kenneth Hagin Ministries, 1988).
20. *The Analytical Greek Lexicon* (Grand Rapids, MI: Zondervan Publishing House, 1970 [Orig. London: Samuel Bagster & Sons, 1852; rev. ed. 1860]), 419, col. 1.
21. Louis Berkhof, *Systematic Theology*, 4th rev. ed. (Grand Rapids, MI: Wm. B. Eerdmans Publishing Co., 1949), 500.

Chapter 6—The Formula of Faith

1. Kenneth Copeland, *The Laws of Prosperity* (Fort Worth, TX: Kenneth Copeland Publications, 1974), 18-29.
2. E.W. Kenyon, *The Two Kinds of Faith: Faith's Secret Revealed* (Lynnwood, WA: Kenyon's Gospel Publishing Society, 1942), 67.
3. Kenneth E. Hagin, *Having Faith in Your Faith* (Tulsa, OK: Kenneth Hagin Ministries, 1988), 4.
4. Ibid., 5.
5. Ibid., 4-5, emphasis in original. Hagin and the other Faith teachers almost always point to this passage to "prove" that Jesus taught His disciples to have faith in their faith so that whatsoever they believe and say will come to pass. That notion, however, is utterly false. The context of the passage makes it clear that we are to place our faith in God and His awesome power, rather than our own frail human devices (v. 22; cf. Chapter 9, "The Faith of God"). Moreover, according to Jesus' own words here, it is *God*, not the believer, who brings about the end results. Thus Jesus says, "It will be done *for* you" (NIV), not "*you* will do it;" "believe that you have *received* it" (NIV), not "believe that you have *taken* it." And this will only happen when we *pray*; that is, when we *ask God*, who answers those requests that are in accordance with His will (1 John 5:14). It is not some substance called faith, but God Himself who ultimately determines which "mountains are thrown into the sea"; He is also the One who carries out the task. If we are to observe the teaching of Scripture, our faith is to be in *God*, not in our faith or in our words.

   Hagin also points to the healing of the woman suffering from a hemorrhage (Mark 5:25-34; see Hagin, *How to Write Your Own Ticket with God* [Tulsa, OK: Kenneth Hagin Ministries, 1979], 7-8, 11-16) to bolster his "faith in faith" error. Yet the careful Bible reader will recognize that the object of the woman's faith—which was responsible for her healing (v. 34)—was not her own faith, but Christ (v. 28); why else would she be determined to get to Him if she really believed that exercising faith in her faith would cure her? She received healing not because she had faith in her faith but because she had *faith in Christ* (vv. 27-29). One commentator writes: "When Jesus attributes the woman's restoration to her faith, i.e., her trust and confidence in Jesus, he does not make her faith the *causa efficiens* [or "efficient cause"], but only the *causa instrumentalis* [or "instrumental cause"]...the hand that receives the gift" (R.C.H. Lenski, *The Interpretation of St. Mark's Gospel* [Minneapolis, MN: Augsburg Publishing House, 1964], 225.)
6. Kenneth E. Hagin, *How to Write Your Own Ticket with God*, 2-3. This booklet has been incorporated as Chapter 6 of Kenneth E. Hagin, *Exceedingly Growing Faith*, 2d ed. (Tulsa, OK: Kenneth Hagin Ministries, 1988), 73-74.
7. Hagin, *How to Write Your Own Ticket with God*, 3.
8. Ibid., 5.
9. Ibid., emphasis deleted.
10. Ibid., 6.
11. Ibid., 6-8 passim.
12. Ibid., 11.
13. Ibid., 12.
14. Ibid., 17.
15. Ibid., 18, emphasis in original.

16. Ibid., 19, emphasis deleted.
17. Ibid., 20.
18. Ibid., 20.
19. Ibid., 21.
20. Ibid., 23, emphasis in original.
21. Charles Capps, *The Tongue—A Creative Force* (Tulsa, OK: Harrison House, 1976), 91.
22. Norvel Hayes on "Praise the Lord" program on TBN (13 November 1990).
23. Paul's use of strong language is also found in such verses as Galatians 5:12 and 1 Timothy 4:1,2.
24. Other instances where Jesus issued harsh condemnations of false teachers can be found in the following passages: Matthew 3:7; 6:2,5,16; 7:5; 12:34; 22:18; 23:13-19,23-29; Luke 3:7; 6:42; 11:39-52; 12:1,56; John 8:44.
25. Kenneth Copeland, "Inner Image of the Covenant" (Fort Worth, TX: Kenneth Copeland Ministries, 1985), audiotape #01-4406, side 2.
26. Ibid.; Kenneth Copeland, "The Forgotten Power of Hope (part II)," *Believer's Voice of Victory*, 20, 3 (March 1992):2-3.
27. Copeland, "Inner Image of the Covenant," side 2.
28. Ibid.
29. Ibid.
30. The Church Universal and Triumphant is one New Age group that greatly emphasizes "the scientific use of the mantra or the dynamic decree of the Word," otherwise known as "the exercise of God's power according to the spoken Word" (Mark and Elizabeth Clare Prophet, *The Lost Teachings of Jesus 2: Mysteries of the Higher Self* [Livingston, MT: Summit University Press, 1988], 144, 207; cf. 103. Also see Mark L. Prophet, *The Soulless One* [Summit University Press, 1981 (orig. 1965)], 34).
31. Copeland, "Inner Image of the Covenant," side 2.
32. Ibid.
33. Kenneth Copeland, "Believer's Voice of Victory" program on TBN (28 March 1991).
34. Paul Yonggi Cho, *The Fourth Dimension*, vols. 1 and 2 (South Plainfield, NJ: Bridge Publishing, 1979, 1983).
35. Cho, *The Fourth Dimension*, vol. 1 (1979), 36-43, 64; vol. 2 (1983), 38-39.
36. Ibid., vol. 1, 64.
37. Ibid., vol. 1, 37.
38. Ibid., vol. 1, 18. This quote does not appear in the second version, vol. 2, 30.
39. Ibid., vol. 2, 30. This comment does not appear in the first version (see vol. 1, 18-19, for first part of the interview) until the end of the question session (vol. 1, 20).
40. Ibid., vol. 2, 30-31. In the first version, the question is phrased differently, and the three choices are "Asian, Caucasian, or Black?" (vol. 1, 19).
41. Ibid., vol. 2, 30. Cf. vol. 1, 19: "Number three: do you want your husband slim and nice looking, or just pleasantly plump?" "I want to have him skinny." The profession is asked as Question No. 5 in the first story.
42. Ibid., vol. 1, 20-21; vol. 2, 30-31.
43. Ibid., vol. 1, 35.
44. Ibid., 65.
45. Ibid., vol. 2, 68.
46. Ibid., vol. 1, ch. 3, "The Creative Power of the Spoken Word," 67-86, passim, e.g., emphasis added: "So men, by exploring their spiritual sphere of the fourth dimension through the development of concentrated visions and dreams in their imaginations, can brood over and *incubate* the third dimension, influencing and changing it. This is what the Holy Spirit taught me" (39-40); "you have the fourth dimension in your heart, and it . . . has *dominion over the three material dimensions.* . . . Through dominion in the fourth dimension—the realm of faith— you can bring order to your circumstances and situations . . . give beauty to the ugly and chaotic, and healing to the hurt and suffering" (66); "*use the spoken word*: to create the power to have a successful personal life" (71-72); "Then God spoke, '. . . Don't just beg and beg for what you need. *Give the word.* . . . As I did when creating the world, *speak* forth. Say "let there be light," or say, "let there be firmament," ' " (73-74); "through the fourth dimension I can incubate the third dimension, and *correct it*" (78); "the *spoken* word has powerful creativity" (87).
47. Rather than teach their followers to walk by the power of the Holy Spirit, a number of Faith teachers encourage them to tap into the same "power source" used by metaphysical practitioners, New Agers, Yogis, Soka Gakkai Buddhists, and other assorted occultists. Sadly enough,

it seems that they are doing so because their methods supposedly work. Yet if the methods used by occult groups are indeed able to produce miraculous results, then these methods should give Christians even greater pause. After all, any supernatural power that energizes anti-Christian groups cannot be of God (cf. Matthew 12:22-28; Deuteronomy 13:1-5). And if the source is not divine, then it can only derive from fallen humanity (in which case it is merely a delusion) or fallen angels (in which case it is demonic) or some combination of the two. Despite such obvious dangers, the Faith teachers persist in promoting such practices.

48. Benny Hinn, "Praise the Lord" program on TBN (1 June 1989). Hinn's story seems odd in light of the fact that wiccans (or witches) generally hold all forms of life to be sacred, due for the most part to their pantheistic worldview (all is God). As such, wiccans typically stand in opposition to rituals, activities, and practices that are harmful to nature in general and animals in particular.

49. See, for example, Charles Capps, *The Tongue—A Creative Force*, 121-28; and Kenneth Copeland, *The Power of the Tongue* (Fort Worth, TX: Kenneth Copeland Ministries, 1980), 3.

50. In one sense it may be said that Proverbs 18:21 has a special relevance to Solomon (see heading in Proverbs 10), as he is the one who penned it. The verse may therefore be legitimately interpreted as an allusion to Solomon's power to pronounce death or life (condemnation or pardon) over his subjects. Others see this text as Solomon's advice to his successor, who would one day take over his father's responsibility. Still another possible way to look at the passage is to consider how our spoken words affect another person's feelings (12:18,25; 16:24), self-image (29:5), and convictions (10:21; 11:9), as well as our own and other people's attitudes toward that person (18:8). There can be no denying that what people say often affects outlooks and perceptions, which in turn may alter intervening and subsequent circumstances; yet nowhere does the Bible teach that humans can speak things into existence (see James Kinnebrew, *The Charismatic Doctrine of Positive Confession: A Historical, Exegetical, and Theological Critique*, [doctoral dissertation, Mid-America Baptist Seminary, 1988], 185-88; and Derek Kidner, *The Proverbs: An Introduction and Commentary*, from the *Tyndale Old Testament Commentary* series, ed. by D.J. Wiseman [Downers Grove, IL: InterVarsity Press, 1964], 15:46-47).

The Faith teachers are also fond of quoting the latter portion of Romans 4:17 ("...even God, who quickeneth the dead, and calleth those things which be not as though they were" [KJV]) in claiming that human speech literally contains the power of creation. However, as is obvious, this verse is a direct reference to God. Applying the passage to humanity, whether redeemed or not, diminishes the sheer magnificence and immensity of God's power. To suggest that believers are capable of performing such acts of creation is tantamount to exalting humanity to godhood, which is clearly unbiblical. There is, after all, only one God, who alone is capable of calling whatever He chooses into existence (Isaiah 43:10; 44:6,24). "Calling into existence" is the literary terminology chosen by the Scripture writers to express what we creatures can never personally accomplish—namely, the creation of something from nothing. "God's voice" does not serve as the substance for material things. Rather, "God's voice" represents His ability or authority to create from nothing.

51. Charles Capps, *The Tongue—A Creative Force*, 67, emphasis in original.

52. Frederick K.C. Price, "Prayer: Do You Know What Prayer Is... and How to Pray?" *The Word Study Bible* (Tulsa, OK: Harrison House, 1990), 1178.

Chapter 7—The Faith of God

1. Kenneth Copeland, *The Force of Faith* (Fort Worth, TX: KCP Publications, 1989), 14.

2. Kenneth Copeland, "Spirit, Soul and Body I" (Fort Worth, TX: Kenneth Copeland Ministries, 1985), audiotape #01-0601, side 1.

3. Kenneth Copeland, "Praise-a-Thon" program on TBN (April 1988).

4. Frederick K.C. Price, "Ever Increasing Faith" program on TBN (1 May 1992), audiotape #PR11; Kenneth Copeland, "God's Covenants with Man II" (Fort Worth, TX: Kenneth Copeland Ministries, 1985), audiotape #01-4404, side 1; Charles Capps, *Authority in Three Worlds* (Tulsa, OK: Harrison House, 1982), 60-61; Kenneth E. Hagin, *Zoe: The God-Kind of Life* (Tulsa, OK: Kenneth Hagin Ministries, 1989), 49; Hagin, *I Believe in Visions* (Old Tappan, NJ: Spire Books/Fleming H. Revell Co., 1972), 81; Paul Yonggi Cho, *The Fourth Dimension* (South Plainfield, NJ: Bridge Publishing, 1979), vol. 1, 83.

5. Richard N. Ostling, "Religion: Power, Glory and Politics," *Time* 127, 7 (17 February 1986):69; cited in D.R. McConnell, *A Different Gospel* (Peabody, MA: Hendrickson Publishers, 1988), 95-96 note 6.

6. Kenneth Copeland, *Holy Bible: Kenneth Copeland Reference Edition* (Fort Worth, TX: Kenneth Copeland Ministries, 1991), NT, 68, emphasis in original. While the conversation with Copeland here is imaginary, the substance of everything he is represented as saying is amply documented.

7. Charles Capps, *God's Creative Power* (Tulsa, OK: Harrison House, 1976), 2-3, emphasis in original.

8. Frederick K.C. Price, *How Faith Works* (Tulsa, OK: Harrison House, 1976), 95.

9. Kenneth Hagin, *Bible Faith Study Course* (Tulsa, OK: Hagin Evangelistic Assoc., ca.1966), 88.

10. Alfred Marshall, *NASB-NIV Parallel New Testament in Greek and English with Interlinear Translation* (Grand Rapids, MI: Regency/Zondervan, 1986), 139.

11. Archibald Thomas Robertson, *Word Pictures in the New Testament* (Nashville: Broadman Press, 1930), 1:361.

12. A.T. Robertson and W. Hersey Davis, *A New Short Grammar of the Greek Testament*, 10th rev. ed. (Grand Rapids, MI: Baker Book House, 1979 [orig. 1933]), 227-28, emphasis added. See also A.T. Robertson, *A Grammar of the Greek New Testament in the Light of Historical Research* (Nashville: Broadman Press, 1934), 500 ("we rightly translate 'have faith *in* God,'" emphasis added).

13. According to renowned Greek scholars Walter Bauer, William F. Arndt, and F. Wilbur Gingrich, Mark 11:22 is an *objective genitive* and is to be translated as "faith *in* God" (*A Greek-English Lexicon of the New Testament and Other Early Christian Literature*, rev. ed. ([Chicago: Univ. of Chicago Press, 1979], 357, emphasis added). Nigel Turner concludes that the genitive "have the faith *of* God" in Mark 11:22 is objective and "surely must mean 'have a faith *in* God'" (*Grammatical Insights into the New Testament* [Edinburgh: T. & T. Clark, 1977], 110, emphasis in original). Likewise, Curtis Vaughan and Virtus E. Gideon, *A Greek Grammar of the New Testament* (Nashville: Broadman Press, 1979), 35. For further confirmation, see: Kurt Aland, ed., *Synopsis of the Four Gospels*, 6th rev. ed. (New York: United Bible Societies, 1983), 240 ("Have faith *in* God," emphasis added); Bruce M. Metzger, *A Textual Commentary on the Greek New Testament*, rev. ed. (London & New York: United Bible Societies, 1975), 109, fn. 1 ("faith *in* God," emphasis added); Joseph Henry Thayer, *The New Thayer's Greek-English Lexicon of the New Testament*, rev. ed. (Peabody, MA: Hendrickson, 1981 [orig. 1889]), 514a ("to trust *in* God," emphasis added); Alexander B. Bruce, "The Synoptic Gospels," *The Expositor's Greek Testament*, ed. by W. Robertson Nicoll (Grand Rapids, MI: Wm. B. Eerdmans Publishing Co., 1979), 1:419, fn. vv. 20-25 ("faith *in* God," emphasis in the original); Otto Michel, "Faith," *The New International Dictionary of New Testament Theology*, ed. by Colin Brown (Grand Rapids, MI: Zondervan, 1975 Eng. transl.), 1:600 ("to have faith *in* God," emphasis added). See also Gerhard Friedrich, ed. (transl. ed. Geoffrey W. Bromiley), *Theological Dictionary of the New Testament* (Grand Rapids, MI: Wm. B. Eerdmans Publishing Co., 1968 Eng. transl.), 6:204 and fn. 230 (*pistin* in Mark 11:22 is objective genitive).

Even the one possible dissenter, Boyce W. Blackwelder, who considers that Mark 11:22 could either be objective or subjective genitive, nevertheless explains that this does not mean that God personally has faith but merely that faith is "divinely imparted" to us (*Light from the Greek New Testament* [Grand Rapids, MI: Baker Book House, 1958], 146).

14. This information was included in an advertisement for Zoe College, Jacksonville, Florida, taken from *Charisma* (May 1992), 82.

15. Kenneth Copeland, *Freedom from Fear* (Fort Worth, TX: KCP Publications, 1983), 11.

16. Ibid., 12, emphasis in original.

17. Kenneth Copeland, *The Power of the Tongue* (Fort Worth, TX: KCP Publications, 1980), 9.

18. Charles Capps, *Authority in Three Worlds*, 80, emphasis in original.

19. Ibid., 82, emphasis added.

20. Ibid., 83, emphasis added.

21. Ibid., 85, emphasis in original.

22. Kenneth Copeland, *The Force of Faith*, 14.

23. Frederick K.C. Price, "Praise the Lord" program on TBN (21 September 1990).

24. Kenneth E. Hagin, *The Name of Jesus* (Tulsa, OK: Kenneth Hagin Ministries, 1981), 16, emphasis in original.

Chapter 8—The Faith Hall of Fame

1. Benny Hinn, "Benny Hinn" program on TBN (3 November 1990).

2. For further injunctions against adding words to Scripture, see Deuteronomy 4:2; 12:32; Galatians 3:15; Revelation 22:18.

3. Benny Hinn, "Benny Hinn" program on TBN (3 November 1990).
4. Kenneth Copeland, sermon recorded at Melodyland Christian Center (Anaheim, CA) (30 March 1983).
5. Charles Capps, *Kicking Over Sacred Cows* (Tulsa, OK: Harrison House, 1987), 37-63.
6. Jerry Savelle, "Framing Your World with the Word of God, Part 1" (Fort Worth, TX: Jerry Savelle Evangelistic Assn., n.d.), audiotape #SS-36, side 1.
7. Paul and Jan Crouch, "Behind the Scenes" program on TBN (12 March 1992).
8. Hinn, along with other Faith teachers, almost always cites Job 3:25 KJV ("For the thing which I greatly feared is come upon me, and that which I was afraid of is come unto me") to demonstrate the devastating impact of "negative confessions." He teaches that Job calls down calamity upon himself by setting in motion the force of fear via his negative confession.

Such an interpretation ignores the fact that Job's lamentation comes *after* his trials (1:6–2:13), not before. His lament was a *product* of his suffering, not its *cause*. At no time before his trials is Job said to have uttered a negative confession—a necessity, according to Faith theology, if the force of fear is to be released. Even after Job had suffered two major trials, the Bible asserts that "in all this, Job did not sin in what he said" (2:10). And do not forget that God judged Job to be "blameless and upright" after he had suffered his first calamity—hardly an apt description for someone who supposedly had unleashed forces hostile to God. In fact, that God chose Job above all others to be tested says much for the man's character, integrity, and devotion to God (Job 1:1,8).

Still, Job was certainly not sinless. He was part of a cursed creation, imperfect and beset with the frailties of fallen humanity. His misfortunes prompted him to lament his birth (chapter 3); to vacillate between desiring God to crush him (6:8,9) and to heal him (7:7-10); to blame God for tormenting him (13:21,25) and treating him unjustly (9:21-24); to question God's treatment of him (chapter 10); to occasionally perceive God as his enemy (7:20; 10:16,17; 16:9); and to virtually demand to have his case presented before God (13:13-19). For these reasons, God rebukes Job (38–42). *But Job is rebuked for challenging God's wisdom and sovereignty and for acting out of ignorance (38:2) and presumption (40:8)—NOT for speaking "negative confessions."*

And don't miss the fact that Job repents! This is why God says to Job's friends in 42:7, "You have not spoken of me what is right, *as my servant Job has.*" No, Job was not perfect; but the book that bears his name makes it clear that, in his day, he was the most righteous man alive on the planet.

9. Benny Hinn, "Benny Hinn" program on TBN (3 November 1990).

Part 3—Little Gods or Little Frauds?
1. I first heard a version of this illustration from D. James Kennedy at Coral Ridge Presbyterian Church, Fort Lauderdale, Florida.

Chapter 9—The Deification of Man
1. M. Scott Peck, *The Road Less Traveled* (New York: Simon & Schuster, 1978), 270.
2. Margot Adler, *Drawing Down the Moon*, rev. ed. (Boston: Beacon Press, 1986), 25, emphasis in original.
3. Bhagwan Shree Rajneesh, quoted in *Fear Is the Master* (Hemet, CA: Jeremiah Films, 1987).
4. Maharishi Mahesh Yogi, *Meditations of Maharishi Mahesh Yogi* (New York: Bantam, 1968), 178; quoted in James W. Sire, *Scripture Twisting* (Downers Grove, IL: InterVarsity Press, 1980), 34.
5. Jim Jones, quoted in James Reston, Jr., and Noah Adams, "Father Cares: The Last of Jonestown," program on National Public Radio (23 April 1981).
6. Kenneth E. Hagin, *Zoe: The God-Kind of Life* (Tulsa, OK: Kenneth Hagin Ministries, Inc., 1989), 35-36, 41.
7. Kenneth Copeland, "Following the Faith of Abraham I" (Fort Worth, TX: Kenneth Copeland Ministries, 1989), tape #01-3001, side 1.
8. John Avanzini with Morris Cerullo, "The Endtime Manifestation of the Sons of God" (San Diego: Morris Cerullo World Evangelism, n.d.), audiotape 1, side 2.
9. Morris Cerullo, "The Endtime Manifestation of the Sons of God," audiotape 1, sides 1 & 2, emphasis in original.
10. Charles Capps, *Authority in Three Worlds* (Tulsa, OK: Harrison House, 1982), 16, emphasis in original.

11. Hebert W. Armstrong, *Mystery of the Ages* (Pasadena, CA: Worldwide Church of God, 1985), 37, 85, emphasis added.
12. Stephen E. Robinson, *Are Mormons Christians?* (Salt Lake City, UT: Bookcraft, 1991), 63.
13. Kenneth Copeland, "The Force of Love" (Fort Worth, TX: Kenneth Copeland Ministries, 1987), audiotape #02-0028, side 1.
14. Benny Hinn, "Praise-a-Thon" program on TBN (6 November 1990).
15. J.N.D. Kelly, *Early Christian Doctrines*, rev. ed. (San Francisco: Harper & Row, 1978), 352, 378, 391, 397, 486.
16. On New Thought, see Charles S. Braden, *Spirits in Rebellion: The Rise and Development of New Thought*, 3rd ed. (Dallas, TX: Southern Methodist University Press, 1970 [orig. 1963]), 10, 13, 38, 71-75, 103-09, 134-36, 151, 198-99. On Christian Science, see Mary Baker Eddy, *Science and Health with Key to the Scriptures* (Boston: First Church of Christ, Scientist, 1971 [orig. 1875]), 109-11, 113-14, 116-17, 119-20, 127, 129, 139, 591; cf. Robert Peel, *Christian Science*, 5th ed. (New York: Henry Holt, 1959), 121-22. On Unity, see H. Emilie Cady et al, *Foundations of Unity*, series 2 (Unity Village, MO: Unity, n.d.), 1:32-36, 41, 50-51; Cady, *God a Present Help* (Lee's Summit, MO: Unity School of Christianity, 1938), 52-53, quoted in Kurt Van Gorden, "The Unity School of Christianity," *Evangelizing the Cults*, ed. by Ronald Enroth (Ann Arbor, MI: Servant Publications, 1990), 148, 190, note 23. On Religious Science, see Ernest Holmes, *The Science of Mind*, rev. ed. (New York: Dodd, Mead & Co., 1938), 98, 100, 362.
17. Henotheism (the belief that ascribes supreme power and devotes worship solely to one god without denying the existence of other gods) can be considered a subcategory of polytheism (the belief in the existence of more than one god). It is often used in discussions of early Hinduism: "Either the particular god of the moment is made to absorb all the others, who are declared to be manifestations of him [a trend toward pantheism]; or else, he is given attributes which in strict logic could only be given to a sole monotheistic deity" (Franklin Edgerton, *The Beginnings of Indian Philosophy* [London: George Allen & Unwin, 1963], 18ff, quoted in John B. Noss, *Man's Religion*, 4th ed. [New York: Macmillan, 1969]), 94.
18. Paul Crouch, "Praise the Lord" program on TBN (7 July 1986).
19. Earl Paulk, *Satan Unmasked* (Atlanta: K Dimension Publishers, 1984), 96.
20. Frederick Buechner, quoted in Philip Yancey and Tim Stafford, *The Student Bible* (Grand Rapids, MI: Zondervan, 1986), 482.
21. Paul Crouch and Benny Hinn, "Praise-a-Thon" program on TBN (November 1990).
22. Kenneth Copeland, "Praise the Lord" program on TBN (5 February 1986).
23. Capps, *Authority in Three Worlds*, 15-16; and Jerry Savelle, "The Authority of the Believer," *The Word Study Bible* (Tulsa, OK: Harrison House, 1990), 1141.
24. R. Laird Harris, Gleason L. Archer, Jr., and Bruce K. Waltke, eds., *Theological Wordbook of the Old Testament*, 2 vols. (Chicago: Moody Press, 1981), 1:192, emphasis added.
25. Cf. James M. Kinnebrew, *The Charismatic Doctrine of Positive Confession: A Historical, Exegetical, and Theological Critique* (doctoral dissertation, Mid-America Baptist Seminary, 1988), 157: "To give the root word, '*dama*,' the meaning that Capps has assigned to it is to make nonsense of many biblical passages. Such a definition would make the psalmist a bird (Psalm 102:7), the neck of the Shulamite a tower (Song of Solomon 4:4), and the armies of God a mere cloud (Ezekiel 38:9)."
26. See also Job chapters 9, 10, 14; 34:20; Psalm 90; 102:11,12; 103:15; Isaiah 40:6-8; James 1:10,11; 1 Peter 1:24,25.
27. See also Jeremiah 32:17; Matthew 19:26; Mark 10:27; Luke 1:37; 18:27.
28. See also 2 Corinthians 12:9; Hebrews 4:15; Job 23.
29. See also Job 11:7-12; 21:22; 36:22-33; 37:5-24; 38:4.
30. See also Psalm 139:7-12; Ephesians 1:23; 4:10; Colossians 3:11.
31. See also Job 23; 37:23; 38–41.
32. Millard J. Erickson, *Christian Theology* (Grand Rapids, MI: Baker Book House, 1988), 510.
33. Ibid., 514.
34. Benny Hinn, "Praise the Lord" program on TBN (26 December 1991). Hinn seems to have derived this idea from Finis J. Dake, *Dake's Annotated Reference Bible* (Lawrenceville, GA: Dake Bible Sales, 1963), Old Testament 1, col. 4 (note on Genesis 1:26), 619, col. 1, note 2; and Dake, *God's Plan for Man* (Lawrenceville, GA: Dake Bible Sales, 1977 [orig. 1949]), 35.
35. Brigham Young, "The Gospel—The One-Man Power" discourse delivered 24 July 1870, reported by D.W. Evans and John Grimshaw, *Journal of Discourses* (London: Horace S. Eldredge, 1966 [orig. 1871]), 13:271.

36. See also Hebrew *mashal* (Psalm 8:6). Harris, Archer, and Waltke, *Theological Wordbook of the Old Testament,* 1:534, 2:833; and Samuel P. Tregelles, translator, *Gesenius' Hebrew and Chaldee Lexicon to the Old Testament Scriptures* (Grand Rapids, MI: Wm. B. Eerdmans Publishing Co., 1976 [orig. 1857]), 517b, 758a.

Chapter 10—The Demotion of God

1. Kenneth Copeland, "Spirit, Soul and Body I" (Fort Worth, TX: Kenneth Copeland Ministries, 1985), audiotape #01-0601, side 1. Some have suggested that Copeland may have simply been referring to Jesus in this statement. However, this creates yet another huge problem—namely, that Jesus had a body prior to His incarnation. Although Jesus *appeared* in the Old Testament in what are appropriately referred to as theophanies (appearances of God), He always did so for the purpose of communicating with men; and in the context of Copeland's sermon, men had not yet been created. For further discussion about theophanies, see Ron Rhodes, *Christ Before the Manger* (Grand Rapids, MI: Baker Book House, 1992), 79-91.

2. Jerry Savelle, "Framing Your World with the Word of God, Part 2" (Fort Worth, TX: Jerry Savelle Evangelistic Association, Inc., n.d.), audiotape #SS-36, side 1.

3. Morris Cerullo, *The Miracle Book* (San Diego, CA: Cerullo World Evangelism, Inc., 1984), x-xi.

4. Benny Hinn and Jan Crouch, "Praise the Lord" program on TBN (13 October 1991).

5. Benny Hinn, "Benny Hinn" program on TBN (3 October 1990).

6. Randy Frame, "Best-selling Author Admits Mistakes, Vows Changes," *Christianity Today* (28 October 1991), 44-45. Hinn resumed teaching that both the Father and the Holy Spirit have bodies (on TBN's October 3, 1991, "Praise the Lord" program) shortly after his supposed change of heart as related in his interview with *Christianity Today*. The interview was conducted one month before the article's October 28 release date. Cf. Randy Frame, "Same Old Benny Hinn, Critics Say," *Christianity Today* (5 October 1992), 53.

7. Ibid.

8. Benny Hinn, "Praise the Lord" program on TBN (23 October 1992). Cf. Hinn, *Good Morning, Holy Spirit* (Nashville: Thomas Nelson Publishers, 1990), 72, 82-84.

9. For a biblical and historical discussion on the doctrine of the trinity, see E. Calvin Beisner, *God in Three Persons* (Wheaton, IL: Tyndale House Publishers, 1984); and Edward H. Bickersteth, *The Trinity* (Grand Rapids, MI: Kregel, 1976).

10. In the case of the Faith teachers' claim that God possesses a literal body—whether some form of physical body or a spirit body—the error is indeed a serious one. For as has already been pointed out, the doctrine itself implies that the Trinity is actually composed of three separate beings. Conversely, the Bible teaches there are three Persons in one Being called God (Deuteronomy 6:4).

    Additionally, since God, according to these Faith teachers, has a body, His presence would be confined to the area occupied by His body. And since God's body supposedly has definite dimensions (e.g., a measurable hand span, height, and weight), it would mean that God cannot truly be at those places which are not currently occupied by His body. In other words, the Faith God cannot be omnipresent. Scripture, on the other hand, presents a God who transcends all such limitations. The one true God is everywhere present in all His fullness: " 'Am I only a God nearby,' declares the Lord, 'and not a God far away? Can anyone hide in secret places so that I cannot see him?' declares the Lord. 'Do not I fill the heaven and earth?' declares the Lord" (Jeremiah 23:23,24; cf. Psalm 139:7-10; Matthew 28:20; Ephesians 1:23; 4:10; Colossians 3:11).

    Copeland apparently reasoned that a God with a physical body needs a physical habitat. So he conveniently transforms heaven into a planet. "Heaven has a north and a south and an east and a west," begins Copeland. "Consequently, it must be a planet." He also says the earth is really "a copy of the mother planet where God lives." How Copeland could squeeze God on any planet is hard to fathom, especially since Solomon pointed out that heaven itself cannot contain God (1 Kings 8:27).

    It seems that the Faith teachers have arrived at their physical God by erroneously taking verses which figuratively describe God in human (anthropomorphic) terms, and reading them literally. Thus God is made out to be a spirit being with a body, complete with eyes and eyelids (Psalm 11:4), ears (Psalm 18:6), nostrils (Psalm 18:8), a mouth (Numbers 12:8), hands and fingers (Psalm 8:3-6), and feet (Exodus 24:10). Yet if these verses were meant to be taken literally, it would also have to be concluded that God has feathers and wings as well (Psalm 91:4)—an obvious absurdity.

The simple fact is that such anthropomorphic descriptions were used primarily to help us understand and relate to our Maker. They were never intended to convey the notion that God possesses physical features like His human creation. The Creator is, after all, "God, and not man" (Hosea 11:9). Jesus made it clear that God is *spirit* (John 4:24), not a spirit being with a body (cf. Deuteronomy 4:12).

Some may try to point to Christ as proof of God having a body. However, all such appeals fail on at least two counts. First, the vast majority of verses cited by such proponents occur in the Old Testament, during a time before Christ took human form (John 1:14; cf. 1 John 4:2; 2 John 7). Second, and even more importantly, the Lord Jesus is not only fully God, but fully man. He is the God-man. His physical attributes are not due to His deity, but to His humanity (Romans 8:3; Philippians 2:7).

11. Kenneth Copeland, "Praise-a-Thon" program on TBN (April 1988).

12. Kenneth Copeland, *Our Covenant with God* (Fort Worth, TX: KCP Publications, 1987), 8-11 passim.

Chapter 11—The Deification of Satan

1. C.S. Lewis, *Mere Christianity*, 22d pr. (New York: Macmillan Publishing Co., 1976), 48.

2. Kenneth Copeland, *The Force of Faith* (Fort Worth, TX: KCP Publications, 1989), 11.

3. Benny Hinn, "Our Position in Christ #2—The Word Made Flesh" (Orlando: Orlando Christian Center, 1991), videotape #255, emphasis added. See also Hinn's claim that believers are "little messiahs" or "little gods" on the "Praise-a-Thon" program on TBN (6 November 1990).

4. Ibid.

5. Kenneth Copeland, "Praise-a-Thon" program on TBN (April 1988).

6. Kenneth Copeland, "Image of God in You III" (Fort Worth, TX: Kenneth Copeland Ministries, 1989), audiotape #01-1403, side 1.

7. Charles Capps, *Authority in Three Worlds* (Tulsa, OK: Harrison House, 1982), 50-51, emphasis added.

8. Kenneth Copeland, "What Happened from the Cross to the Throne" (Fort Worth, TX: Kenneth Copeland Ministries, 1990), audiotape #02-0017.

Chapter 12—The Demotion of Christ

1. Kenneth Copeland, "Authority of the Believer IV" (Fort Worth, TX: Kenneth Copeland Ministries, 1987), audiotape #01-0304, side 1.

2. Kenneth Copeland, "Take Time to Pray," *Believer's Voice of Victory* 15, 2 (February 1987):9.

3. Kenneth Copeland, "Question & Answer," *Believer's Voice of Victory* 16, 8 (August 1988):8, emphasis in original.

4. Kenneth Copeland, "The Incarnation" (Fort Worth, TX: Kenneth Copeland Ministries, 1985), audiotape #01-0402, side 1, emphasis in original. We should note that while Copeland, in this tape, speaks of Jesus as the God-man, his statement, "He cannot be a God," clearly indicates otherwise.

5. For further study on the deity of Christ, see Josh McDowell and Bart Larson, *Jesus: A Biblical Defense of His Deity* (San Bernardino, CA: Here's Life Publishers, 1983).

6. Benny Hinn, *Good Morning, Holy Spirit* (Nashville: Thomas Nelson, 1990), 135-36, emphasis added. In the seventh printing, certain unannounced changes were made in the text in response to criticism from CRI so that the passage now reads (changes emphasized): "And let me add this: Had the Holy Spirit not been with Jesus, He *may have likely* sinned. That's right. It was the Holy Spirit *who* was the power that kept Him pure. He was not only sent from heaven, but He was called the Son of Man—and as such He was capable of sinning. . . . Without the Holy Ghost, Jesus *may* have never made it." The "Can you imagine . . ." sentence was deleted entirely. But even with the changes, Christ is still made out to depend on the Holy Spirit to keep Him from sinning, thus denying Christ the sinlessness that is an essential attribute of God.

7. For the significance of the title "Son of Man" in Daniel, see Gleason L. Archer, Jr., *Encyclopedia of Bible Difficulties* (Grand Rapids, MI: Zondervan, 1982), 322-24; and Robert L. Reymond, *Jesus, Divine Messiah* (Phillipsburg, NJ: Presbyterian and Reformed Publishing, 1990), 52-61.

8. Kenneth Copeland, "Substitution and Identification" (Fort Worth, TX: Kenneth Copeland Ministries, 1989), audiotape #00-0202.

9. Charles Capps, *Authority in Three Worlds* (Tulsa, OK: Harrison House, 1982), 189.

10. Charles Capps, *Dynamics of Faith & Confession* (Tulsa, OK: Harrison House, 1987), 86.

11. Copeland, "The Image of God in You III" (Fort Worth, TX: Kenneth Copeland Ministries, 1989), audiotape #01-1403, side 2.

12. Ibid.
13. Copeland, "What Happened from the Cross to the Throne," emphasis in original.

Part 4—Atonement Atrocities
1. Kenneth Copeland, "What Happened from the Cross to the Throne" (Fort Worth, TX: Kenneth Copeland Ministries, 1990), tape #02-0017, side 1.
2. According to a number of Faith teachers, God was able to get a foothold back on the earth after arranging a deal with Abraham. However, according to this peculiar theology, it was not until God caught Satan committing an "illegal move" that He was able to regain control of the universe (see pages 169-70). This highly unusual view stands in marked contrast to the historical ransom theory as set forth by such figures as Origen, Gregory of Nyssa, Augustine, and Anselm (see Millard J. Erickson, *Christian Theology* [Grand Rapids, MI: Baker Book House, 1988], 792-96, 821-22).

Chapter 13—Re-Creation on the Cross
1. The classic Faith work on this subject is E.W. Kenyon, *What Happened from the Cross to the Throne*, 12th ed. (Lynnwood, WA: Kenyon's Gospel Publishing Society, 1969).
2. Benny Hinn, "Benny Hinn" program on TBN (15 December 1990, emphasis in original). This message, titled "The Person of Jesus" (delivered during Orlando Christian Center's Sunday morning service on December 2, 1990), comprises part four of Hinn's six-part series on *The Revelation of Jesus* (Orlando: Orlando Christian Center, 1991), videotape #TV-292. Although Hinn was quoted in October 1991 by *Christianity Today* as confessing he "no longer believe[s] the faith message," it was not long before Hinn was back on the air teaching, once again, the Faith doctrines of prosperity ("Praise the Lord" on TBN [17 April 1992]) and guaranteed healing ("Praise the Lord" programs on TBN [26 December 1991 and 16 April 1992]). To what degree Hinn has "returned" to the Faith camp remains uncertain, though his favorable allusions to both Oral Roberts and Kenneth Hagin (in the programs mentioned) indicate disturbing tendencies.
3. Kenneth E. Hagin, *The Name of Jesus* (Tulsa, OK: Kenneth Hagin Ministries, 1981), 31, emphasis in original.
4. Kenneth Hagin, Jr., personal letter to the author (4 January 1991), 2, emphasis in original. Despite our theological differences, I commend Hagin Jr. for having written his letter to me in a very diplomatic tone.
5. Indications are that the "I" in the attached statement refers to Hagin Sr., since this portion of the correspondence appears to be the standard question-and-answer material which Kenneth Hagin Ministries sends out in response to inquiries (as mentioned in the beginning portion of Hagin Jr.'s letter).
6. Frederick K.C. Price, "Identification #3" (Inglewood, CA: Ever Increasing Faith Ministries, 1980), tape #FP545, side 1.
7. Think for a moment of what it would mean for Christ to have been re-created from the nature of God to the nature of Satan in the Garden of Gethsemane. Among other things, it would mean that a being with the nature of Satan, rather than the spotless Lamb, suffered the Roman scourge and the crown of thorns, along with the crucifixion. It would also mean that the finished work of Christ on the cross is further diminished, as the culmination of the Lord's mission is summarily displaced from Calvary to Gethsemane.
8. Glenn W. Gohr, "Price, Frederick K.C.," *Dictionary of Pentecostal and Charismatic Movements*, eds. Stanley M. Burgess, Gary B. McGee, and Patrick H. Alexander (Grand Rapids, MI: Regency/Zondervan, 1988), 727.
9. See James E. Talmage, *Jesus the Christ* (Salt Lake City: Deseret Book Co., 1969), 613-14. Cf. *What the Mormons Think of Christ*, pamphlet (Salt Lake City: Deseret New Press, n.d.), 31-32; and Joseph Fielding Smith, *Doctrines of Salvation*, compiled by Bruce R. McConkie (Salt Lake City: Bookcraft, 1975 [orig. 1954]), 1:121-38, especially p. 130.
10. Kenneth Copeland, "What Happened from the Cross to the Throne" (Fort Worth, TX: Kenneth Copeland Ministries, 1990), audiotape #02-0017, side 2.
11. For more on this point, see Brian Onken, "The Atonement of Christ and the 'Faith' Message," *Forward* 7, 1 (1984):11-12.
12. Thomas J. Crawford, *The Doctrine of Holy Scripture Respecting the Atonement* (Grand Rapids, MI: Baker Book House, 1954), v; quoted in Onken, "The Atonement," 12.
13. Phillip E. Hughes, *Paul's Second Epistle to the Corinthians*, from *The New International Commentary on the New Testament* series, ed. by Ned B. Stonehouse (Grand Rapids, MI:

Wm. B. Eerdmans Publishing Co., 1962), 213-14. For similar comments, see R.V.G. Tasker, *The Second Epistle of Paul to the Corinthians*, from the *Tyndale New Testament Commentaries* series (Wm. B. Eerdmans Publishing Co., 1977 [orig. 1958]), 90-91.

14. Noted Bible scholar Merrill C. Tenney says of this passage: "The use of the perfect tense in 'It is finished' (*tetelestai*) signifies full completion of Jesus' work and the establishment of a basis for faith. Nothing further needed to be done. Jesus' act was voluntary and confident, for he had discharged perfectly the Father's purpose and was leaving the scene of his human struggle" ("The Gospel of John" from *The Expositor's Bible Commentary* series, gen. ed. Frank E. Gaebelein [Grand Rapids, MI: Regency/Zondervan, 1981], 9:184).

Chapter 14—Redemption in Hell

1. Robert Tilton, "Success-N-Life" program (18 July 1991).
2. Frederick K.C. Price, *Ever Increasing Faith Messenger* (June 1980), 7; quoted in D.R. McConnell, *A Different Gospel* (Peabody, MA: Hendrickson Publishers, 1988), 120.
3. Frederick K.C. Price, "Identification #9" (Los Angeles: Ever Increasing Faith Ministries, 1980), tape #FP551, side 1.
4. For the case against Hagin, see McConnell, *A Different Gospel*, 3-14.
5. Kenneth E. Hagin, "How Jesus Obtained His Name" (Tulsa, OK: Kenneth Hagin Ministries, n.d.), tape #44H01, side 1. Also, see Hagin's article "Made Alive," *The Word of Faith* 15, 4 (April 1982):3, where he writes: "Jesus died as our Substitute. He who knew no sin was made to be sin. He took upon Himself our sin nature. And He died—He was separated and cut off from God. He went down into the prison house of suffering in our place. He was there three days and nights."
6. Kenneth Copeland, "Jesus—Our Lord of Glory," *Believer's Voice of Victory* 10, 4 (April 1982):3.
7. Paul E. Billheimer, *Destined for the Throne*, special edition for TBN (Fort Washington, PA: Christian Literature Crusade, 1988 [orig. 1975]), 83-84, emphasis in original; quoted at length by Jan Crouch during the "Praise the Lord" program on TBN (20 August 1987).
8. Charles Capps, in a manner similar to Fred Price, offers the rationale that "He [Christ] suffered hell for us so that we won't have to" (*Authority in Three Worlds* [Tulsa, OK: Harrison House, 1982], 138).
9. It is more than likely that the word "hell," with all its connotations, was inadvertently substituted for the word "hades" (see Phillip Schaff, *The Creeds of Christendom* [Baker, 1985], 45-46, 69).
10. Strangely enough, some Faith teachers use the same line of argumentation employed by Jehovah's Witnesses to try to get around this point—namely, by claiming that the word—"today" indicates when Jesus uttered His statement to the thief, and not when the thief would be with the Lord in paradise (see, for example, E.W. Kenyon, *What Happened from the Cross to the Throne*, 12th ed. [Lynnwood, WA: Kenyon's Gospel Publishing Society, 1969], 60). For a solid biblical response, see David A. Reed, *Jehovah's Witnesses Answered Verse-By-Verse* (Baker, 1986), 67-69.

Part of the argument also hinges on the distinction between *Hades* and *Gehenna*. I understand the terms to convey distinct ideas. In simple terms, *Hades* is the Greek equivalent for the Hebrew word *Sheol*. It is depicted as the place of disembodied spirits or souls. The Bible portrays it as containing two distinct areas. One area is a place of torment for the wicked; the other is a place of conscious bliss for the righteous (referred to as "paradise" or "Abraham's Bosom"). Both were but a foretaste of what was to come.

That Jesus went to Hades (specifically, the section of Hades called paradise) is evident from 1 Peter 3:18-20. Here Jesus proclaims the completion of His atonement on the cross to the "spirits in prison." And then, as we read in Ephesians 4:8,9, He took the righteous out of Hades (that is, Abraham's Bosom or paradise) and brought them to the very throne room of God. In fact, 2 Corinthians 12:2-4 teaches that paradise is no longer in Hades but is now in the very throne room of God.

The unrighteous who remain in Hades await the day of judgment, when they will stand before God and receive final sentencing. Then death and Hades will be thrown into the lake of fire, which is the second death (Revelation 20:14). It is this lake of fire which Scripture refers to as hell or *Gehenna*—the future place of punishment in the eternal state. While Bible students differ as to exactly what occurred when Jesus went to paradise or Hades, one thing they do agree upon: Jesus did not go to hell to be tortured by Satan and his minions.

Chapter 15—Rebirth in Hell

1. Kenneth Copeland, *Walking in the Realm of the Miraculous* (Fort Worth, TX: Kenneth Copeland Ministries, 1979), 77.
2. Kenneth Copeland, "What Happened from the Cross to the Throne" (Fort Worth, TX: Kenneth Copeland Ministries, 1990), audiotape #02-0017, side 2.
3. Kenneth Copeland, "Believer's Voice of Victory" program (21 April 1991). This message was originally delivered at the Full Gospel Motorcycle Rally Association 1990 Rally at Eagle Mountain Lake, Texas.
4. Kenneth Copeland, "The Price of it All," *Believer's Voice of Victory* 19, 9 (September 1991):4-6.
5. Charles Capps, *Authority in Three Worlds* (Tulsa, OK: Harrison House, 1982), 212-13, emphasis in original.
6. Kenneth E. Hagin, *The Name of Jesus* (Tulsa, OK: Harrison House, 1981), 29.
7. Cf. note 6.
8. The term "firstborn" in Romans 8:29 has also received similar mistreatment from the Faith teachers. See, for example, Frederick K.C. Price, "Identification #8" (Los Angeles: Ever Increasing Faith Ministries, 1980), tape #FP550, side 1.
9. For additional discussions on this point, see J.B. Lightfoot, *St. Paul's Epistles to the Colossians and to Philemon* (Peabody, MA: Hendrickson Publishers, Inc., 1981), 156-58; cf. 146-47; and Herbert M. Carson, *The Epistles of Paul to the Colossians and Philemon*, from the *Tyndale New Testament Commentaries* series (Grand Rapids, MI: Wm. B. Eerdmans Publishing Co., 1977), 43-44.
10. This line of reasoning and exegesis of Colossians 1:18 is applicable to Revelation 1:5 ("the firstborn from the dead") as well.
11. Paul E. Billheimer, *Destined for the Throne*, special edition for TBN (Fort Washington, PA: Christian Literature Crusade, 1988 [orig. 1975]), 86; quoted at length by Jan Crouch during the "Praise the Lord" program on TBN (20 August 1987).
12. See, for example, R.C.H. Lenski, *The Interpretation of the Epistles of St. Peter, St. John and St. Jude* (Minneapolis, MN: Augsburg Publishing House, 1966), 159.
13. Kenneth Copeland, "Substitution and Identification" (Ft. Worth, TX: Kenneth Copeland Ministries, 1989), tape #00-0202, side 2.
14. Benny Hinn, "Our Position 'In Christ,' Part 1" (Orlando, FL: Orlando Christian Center, 1991), videotape #TV-254.

Chapter 16—Reincarnation

1. Paul Crouch, "Praise-a-Thon" program on TBN (6 November 1990).
2. Kenneth E. Hagin, "The Incarnation," *The Word of Faith* 13, 12 (December 1980):14. Hagin's entire article was taken almost word for word from the first half of a chapter titled "The Incarnation or the Humanity and Deity of Jesus," in E.W. Kenyon's book *The Father and His Family*, 12th ed. (Lynnwood, WA: Kenyon's Gospel Publishing Society, 1964), 97-101.
3. See, for example, Bruce R. McConkie, *Mormon Doctrine*, 2d ed. (Salt Lake City: Bookcraft, 1974 [orig. 1966]), 216-17, 278, 282, 590, 750-51.

Chapter 17—Cultural Conformity

1. Quentin J. Schultze, *Televangelism and American Culture* (Grand Rapids, MI: Baker Book House, 1991), 132-33. Cf. Dennis Hollinger, "Enjoying God Forever: An Historical/Sociological Profile of the Health and Wealth Gospel," *Trinity Journal* 9, 2 (Fall 1988): 145-48.
2. Robert Tilton, "Success-N-Life" television program (27 December 1990).
3. See pages 381-82, notes 34-37.
4. John Avanzini, "Was Jesus Poor?" videotape (Hurst, TX: His Image Ministries, n.d.).
5. Frederick K.C. Price, "Ever Increasing Faith" program on TBN (9 December 1990).
6. Avanzini, "Was Jesus Poor?" videotape.
7. John Avanzini, "Praise the Lord" program on TBN (1 August 1989).
8. In discussing the role of biblical interpretation in the "gospel" of prosperity, noted Bible scholar Gordon Fee pointedly remarked that "the plain meaning of the text is *always* the first rule, as well as the ultimate goal, of all valid interpretation. But 'plain meaning' has first of all to do with the author's original *intent*, it has to do with what would have been plain to those to whom the words were originally addressed. It has *not* to do with how someone from a suburbanized white American culture of the late 20th century reads his own cultural setting

back into the text through the frequently distorted prism of the language of the early 17th century" (*The Disease of the Health and Wealth Gospels*, 3d pr. [Beverly, MA: Frontline Publishing, 1985], 5-6, emphasis in original).

9. John Avanzini, "Believer's Voice of Victory" program on TBN (20 January 1991).

10. For a brief yet forceful critique of materialism within Christianity today, see David L. Larsen, "The Gospel of Greed Versus the Gospel of Grace," *Trinity Journal* 9, 2 (Fall 1988):211-20.

11. T.L. and Daisy Osborn, *She & He Photo-Book—Go for It!* (Tulsa, OK: Osborn Foundation, 1983), 62.

12. Ibid., 65, capitalization in original.

13. Frederick K.C. Price, *Faith, Foolishness, or Presumption?* (Tulsa, OK: Harrison House, 1979), 34.

14. Frederick K.C. Price, "Ever Increasing Faith" program on TBN (29 March 1992).

15. Patti Roberts with Sherry Andrews, *Ashes to Gold* (Waco, TX: Word Books, 1983), 110-11.

Chapter 18—Cons and Cover-Ups

1. Philip Schaff, *History of the Christian Church*, 8 vols. (New York: n.p., 1888 [reprint n.p.: AP & A, n.d.]), 7:69.

2. Ibid., 72.

3. Ibid., 73-74.

4. Ibid., 73.

5. Ibid., 75.

6. Ibid., 78.

7. Quote collated from Kenneth Scott Latourette, *A History of Christianity*, rev. ed., 2 vols. (New York: Harper & Row, 1975), 2:717; and R. Tudor Jones, *The Great Reformation* (Downers Grove, IL: InterVarsity Press, 1985), 44. For additional bibliographic data and discussion of variant renderings, see Schaff, *History of the Christian Church*, 7:139, 141.

8. Patti Roberts with Sherry Andrews, *Ashes to Gold* (Waco, TX: Word Books, 1983), 121.

9. Oral Roberts, *A Daily Guide to Miracles* (Tulsa, OK: Pinoak Publications, 1975), 63, capitalization in original.

10. David Lane, president and general manager of WFAA-TV in Dallas, quoted in Associated Press dispatch from Tulsa, Oklahoma, printed as: "TV Ban Won't End Oral Roberts' Vow of 'Cash or Death,' " *Toronto Star* (14 January 1987), A11; and "Despite TV Stations' Protests, Oral Roberts Won't Stop Life-or-Death Appeal for Funds," *Orange County [California] Register* (14 January 1987), A19.

11. Ibid.

12. Oral Roberts, direct-mail letter, undated (ca. 1 March 1987). For the "end of March" deadline, see Oral Roberts, "God's Mandate to Me," *Abundant Life* 41, 2 (March/April 1987):3.

13. Oral Roberts letter (ca. 1 March 1987), 2.

14. Ibid., 4.

15. Richard Roberts, direct-mail letter, undated (ca. 1 January 1987), 1-3 passim. Oral Roberts' 69th birthday was on January 24, 1987.

16. Ibid., capitalization in original.

17. Oral Roberts, direct-mail letter, undated (ca. 1 January 1985), 1-2, emphasis in original.

18. Ibid., 1.

19. Ibid., 2, capitalization in original.

20. Ibid., 3, capitalization in original.

21. Ibid., 1, 3, capitalization in original.

22. Ibid., 2, capitalization in original.

23. Oral Roberts, presentation at the World Charismatic Conference, Melodyland Christian Center, Anaheim, CA (7 August 1992), audiotape excerpt on file at Christian Research Institute, emphasis added.

24. See Charles Fillmore, *Prosperity* (Lee's Summit, MO: Unity Books, 1967 [orig. 1936]).

25. The item referred to here is a poem, presented as the day's devotional, that was previously published in *Unity Magazine*. R.H. Grenville, "Whatever Good," *Daily Blessing: A Guide to Seed-Faith Living*, 24, 1 (January-February-March 1982):46.

26. Gloria Copeland, *God's Will Is Prosperity* (Tulsa, OK: Harrison House, 1978), 54.

27. Ibid.

28. "Praise-a-Thon" program on TBN (5 November 1990).

29. Ibid.

30. Ibid.
31. Ibid.
32. Ibid.
33. Ibid.
34. Paul Crouch, "Praise the Lord" program on TBN (21 July 1992).
35. Oral Roberts, *Oral Roberts' Best Sermons and Stories* (Tulsa, OK: Oral Roberts, 1956), 46; *101 Questions and Answers* (Tulsa, OK: Oral Roberts, 1968), 18; quoted in David Edwin Harrell, Jr., *Oral Roberts: An American Life* (Bloomington, IN: Indiana University Press, 1985), 451, 604, note 110.
36. Robert Tilton, direct-mail letter with enclosures (1990), 6.
37. Ibid.
38. Ibid., 5, 6.
39. Ibid., 2, 3, capitalization and emphasis in original.
40. Ibid., 4.
41. Marilyn Hickey, direct-mail letter, undated (ca. December 1988), 4, emphasis in original.
42. Oral and Richard Roberts, direct-mail letter (August 1984), 2-3.
43. Ibid., 3.
44. Ibid., capitalization in original.
45. Ibid.
46. Ibid., 4, capitalization in original.
47. Ibid., capitalization in original.
48. Ibid.
49. Ibid.
50. Oral Roberts, *A Daily Guide to Miracles*, 64.
51. Ibid., 66.
52. Ibid., 68.
53. Ibid., 65.
54. Marilyn Hickey, direct-mail letter, undated (ca. 1992), 3.
55. John Avanzini, *It's Not Working, Brother John!* (Tulsa, OK: Harrison House, 1992), 13, emphasis in original.
56. Subtitle of Avanzini's book (ibid.).
57. Ibid., 45-53.
58. Ibid., 49-52; also see previous chapter on "Cultural Conformity."
59. Ibid., 52 (footnote).
60. Ibid., 141-42, capitalization in original.
61. Ibid., 142.
62. Ibid., 145, capitalization in original.
63. Ibid., 143.
64. Ernest Holmes, *Creative Mind and Success*, rev. ed. (New York: Dodd, Mead & Co., 1967 [orig. 1919]), 84.
65. Avanzini, *It's Not Working, Brother John!*, 213, back cover.
66. Ibid., 124, 122, emphasis in original.
67. Ibid., 122, emphasis in original.
68. Ibid., 123, emphasis in original.

Chapter 19—Covenant-Contract
1. Kenneth Copeland, *Our Covenant with God* (Fort Worth, TX: KCP Publications, 1987), 10.
2. Benny Hinn, sermon at the World Charismatic Conference, Melodyland Conference Center, Anaheim, CA (7 August 1992), audiotape excerpt on file at Christian Research Institute.
3. Kenneth Copeland, "God's Covenants with Man II" (Fort Worth, TX: Kenneth Copeland Ministries, 1985), audiotape #01-4404, side 2.
4. E.W. Kenyon, *The Blood Covenant* (Lynnwood, WA: Kenyon's Gospel Publishing Society, 1969), 14, 16.
5. The Faith movement clearly promotes a view of covenants which better fits the description of contracts than the biblical idea of covenants. Consider these key features which distinguish covenants from contracts:

   1) Contracts are *thing-oriented* (focusing largely on the benefits to which each party is entitled), whereas covenants are *person-oriented* (arising out of a desire to form an intimate relationship, one party to another).

2) Contracts arise from a *mutual agreement* between two parties (thereby involving some form of *negotiation*), whereas covenants are initiated by the *stronger party* (who offers non-negotiable help, not of necessity, but out of grace or as a gift).

3) Contracts have conditions that are *performance-oriented* (focusing on the fulfillment of certain terms), whereas covenants stipulate obligations in terms of *personal loyalty*.

(Adapted from Elmer A. Martens, *God's Design: A Focus on Old Testament Theology* [Grand Rapids, MI: Baker Book House, 1981], 72-73.)

The divine covenants discussed in the Old Testament (i.e., between God and humanity) are comprised of elements that are strikingly similar to those found in suzerainty treaties of the ancient Near East. In light of this fact, one may well contend that the Faith teaching of "covenant-contracts" has been proven false by the archaeological and historical records. (On the relationship between ancient Near Eastern suzerainty treaties and Old Testament covenants, see William Dyrness, *Themes in Old Testament Theology* [Downers Grove, IL: InterVarsity Press, 1979], 114-16; the classic treatment on this subject is George E. Mendenhall, Covenant Forms in Israelite Tradition, *The Biblical Archaeologist* 17, 3 [September 1954]: 50-76.)

6. Kenneth Copeland, "Christianity, A Series of Decisions" (Fort Worth, TX: Kenneth Copeland Ministries, 1985), audiotape #01-0406, side 2; "Origin of the Blood Covenant" (Fort Worth, TX: Kenneth Copeland Ministries, 1985), audiotape #01-4401, side 2.

7. Charles Capps, *Authority in Three Worlds* (Tulsa, OK: Harrison House, 1982), 66, emphasis in original.

8. Kenneth Copeland, *The Power of the Tongue* (Fort Worth, TX: KCP Publications, 1980), 10.

9. Kenneth Copeland, *The Laws of Prosperity* (Fort Worth, TX: Kenneth Copeland Publications, 1974), 51, emphasis in original.

10. Frederick K.C. Price, *Prosperity on God's Terms* (Tulsa, OK: Harrison House, 1990), 36-37, emphasis in original.

11. Copeland, *The Laws of Prosperity*, 50-51. Copeland is here referring to Galatians 3:13,14 to argue that Jesus has redeemed all Christians from the curse of the law (which the Faith teachers wrongly associate with the curses listed in Deuteronomy 28) and has procured for them the material blessings of Abraham. However, the context of the passage militates against any such interpretation, as the discussion involves spiritual redemption and not earthly riches.

The message of Galatians 3 is straightforward and simple: Fallen humanity can achieve a right standing with God only through faith in Christ. God's law demands nothing short of perfection; hence it becomes a curse for those who attempt to attain a righteous standing by striving to fulfill it through sheer human effort (verses 10-12). Sinful humanity is wholly incapable of coming close to meeting such high standards (verse 3). The good news is that Christ redeemed the elect from that curse by His perfect obedience and sacrifice to the Father. Our faith or trust in Christ's finished work is credited as righteousness and justifies us before God (verses 26-28), which is precisely the blessing Abraham received (verses 6-9).

The Faith teachers diminish the infinite value and worth of Christ's sacrifice by falsely asserting that He died so that we may pamper ourselves in material indulgences. Far from concerning itself with such triflings, Galatians 3 calls attention to the grace of God, who, knowing that we could never be righteous in His sight through our own works, offered the supreme sacrifice so that we might be reconciled to Him.

12. Robert Tilton, "Success-N-Life" program (27 December 1990).

13. Jim Bakker, quoted in Terry Mattingly, " 'Prosperity Christian' Sings a Different Tune," *Rocky Mountain News* (16 August 1992), 158.

14. Ibid.

15. Ibid.

16. Ibid.

17. Ibid.

18. Paraphrased from Charles H. Spurgeon, "A Sermon from a Rush" [commenting on Job 8:11-13, sermon 651 of sermons preached during 1865] in *Metropolitan Tabernacle Pulpit*, 63 vols. (Pasadena, TX: Pilgrim Publications, 1989), 11:537.

Chapter 20—Context, Context, Context

1. Paul Crouch, "Praise-a-Thon" program on TBN (2 April 1991).

2. Ibid.

3. Ibid. Other opponents of orthodox Christianity have also received a warm welcome on TBN. Anti-Trinitarians who have been given a platform include Roy Blizzard, Joseph Good, and at least one minister from the United Pentecostal Church (UPC). William DeArteaga, who wrote a book advocating a form of "Christian" reincarnation (*Past Life Visions: A Christian Exploration* [New York: Seabury Press, 1983]; cf. Norman Geisler and J. Yutaka Amano, *The Reincarnation Sensation* [Wheaton, IL: Tyndale House Publishers, 1986], 52-53), has also appeared on TBN to promote his latest book dealing with the Charismatic movement and the Faith controversy. Although DeArteaga has claimed that he has since abandoned his metaphysical ideas, it is uncertain whether this includes his views regarding reincarnation (cf. *Quenching the Spirit* [Lake Mary, FL: Creation House, 1992], 13, 279, note 25).

4. Ibid.

5. Ibid.

6. For a discussion on this topic, see Ron Rhodes, "Esotericism and Biblical Interpretation," *Christian Research Journal* 14, 3 (Winter 1992).28-31.

7. For a short list of helpful aids and resources, see R.C. Sproul, *Knowing Scripture* (Downers Grove, IL: InterVarsity Press, 1977), 123-25.

8. John Avanzini, "Praise-a-Thon" program on TBN (5 November 1990).

9. Walter Bauer, William F. Arndt, F. Wilbur Gingrich, *A Greek-English Lexicon of the New Testament and Other Early Christian Literature*, 4th rev. and aug. ed. (Chicago: The University of Chicago Press, 1957), 857a; U. Wilckens, "hysterema, hysteresis," *Theological Dictionary of the New Testament*, abridged in one vol. and ed. by Geoffrey W. Bromiley (Grand Rapids, MI: Eerdmans/Paternoster Press, 1985), 1241; W.E. Vine, *An Expository Dictionary of New Testament Words* (Old Tappan, NJ: Fleming H. Revell Co., 1966), 196.

10. Roberts, *A Daily Guide to Miracles* (Tulsa, OK: Pinoak Press, 1975), 36-38 passim.

11. Gordon D. Fee, *The Disease of the Health and Wealth Gospels* (Beverly, MA: Frontline Publishing, 1985), 6, emphasis in original.

12. Ibid.

13. Ibid.

14. John Piper, *Desiring God* (Portland, OR: Multnomah Press, 1986), 163, 167.

Part 6—Sickness and Suffering

1. Paraphrasing Job 8:6 (Bildad the Shuhite); 11:4-6,14,15 (Zophar the Naamathite); 15:5,6; 22:5-7,9,23 (Eliphaz the Temanite). Elihu the son of Barachel the Buzite was not described as a "friend" of Job's, but he too attacked Job for alleged sin (Job 34:37). Some Faith commentators try to twist these passages around to argue that since God seemingly did not condemn Elihu at the end, but only Job's three "friends" (Job 42:7,8; cf. 2:11), this means that Elihu's charges against Job still stand. This argument fails because God not only condemns the three friends but also adds repeatedly that they had "not spoken of me what is right, as my servant Job has" (Job 42:7,8, emphasis added). Thus, regardless of the reason for omitting reference to Elihu at the end of the book, Job was still upheld by God Himself as having told the truth, obviously including Job's many statements that he had not sinned against God.

2. Frederick K.C. Price, *Is Healing for All?* (Tulsa, OK: Harrison House, 1976), 20.

3. Betty Price, "A Praise Report," *Ever Increasing Faith Messenger*, 12:3 (Summer 1991); see also Pat Hays, "Betty Price Speaks At 1991 'Wisdom from Above' Luncheon," *Ever Increasing Faith Messenger*,13:1 (Winter 1992), 12-13; and Betty Price, "Health Update...then... and...now from Betty Price," *Ever Increasing Faith Messenger*, 13:4 (Fall 1992), 5.

4. Kenneth Hagin: "...I've been able to live for nearly sixty years without having a headache. I didn't say headache symptoms never tried to attack me. I said I haven't had a headache in nearly sixty years because when a symptom came, I demanded that it leave in Jesus' Name, and it left!...When you exercise your authority by faith in the Name of Jesus, sickness or disease must go!" (*Classic Sermons*, Word of Faith 25th Anniversary 1968-1992 Commemorative Edition [Tulsa, OK: Kenneth Hagin Ministries, 1992], 159, emphasis added.) "I have not had one sick day in 45 years. I did not say that the devil hadn't attacked me. But before the day is out, I am healed" (*The Name of Jesus* [Tulsa, OK: Kenneth Hagin Ministries, 1979], 133.) In the early days, Hagin was not so sure he was always healed by the end of the day: "Perhaps the next day it [the healing] has not yet materialized, but we have to walk by faith and hold fast to our confession" (*Right and Wrong Thinking* [Tulsa, OK: Kenneth Hagin Ministries, 1966], 21.) Later, Hagin was not only sure he had always been healed by the end of the day, but that it in fact took no more than 1½ hours (Kenneth E. Hagin, *Seven Things You Should Know About*

Divine Healing [Tulsa, OK: Kenneth Hagin Ministries, 1979], 68, emphasis added.) Now, Hagin maintains that he has been healed "within just a few seconds," evidently referring to a 1942 instance of heart trouble (Hagin, "God's Best Belongs to You!" *Word of Faith*, 26:1 [December 1992], 5c).

On Hagin's "no headache" since 1933/4 comment, see Kenneth E. Hagin, sermon at the "All Faith's Crusade," Anaheim [CA] Convention Center (21 March 1991); and Kenneth E. Hagin, *Name of Jesus* (Tulsa, OK: Kenneth Hagin Ministries, 1981), 44. "Forty-five years have come and gone, and I haven't had a headache. Not one. The last headache I can actually remember having was in August 1933. I haven't had a headache, and I'm not expecting to have one. But if I had a headache, I wouldn't tell anybody. And if somebody asked me how I was feeling, I would say, 'I'm fine, thank you'" (Kenneth E. Hagin, *Words* [Tulsa, OK: Kenneth Hagin Ministries, 1979], 6-7.)

Hagin claims he was healed of his "deformed heart," "paralysis," and "incurable blood disease." In case he missed something, he declared his "healing from the top of my head to the soles of my feet" on August 7, 1934, so that "every symptom of distress, deficiency and physical wrongness was driven out of my body," perpetually. "I'm still healed after 49 years," Hagin said. (Kenneth E. Hagin, *Exceedingly Growing Faith*, 2d rev. ed. [Tulsa, OK: Kenneth Hagin Ministries, 1990], 82-83.) See also Kenneth E. Hagin, *Understanding How to Fight the Good Fight of Faith* (Tulsa, OK: Kenneth Hagin Ministries, 1987), 6; Kenneth E. Hagin, *What Faith Is*, rev. ed. (Tulsa, OK: Kenneth Hagin Ministries, 1983), 18-19; Kenneth E. Hagin, *How to Write Your Own Ticket with God* (Tulsa, OK: Kenneth Hagin Ministries, 1979), 16-17; Kenneth E. Hagin, *Faith Food for Spring* (Tulsa, OK: Kenneth Hagin Ministries, 1978), 9; Kenneth E. Hagin, *I Believe in Visions* (Old Tappan, NJ: Revell, 1972), 27-30 (apparently his healing occurred on Tuesday of the "second week" of August 1934, or August 7, which was not the same date as the "second Tuesday" that month [August 14]). Elsewhere Hagin gives various dates, such as "6 days before my 17th birthday [August 20, 1934]," which would be August 14, the "second Tuesday of August 1934": (Kenneth E. Hagin, *El Shaddai* [Tulsa, OK: Kenneth Hagin Ministries, 1980], 24-25.) But see Kenneth E. Hagin, *How You Can Be Led by the Spirit of God* (Tulsa, OK: Kenneth Hagin Ministries, 1978), 87 (healing on a "Thursday" in August 1934). In still another place Hagin claims his healing was on "August 8, 1934," which was a Wednesday (Kenneth E. Hagin, *Zoe: The God-Kind of Life* [Tulsa, OK: Kenneth Hagin Ministries, 1981], 13.) The blood disease may have been a form of hemolytic anemia (Hagin, *How You Can Be Led*, ibid., 88).

5. Hagin suffered heart-crisis episodes in 1939, 1942, 1949, and 1973:

> (1) Ca. May 1939: "...I attended a Full Gospel convention....As I sat in the service, I began to have sharp pains around my heart. It seemed to quiver and stop. It even felt as if my breath were being cut off" (Hagin, *Right and Wrong Thinking*, 20-21).
>
> (2) 1942: "...While pastoring a church in East Texas, I had a battle in my body....I didn't tell anyone about it. I just told the Lord and believed He would heal me. Then I stood my ground. There were some trying moments in the nighttime when it seemed as if I wouldn't make it....I had fought this battle for about six weeks....I had been fighting this battle for a long time" (Kenneth E. Hagin, *Authority of the Believer* [Tulsa, OK: Kenneth Hagin Ministries, 1967], 9). "In the nighttime I would be awakened with alarming heart symptoms....I battled that thing for about six weeks" (Kenneth E. Hagin, *The Believer's Authority*, 2d rev. ed. [Tulsa, OK: Kenneth Hagin Ministries, 1991], 8). "...I had a battle with symptoms in my body....At times it looked like I wasn't going to make it" (Kenneth E. Hagin, *Faith Food for Spring* [Tulsa, OK: Kenneth Hagin Ministries, 1978], 29).
>
> This is apparently the same incident as the following: "The heart symptoms did come back on me....I struggled with it in the nighttime.... 'Yes, I've got heart symptoms. In fact, if it gets any worse, I don't know what I'm going to do'" (*The Name of Jesus*, 138). "...some alarming heart symptoms tried to come back on me....I knew that these symptoms could mean death, but I never budged an inch. I didn't discuss it with anyone. The devil kept telling me, 'You are not going to make it. You're going to die....' I...took my Bible and put it on the floor, and put both my feet on it" (Kenneth E. Hagin, *The Real Faith* [Tulsa, OK: Kenneth Hagin Ministries, 1982], 27). "I remember many years ago after I was healed, physical symptoms came back....The devil said to me, '...You're going to die...!'...I laid my Bible on the floor and literally stood on it...." (Kenneth E. Hagin, "God's Best," *Word of Faith* [December 1992], 5c).

(3) July 10, 1949: "... I was planning to preach at a church in East Texas ... and I attended a men's Bible class before the service. I was sitting on a bench and suddenly my heart stopped and I pitched over on the floor on my face. I fell right at the pastor's feet. He picked me up and my heart began to race. You couldn't detect the beating. It felt like something shaking like a bowl full of gelatin.... They told me later, 'We knew you were dead.' I was cold all over and white as a sheet. Death was upon my brow" (Kenneth E. Hagin, *Must Christians Suffer?* [Tulsa, OK: Kenneth Hagin Ministries, 1982], 38). "Sitting in [Sunday school] class my heart suddenly stopped beating. I fell from my seat to the floor. Then my heart started beating erratically with a rapid pulse.... When some ministers ... felt my pulse they said, 'We cannot distinguish a beat—all we can feel is a flutter.' It seemed to me as if it were racing two or three hundred times a minute.... I became as cold as ice all over.... I knew when death came over me.... [I] nearly died..." (Kenneth E. Hagin, *The Human Spirit* [Tulsa, OK: Kenneth Hagin Ministries, 1974], 24-25).

(4) 1973 heart episode: "[Hagin] had a heart attack, and like to died. God told him, says, 'You gonna die at the age of 55 [1972-73] if you don't start prophesying.' ... It come real close of costing Kenneth Hagin his whole life.... That was the year before Rhema was started [in 1974]" (Norvel Hayes, presentation at the East Coast Believers' Convention [24 May 1982], audiotape). Possibly this is the same incident described by Hagin in 1978: "I was awakened at 1:30 A.M., several years ago, with severe symptoms in my heart and chest. I knew something about them because I'd been bedfast and expected to die with a heart condition as a teenager" (*Faith Food for Spring*, 89). In 1989 Hagin added some details about this occurrence: "... I was holding a meeting in Pasadena, Texas. After one of the evening meetings, I had just gotten off to sleep, when I was awakened about 1:30 in the morning with severe heart pains. It seemed as if the incurable heart disease I'd had as a teenager had come back on me.... I lay in bed that night with severe heart pain gripping me..." (Kenneth E. Hagin, *Knowing What Belongs to Us* [Tulsa, OK: Kenneth Hagin Ministries, 1989], 13-14).

(5) No date: "... twice in my life it seemed that death had come and fastened itself upon me. Both times I just started laughing." One of the incidents is described above (Pasadena, Texas, no date) (Hagin, *Knowing What Belongs to Us*, 13).

(6) Possible heart condition for three days, no date: "One time when I was attending a convention, I was having physical problems. I didn't say anything to my wife, but I couldn't sleep. Three nights I got down by the bed praying, but my healing would not come into manifestation. The symptoms would not leave me" (Kenneth E. Hagin, *Three Big Words* [Tulsa, OK: Kenneth Hagin Ministries, 1983], 24).

(7) One-night episode, no date: "A number of years ago, just before bedtime I was troubled with physical symptoms of alarming proportions.... I got into bed, but these symptoms only grew worse. I continued to praise God for healing and finally managed to fall asleep. Almost immediately I was awakened with these symptoms. I finally said, 'Lord, I just don't know how much longer I can take this.' ... Awakened by serious symptoms for the third time, I heard in my spirit the words, 'Consider not.' ... My struggle was with appropriating physical healing in my body as alarming symptoms persisted.... Symptoms and pain persisted" (Kenneth E. Hagin, *The Key to Scriptural Healing* [Tulsa, OK: Kenneth Hagin Evangelistic Assoc., 1977], 27-28, [1984 rev.], 25-26).

6. Hagin, "God's Best," 5c.

7. "God's Bountiful Double Portion," *Word of Faith* (December 1992), 10b-c.

8. Bruce Barron, *The Health and Wealth Gospel* (Downers Grove, IL: InterVarsity Press, 1987), 14-34.

9. Marla Cone, "Oral Roberts Stable After Heart Problem," *The Los Angeles Times* (8 October 1992), B1, B9; Oral Roberts and Paul Crouch on "Praise the Lord" show on TBN (6 October 1992). When Crouch laid hands on Roberts to minister to Roberts' chest pains, the latter exclaimed, "I feel the healing power of Jesus!" and said it felt like an "electric current." Less than four hours later, while visiting a home in Newport Beach, Roberts felt more pains and was hospitalized at Hoag Presbyterian Memorial Hospital (also in Newport Beach), shortly after midnight. Subsequent articles report that Roberts's heart attack was "near fatal" ("Evangelist Has Tests," *The Orange County [CA] Register* [16 December 1992], A-7) and resulted in the evangelist receiving a pacemaker ("Roberts Out of Hospital," *The Orange County [CA] Register* [21 December 1992], A-30).

Paul Crouch's heart trouble: "Just this week ... Paul [Crouch] just had the awfullest heart pains for two days. Just the awfullest heart pains. His heart would beat and stop, and stop and flutter and go and pain and pain and pain" (Jan Crouch, "Praise the Lord" program on TBN [31 July 1992]).

10. Letter from L.E. [name withheld for privacy] (25 August 1992).
11. Author's letter to L.E. [name withheld for privacy] (31 August 1992).
12. Letter from D.B. [name withheld for privacy] (13 July 1992).

Chapter 21—Symptoms and Sickness

1. Kenneth Copeland, *The Troublemaker* (Fort Worth, TX: Kenneth Copeland Publications, n.d. [ca. 1970]), 6.
2. Kenneth Copeland, *Healed... to Be or Not to Be* (Fort Worth, TX: Kenneth Copeland Ministries, 1979), 25.
3. Ibid., 31-32, emphasis in original.
4. Benny Hinn, *"Rise & Be Healed!"* (Orlando, FL: Celebration Publishers, 1991), 44.
5. Ibid., 14.
6. Ibid., 32, emphasis in original.
7. Ibid., 65.
8. Jerry Savelle, *If Satan Can't Steal Your Joy...* (Tulsa, OK: Harrison House, 1982), 9.
9. Ibid., 9-10, emphasis in original.
10. "I also have successfully resisted the flu all these years," claims Hagin. The longest any symptoms ever stayed was an hour and a half. Generally speaking, we Christians do not do that [resist illness]. At the first little *symptom of flu* that shows up (a headache or whatever) we will say, 'Oh, yes, I've got it.' " (*Seven Things You Should Know About Divine Healing* [Tulsa, OK: Kenneth Hagin Ministries, 1979], 68, emphasis added). "Someone asked, 'Brother Hagin, are you ever sick?' 'No' " (Kenneth E. Hagin, *God's Medicine* [Tulsa, OK: Kenneth Hagin Ministries, 1977], 17).

Hagin once declared during a 1957 flu epidemic, "This epidemic doesn't worry me. I will never have the Asian flu" (*Understanding How to Fight the Good Fight* [Tulsa, OK: Kenneth Hagin Ministries, 1987], 119). In another version Hagin asserts, "I'll *never* [Hagin's emphasis] have the Asian flu" (*El Shaddai* [Tulsa, OK: Kenneth Hagin Ministries, 1980], 35-36). See also Hagin's son's report of the incident (Kenneth E. Hagin, Jr., *Blueprint for Building Strong Faith* [Tulsa, OK: Kenneth Hagin Ministries, 1980], 27). Hagin's son mentioned that his own young son (senior Hagin's grandson) was "diagnosed as having a brain tumor that required immediate surgery," but there is no mention of any faith healing whatsoever (Kenneth E. Hagin, Jr., *The Answer for Oppression* [Tulsa, OK: Kenneth Hagin Ministries, 1983], 14-16, 23).

However, during another flu epidemic, in Texas in 1960, Hagin admits: "Everyone [sic] of those symptoms passed over my body in the night time, but I never told a person." (*Bible Faith Study Course* [Tulsa, OK: Hagin Evangelistic Assoc., n.d. (ca. 1966)], 6). Elsewhere Hagin admits, "At times when I've had symptoms of a cold, some have said to me, 'Oh, you're getting a cold.' I say, 'No, I don't have a cold and I'm not going to have one.' " (*Understanding How to Fight*, 129).

Jesus supposedly told Hagin in January 1950: "Sometimes even while you were preaching any symptoms you had would disappear." (Kenneth E. Hagin, *How God Taught Me About Prosperity* [Tulsa, OK: Kenneth Hagin Ministries, 1985], 11.)
11. Frederick K.C. Price, *Faith, Foolishness, or Presumption?* (Tulsa, OK: Harrison House, 1979), 76-77.
12. Savelle, *If Satan*, 10-11, emphasis in original.
13. Kenneth Copeland, "West Coast Believer's Convention," recorded in Anaheim, CA, on June 13, 1991.
14. Kenneth E. Hagin, *Right and Wrong Thinking* (Tulsa, OK: Kenneth Hagin Ministries, 1966), 20-21.
15. Ibid., 21.
16. Paul Brand and Philip Yancey, *Healing: What Does God Promise?* (Portland, OR: Multnomah Press, 1984 [Guideposts reprint, Carmel, NY]), 7.
17. Ibid.
18. Ibid.
19. Mary Baker Eddy, *Science and Health with Key to the Scriptures* (Boston: First Church of Christ, Scientist, 1971 [orig. 1875]), 390.
20. Phineas Quimby, *The Quimby Manuscripts*, ed. by Horatio W. Dresser (New Hyde Park, NY: University Books, 1961 [orig. 1859]), 186.
21. Hagin, *Right and Wrong Thinking*, 19, 24.

22. Kenneth Copeland, *Walking in the Realm of the Miraculous* (Fort Worth, TX: Kenneth Copeland Ministries, 1979), 37.
23. Price, *Faith, Foolishness*, 93. Also see Frederick K.C. Price, *How Faith Works* (Tulsa, OK: Harrison House, 1976), 92-93, quoted in D.R. McConnell, *A Different Gospel* (Peabody, MA: Hendrickson Publishers, 1988), 154, 167, note 31.
24. Price, *Faith, Foolishness*, 88.
25. Hagin, "Healing: The Father's Provision," *Word of Faith* (August 1977), 9; quoted in McConnell, *A Different Gospel*, 157, 168, note 41.
26. Hinn, *"Rise & Be Healed!"*, 64, emphasis in original.
27. Paul Crouch letter to M.A. [name withheld for privacy], 28 August 1992, emphasis added.
28. Copeland, *Healed...to Be*, 12.
29. Ibid., 12-13.
30. For additional treatment of the Faith movement's misuse of Isaiah 53:5 and other verses, see Elliot Miller, *Healing: Does God Always Heal?* (San Juan Capistrano: CRI, 1979), 3-5.

Chapter 22—Satan and Sickness
1. Kenneth Copeland, *The Power of the Tongue* (Fort Worth, TX: Kenneth Copeland Ministries, 1980), 20, emphasis in original.
2. Ibid., 30, emphasis in original.
3. Ibid., 23-24, emphasis in original.
4. Finis J. Dake, *God's Plan for Man* (Lawrenceville, GA: Dake Bible Sales, 1977 [orig. 1949]), 241.
5. Frederick K.C. Price, *Faith, Foolishess, or Presumption?* (Tulsa, OK: Harrison House, 1979), 88, 94.
6. Frederick K.C. Price, *Is Healing for All?* (Tulsa, OK: Harrison House, 1976), 113, emphasis in orig.
7. Kenneth E. Hagin, *I Believe in Visions* (Old Tappan, NJ: Spire Books/Revell, 1972), 65.
8. Ibid., 67.
9. Robert Tilton, "Success-N-Life" program (ca. 1991), video on file at Christian Research Institute.
10. Matthew, in context, is saying that when church members sin and repent, the church must "loose" or restore them to fellowship; but when they cannot, they should "bind" or remove them. (See Hendrik H. Hanegraaff, "CRI Perspective: 'Binding and Loosing'" [Irvine, CA: CRI, 1991], order no. CP-0610; Eric Villanueva, "Territorial Spirits and Spiritual Warfare: A Biblical Perspective," *Christian Research Journal*, 15:1 [Summer 1992], 39.)
11. Frederick K.C. Price, *How Faith Works* (Tulsa, OK: Harrison House, 1976), 23.
12. Kenneth E. Hagin, *Faith Food for Spring* (Tulsa, OK: Kenneth Hagin Ministries, 1978), 72, 73, 79, emphasis in original.
13. Gloria Copeland, "Believer's Voice of Victory" program on TBN (25 October 1992).
14. Frederick K.C. Price, "Is God Glorified Through Sickness?" (Los Angeles: Crenshaw Christian Center, n.d.), audiotape #FP605, emphasis added.

Chapter 23—Sin and Sickness
1. Letter from S.C. [name withheld for privacy] (25 September 1991), 2.
2. Letter from H.C. [name withheld for privacy] (ca. 6 August 1991).
3. Letter from C.C. [name withheld for privacy] (19 June 1992).
4. Kenneth Copeland, presentation at Melodyland Christian Center, Anaheim, CA (30 March 1983), emphasis in original.
5. Frederick K.C. Price, *How Faith Works* (Tulsa, OK: Harrison House, 1976), 77.
6. Frederick K.C. Price, "Paul's Thorn #1" (Los Angeles: Ever Increasing Faith Ministries, 1980), audiotape #FP606, side 2. See also Price's statement, "Paul was a man who was prone to brag and boast." (*Is Healing for All?* [Tulsa, OK: Harrison House, 1976], 12.)
7. It is even more obvious in the original Greek than it is in English that Paul was *given* a thorn in the flesh, as opposed to giving it to himself. In Greek, the passive verb (*edothe*) is used to make it clear that Paul was the *recipient of the giving*. In other words, the giving came from somewhere else. If the Holy Spirit had intended to indicate that Paul's own sin was responsible for his sickness or affliction, the middle voice (*edoto*) would have been used.
8. Gordon D. Fee, *The Disease of the Health and Wealth Gospels* (Beverly, MA: Frontline Publishing, 1985), 28-30, emphasis in original.
9. Benny Hinn, *"Rise & Be Healed!"* (Orlando, FL: Celebration Publishers, 1991), 62.
10. Darrel W. Amundsen, "The Anguish and Agonies of Charles Spurgeon," *Christian History* 10, 1 (1991):22-25 at 25b-c.

11. Kenneth Copeland, *The Troublemaker* (Fort Worth, TX: Kenneth Copeland Publications, ca. 1970), 12.
12. Mary Ann Jeffreys, "Sayings of Spurgeon," *Christian History* 10, 1 (1991):12a.
13. Price, *Is Healing for All?*, 14-15.
14. George M. Lamsa, *Holy Bible: From the Ancient Eastern Text* (New York: A.J. Holman, 1933 [San Francisco: Harper & Row, n.d., 1984 reprint]), 1065a.
15. See John P. Juedes, "George M. Lamsa: Christian Scholar or Cultic Torchbearer?" *Christian Research Journal* 12, 2 (Fall 1989):8-14.
16. Price, *Is Healing for All?*, 15 (footnote).
17. Kenneth Copeland, *The Power of the Tongue* (Fort Worth, TX: Kenneth Copeland Ministries, 1980), 22.
18. Kenneth Copeland, *Welcome to the Family* (Fort Worth, TX: Kenneth Copeland Ministries, 1979), 25, emphasis in original.

Chapter 24—Sovereignty and Sickness
1. Benny Hinn, *"Rise & Be Healed!"* (Orlando, FL: Celebration Publishers, 1991), 47-48.
2. Frederick K.C. Price, "Ever Increasing Faith" program on TBN (16 November 1990).
3. Matthew 26:42; Mark 14:36; Luke 22:42; John 4:34; 5:30; 6:38; Acts 18:21; 1 Corinthians 4:19; Hebrews 10:7; Psalm 40:8; 143:10.
4. Gordon D. Fee, *The Disease of the Health and Wealth Gospels* (Beverly, MA: Frontline Publishers, 1985), 22.

Part 7—Back to Basics
1. Associated Press release, "4 Killed When Balloon Hits Wires And Burns," *St. Louis Post-Dispatch* (16 December 1979), 14A.
2. Additional details about the author's Christian conversion can be found in Hendrik Hanegraaff, "Testimony of a Former Skeptic," *Acts & Facts: Impact* 202 (April 1990), available from the Christian Research Institute, Box 500, San Juan Capistrano, CA 92693-0500.

Chapter 25—A = Amen
1. Frederick K.C. Price, "Ever Increasing Faith" program on TBN (16 November 1990).
2. Frederick K.C. Price, *What Every Believer Should Know About Prayer*, pamphlet (Los Angeles: Ever Increasing Faith Ministries, 1990), [4]. In light of the fact that the Faith teachers promote the error that "confession brings possession," their dim view of adding "Thy will be done" to prayer is not too surprising. Their system, implicitly if not explicitly, opposes the biblical teaching of submitting prayer petitions to the will of God. After all, petitions in prayer are *requests* that are subject to God's will, while confessions in Faith theology are outright *demands* supposedly guaranteed by God to bring each individual's personal desires into being. As Price's role model wrote: "I have found that the most effective way to pray can be when you demand your rights. That's the way I pray: 'I demand my rights!' " (Kenneth E. Hagin, *The Believer's Authority*, 2d ed. [Tulsa, OK: Kenneth Hagin Ministries, 1991], 22).
3. Frederick K.C. Price, *Petition Prayer, or the Prayer of Faith*, pamphlet (Los Angeles: Ever Increasing Faith Ministries, 1991), [1], emphasis in original.
4. Price, *What Every Believer Should Know About Prayer*, [4].
5. Frederick K.C. Price, letter to B.G. [name withheld for privacy] (14 October 1992).
6. Price, *Petition Prayer, or the Prayer of Faith*, [1], capitalization in original.
7. Ibid., [3], capitalization in original.
8. Ibid., [4], capitalization and emphasis in original.
9. R.A. Torrey, *The Power of Prayer* (Grand Rapids, MI: Zondervan, 1981) 123-24, emphasis in original.

Chapter 26—B = Bible
1. Charles R. Swindoll, *Growing in the Seasons of Life* (Portland. OR: Multnomah Press, 1983), 53, emphasis in original.
2. A number of Faith teachers have seized upon this verse and twisted it to justify their grossly unbiblical doctrine of wealth and prosperity. However, the context of the passage (and the entire book, for that matter) does not allow for any such interpretation. The prosperity and success mentioned in verse 8 pertain to Joshua's conquest of Canaan. God's command to remember and meditate upon the Book of the Law was given to bolster the Israelites' strength and courage as

they prepared to do battle in Canaan (cf. verses 6,7). It served to remind them that God would be with them wherever they went (verse 9). As one observer rightly noted, "Joshua was a general, not a banker; financial prosperity is simply not in view here" (Ken L. Sarles, "A Theological Evaluation of the Prosperity Gospel," *Bibliotheca Sacra* 143, 572 [October-December 1986]:338).

3. Cited in Bernard Ramm, *Protestant Biblical Interpretation* (Grand Rapids, MI: Baker Book House, 1978), 14. We should note that many if not all the Faith teachers bank on "new revelations" comparable to Scripture. Benny Hinn on one occasion made the following remark: "Don't think OCC [Orlando Christian Center] is here to repeat something you heard for the last fifty years. If God called me to repeat things you heard, I shouldn't be here. If *we quit giving you new revelations, we're dead.*" He then proceeded to tell his congregation and the larger viewing audience that Jesus was simply the product of God's positive confession. (See Hinn, "Benny Hinn" program on TBN [15 December 1991], from "The Revelation of Jesus [part 4]—The Person of Jesus" [Orlando, FL: Orlando Christian Center, 1991], videotape #TV-292, emphasis added.)

4. Walter M. Martin, *The Kingdom of the Cults*, rev. ed. (Minneapolis: Bethany House, 1985), 67-125; "The New World Translation," *Christian Research Newsletter* 3, 3 (1990):5.

5. John P. Juedes, "George M. Lamsa: Christian Scholar or Cultic Torchbearer?" *Christian Research Journal* 12, 2 (Fall 1989):8-14.

6. Finis J. Dake, ed., *Dake's Annotated Reference Bible* (Lawrenceville, GA: Dake Bible Sales, 1963), NT pp. 96 col. 1, 97 cols. 1-2, emphasis in original; OT pp. 388 col. 1b, 467 col. 1f.

7. Ibid., NT p. 1 col. 1a.

Chapter 27—C = Church

1. I believe I first heard a version of this illustration from D. James Kennedy.

Chapter 28—D = Defense

1. Paul Crouch, "Praise-a-Thon" program on TBN (10 November 1987).
2. John Avanzini, "Praise-a-Thon" program on TBN (5 November 1990).
3. Henry M. Morris and Gary E. Parker, *What Is Creation Science?* rev. (El Cajon, CA: Master Books, 1987), 154-57.
4. See Duane T. Gish, *Evolution: The Challenge of the Fossil Record* (El Cajon, CA: Creation-Life Publishers, 1991), 180-84; and Marvin L. Lubenow, *Bones of Contention* (Grand Rapids, MI: Baker Book House, 1992), 86-120.

Chapter 29—E = Essentials

1. Paul Crouch, "Praise the Lord" program on TBN (5 September 1991).
2. This is an illustration that Walter Martin used throughout his ministry and which he cited in *Kingdom of the Cults* (Minneapolis: Bethany House Publishers, 1982), 16-17.
3. Although the Athanasian Creed bears the name of Athanasius, the great fourth-century Trinitarian defender of the faith, most scholars today do not believe this creed was written by Athanasius, although they do affirm its universal acceptance by the church.
4. The statistical illustration is pertinent even though it is not meant to convey that everyone who is evangelized will become a believer.
5. Merrill F. Unger, *The New Unger's Bible Handbook*, rev. by Gary N. Larson (Chicago: Moody Press, 1984), p. 708.

Epilogue

1. Benny Hinn, "Praise-a-Thon" program on TBN (2 April 1991).
2. Jerry Savelle, "Framing Your World with the Word of God, Part 1" (Fort Worth, TX: Jerry Savelle Evangelistic Association, n.d.), tape #SS-36, side 1.

Kenyon and the Leading Proponents of a Different Gospel

1. E.W. Kenyon, *The Hidden Man*, 5th ed. (Lynnwood, WA: Kenyon's Gospel Publishing Society, 1970), 98.
2. Notable works include Charles Farah, "A Critical Analysis: The 'Roots' and 'Fruits' of Faith-Formula Theology" (paper presented at the Society for Pentecostal Studies, November 1980); James M. Kinnebrew, *The Charismatic Doctrine of Positive Confession: A Historical, Exegetical, and Theological Critique* (doctoral dissertation, Mid-America Baptist Theological

Seminary, 1988); D.R. McConnell, *The Kenyon Connection: A Theological and Historical Analysis of the Cultic Origins of the Faith Movement* (master's thesis, Oral Roberts University, 1982) and *A Different Gospel* (Peabody, MA: Hendrickson Publishers, Inc., 1988); H. Terris Neuman, *An Analysis of the Sources of the Charismatic Teaching of Positive Confession* (unpublished paper, Wheaton Graduate School, 1980); "Cultic Origins of Word-Faith Theology Within the Charismatic Movement" (*Pneuma: The Journal of the Society for Pentecostal Studies*, 12, 1, Spring 1990:3-55); and Dale H. Simmons, *A Theological and Historical Analysis of Kenneth E. Hagin's Claim to Be a Prophet* (master's thesis, Oral Roberts University, 1985).

3. See McConnell, *A Different Gospel*, 35-43.

4. See chapter 1, endnote 9, 384; also McConnell, 23.

5. Ibid., 23, 28, note 23, 33.

6. Ibid., 23, 33.

7. Ibid., 100.

8. Vinson Synan, "The Faith of Kenneth Hagin," *Charisma & Christian Faith*, 15:11 (June 1990), 68.

9. Ibid.

10. Hagin's "demon monkey" story is recounted in the following: Kenneth E. Hagin, *I Believe in Visions* (Old Tappan, NJ: Spire Books/Fleming H. Revell Co., 1972), 80-82; *Demons and How to Deal with Them* (Tulsa, OK: Kenneth Hagin Evangelistic Assoc., 1976, 23-24; Kenneth Hagin Ministries, 2nd rev. 1983, 24-25); *Zoe: The God-Kind of Life* (Tulsa, OK: Kenneth Hagin Ministries, 1989), 47-49; *The Believer's Authority*, 2d rev. ed. (Tulsa, OK: Kenneth Hagin Ministries, 1991), 29-31.

11. The demonic entity was described as "an evil spirit" (*I Believe in Visions*, 80); as "an evil spirit that looked like a monkey" (*Zoe*, 47; *Visions*, 80); and as "an evil spirit that looked like a little monkey or elf" (*The Believer's Authority*, 29).

Hagin claims to have seen a "demon monkey" on another occasion, when it was oppressing a woman with cancer: "I saw a demon or an evil spirit hanging on to her body from the outside. It was like a little monkey hanging onto a tree limb. It looked like pictures we've seen of little elves" (*Ministering to the Oppressed* [Tulsa, OK: Kenneth Hagin Evangelistic Association, 7th pr. 1977], 23. A pastor told Hagin of seeing a similar entity oppressing his church: "There sitting above the ceiling on a rafter was a spirit that looked like a big ape or baboon" (*The Interceding Christian* [Tulsa, OK: Kenneth Hagin Ministries, 1978], 17).

12. "Now understand," explains Hagin, "'that' doesn't just include the demon; it included the dark cloud that shut off the vision of Jesus and heaven. It included communication that didn't get through—prayers, or whatever" (See Hagin, *Zoe*, 49).

13. Hagin, *I Believe in Visions*, 81.

14. Ibid.

15. Hagin, *Zoe*, 57. Hagin also says euphemistically that he received "the left foot of fellowship" from the Baptists (Kenneth E. Hagin, *Casting Your Cares Upon the Lord* [Tulsa, OK: Kenneth Hagin Ministries, 1981], 13; Kenneth E. Hagin, *Seven Things You Should Know About Divine Healing* [Tulsa, OK: Kenneth Hagin Ministries, 1979], 21; Kenneth E. Hagin, *What to Do When Faith Seems Weak & Victory Lost* [Tulsa, OK: Kenneth Hagin Ministries, 1979], 47).

16. Kenneth Hagin, Jr., *Faith Worketh by Love* (Tulsa, OK: Kenneth Hagin Ministries, 1979), 21, emphasis added.

17. Kenneth E. Hagin, *Obedience in Finances* (Tulsa, OK: Kenneth Hagin Ministries, 1983), 8.

18. H. Vinson Synan, "Capps, Charles Emmitt," *Dictionary of Pentecostal & Charismatic Movements*, ed. by Stanley M. Burgess, Gary B. McGee, and Patrick H. Alexander (Grand Rapids, MI: Regency/Zondervan, 1988), 107; Russ White, "Congregation Keeps the Faith with Spellbinding Benny Hinn," *Orlando Sentinel* (11 October 1987), F6.

19. Hagin's daily broadcast, "Faith Seminar of the Air," radio station listings in *The Word of Faith*, 25, 6 (June 1992):18-19. Additionally, Hagin's son, Kenneth Jr., has his own separate weekly radio program, "Rhema Radio Church."

20. "Graduation '92—A Gateway to the Nations!" *The Word of Faith* 25, 7 (July 1992):8; "RHEMA's First Russian Graduate!" ibid., 10-11.

21. Kenneth Hagin, Jr., "Trend Toward Faith Movement," *Charisma & Christian Life* (August 1985), 67-70, cited in James M. Kinnebrew, *The Charismatic Doctrine of Positive Confession* (doctoral dissertation, Mid-America Baptist Theological Seminary, September 1988 [Ann Arbor, MI: University Microfilms, 1992 reprint]), 16 and note 20; cf. discrepant figures in Bruce Barron, *The Health and Wealth Gospel* (Downers Grove, IL: InterVarsity Press, 1987), 55.

22. According to Ron Wilson, Executive Director of the Evangelical Press Association, *The Word of Faith* magazine has a circulation total of 396,259 (CRI telephone interview on 24 July 1992).

23. Hagin, *Classic Sermons, Word of Faith 25th Anniversary 1968-92 Commemorative Edition* (Tulsa, OK: Kenneth Hagin Ministries, 1992), Preface [ix]. According to Hagin's October 1990 Ministry Partner letter, more than 40,000 cassette tapes are duplicated and mailed every month; according to Hagin's *Classic Sermons* (112), some 40,000 to 50,000 tapes are sent out monthly now.

24. "Faith Library Catalog" (Tulsa, OK: Kenneth Hagin Ministries, 1991).

25. Synan, "The Faith of Kenneth Hagin," 63.

26. Hagin, *I Believe in Visions*, 14-16.

27. See, for example, Kenneth E. Hagin, *I Went to Hell* (Tulsa, OK: Kenneth Hagin Ministries, 1982), 5, 9, 14, 18, 23. Hagin attempts to cite still other biblical precedents for his own experience (*Exceedingly Growing Faith,* 36). Hagin refers to Paul's description of a journey by someone (most commentators believe Paul was referring to himself) to the third heaven, in which Paul states that he did not know whether this vision occurred in or out of the body and that only God knows which it was (2 Corinthians 12:1-4). But Hagin clearly describes himself as knowing that he was *out of his body*, despite his clever statement, "I know what Paul meant when he said that he didn't know if he was in the body, or out of the body" (*Exceedingly*, 36)—a statement that does not actually say Hagin was incapable of telling whether he was in or out of his body, only that Hagin knew how Paul must have felt, that he could sympathize.

    Hagin in fact describes his exact locations outside of his "partially paralyzed" body lying on his sickbed with his heart stopped (*Visions*, 12; *Exceedingly*, 35): "*I knew I was outside of my body*. I could see my family in the room..." (*Hell*, 5 [emphasis added]). "*I knew I was out of my body*.... I came up head first to the porch outside that south bedroom. Just for a second *I knew that I was standing up on the porch*. Then I went right through the wall. I seemed to *leap inside my body*. Back inside my body, I could contact the physical again" (*Exceedingly*, 35-37 [emphasis added]). "I came back into that room *just as real as at any other time* ..." (*Visions*, 12 [emphasis added]). In another deathbed experience soon after, Hagin writes: "... I had the *same sensation I'd had before*.... As I leaped *out of my body* and left it, I began to ascend. ... When I got up to about where the roof of the house should have been, *approximately 16 feet above the bed*, my ascent stopped and I seemed to stand there. *I was fully conscious and knew everything that was going on*. Looking back into the room, *I saw my body lying on the bed and my mother stooped over it holding my hand in hers* (*Exceedingly*, 37 [emphasis added]).

28. Hagin, *I Believe in Visions* (Tulsa, OK: Spire Books/Revell, 1972), 12-16; also *I Went to Hell*, 14; and *The Name of Jesus* (Tulsa, OK: Kenneth Hagin Ministries, 1981), 68. McConnell calls this Hagin's "out-of-body descent into hell" (McConnell, 74 n. 2). Other Faith teachers who have reported out-of-body experiences include Benny Hinn, Norvel Hayes, and Kenneth Copeland.

    The ancient Egyptians believed that the human soul or spirit exits and enters through the mouth: E.A. Wallis Budge, *Osiris: The Egyptian Religion of Resurrection*, 2 vols. (London: Warner, 1911 [New York: University Books, 1961 reprint]), 1:399; cf. 1:333; 2:128; Budge, *From Fetish to God in Ancient Egypt* (London: Oxford University Press, 1934 [New York: Dover, 1988 reprint]), 331-33.

29. Kenneth E. Hagin, *The Glory of God* (Tulsa, OK: Kenneth Hagin Ministries, 1987), 13-15.

30. Ibid., 16.

31. Hagin, *I Believe in Visions*, 51.

32. Ibid., 50.

33. See Henry George Liddell and Robert Scott (rev. Henry Stuart Jones), *A Greek-English Lexicon* (Oxford, England: Oxford University Press, 1968 rev. ed.), 1983b-84a, "*cheir*" items I.1, II.6.c, III.1; Gerhard Friedrich, ed.-trans. Geoffrey W. Bromiley, *Theological Dictionary of the New Testament* (Grand Rapids, MI: Wm. B. Eerdmans Publishing Co., 1974), 9:424-25, 430, items A.1.a. and fn. 4, C.1.b.; and Walter Bauer, William F. Arndt, and F. Wilbur Gingrich, *A Greek-English Lexicon of the New Testament* (Chicago: University of Chicago Press, 1979 rev. ed.), 880a. See also Kenneth E. Stevenson and Gary R. Habermas, *The Shroud and the Controversy* (Nashville, TN: Thomas Nelson, 1990), 152.

34. Dr. Pierre Barbet was the chief surgeon at St. Joseph's Hospital in Paris. He performed experiments on cadavers in the 1930's which showed that crucifixion by nails through the palms could not have supported the weight of the body on the cross. The nails would have ripped through the flesh. See Pierre Barbet, *A Doctor at Calvary*, Eng. transl. (New York: P.J. Kenedy and Doubleday, 1953 [French orig. 1950]), cited in Ian Wilson, *The Mysterious Shroud* (Garden

City, NY: Doubleday, 1986), 17, 20; and Frank C. Tribbe, *Portrait of Jesus?* (New York: Stein & Day, 1983), 80, 99-104.

Interestingly, an actual crucifixion victim of the Roman destruction of Jerusalem in A.D. 70, named Yohanon ben ha-Galgol, was excavated by Israeli archaeologists in a New Testament-era cemetery just outside Jerusalem in 1968. Yohanon was crucified with a nail through the radius and ulna bones of the forearm, as evidenced by grinding found on the inside of the radius bone at the wrist end (Wilson, 32-33; and Tribbe, 86-87).

Barbet's experiments with cadavers have recently been repeated and confirmed by Paris orthopedic surgeon Dr. Pierre Merat ("Critical Study: Anatomy and Physiology of the Shroud," *The Catholic Counter-Reformation in the XXth Century*, no. 218 [April 1989], 3-4).

35. "Special Report: Campmeeting '83," *Word of Faith*, 16, 10 (October 1983):3.
36. Hagin, *I Believe in Visions*, 115.
37. Ibid.
38. Kenneth E. Hagin, *Why Do People Fall Under the Power?* (Tulsa, OK: Kenneth Hagin Ministries, 1981), 10.
39. Ibid., 11-12.
40. Benny Hinn, "Praise-a-Thon," program on TBN (8 November 1990).
41. See Randy Frame, "Best-selling Author Admits Mistakes, Vows Changes," *Christianity Today* (28 October 1991), 44.
42. Benny Hinn, sermon delivered during "Miracle Invasion Rally" at the Anaheim [CA] Convention Center (22 November 1991).
43. John Avanzini, "Praise-a-Thon" program on TBN (Spring 1990).
44. Paul Crouch, "Praise-a-Thon" program on TBN (2 April 1991).
45. Kenneth Copeland, "Why All Are Not Healed" (Fort Worth, TX: Kenneth Copeland Ministries, 1990), audiotape #01-4001, side 1.
46. Barron, *Health & Wealth Gospel*, 56-57; see also Kenneth Hagin, Jr., *Faith Worketh by Love* (Tulsa, OK: Kenneth Hagin Ministries, 1979), 21.
47. Ibid., 183 note 59.
48. Richard M. Riss, "Copeland, Kenneth," *Dictionary of Pentecostal & Charismatic Movements*, 226; cf. Gloria Copeland, *God's Will for You* (Fort Worth, TX: Kenneth Copeland Publications, 1972), xii.
49. Kenneth Copeland, *Living to Give* [brochure] (Fort Worth, TX: Kenneth Copeland Ministries, n.d. [ca. 1988]), [4].
50. Ibid., [5-6].
51. Kenneth Copeland, *Walking in the Realm of the Miraculous* (Fort Worth, TX: Kenneth Copeland Ministries, 1979), 8.
52. Ibid., [8], emphasis in original.
53. Kenneth Copeland, "Following the Faith of Abraham I" (Fort Worth, TX: Kenneth Copeland Ministries, 1989), audiotape #01-3001, side 1; compare also Finis J. Dake, *Dake's Annotated Reference Bible* (Lawrenceville, GA: Dake Bible Sales, 1963), OT pp. 388 col. 1b, 467 col. 1f.
54. Brigham Young, "Discourse...June 8th, 1873," *Deseret News* [Salt Lake City, UT] (18 June 1873), 308; Brigham Young, sermon, 9 April 1852; G.D. Watt, ed., *Journal of Discourses* (Liverpool, England: F.D. Richards, 1855), 1:50.
55. Kenneth Copeland, "Spirit, Soul and Body I" (Fort Worth, TX: Kenneth Copeland Ministries, 1985), audiotape #01-0601, side 1.
56. Joseph Smith, "The King Follett Sermon" (7 April 1844), *History of the Church* 8th pr. (Salt Lake City, UT: Deseret Book Co., 1975), 6:305; Joseph Smith, "The King Follett Discourse," *Teachings of the Prophet Joseph Smith*, 21st pr., in Joseph Fielding Smith, ed. (Salt Lake City, UT: Deseret Book Co., 1972), 345.
57. Kenneth Copeland, "Following the Faith of Abraham I" (Fort Worth, TX: Kenneth Copeland Ministries, 1989), audiotape #01-3001, side 1.
58. Ibid.
59. Copeland, "Following the Faith of Abraham I."
60. Copeland, "Praise-a-Thon" program on TBN (April 1988).
61. Copeland, *Holy Bible: Kenneth Copeland Reference Edition* (Fort Worth, TX: Kenneth Copeland Ministries, 1991), 129, emphasis in original.
62. Copeland, "Believer's Voice of Victory" program (21 April 1991).
63. Kenneth Copeland, "Inner Image of the Covenant" (Fort Worth, TX: Kenneth Copeland Ministries, 1985), audiotape #01-4406, side 2.

64. Ibid.
65. Ibid.
66. Kenneth Copeland, "Believer's Voice of Victory" program on TBN (28 March 1991).
67. Copeland, "Inner Image of the Covenant," side 2.
68. Gloria Copeland, "Paul's Thorn in the Flesh," *Believer's Voice of Victory* 11:11 (November 1983), 5:8.
69. Benny Hinn, "Benny Hinn" program on TBN (8 June 1992).
70. Benny Hinn, *The Anointing* (Nashville, TN: Thomas Nelson, 1992), 86, 94.
71. Ibid., 94-95.
72. Russ White, "Congregation Keeps the Faith With Spellbinding Benny Hinn," *Orlando Sentinel* (11 October 1987), F6. "Hinn claims that . . . he helped heal even those who have AIDS. . . . He doesn't say whom he has healed or present documented proof." See also Mike Thomas, "The Power and the Glory," 12; Michael McAteer, "Debunkers Put No Faith in Healer's 'Miracles,' " *Toronto Star*, 24 September 1992, A2. Cf. Hinn's "hundreds of verified healings," *Anointing*, 94-95.
73. Mike Thomas, "The Power and the Glory," 12. Hinn and his spokesman/personal aide, Gene Polino, Administrator of Orlando Christian Center, later denied that Susan Smith documents healings for the church, asserting that she merely works in the video department and that Kent Mattox does the miracle documentation instead (Benny Hinn and Gene Polino meeting with CRI President Hanegraaff and Vice President Research Robert Lyle, 21 August 1992; Gene Polino interview by Renee Munshi, freelance reporter for *Bookstore Journal*, 1 September 1992; CRI interview with Munshi, 1 September 1992; Renee Munshi, "Benny Hinn: An Enigma," revised draft article faxed to CRI and Hinn Ministries, 2 September 1992).

    However, on September 4, 1992, Hinn provided CRI some medical records allegedly documenting three of his healing miracles, and among them were standardized forms used by the Hinn ministries for recording information in interviews with people thought to have been healed. Susan Smith's name appears on the form as the interviewer (the exact role stated by *Florida* magazine in the first place and admitted by Polino to Munshi). Thus Smith does appear to help document miracles for Hinn's ministry.
74. "But despite all the thousands of miracles claimed by Hinn, the church seems hard pressed to come up with any that would convince a serious skeptic. . . . [Susan] Smith also said there was a documented AIDS cure, but when pressed for details, she later said the final tests weren't in yet," according to Mike Thomas in "The Power and the Glory," *Florida*, 12. No such test results proving the AIDS cure were forthcoming nearly a year later when Hinn talked about the subject, and he sounded like he was only then starting to investigate for the first time: "Hinn said he does not know if there is documentation that authenticates the healing of people with AIDS but promised a 'thorough search' to see if such documentation exists." (Michael McAteer, "Debunkers Put No Faith in Healer's 'Miracles,' " *Toronto Star* [24 September 1992], A2.)
75. Medical records and other documents enclosed with cover letter from Benny Hinn, 4 September 1992.
76. Dr. Preston Simpson, M.D., medical analysis report, 28 October 1992; CRI telephone interviews with Dr. Preston Simpson, 6 and 23 October 1992. Although Hinn's medical documentation assistant or "pastor for followup," Kent Mattox, claims he has compiled "proof" of Hinn's healings from the records of physicians who have conducted "*before-and-after examinations,*" Dr. Simpson found there were virtually no before-miracle medical records to make a "before-and-after" comparison (Mattox interview by Renee Munshi for *Bookstore Journal*, 1 September 1992; CRI interview with Munshi, 1 September 1992; Munshi, "Benny Hinn: An Enigma," revised draft article [2 September 1992]).
77. "We do not know whether this man was cured by a miracle or by standard surgical treatment," according to Simpson, medical analysis, 28 October 1992. Cf. CRI telephone interviews with Dr. Simpson, 6 and 23 October 1992. It is also unclear whether the tumor started diminishing in size before or after the Hinn Miracle Crusade.
78. Simpson, medical analysis, 28 October 1992. For the effects of lupus, see Robert Berkow, ed., *The Merck Manual*, 15th rev. ed. (Rahway, NJ: Merck, 1987), 1276-77.
79. This case involves a three-inch tumor which invaded the lower spinal vertebrae and caused two of them to fracture and collapse. The net result was that the 40-year-old woman in question apparently was unable to walk, but the medical records provided do not explicitly document this fact. Nearly two years into the case, her doctors did not seem to know what diagnoses or tests

had been run previously or what treatments had been given. It is not even clear from the records provided whether the tumor was cancerous or caused by a viral or bacterial infection. One medical report (dated December 30, 1991) suggested polio or TB infections as possible causes, yet this was nearly *two years* after some form of cancer was supposedly first diagnosed on January 19, 1990 (seemingly in the lymphatic system). Although it is unclear from the records exactly when the spinal tumor was discovered, surely it should have been diagnosed as cancerous or not after the November 19, 1991, spinal X-rays mentioned in the incomplete records provided by Hinn (there is no actual radiology report for that date. The X-rays are mentioned in later reports). (Medical records supplied to CRI by Benny Hinn, 4 September 1992.)

80. Radiology report, 2 July 1992.
81. The Hinn Miracle Crusade was on May 14, 1992, in Tulsa, Oklahoma, but the tumor was still present at the examination on July 2, 1992.
82. Michael McAteer, "Debunkers Put No Faith in Healer's 'Miracles,' " *Toronto Star*, 24 September 1992, A2; cf. Hinn's "hundreds of verified healings," *Anointing*, 94-95. However, Benny Hinn's medical documentation assistant, Kent Mattox, told a freelance reporter for *Bookstore Journal* on September 1, 1992, that the upcoming Hinn book will contain only 10 to 15 "documented" cases of healing by Hinn (Mattox interview by Renee Munshi, for *Bookstore Journal*, 1 September 1992; CRI interview with Munshi, 1 September 1992; Munshi, "Benny Hinn: An Enigma" [2 September 1992]).
83. Hinn, "Our Position in Christ #5—An Heir of God" (Orlando, FL: Orlando Christian Center, 1990), audiotape #A031190-5, side 2.
84. Hinn, "Double Portion Anointing, Part #3" (Orlando, FL: Orlando Christian Center, n.d.), audiotape #A031791-3, sides 1-2; aired on TBN, 7 April 1991.
85. Benny Hinn, sermon delivered at Orlando Christian Center, 31 December 1989; partial transcript in Albert James Dager, "Special Report: Benny Hinn Pros & Cons," *Media Spotlight* (May 1992).
86. G. Richard Fisher, "Benny Hinn's Anointing: Heaven Sent or Borrowed?", 1.
87. Figure based on latest TBN potential viewer tally reported in *Praise the Lord* [TBN newsletter] 19, 8 (August 1992):[4]. In addition to cable television, TBN's programs are also broadcast on local and network television (some 312 stations) and shortwave radio. (See also *Praise the Lord*, 19, 11 (November 1992):[1].)
88. Cf. Ken Garfield, "Faith Healer from Florida Draws Crowds, and Questions," *Charlotte Observer* (15 October 1992), 1C (one million-plus copies of *Good Morning, Holy Spirit*); Randy Frame, "Same Old Benny Hinn, Critics Say," *Christianity Today*, 36:11 (5 October 1992):54 (1.7 million copies of both books combined).
89. Hinn, *Good Morning, Holy Spirit*, 56.
90. Ibid., 42.
91. The following account of Hinn's Oshawa sermon of December 7, 1974, is taken from Hinn, *Anointing*, 23-27; and Hinn, *Good Morning, Holy Spirit*, 44-46.
92. Hinn, *Anointing*, 26.
93. Hinn, *Anointing*, 27.
94. See the author's detailed book review, *"The Anointing* by Benny Hinn," *Christian Research Journal*, 15, 2 (Fall 1992):38.
95. Hinn, *Anointing*, 31.
96. Ibid., 79.
97. Ibid., 177-78.
98. Randy Frame, "Best-selling Author Admits Mistakes, Vows Changes," *Christianity Today* (28 October 1991), 44-45.
99. Ibid., 44, emphasis added.
100. Ibid.
101. Ibid.
102. Benny Hinn, "Praise the Lord" program on TBN, aired live, 3 October 1991. The *Christianity Today* interview was conducted about 25 September 1991, a month before the article's actual release (28 October 1991).
103. Benny Hinn on "Praise the Lord" program on TBN (23 October 1992). On that program Paul Crouch said to Hinn: "You have been attacked on some statements that you have made concerning the Trinity and the members of the Godhead." Hinn replied, "Especially on that one, yes." They both agreed there are three members of the Trinity. Then Crouch said, "Not

nine." Hinn laughed, "No, goodness sake!" Crouch asked, "Where did they get that silly idea anyway?" Hinn ignored the question.

The answer is that the idea came from Benny Hinn's own lips, and we have it on tape (Hinn program on TBN [13 October 1990]).

104. Hinn, "Miracle Invasion," Anaheim, California, Convention Center (22 November 1991). Hinn was responding to the previous night's ABC "PrimeTime Live" exposé of Robert Tilton, Larry Lea, and W.V. Grant, but he seemed oblivious to the bad timing of making dire threats on the anniversary of a Presidential assassination.

105. Benny Hinn, presentation at World Charismatic Conference, Melodyland Christian Center, Anaheim, California (7 August 1992), CRI audiotape.

106. Benny Hinn interview by Randy Frame, *Christianity Today*, 3 September 1992; my interview with Frame, 3 September 1992; see also Frame, "Same Old Benny Hinn," *Christianity Today* (5 October 1992), 52-53.

107. Even without his admission, it was clear that Hinn referred to CRI's "Bible Answer Man" radio program, broadcast nationwide in the afternoons from Southern California and heard evenings in East Coast time (Hinn's locale). Hinn had no explanation as to why CRI might be about to physically harm him. This makes no sense except as after-the-fact damage control, since CRI poses no threat to Hinn's personal safety.

108. Russ White, "Congregation Keeps the Faith With Spellbinding Benny Hinn," *Orlando Sentinel* (11 October 1987), F-6.

109. "Benny Hinn" program on TBN (8 June 1992).

110. "Benny Hinn" program on TBN (29 June 1992).

111. "Benny Hinn" program on TBN (6 July 1992).

112. McConnell, *A Different Gospel*, 4.

113. John Dart, "Huge 'FaithDome' in L.A.," *Los Angeles Times* (9 September 1989), Part II, 9-10; cf. Glenn W. Gohr, "Price, Frederick K.C.," *Dictionary of Pentecostal & Charismatic Movements*, 727.

114. Stephen Strang, "The Ever Increasing Faith of Fred Price," *Charisma & Christian Life* (May 1985), 23; cf. Gohr, "Price, Frederick K.C.," 727.

115. See Strang, "The Ever Increasing Faith of Fred Price," 24-25; Gohr, "Price," *Dictionary of Pentecostal & Charismatic Movements*, 727; Brad Darrach, "Masking His Biblical Teaching in Theatrics, Pastor Fred Price Gets His Message Across Swimmingly," *People* (10 October 1983), 48, 53; John Dart, "Scholarly Black Pastor Has a Burgeoning Flock," *Los Angeles Times* (7 December 1981), 6-8.

116. "Special Report: Campmeeting '83," *Word of Faith* 16, 10 (October 1983), 11b.

117. Strang, "The Ever Increasing Faith of Fred Price," 25; John Dart, "Scholarly Black Pastor Has a Burgeoning Flock," 8.

118. Frederick K.C. Price, "Name It and Claim It! What Saith the WORD?...", *Ever Increasing Faith Messenger* 10, 3 (Summer 1989):2, capitalization in original.

119. Flo Jenkins-Bryant, "We've Come This Far by Faith!...And It's Time to Rejoice!!!" *Ever Increasing Faith Messenger* 11, 1 (Winter 1990):8.

120. Frederick K.C. Price, "Ever Increasing Faith," program on TBN (9 December 1990), available from Crenshaw Christian Center (audiotape #CR-A2).

121. Frederick K.C. Price, *Is Healing for All?* (Tulsa, OK: Harrison House, 1976), 20.

122. Frederick Price, *Faith, Foolishness, or Presumption?* (Tulsa, OK: Harrison House, 1979), 88.

123. Betty Price, "A Praise Report," *Ever Increasing Faith Messenger* 12, 3 (Summer 1991); Pat Hays, "Betty Price Speaks at 1991 'Wisdom from Above' Luncheon," ibid., 13, 1 (Winter 1992):12-13.

124. CRI telephone interview with Crenshaw Christian Center staff member (31 July 1992). See also Betty Price, "Health Update...then...and...now from Betty Price," *Ever Increasing Faith Messenger* 13, 4 (Fall 1992):5.

125. Price, "Ever Increasing Faith" program on TBN (16 November 1990).

126. Frederick K.C. Price, "Ever Increasing Faith" television program (3 May 1992).

127. Frederick K.C. Price, "Identification #3" (Inglewood, CA: Ever Increasing Faith Ministries, 1980), audiotape #FP545, side 1.

128. Frederick K.C. Price, *Ever Increasing Faith Messenger* (June 1980), 7; quoted in McConnell, *A Different Gospel*, 120.

129. Frederick Price, "Ever Increasing Faith" program on TBN (23 November 1990).

130. Ibid.

131. John Avanzini, "Believer's Voice of Victory" program on TBN (20 January 1991).
132. The Greek word in the passage, *chiton*, is properly defined as a *"tunic, shirt*, a garment worn next to the skin, and by both sexes" (see Walter Bauer, William F. Arndt, and F. Wilbur Gingrich, *A Greek-English Lexicon of the New Testament and Other Early Christian Literature*, rev. ed. [Chicago: University of Chicago Press, 1952], 890b, emphasis in original); cf. F.F. Bruce, *The Gospel of John* (Grand Rapids, MI: Wm. B. Eerdmans Publishing Co., 1983), 370; and Merrill C. Tenney, "The Gospel of John," ed. by Frank E. Gaebelein, in *The Expositor's Bible Commentary* (Grand Rapids, MI: Zondervan, 1981), 9:81.
133. John Avanzini, "Believer's Voice of Victory" program on TBN (20 January 1991).
134. John Avanzini, "Praise the Lord" program on TBN (1 August 1989).
135. John Avanzini, "Praise-a-Thon" program on TBN (15 September 1988).
136. John Avanzini, "Praise-a-Thon" program on TBN (April 1991).
137. John Avanzini, *It's Not Working, Brother John!* (Tulsa, OK: Harrison House, 1992).
138. John Avanzini, "Praise-a-Thon" program on TBN (5 November 1990).
139. John Avanzini, "Praise-a-Thon" program on TBN (10 April 1992).
140. Ibid.
141. John Avanzini, "Praise-a-Thon" program on TBN (7 July 1992).
142. John Avanzini, "Praise-a-Thon" program on TBN (April 1991).
143. Benny Hinn, "Praise-a-Thon" program on TBN (6 November 1990).
144. Scott Baradell, "Robert Tilton's Heart of Darkness," *Dallas Observer* (6 February 1992), 13, 18.
145. Ibid., 18.
146. Ibid., 19-20.
147. Ibid., 13, 18, 19-20.
148. Ibid., 13.
149. [Religious News Service], "TV Preachers Seen As 'Beggars': Public Dislikes Evangelists' Onscreen Methods, Professor Says," *Dallas Morning News* (21 November 1992); Ari L. Goldman, "Religion Notes," *New York Times* [Nat. Ed.] (21 November 1992), 8.
150. Howard Swindle and Allen Pusey, "Tilton Ends Syndication of His Sunday Services," *Dallas Morning News* (13 August 1992), 1A, 28A; Terry Box, "Backers Think Tilton Will Endure" (16 February 1992), 1A, 12A-13A; Jim Jones, "The Undercover Thorn in Robert Tilton," *Fort Worth Star-Telegram* (26 January 1992), 1A, 20A.

Recently, Tilton's Arbitron ratings dropped 39 percent following the ABC television exposé in November 1991. (See Allen Pusey and Howard Swindle, "Tilton Bankrolled '83 TV License Bid, Source and Files Say" [12 July 1992], 1A, 29A.)
151. Baradell, "Robert Tilton's Heart of Darkness," 13; Nancy St. Pierre, "Tilton's Lawyer Has Key Role," *Dallas Morning News* (17 February 1992), 1A, 14A. In September 1992, Tilton spokesman and attorney J.C. Joyce stated that as many as 400 Tilton employees had lost their jobs due to decreased contributions following the media exposés, which if correct would reduce the 850 employees figure to perhaps 450 (Jim Jones, "Tilton Ministry Still Strong Despite Layoffs, Assistant Says," *Fort Worth Star-Telegram* [23 November 1992]).
152. Nancy St. Pierre, "Tilton's Wife Tells of Finances," *Dallas Morning News* (5 March 1992), 1A, 7A; Terry Box, "Tax Appraiser Is Scrutinizing Tilton's Church" (22 March 1992), 1A; see similar estimates of Tilton's ministry income in Trinity Foundation release, "Does Word of Faith = Wheel of Fortune?" (9 December 1991); Box, "Backers Think Tilton Will Endure," *Dallas Morning News* (16 February 1992), 1A, 12A-13A.
153. "Guilt prompts Tilton worker to quit" [Associated Press report from Tulsa, OK] *Denton [Texas] Record Chronicle* (16 December 1991). On July 9, 1992, ABC "PrimeTime Live" interviewed two close assistants of Tilton who have come forward since the first report. Brenda Reynolds said she had been the nanny to the Tiltons' children for six years. When she tried to bring prayer request letters from the garage into the house for Tilton to pray over them, she said Tilton told her to throw them away. "I know for a fact he didn't pray over them and I took them to the trash myself," said Reynolds.

Associated Press reported in December 1991 that an assistant manager of a paper-recycling plant in Tulsa had found thousands of prayer requests sent to Tilton. (See John Archer, "PrimeTime Lies?", *Charisma & Christian Life*, 17, 7 [February 1992]:30-31.) Another account states that a CNN camera crew found "tons" of requests in a recycling bin in Tulsa. (See Trinity Foundation release, "Tons of Tilton Prayer Requests Discovered in Recycle Center" [9 December 1991].)

Televangelist-watchdog Ole Anthony, President of the Trinity Foundation in Dallas, testified at a federal court hearing that he too found evidently unanswered prayer requests in trash bins outside Tulsa businesses. Anthony said he turned the evidence over to the Texas Attorney General in November 1991. (See Nancy St. Pierre, "Man Sifted Tilton's Trash for Evidence," *Dallas Morning News* [6 March 1992], 1A, 6A.)

Tilton has always denied publicly he threw away unread prayer requests, but admitted in a videotaped court deposition for the Texas Attorney General's office in March 1992—made public by ABC over Tilton's objections—that he did not pray over every letter, but prayed over computer printout lists of some letters. What did he do with these letters? "I threw them away," said Tilton.

154. Paul Carden, "Special Report: Tilton's Tottering TV Empire," *Christian Research Journal*, 15, 1 (Summer 1992):5.

155. Beverly Crowley of Wynona, Oklahoma, has reportedly sued Tilton for 40 million dollars for continuing to receive mail from Tilton promising to heal her husband five months after he had died—if he would "sow the new seed for the miracle you need" by sending money. The letters kept coming despite a January 1, 1992, letter to Tilton from Mrs. Crowley saying, "Punch the computer to cancel the mail that is coming to Tom Crowley. You see, Tom passed away Sept. 30, 1991, 3 months ago. I guess God forgot to tell you that." (See Risa Robert, "Tilton Sent Dead Man 'Personal' Mail," *Tulsa Tribune* [27 February 1992], 7A; Howard Swindle, "Tilton Letters to Dead Man Prompt Widow to File Suit," *Dallas Morning News* [28 February 1992], 1A, 18A; Scott Baradell, "Under the Tilton Hearing Big Top," *Dallas Observer* [12 March 1992], 18-19; Scott Baradell, "The Man Who Could Topple Tilton," *Dallas Observer* [19 March 1992]; and Terry Box, "Tax Appraiser Is Scrutinizing Tilton's Church," *Dallas Morning News* [22 March 1992], 1A, 10A.)

Dorothy Ries of Tulsa also has filed suit for 40 million dollars for a similar claim against Tilton. Like Mrs. Crowley, Mrs. Ries claims she wrote to Tilton informing him her husband had died, but that the healing/fund-raising letters addressed to the dead man kept coming. (See Nancy St. Pierre, "2nd Widow Sues Tilton Over Letters," *Dallas Morning News* [18 March 1992], 28A; and Nancy St. Pierre, "U.S. Court Judge Criticizes Morals in Tilton Inquiry," *Dallas Morning News* [19 March 1992], 1A, 13A.)

ABC "PrimeTime Live" reported on July 9, 1992, that a total of nine people are now suing Tilton, though it was not stated what types of claims were alleged.

156. Nine civil actions totaling 500 million dollars had reportedly been filed: Nancy St. Pierre, "Judge Rejects Tilton Bid for Restraining Order," *Dallas Morning News* (15 May 1992), 1A, 8A; St. Pierre, "Judge Rejects Tilton's Suit Against Foes" (25 June 1992), 29A, 32A.

A tenth lawsuit (assuming we have a complete count) was filed in federal court in Dallas on November 13, 1992, by Mike and Vivian Elliott. They charged that in a January 1991 testimonial video production Tilton misrepresented Mrs. Elliott's story of God's deliverance from attempted suicide in October 1990, crediting Tilton for rescuing her instead of God. The Elliotts say that Tilton's ministry promised Mrs. Elliott that the video would be used to raise money for a professional "crisis center." But the center was never set up, and her $3500 pledge money and money raised by the video were misused, the suit claims. The changes in the testimonial were made to "satisfy defendants' greed," the suit alleges (Allen Pusey, "Florida Couple Sues Tilton Organization: Suit Says Story Misrepresented, Funds Misused," *Dallas Morning News* [14 November 1992]).

"Several" of the first nine suits have been dismissed, though legally they may be subject to reinstatement later if appealed (Sylvia Martinez, "Tilton Sues ABC News, 'PrimeTime,'" *Dallas Morning News* [11 November 1992], 33A).

157. Tilton filed an unusual suit in Tulsa federal court on May 14, 1992, against his two fiercest critics as well as the attorneys representing several clients suing Tilton—but it was thrown out on June 24, 1992 (St. Pierre, "Judge Rejects Tilton Bid," *Dallas Morning News* [15 May 1992], 1A; St. Pierre, "Judge Rejects Tilton's Suit" [25 June 1992], 29A).

158. "PrimeTime Lies," program broadcast in place of Robert Tilton's regular "Success-N-Life" television program (18 August 1992).

The ABC charges against Tilton were not very convincingly rebutted in Tilton's response. For example, the rebuttal video tried to portray the Tiltons' former housekeeper/nanny, Brenda Reynolds, as somehow not in the position to have knowledge of Tilton throwing away unread prayer-request letters stored in the family home where she worked for six years.

Tilton has sued ABC News, its "PrimeTime Live" show, anchor Diane Sawyer, and others for libel (Sylvia Martinez, "Tilton Sues ABC News, 'PrimeTime,'" *Dallas Morning News* [11 November 1992], 29A, 33A).

159. Robert Tilton, "Success-N-Life" program (22 November 1991).
Since the first ABC exposé in November 1991, Tilton and his ministry have come under investigation by the FBI, IRS, U.S. Postal Service, and Texas Attorney General for possible wrongdoing (St. Pierre, "Judge Rejects Tilton Bid," *Dallas Morning News* [15 May 1992], 8A; St. Pierre, "Judge Rejects Tilton's Suit" [25 June 1992], 32A; Martinez, "Tilton Sues ABC News" [11 November 1992], 33A).

160. Robert Tilton, "Success-N-Life" program (22 November 1991). Tilton has also alleged that the dumpster full of prayer requests found by ABC was actually planted by enemies to discredit him. (See Christopher Lee, "Tilton's Wife Defends Ministry, Blasts TV Exposé of Husband," *Dallas Morning News* [25 November 1991], 1A, 12A.) Excerpts from Tilton's televised replies about "ink poisoning" and the "stolen and planted" letters were aired on ABC's "PrimeTime Live" update on July 9, 1992.

161. Ibid. Tilton quoted Jim Moore, President of Response Media, which processes Tilton ministry's mail, as saying his employees became ill due to an allergy to a certain type of yellow ink. None of Moore's employees evidently reported getting "strokes in the brain" or having to undergo plastic surgery, as Tilton claimed for himself.

162. Marilyn Hickey Ministries, direct-mail piece (n.d. [ca. 1992]), emphasis in original.

163. Marilyn Hickey Ministries, direct-mail piece (n.d.).

164. Marilyn Hickey, "Claim Your Miracles" (Denver: Marilyn Hickey Ministries, n.d.), audiotape #186, side 2.

165. Marilyn Hickey, "Today with Marilyn" program on TBN (11 April 1991).

166. Hickey, "Breakthroughs to Faith" (Denver: Marilyn Hickey Ministries, n.d.), audiotape #1105, side 2.

167. Stephen Strang, "Hickey, Marilyn Sweitzer," *Dictionary of Pentecostal & Charismatic Movements*, 389. *Outpouring* magazine was formerly called *Time With Him*.

168. "Yesterday, Today, and Tomorrow: 15 Years of Covering the Earth with the Word," *Outpouring*, 15:1 (Special ed.), [4].

169. Hickey, "Claim Your Miracles" audiotape, side 1.

170. Ibid., side 2.

171. "Yesterday, Today, and Tomorrow," *Outpouring*, [4].

172. CRI telephone information from C. Peter Wagner, School of World Missions, Fuller Theological Seminary (30 July 1992); cf. "Cho Starts Newspaper," *Charisma & Christian Life*, 16, 5 (December 1990):33.

173. Soka Gakkai claims some 11 million members worldwide. See Leslie Helm, "Religious Battle Taking Shape in Foothills of Mt. Fuji," *Los Angeles Times* (16 December 1991), A21. See also Mamoru Billy Ogata, "A Comparison Between Paul Yonggi Cho's Church (Korea) and the Soka Gakkai (Japan)," [Appendix A] in *A Comparative Study of Church Growth in Korea and Japan with Special Application to Japan* (Fuller Theological Seminary thesis, 1984).

174. Paul Yonggi Cho, *The Fourth Dimension, Volume Two* (So. Plainfield, NJ: Bridge Publishing, 1983), xiii.

175. Dwight J. Wilson, "Cho, Paul Yonggi," *Dictionary of Pentecostal & Charismatic Movements* (1988), 161.

176. "Yonggi Cho Changes His Name," *Charisma & Christian Life* 18:4 (November 1992), 80.

177. Wilson, "Cho," *Dictionary of Pentecostal & Charismatic Movements*, 162.

178. Paul Yonggi Cho, *The Fourth Dimension*, [vol. 1] (So. Plainfield, NJ: Bridge Publishing, 1979), 83.

179. Ibid., 38-39.

180. Ibid., 39-40.

181. Ibid., 9-35; vol. 2, 18-33.

182. Ibid., vol. 1, 44.

183. Ibid., 43.

184. Ibid., 40-41.

185. Ibid., 64.

186. Ibid., 36-37; vol. 2, 36.

187. Ibid., vol. 1, 37, 41.

188. Charles Capps, *The Tongue—A Creative Force* (Tulsa, OK: Harrison House, 1976), 91.

189. Charles Capps, *Dynamics of Faith & Confession* (Tulsa, OK: Harrison House, 1987), 86-87, emphasis added; cf. Charles Capps, *Authority in Three Worlds* (Tulsa, OK: Harrison House, 1982), 76, 85.

190. Ibid., 83, emphasis added; cf. Capps, *Dynamics of Faith*, 88; Capps, *The Tongue*, 19.
191. Capps, *Dynamics of Faith*, 79-80.
192. See McConnell, 4. Capps claims that Kenneth Hagin's book *Right and Wrong Thinking* was responsible for his move into positive confession. "It went off inside me like a bombshell," says Capps. "I knew instantly that this was truth" (Capps, *The Tongue*, 66).
193. H. Vinson Synan, "Capps, Charles Emmitt," *Dictionary of Pentecostal & Charismatic Movements*, 107.
194. Printing figures totaling at least 3,162,000 are given on the copyright pages of the following Capps books and booklets: *God's Creative Power* (Tulsa, OK: Harrison House, 1976 [n.d., 27th printing]) (2,365,000 copies); *The Tongue—A Creative Force* (Tulsa, OK: Harrison House, 1976 [n.d., 25th printing]) (595,000 copies); *Changing the Seen & Shaping the Unseen* (Tulsa, OK: Harrison House, 1981 [n.d., 11th printing]) (102,000 copies); *Angels* (Tulsa, OK: Harrison House, 1984 [n.d., 6th printing]) (100,000 copies).
195. Ibid.
196. Charles Capps, *The Substance of Things* (Tulsa, OK: Harrison House, 1990), 41-42.
197. Ibid., 42.
198. Kenneth Copeland, "Spirit, Soul and Body I" (Fort Worth, TX: Kenneth Copeland Ministries, 1985), audiotape #01-0601, side 1.
199. Jerry Savelle, "Framing Your World with the Word of God, Part 2" (Fort Worth, TX: Jerry Savelle Evangelistic Association, Inc., n.d.), audiotape #SS-36, side 1.
200. Ibid.
201. Ibid., side 2.
202. Ibid., side 1.
203. Jerry Savelle, *If Satan Can't Steal Your Joy...* (Tulsa, OK: Harrison House, 1982), 17, 19.
204. Ibid., 18.
205. Morris Cerullo, *The Miracle Book* [special charter ed.] (San Diego, CA: Morris Cerullo World Evangelism, 1984), ix.
206. *God's Faithful, Anointed Servant, Morris Cerullo* [brochure] (San Diego, CA: Morris Cerullo World Evangelism, n.d.).
207. Cerullo, *Miracle Book*, ix.
208. *7 Point Outreach—World Evangelism and You* (San Diego: Morris Cerullo World Evangelism, n.d.), [4].
209. Cerullo, *Miracle Book*, xi.
210. *7 Point Outreach*, [4].
211. Cerullo, *Miracle Book*, xi.
212. Ibid.
213. Ibid., xii.
214. *God's Faithful, Anointed Servant, Morris Cerullo.*
215. Cerullo, *Miracle Book*, x.
216. Morris Cerullo, "Few Are Chosen," *Deeper Life* 21, 5 (June 1981):2.
217. Morris Cerullo, "The Greatest Message in the World," *Deeper Life* 21, 3 (April 1981):8.
218. Morris Cerullo, "The Endtime Manifestation of the Sons of God" (San Diego: Morris Cerullo World Evangelism, Inc., n.d.), audiotape 1, sides 1 & 2, emphasis in original.
219. *God's Faithful, Anointed Servant, Morris Cerullo.*
220. Laura Monteros, "The Rebirth of Morris Cerullo," *Los Angeles Herald-Examiner* (18 November 1978).
221. Morris Cerullo, "From the Heart," *Victory* (January/February 1992), 6, emphasis in original.
222. Morris Cerullo, "A Word from God at the Deeper Life World Conference," *Deeper Life* 22, 2 (March 1982):15.
223. Mark Pinsky, "FCC Reviewing Trinity's Minority Subsidiary," *Los Angeles Times* (29 September 1991), B7.
224. Paul Crouch, *Praise the Lord* [TBN newsletter] 19:8 (August 1992), [2]; 19:11 (November 1992), [1] (312 stations). Another source reports that TBN, "with more than 285 stations, is the largest purveyor of religious programming in the world" (Kenneth L. Woodward and Lynda Wright, "The T Stands for Troubled," *Newsweek* 99, 13 [30 March 1992]:60).
225. *Praise the Lord* (August 1992), [4].
226. Paul Crouch, *Praise the Lord* [TBN newsletter] 19, 7 (July 1992):[1], emphasis in original.
227. Many of today's most well-known Faith and prosperity preachers have their own programs on TBN, including Kenneth Copeland, Frederick K.C. Price, Benny Hinn, Marilyn Hickey, John Avanzini, Dwight Thompson, T.L. Osborn, and Oral and Richard Roberts.

228. John Avanzini, "Praise-a-Thon" program on TBN (6 November 1990).
229. Roy Blizzard has appeared on the "Praise the Lord" program and had his own weekly show, "Treasures of the Jewish World," sponsored by TBN. On Blizzard's antitrinitarian stance, see Roy Blizzard, "The fact of the matter..." *Through Their Eyes* 2, 1 (January 1987):19.
230. Joseph Good is a frequent guest on the "Praise the Lord" program and has two weekly shows, "Footsteps of the Messiah" and "Ancient Israel," sponsored by TBN. On Good's denial of Christ's deity during His incarnation and after the resurrection, see Joseph Good, "Difficult Verses" (Port Arthur, TX: Hatikva Ministries, April 1990), audiotape #5.
231. Paul Crouch, "Praise the Lord" program on TBN (5 September 1991).
232. Paul Crouch, "Praise-a-Thon" program on TBN (2 April 1991), emphasis added.
233. Ibid. On Crouch praying for the death of his network's enemies, see Mark I. Pinsky, "He Wished Death on Foes—Theologians Fault Prayer by Crouch," *Los Angeles Times* [Orange County ed.] (16 May 1991), II-1, II-10.
234. Paul Crouch, "Praise-a-Thon" program on TBN (April 1990).
235. My letter to Paul Crouch (6 December 1991). The letter served to follow up a discussion of the Faith movement's view of the atonement, brought up during a meeting between Crouch and me (6 November 1991).
236. Paul Crouch, "Praise-a-Thon" program on TBN (2 April 1991).
237. Paul Crouch letter to R.C. [name withheld for privacy] (22 January 1992).
238. Walter Martin, "The Warnings of God (Kenneth Copeland's False Prophecy)" (San Juan Capistrano, CA: CRI, 1987), audiotape #C-210, side 1.
239. Paul Crouch, "Praise the Lord" program on TBN (31 July 1992).
240. Paul Crouch, "Praise the Lord" program on TBN (18 February 1986, rebroadcast on 6 August 1991).
241. Notable individuals include Norvel Hayes, Lester Sumrall, Oral and Richard Roberts, Dwight Thompson, Charles and Frances Hunter, Doyle "Buddy" Harrison, "Happy" Caldwell, Don Gossett, Andrew Womack, and Earl Paulk.
242. Casey Treat, *Renewing the Mind* (Seattle, WA: Casey Treat Ministries, 1985), 90.
243. John Osteen, *The 6th Sense... Faith* (Houston, TX: John Osteen Publications, 1980), 13.
244. T.L. Osborn, *Faith Digest* XXII E34-77, 11, emphasis in original.

Appendix B—Apologetics: The Defense of the Faith

1. Stephen Jay Gould, "Evolution's Erratic Pace," *Natural History* Vol. 86, no. 5 (May 1977), 14.
2. Adapted from Ken Boa, *I'm Glad You Asked* (Wheaton, IL: Victor Books, 1982), 36.
3. Evolutionists typically raise two objections to the use of entropy as an argument against evolution.

    A) *Entropy applies only in a closed system.* There are two main problems with this objection. First, the universe is a closed system; second, while the earth may be an open system, energy from the sun does not decrease entropy.

    B) *The second law of thermodynamics (entropy) cannot be invoked because it merely deals with energy relationships of matter, and evolution deals with the issue of complex life-forms arising from simpler life-forms.* Entropy, however, is not limited to energy relationships of matter. Shannon's Law deals with information entropy and militates against evolution on a genetic level.
4. Simon Greenleaf, *The Testimony of the Evangelists* (Grand Rapids, MI: Baker Book House, 1984 [orig. New York: Cockcroft & Company, 1874]), 29-30.

Bibliography

Adler, Margot, *Drawing Down the Moon* (Boston: Beacon Press, 1986 rev.).

Aland, Kurt, ed., *Synopsis of the Four Gospels* ([New York]: United Bible Societies, 6th rev., 1983).

Amundsen, Darrel W., The Anguish and Agonies of Charles Spurgeon, *Christian History*, 10:1 (1991), 22-25.

Anastasios, Archimandrite, President of Ecclesiastical Court Jaffa, Greek Orthodox Patriarchate Certificate of baptism of Issa Nabil Benedictos [Christopher N. Hinn], son of Costandi Hin and Clemence Salameh, born in Jaffa, 20 May 1954, baptized in Jaffa, 19 October 1957, signed by Secretary L. Hanna (9 July 1968).

Arbitron, Top 20 Syndicated Religious Programs [May 1992], *Religious Broadcasting* (October 1992), 38.

Arbitron, Top 20 Syndicated Religious Programs [July 1992], *Religious Broadcasting* (December 1992), 34.

Archer, Gleason L., Jr., *Encyclopedia of Bible Difficulties* (Grand Rapids, MI: Zondervan, 1982).

Archer, John, PrimeTime Lies? *Charisma & Christian Life*, 17:7 (February 1992), 30-31.

Armstrong, Herbert W., *Mystery of the Ages* (Pasadena, CA: Worldwide Church of God, 1985).

Armstrong, M., She Trusted God to Save Her, *Woman's World* (27 October 1992).

Associated Press, Despite TV Stations' Protests, Oral Roberts Won't Stop Life-or-Death Appeal for Funds, *Orange County Register* [Santa Ana, CA] (14 January 1987), A19.

Associated Press, 4 Killed When Balloon Hits Wires And Burns, *St. Louis Post-Dispatch* (16 December 1979), 14A.

Associated Press (Tulsa, OK), Guilt Prompts Tilton Worker to Quit, *Denton [Texas] Record Chronicle* (16 December 1991).

Associated Press, TV Ban Won't End Oral Roberts' Vow of Cash or Death, *Toronto Star* (14 January 1987), A11.

Avanzini, John, Believer's Voice of Victory program on TBN (20 January 1991).

Avanzini, *It's Not Working, Brother John!* (Tulsa, OK: Harrison House, 1992).

Avanzini, Praise-a-Thon program on TBN (15 September 1988).

Avanzini, Praise-a-Thon program on TBN (April 1990).

Avanzini, Praise-a-Thon program on TBN (Spring 1990).

Avanzini, Praise-a-Thon program on TBN (5 November 1990).

Avanzini, Praise-a-Thon program on TBN (6 November 1990).

Avanzini, Praise-a-Thon program on TBN (April 1991).

Avanzini, Praise-a-Thon program on TBN (10 April 1992).

Avanzini, Praise-a-Thon program on TBN (7 July 1992).

Avanzini, Praise the Lord program on TBN (15 September 1988).

Avanzini, Praise the Lord program on TBN (1 August 1989).

Avanzini, Was Jesus Poor? videotape (Hurst, TX: His Image Ministries, n.d.).

Avanzini with Morris Cerullo, "The Endtime Manifestation of the Sons of God" (San Diego: Morris Cerullo World Evangelism, n.d.), audiotape 1.

Bakker, Jim, letter quoted in Terry Mattingly, Prosperity Christian sings a different tune, *Rocky Mountain News* (16 August 1992), 158.

Baradell, Scott, Robert Tilton's Heart of Darkness, *Dallas Observer* (6 February 1992), 13ff.

Baradell, Scott, The Man Who Could Topple Tilton, *Dallas Observer* (19 March 1992).

Baradell, Scott, Under the Tilton Hearing Big Top, *Dallas Observer* (12 March 1992), 18-19.

Barbet, Pierre, *A Doctor at Calvary* (New York: P.J. Kenedy/Doubleday, 1953 Eng. transl. [French orig. 1950]).

Barbour, Bruce, Publisher, Thomas Nelson Publishers, G. Richard Fisher telephone interview (8 May 1992).

Barbour, Bruce, Publisher, Thomas Nelson Publishers, telephone interview by Hanegraaff (20 July 1992).

Barron, Bruce, *The Health and Wealth Gospel* (Downers Grove, IL: InterVarsity Press, 1987).

Barron, Bruce, Why Settle for Riches If You Can Be a God? Updating the Word-Faith Controversy (paper presented to the Society for Pentecostal Studies, November 1988).

Bauer, Walter, William F. Arndt, and F. Wilbur Gingrich, *A Greek-English Lexicon of the New Testament and Other Early Christian Literature* (Chicago: University of Chicago Press, 1952 rev.) (1979 rev.).

Beik, Stephen W. (Benny Hinn attorney), letter to Kurt Goedelman and G. Richard Fisher, Personal Freedom Outreach (PFO) (9 October 1992).

Berkhof, Louis, *Systematic Theology* (Grand Rapids: Eerdmans, 4th rev., 1949).

Berkow, Robert, M.D., ed., *The Merck Manual* (Rahway, NJ: Merck, 16th rev. 1992).

Best, Paul, telephone interview by CRI-Canada (3, 14 September 1992).

Bickersteth, Edward H., *The Trinity* (Grand Rapids, MI: Kregel, 1976).

Billheimer, Paul E., *Destined for the Throne* [TBN edition] (Fort Washington, PA: Christian Literature Crusade, 1988 reprint [1975]).

Blackwelder, Boyce W., *Light from the Greek New Testament* (Grand Rapids, MI: Baker Book House, 1958).

Blizard, Paul R., The Orlando Christian Center: Where you're only a visitor once, *Personal Freedom Outreach [PFO] Quarterly Journal,* 13:1 (January-March 1993), 8-9.

Blizzard, Roy, The fact of the matter... *Through Their Eyes,* 2:1 (January 1987), 19.

Boa, Kenneth, and Larry Moody, *I'm Glad You Asked* (Wheaton, IL: Victor Books, 1982).

Bowman, Robert M., Jr., A Summary Critique: Good Morning, Holy Spirit, *Christian Research Journal,* 13:4 (Spring 1991), 36-38.

Box, Terry, Backers Think Tilton Will Endure, *Dallas Morning News* (16 February 1992), 1A, 12A-13A.

Box, Terry, Tax Appraiser Is Scrutinizing Tilton's Church, *Dallas Morning News* (22 March 1992), 1A, 10A.

Braden, Charles S., *Spirits in Rebellion: The Rise and Development of New Thought* (Dallas, TX: Southern Methodist University Press, 3rd ed. 1970 [1963]).

Brand, Paul, and Philip Yancey, *Healing: What Does God Promise?* (Portland, OR: Multnomah Press, 1984 [Guideposts reprint, Carmel, NY]).

Brayley, Manuel, telephone interview by CRI-Canada (13 September 1992).

Bromiley, Geoffrey W., ed., *Theological Dictionary of the New Testament* (Grand Rapids, MI: Eerdmans/Paternoster Press, 1985).

Brown, Colin, gen. ed., *The New International Dictionary of New Testament Theology* (Grand Rapids, MI: Zondervan, 1975 Eng. transl.).

Bruce, Alexander B., The Synoptic Gospels, in W. Robertson Nicoll, ed., *The Expositor's Greek Testament* (Grand Rapids, MI: Eerdmans, 1979 reprint).

Bruce, F.F., *The Gospel of John* (Grand Rapids, MI: Eerdmans, 1983).

Budge, E.A. Wallis, *From Fetish to God in Ancient Egypt* (London: Oxford University Press, 1934 [New York: Dover, 1988 reprint]).

Budge, E.A. Wallis, *Osiris: The Egyptian Religion of Resurrection,* 2 vols. (London: Warner, 1911 [New York: University Books, 1961 reprint]).

Burgess, Stanley M., Gary B. McGee, and Patrick H. Alexander, eds., *Dictionary of Pentecostal and Charismatic Movements* (Grand Rapids, MI: Regency/Zondervan, 1988).

C.C. [name withheld for privacy], letter, 19 June 1992.

Cady, H. Emilie, *God a Present Help* (Lee's Summit, MO: Unity School of Christianity, 1938).

Cady, H. Emilie, et al, *Foundations of Unity*, series 2 (Unity Village, MO: Unity, n.d.).

Capps, Charles, *Angels* (Tulsa, OK: Harrison House, 1984 [n.d. 1991, 6th printing]).

Capps, *Authority in Three Worlds* (Tulsa, OK: Harrison House, 1982).

Capps, *Changing the Seen & Shaping the Unseen* (Tulsa, OK: Harrison House, 1980), (1981 [n.d., 1991? 11th ed.]).

Capps, *Dynamics of Faith & Confession* (Tulsa, OK: Harrison House, 1987).

Capps, *God's Creative Power* (Tulsa, OK: Harrison House, 1976 [n.d. 1991?, 27th ed.]).

Capps, *Kicking Over Sacred Cows* (Tulsa, OK: Harrison House, 1987).

Capps, *The Substance of Things* (Tulsa, OK: Harrison House, 1990).

Capps, *The Tongue—A Creative Force* (Tulsa, OK: Harrison House, 1976 [n.d., 1991?, 25th ed.]).

Carden, Paul, Special Report: Tilton's Tottering TV Empire, *Christian Research Journal*, 15:1 (Summer 1992), 5.

Carson, Herbert M., *The Epistles of Paul to the Colossians and Philemon* [*Tyndale New Testament Commentaries*] (Grand Rapids, MI: Eerdmans, 1977).

Cerullo, Morris, A Word from God at the Deeper Life World Conference, *Deeper Life*, 22:2 (March 1982), 15.

Cerullo, The Endtime Manifestation of the Sons of God (San Diego: Morris Cerullo World Evangelism, n.d.), audiotape 1.

Cerullo, Few Are Chosen, *Deeper Life* 21:15 (June 1981), 2.

Cerullo, From the Heart, *Victory* (January/February 1992), 6.

Cerullo, The Greatest Message in the World, *Deeper Life* 21:3 (April 1981), 8.

Cerullo, *The Miracle Book* [special charter ed.] (San Diego: Morris Cerullo World Evangelism, 1984).

[Cerullo, Morris, World Evangelism], *God's faithful, anointed servant, Morris Cerullo* [brochure] (San Diego, CA: Morris Cerullo World Evangelism, n.d.).

[Cerullo, Morris, World Evangelism], *7 Point Outreach—World Evangelism and You* (San Diego, CA: Morris Cerullo World Evangelism, n.d.).

Cho, Paul Yonggi, *The Fourth Dimension* [vol. 1] (So. Plainfield, NJ: Bridge Publishing, Inc., 1979).

Cho, *The Fourth Dimension, Volume Two* (So. Plainfield, NJ: Bridge Publishing, Inc., 1983).

Cho Starts Newspaper, *Charisma & Christian Life*, 16:5 (Dec. 1990), 33.

Christian Research Journal, 12:2 (Fall 1989), 27.

Cone, Marla, Oral Roberts Stable After Heart Problem, *Los Angeles Times* (8 October 1992), B1, B9.

Copeland, Gloria, Believer's Voice of Victory program on TBN (25 October 1992).

Copeland, Gloria, *God's Will for You* (Fort Worth, TX: Kenneth Copeland Publications, 1972).

Copeland, Gloria, *God's Will Is Prosperity* (Tulsa, OK: Harrison House, 1978).

Copeland, Gloria, Paul's Thorn in the Flesh, *Believer's Voice of Victory*, 11:11 (November 1983), 5, 8.

Copeland, Gloria, Praise-a-Thon program on TBN, 5 November 1990.

Copeland, Kenneth, The Abrahamic Covenant (Fort Worth, TX: Kenneth Copeland Ministries, 1985), audiotape #01-4405.

Copeland, *Authority of the Believer IV* (Fort Worth, TX: Kenneth Copeland Ministries, 1987), audiotape #01-0304, side 1.

Copeland, Believer's Voice of Victory program on TBN (28 March 1991).

Copeland, Believer's Voice of Victory program on TBN (21 April 1991), [originally delivered at Full Gospel Motorcycle Rally Association 1990 Rally, Eagle Mt. Lake, TX].

Copeland, *Christianity, A Series of Decisions* (Fort Worth, TX: Kenneth Copeland Ministries, 1985), audiotape #01-0406.

Copeland, Following the Faith of Abraham I (Fort Worth, TX: Kenneth Copeland Ministries, 1989), audiotape #01-3001.

Copeland, *The Force of Faith* (Fort Worth, TX: KCP Publications, 1989).

Copeland, "The Force of Love" (Fort Worth, TX: Kenneth Copeland Ministries, 1987), audiotape #02-0028.

Copeland, *Forces of the Recreated Human Spirit* (Fort Worth, TX: Kenneth Copeland Ministries, 1982).

Copeland, The Forgotten Power of Hope, *Believer's Voice of Victory*, 20:3 (March 1992), 2-3.

Copeland, *Freedom from Fear* (Fort Worth, TX: KCP Publications, 1983).

Copeland, God's Covenants with Man II (Fort Worth, TX: Kenneth Copeland Ministries, 1985), audiotape #01-4404.

Copeland, *Healed...to Be or Not to Be* (Fort Worth, TX: Kenneth Copeland Ministries, 1979).

[Copeland, ed.], *Holy Bible: Kenneth Copeland Reference Edition* (Fort Worth, TX: Kenneth Copeland Ministries, 1991).

Copeland, "The Image of God in You III" (Fort Worth, TX: Kenneth Copeland Ministries, 1989), audiotape #01-1403.

Copeland, *The Incarnation* (Fort Worth, TX: Kenneth Copeland, 1985), audiotape #01-0402.

Copeland, Inner Image of the Covenant (Fort Worth, TX: Kenneth Copeland Ministries, 1985), audiotape #01-4406.

Copeland, Jesus Our Lord of Glory, *Believer's Voice of Victory* (April 1982), 3.

Copeland, *The Laws of Prosperity* (Fort Worth, TX: Kenneth Copeland Publications, 1974).

Copeland, Legal and Vital Aspects of Redemption (Fort Worth, TX: Kenneth Copeland Ministries, 1985), audiotape #01-0403.

Copeland, *Living to Give* [brochure] (Fort Worth, TX: Kenneth Copeland Ministries, n.d. [ca. 1988]).

Copeland, *Origin of the Blood Covenant* (Fort Worth, TX: Kenneth Copeland Ministries, 1985), audiotape #01-4401.

Copeland, *Our Covenant with God* (Fort Worth, TX: KCP Publications, 1987 reprint [1976]).

Copeland, *The Power of the Tongue* (Fort Worth, TX: KCP Publications, 1980).

Copeland, Praise the Lord program on TBN (5 February 1986).

Copeland, Praise the Lord program on TBN (6 February 1986).

Copeland, Praise-a-Thon broadcast on TBN (1988).

Copeland, Praise-a-Thon program on TBN (April 1988).

Copeland, presentation at Melodyland Christian Center, Anaheim, CA (30 March 1983), audiotape.

Copeland, The Price of It All, *Believer's Voice of Victory* 19:9 (September 1991), 4-6.

Copeland, Question & Answer, *Believer's Voice of Victory*, 16:8 (August 1988), 8.

Copeland, *Sensitivity of Heart* (Fort Worth, TX: KCP Publications, 1984).

Copeland sermon tape supplied by Dave Hunt (n.d.).

Copeland, Spirit, Soul and Body I (Fort Worth, TX: Kenneth Copeland Ministries, 1985), audiotape #01-0601.

Copeland, Substitution and Identification (Fort Worth, TX: Kenneth Copeland Ministries, 1989), audiotape #00-0202.

Copeland, Take Time to Pray, *Believer's Voice of Victory* 15:2 (February 1987), 9.

Copeland, *The Troublemaker* (Fort Worth, TX: Kenneth Copeland Publications, n.d. [ca. 1970]).

Copeland, *Walking in the Realm of the Miraculous* (Fort Worth, TX: Kenneth Copeland Ministries, 1979).

Copeland, *Welcome to the Family* (Fort Worth, TX: Kenneth Copeland Ministries, 1979).

Copeland, What Happened from the Cross to the Throne (Fort Worth, TX: Kenneth Copeland Ministries, 1990), audiotape #02-0017.

Copeland, Why All Are Not Healed (Fort Worth, TX: Kenneth Copeland Ministries, 1990), audiotape #01-4001.

Covey, Stephen, *The 7 Habits of Highly Effective People* (New York: Simon & Schuster, 1990).

Crawford, Thomas J., *The Doctrine of Holy Scripture Respecting the Atonement* (Grand Rapids, MI: Baker Book House, 1954).

Crenshaw Christian Center staff member, CRI telephone interview (31 July 1992).

Crouch, Jan, Behind the Scenes program on TBN (12 March 1992).

Crouch, Jan, Praise the Lord program on TBN (20 August 1987).

Crouch, Jan, Praise the Lord program on TBN (5 February 1986).

Crouch, Jan, Praise the Lord program on TBN (31 July 1992).

Crouch, Paul, Behind the Scenes program on TBN (12 March 1992).

Crouch letter to M.A. [name withheld for privacy], 28 August 1992.

Crouch letter to R.C. [name withheld for privacy], (22 January 1992).

Crouch, Praise-a-Thon program on TBN (April 1990).

Crouch, Praise-a-Thon program on TBN (6 November 1990).

Crouch, Praise-a-Thon program on TBN (2 April 1991).

Crouch, Praise the Lord program on TBN (5 February 1986).

Crouch, Praise the Lord program on TBN (18 February 1986, rebroadcast on 6 August 1991).

Crouch, Praise the Lord program on TBN (7 July 1986).

Crouch, Praise the Lord program on TBN (5 September 1991).

Crouch, Praise the Lord program on TBN (21 July 1992).

Crouch, Praise the Lord program on TBN (31 July 1992).

Crouch, Praise the Lord program on TBN (6 October 1992).

Crouch, Praise the Lord program on TBN (23 October 1992).

Crouch, *Praise the Lord* [TBN newsletter] 19:7 (July 1992), [1].

[Crouch], *Praise the Lord* [TBN newsletter] 19:8 (August 1992).

[Crouch], *Praise the Lord* [TBN newsletter] 19:11 (November 1992).

Crouch and Benny Hinn, "Praise-a-Thon" program on TBN (November 1990).

D.B. [name withheld for privacy], letter, 13 July 1992.

Dager, Albert James, Special Report: Benny Hinn Pros & Cons, *Media Spotlight* (May 1992).

Dake, Finis J., ed., *Dake's Annotated Reference Bible* (Lawrenceville, GA: Dake Bible Sales, 1963).

Dake, Finis J., *God's Plan for Man* (Lawrenceville, GA: Dake Bible Sales, 1949 [1977 reprint]).

Darrach, Brad, Masking His Biblical Teaching in Theatrics, Pastor Fred Price Gets His Message Across Swimmingly, *People* (10 October 1983), 48, 53.

Dart, John, Huge FaithDome in L.A., *Los Angeles Times* (9 September 1989), Part II, 9-10.

Dart, John, Scholarly Black Pastor Has a Burgeoning Flock, *Los Angeles Times* (7 December 1981), 6-8.

DeArteaga, William, *Past Life Visions: A Christian Exploration* (New York: Seabury Press, 1983).

DeArteaga, William, *Quenching the Spirit* (Lake Mary, FL: Creation House, 1992).

Dorst, Karen MacIntire, telephone interview by CRI-Canada (23 August 1992).

Eddy, Mary Baker, *Science and Health with Key to the Scriptures* (Boston: First Church of Christ, Scientist, 1971 reprint [1875]).

Edgerton, Franklin, *The Beginnings of Indian Philosophy* (London: George Allen & Unwin, 1963).

Enroth, Ronald, *What Is a Cult? A Guide to Cults and New Religions* (Downers Grove, IL: InterVarsity Press, 1983).

Enroth, Ronald, ed., *Evangelizing the Cults* (Ann Arbor, MI: Servant Publications, 1990).

Enroth, Ronald M., and J. Gordon Melton, *Why Cults Succeed Where the Church Fails* (Elgin, IL: Brethren Press, 1985).

Erickson, Millard J., *Christian Theology* (Grand Rapids, MI: Baker Book House, 1988).

Evans, D.W., and John Grimshaw, *Journal of Discourses* (London: Horace S. Eldredge, 1871 [reprint 1966]).

Farah, Charles, A Critical Analysis: The Roots and Fruits of Faith-Formula Theology (unpublished paper for Soc. for Pentecostal Studies, November 1980).

Farah, Charles, *From the Pinnacle of the Temple* (Plainfield, NJ: Logos, 1978).

Fear Is the Master (Hemet, CA: Jeremiah Films, 1987).

Fee, Gordon D., *The Disease of the Health and Wealth Gospels* (Beverly, MA: Frontline Publishing, 1985).

Fillmore, Charles, *Prosperity* (Lee's Summit, MO: Unity Books, 1967 reprint [1936]).

Fisher, G. Richard, Editorial: A History Lesson for Benny Hinn, *Personal Freedom Outreach [PFO] Quarterly Journal,* 12:4 (October-December 1992), 2, 9-10.

Fisher, G. Richard, with Stephen F. Cannon and M. Kurt Goedelman, "Benny Hinn's Anointing: Heaven Sent or Borrowed?" *Personal Freedom Outreach [PFO] Quarterly Journal* 12:3 (July-September 1992), 1, 10-14.

Fisher, G. Richard, telephone interview by CRI (9 October 1992).

Fisher, G. Richard, Paul R. Blizard and Kurt Goedelman, Benny Hinn: Mr. Confusion: The Demystification of the Miracle Man, *Personal Freedom Outreach [PFO] Quarterly Journal,* 13:1 (January–March 1993), 5-12.

Frame, Randy, Best-selling Author Admits Mistakes, Vows Changes, *Christianity Today* (28 October 1991), 44-45.

Frame, Randy, Same Old Benny Hinn, Critics Say, *Christianity Today,* 36:11 (5 October 1992), 52-54.

Frame, Randy, telephone interview by CRI (3 September 1992).

Frame, Randy, telephone interview with Hanegraaff, 3 September 1992.

Friedrich, Gerhard, ed. (transl. ed. Geoffrey W. Bromiley), *Theological Dictionary of the New Testament* (Grand Rapids, MI: Eerdmans, 1968 Eng. transl.), (1974 ed.).

Gaebelein, Frank E., ed., *The Expositor's Bible Commentary* [vol. 9] (Grand Rapids, MI: Zondervan, 1981).

Garfield, Ken, Faith Healer from Florida Draws Crowds, and Questions, *Charlotte Observer* (15 October 1992), 1C.

Geisler, Norman, and J. Yutaka Amano, *The Reincarnation Sensation* (Wheaton, IL: Tyndale House Publishers, 1986).

Germain, Annabeth, telephone interview by Hanegraaff (21 October 1992).

Gish, Duane T., *Evolution: The Challenge of the Fossil Record* (El Cajon, CA: Creation-Life Publishers, 1991).

God's Bountiful Double Portion, *Word of Faith,* 26:1 (December 1992).

Gohr, Glenn W., and Frederick K.C. Price, in Stanley M. Burgess, Gary B. McGee, and Patrick H. Alexander, eds., *Dictionary of Pentecostal and Charismatic Movements* (Grand Rapids, MI: Regency/Zondervan, 1988), 727.

Goldman, Ari L., Religion Notes, *New York Times* [Nat. Ed.] (21 November 1992), 8.

Good, Joseph, Difficult Verses (Port Arthur, TX: Hatikva Ministries, April 1990), audiotape #5.

Gregorios, Archimandrite, President of the Greek Orthodox Patriarchate Ecclesiastical Court, Certificate (26 January 1967), no. 56/vol. 67, Jaffa.

H.C. [name withheld for privacy], letter, ca. 6 August 1991.

Hagin, Kenneth E., Jr., *The Answer for Oppression* [Tulsa, OK: Kenneth Hagin Ministries, 1983).

Hagin Kenneth E., Jr., *Blueprint for Building Strong Faith* (Tulsa, OK: Kenneth Hagin Ministries, 1980).

Hagin, Kenneth E., Jr., *Faith Worketh by Love* (Tulsa, OK: Kenneth Hagin Ministries, 1979).

Hagin, Kenneth E., Jr., letter to the author (4 January 1991).

Hagin, Kenneth, E., Jr., Trend Toward Faith Movement, *Charisma & Christian Life* (August 1985), 67-70.

Hagin, Kenneth E. (Sr.), letter to H. Robert Cowles, Executive Vice-President of Christian Publications, Inc. (28 February 1984).

Hagin, *Authority of the Believer* (Tulsa, OK: Kenneth Hagin Ministries, 1967).

Hagin, *Believer's Authority* (Tulsa, OK: Kenneth Hagin Ministries, 2d rev. 1991).

Hagin, *Bible Faith Study Course* (Tulsa, OK: Hagin Evangelistic Assoc., n.d. [ca. 1966]).

Hagin, *Casting Your Cares Upon the Lord* (Tulsa, OK: Kenneth Hagin Ministries, 1981).

Hagin, *Classic Sermons: Word of Faith 25th Anniversary 1968-1992 Commemorative Edition* (Tulsa, OK: Kenneth Hagin Ministries, 1992).

Hagin, *Demons and How to Deal with Them* (Tulsa, OK: Kenneth Hagin Evangelistic Assoc., 1976), (Kenneth Hagin Ministries, 2d rev. 1983).

Hagin, *El Shaddai* (Tulsa, OK: Kenneth Hagin Ministries, 1980).

Hagin, *Exceedingly Growing Faith* (Tulsa, OK: Kenneth Hagin Ministries, 1983 [2d ed. 1990]).

Hagin, *Faith Food for Spring* (Tulsa, OK: Kenneth Hagin Ministries, 1978).

Hagin, *The Glory of God* (Tulsa, OK: Kenneth Hagin Ministries, 1987).

Hagin, God's Best Belongs to You! *Word of Faith*, 26:1 (December 1992).

Hagin, *God's Medicine* (Tulsa, OK: Kenneth Hagin Ministries, 1977).

Hagin, *Having Faith in Your Faith* (Tulsa, OK: Kenneth Hagin Ministries, 1980 [1988 reprint]).

Hagin, Healing: The Father's Provision, *Word of Faith* (August 1977).

Hagin, *How God Taught Me About Prosperity* (Tulsa, OK: Kenneth Hagin Ministries, 1985).

Hagin, How Jesus Obtained His Name (Tulsa, OK: Kenneth Hagin Ministries, n.d.), audiotape #44H01.

Hagin, *How to Write Your Own Ticket with God* (Tulsa, OK: Kenneth Hagin Ministries, 1979).

Hagin, *How You Can Be Led by the Spirit of God* (Tulsa, OK: Kenneth Hagin Ministries, 1978).

Hagin, *The Human Spirit* (Tulsa, OK: Kenneth Hagin Ministries, 1974).

Hagin, *I Believe in Visions* (Old Tappan, NJ: Spire Books/Revell, 1972).

Hagin, *I Went to Hell* (Tulsa, OK: Kenneth Hagin Ministries, 1982).

Hagin, The Incarnation, *Word of Faith*, 13:12 (December 1980), 14.

Hagin, *The Interceding Christian* (Tulsa, OK: Kenneth Hagin Ministries, 1978 printing).

Hagin, *The Key to Scriptural Healing* (Tulsa, OK: Kenneth Hagin Evangelistic Assoc., 1977) (1984 rev. ed.).

Hagin, *Knowing What Belongs to Us* (Tulsa, OK: Kenneth Hagin Ministries, 1989).

Hagin, Made Alive, *Word of Faith* (April 1982), 3.

Hagin, *Ministering to the Oppressed* (Tulsa, OK: Kenneth Hagin Evangelistic Assoc., 7th ed. 1977).

Hagin, *Must Christians Suffer?* (Tulsa, OK: Kenneth Hagin Ministries, 1982).

Hagin, *The Name of Jesus* (Tulsa, OK: Kenneth Hagin Ministries, 1979, 1981).

Hagin, *Obedience in Finances* (Tulsa, OK: Kenneth Hagin Ministries, 1983).

Hagin, *The Real Faith* (Tulsa, OK: Kenneth Hagin Ministries, 1970 [1982 reprint]).

Hagin, *Right and Wrong Thinking for Christians* (Tulsa, OK: Kenneth Hagin Ministries, 1966).

Hagin, *Seven Steps for Judging Prophecy* (Tulsa, OK: Kenneth Hagin Ministries, 1982).

Hagin, *Seven Things You Should Know About Divine Healing* (Tulsa, OK: Kenneth Hagin Ministries, 1979).

Hagin, *Three Big Words* (Tulsa, OK: Kenneth Hagin Ministries, 1983).

Hagin, *Understanding How to Fight the Good Fight of Faith* (Tulsa, OK: Kenneth Hagin Ministries, 1987).

Hagin, *What Faith Is* (Tulsa, OK: Kenneth Hagin Ministries, 1983 rev.), (1966 orig. ed.).

Hagin, *What to Do When Faith Seems Weak & Victory Lost* (Tulsa, OK: Kenneth Hagin Ministries, 1979).

Hagin, *Why Do People Fall Under the Power?* (Tulsa, OK: Kenneth Hagin Ministries, 1981).

Hagin, *Words* (Tulsa, OK: Kenneth Hagin Ministries, 1979).

Hagin, *Zoe: The God-Kind of Life* (Tulsa, OK: Kenneth Hagin Ministries, 1981); (1989).

[Hagin Ministries], Faith Library Catalog (Tulsa, OK: Kenneth Hagin Ministries, 1991).

[Hagin Ministries], Faith Seminar of the Air, radio station listings in *Word of Faith* 25:6 (June 1992), 18-19.

[Hagin Ministries], Graduation 92: A Gateway to the Nations! *Word of Faith* 25:7 (July 1992), 8ff.

[Hagin Ministries], RHEMA's First Russian Graduate! *Word of Faith* 25:7 (July 1992), 10-11.

Hanegraaff, Hendrik (Hank), certified letter to Bruce Barbour, Thomas Nelson Publishers (28 July 1992).

Hanegraaff, CRI Perspective: Binding and Loosing (Irvine, CA: CRI, n.d. [1991]), order no. CP-0610.

Hanegraaff, *The F-A-C-E that demonstrates the Farce of Evolution* (San Juan Capistrano, CA: Memory Dynamics, 1993).

Hanegraaff, *The F-E-A-T that demonstrates the Fact of the Resurrection* (San Juan Capistrano, CA: Memory Dynamics, 1993).

Hanegraaff, letter to L.E. [name withheld for privacy], 31 August 1992.

Hanegraaff, letter to Paul Crouch (6 December 1991).

Hanegraaff, *MAPS to Chart Our Course to Biblical Reliability* (San Juan Capistrano, CA: Memory Dynamics, 1993).

Hanegraaff, *Personal Witness Training: Your Handle on the Great Commission* (San Juan Capistrano, CA: Memory Dynamics, 1993).

Hanegraaff, A Summary Critique: The Anointing [by] Benny Hinn, *Christian Research Journal*, 15:2 (Fall 1992), 38.

Hanegraaff, Testimony of a Former Skeptic, *Acts & Facts: Impact* no. 202 (April 1990).

Happy Church Buys Shopping Mall, *Charisma & Christian Life*, 15:12 (July 1990), 26.

Harrell, David Edwin, Jr., *Oral Roberts: An American Life* (Bloomington, IN: Indiana Univ. Press, 1985).

Harris, R. Laird, Gleason L. Archer, Jr., and Bruce K. Waltke, eds., *Theological Wordbook of the Old Testament*, 2 vols. (Chicago: Moody Press, 1981).

Hayes, Norvel, Praise the Lord program on TBN (13 November 1990).

Hayes, Norvel, presentation at East Coast Believer's Convention, 24 May 1992, audiotape.

Hays, Pat, Betty Price Speaks at 1991 Wisdom from Above Luncheon, *Ever Increasing Faith Messenger*, 13:1 (Winter 1992), 12-13.

Hays, Pat, Farewell Old Sanctuary, Welcome Kenneth E. Hagin Auditorium! *Ever Increasing Faith Messenger*, 11:2 (Spring 1990), 13.

Helm, Leslie, Religious Battle Taking Shape in Foothills of Mt. Fuji, *Los Angeles Times* (16 December 1991), A21.

Hexham, Irving, and Karla Poewe, *Understanding Cults and New Religions* (Grand Rapids, MI: Eerdmans, 1986).

Hickey, Marilyn, Breakthroughs to Faith (Denver, CO: Marilyn Hickey Ministries, n.d.), audiotape #1105.

Hickey, Claim Your Miracles (Denver, CO: Marilyn Hickey Ministries, n.d.), audiotape #186.

Hickey, direct-mail letter, undated (ca. 1992).

Hickey, direct-mail letter, undated (ca. December 1988).

Hickey, Today With Marilyn program on TBN (11 April 1991).

Hickey Ministries, direct-mail piece (n.d. [1992]).

Hickey Ministries, direct-mail piece (n.d.).

Hinn, *The Anointing* (Nashville, TN: Thomas Nelson, 7th ed. 1992).

Hinn, Double Portion Anointing, Part #3 (Orlando, FL: Orlando Christian Center, n.d.), audiotape #A031791-3, aired on TBN (7 April 1991).

Hinn, *Good Morning, Holy Spirit*, draft manuscript (ca. September 1989).

Hinn, *Good Morning, Holy Spirit* (Nashville, TN: Thomas Nelson Publishers, 7th ed. 1990).

Hinn letter to Hanegraaff with medical records (4 September 1992).

Hinn letter to S.R. [name withheld for privacy], 14 September 1992.

Hinn, Miracle Invasion, Anaheim, California, Convention Center, 22 November 1991.

Hinn, Our Position in Christ, Part 1 (Orlando, FL: Orlando Christian Center, 1991), videotape #TV-254.

Hinn, Our Position in Christ #5: An Heir of God (Orlando, FL: Orlando Christian Center, 1990), audiotape #A031190-5.

Hinn, Our Position in Christ #2: The Word Made Flesh (Orlando, FL: Orlando Christian Center, 1991), audiotape #A031190-2.

Hinn, personal interviews by Hanegraaff and CRI Vice President–Research Robert Lyle (21 August 1992).

Hinn, Personal Testimony, audiotape, recorded at Orlando Christian Center (19 July 1987).

Hinn, program on TBN (15 December 1990), The Person of Jesus (delivered during Orlando Christian Center's Sunday morning service on 2 December 1990), comprises Part 4 of Hinn's six-part series on *The Revelation of Jesus* (Orlando: Orlando Christian Center, 1991), videotape #TV-292.

Hinn, Praise-a-Thon program on TBN (6 November 1990).

Hinn, Praise-a-Thon program on TBN (8 November 1990).

Hinn, Praise-a-Thon program on TBN (April 1991).

Hinn, Praise-a-Thon program on TBN (2 April 1991).

Hinn, Praise the Lord program on TBN (3 October 1991).

Hinn, Praise the Lord program on TBN (26 December 1991).

Hinn, Praise the Lord program on TBN (16 April 1992).

Hinn, Praise the Lord program on TBN (17 April 1992).

Hinn, Praise the Lord program on TBN (8 October 1992).

Hinn, Praise the Lord program on TBN (23 October 1992).

Hinn, presentation at World Charismatic Conference, Melodyland Christian Center, Anaheim, California, 7 August 1992, CRI audiotape.

Hinn, program on TBN (13 October 1990).

Hinn, program on TBN (20 October 1990).

Hinn, program on TBN (3 November 1990).

Hinn, program on TBN (15 December 1991), from *The Revelation of Jesus*, Part 4: The Person of Jesus (Orlando, FL: Orlando Christian Center, 1991), videotape #TV-292.

Hinn, program on TBN (8 June 1992).

Hinn, program on TBN (29 June 1992).

Hinn, program on TBN (6 July 1992).

Hinn, The Person of Jesus [delivered during Orlando Christian Center's Sunday morning service on 2 December 1991]: The Revelation of Jesus, Part 4 (Orlando, FL: Orlando Christian Center, 1991), videotape #TV-292.

Hinn, *"Rise & Be Healed!"* (Orlando, FL: Celebration Publishers, 1991).

Hinn, sermon at Miracle Invasion Rally, Anaheim [California] Convention Center (22 November 1991).

Hinn, sermon at Orlando Christian Center (31 December 1989).

Hinn, telephone interview by Hanegraaff (19 August 1992).

Hinn, telephone interview by Randy Frame, *Christianity Today* (3 September 1992).

Hinn, telephone interview by Renee Hooley Munshi, freelance reporter for *Bookstore Journal* (26 August 1992).

Hinn, videotaped sermon (3 November 1990).

Hinn, Christopher N., telephone interview by Hanegraaff (30 September 1992).

Hinn Ministries/Orlando Christian Center spokesman Steve, telephone interview by G. Richard Fisher (PFO) (21 April 1992).

Hinn, Mrs. E., CRI telephone interview (27 July 1992).

Hollinger, Dennis, Enjoying God Forever: An Historical/Sociological Profile of the Health and Wealth Gospel, *Trinity Journal* 9:2 (Fall 1988), 145-48.

Holmes, Ernest, *Creative Mind and Success* (New York: Dodd, Mead & Co., 1967 rev. [1919]).

Holmes, Ernest, *The Science of Mind* (New York: Dodd, Mead & Co., 1938 rev.).

Horton, Michael, ed., *The Agony of Deceit* (Chicago: Moody Press, 1990).

Hughes, Phillip E., *Paul's Second Epistle to the Corinthians* [Ned B. Stonehouse, ed., *The New International Commentary on the New Testament*] (Grand Rapids, MI: Eerdmans, 1962).

Hunt, Rev. Garth, telephone interview by CRI-Canada (13 September 1992).

Hutchinson, Steve, and Michelle (O'Connor), Hutchinson, telephone interviews by CRI-Canada (30 August 1992).

Jeffreys, Mary Ann, Sayings of Spurgeon, *Christian History*, 10:1 (1991).

Jenkins-Bryant, Flo, We've Come This Far by Faith!...And It's Time to Rejoice!!! *Ever Increasing Faith Messenger*, 11:1 (Winter 1990), 8.

Jones, Jim, Tilton Ministry Still Strong Despite Layoffs, Assistant Says, *Fort Worth Star-Telegram* (23 November 1992).

Jones, Jim, The Undercover Thorn in Robert Tilton, *Fort Worth Star-Telegram* (26 January 1992), 1A, 20A.

Jones, R. Tudor, *The Great Reformation* (Downers Grove, IL: InterVarsity Press, 1985).

Juedes, John P., George M. Lamsa: Christian Scholar or Cultic Torchbearer? *Christian Research Journal* 12:2 (Fall 1989), 8-14.

Kelly, J.N.D., *Early Christian Doctrines* (San Francisco: Harper & Row, 1978 rev.).

Kenyon, E.W., *The Blood Covenant* (Lynnwood, WA: Kenyon's Gospel Publishing Society, 1969).

Kenyon, *The Father and His Family* (Lynnwood, WA: Kenyon's Gospel Publishing Society, 17th ed. 1964).

Kenyon, *The Father and His Family* (Seattle: Kenyon's Gospel Publishing Society, 1964).

Kenyon, *The Hidden Man* (Kenyon's Gospel Publishing Society, 5th ed. 1970).

Kenyon, *The Two Kinds of Faith: Faith's Secret Revealed* (Seattle: Kenyon's Gospel Publishing Society, 1942 [1969 reprint]).

Kenyon, *What Happened from the Cross to the Throne* (Lynnwood, WA: Kenyon's Gospel Publishing Society, 12th ed. 1969).

Kinnebrew, James M., *The Charismatic Doctrine of Positive Confession: A Historical, Exegetical, and Theological Critique* (doctoral dissertation, Mid-America Baptist Theological Seminary, September 1988 [Ann Arbor, MI: University Microfilms, 1992 reprint]).

L.E. [name withheld for privacy], letter, 25 August 1992.

Lamsa, George M., transl., *Holy Bible: From the Ancient Eastern Text* (New York: A.J. Holman, 1933 [San Francisco: Harper & Row, n.d. 1984, reprint]).

Larsen, David L., The Gospel of Greed Versus the Gospel of Grace, *Trinity Journal* 9:2 (Fall 1988), 211-20.

Latourette, Kenneth Scott, *A History of Christianity* (New York: Harper & Row, 1975 rev.).

Lee, Christopher, Tilton's Wife Defends Ministry, Blasts TV Exposé of Husband, *Dallas Morning News* (25 November 1991), 1A, 12A.

Lenski, R.C.H., *The Interpretation of the Epistles of St. Peter, St. John and St. Jude* (Minneapolis: Augsburg Publishing House, 1966).

Lewis, Gordon R., *Confronting the Cults* (Grand Rapids, MI: Baker Book House, 1975).

Liddell, Henry George, and Robert Scott (rev. Henry Stuart Jones), *A Greek-English Lexicon* (Oxford, Eng.: Oxford Univ. Press, 1968 rev.).

Lightfoot, John B., *St. Paul's Epistles to the Colossians and to Philemon* (Peabody, MA: Hendrickson, 1981).

Lockman Foundation, *The Amplified Bible* (Grand Rapids, MI: Zondervan, 1965).

Lockwood, David, telephone interview by G. Richard Fisher (PFO) (26 July 1992).

Lubenow, Marvin L., *Bones of Contention* (Grand Rapids, MI: Baker Book House, 1992).

MacArthur, John, *Charismatic Chaos* (Grand Rapids, MI: Zondervan Publishing House, 1992).

MacLean, Mike and Anne, telephone interviews by CRI-Canada (13 September 1992).

MacLean, Mike, telephone interview by G. Richard Fisher (PFO) (10 November 1992).

MacMillan, John A., *The Authority of the Believer* (Harrisburg, PA: Christian Publications, 1980 reprint [1932]).

Marshall, Alfred, *NASB-NIV Parallel New Testament in Greek and English with Interlinear Translation* (Grand Rapids, MI: Regency/Zondervan, 1986).

Martin, Walter, The Errors of Positive Confession (Christian Research Institute, n.d.), audiotape #C-100.

Martin, Walter, Healing: Does God Always Heal? (Christian Research Institute, n.d.), audiotape #C-95.

Martin, Walter, The Health and Wealth Cult (San Juan Capistrano, CA: Christian Research Institute, n.d.), audiotape #C-152.

Martin, Walter, *The Kingdom of the Cults* (Minneapolis: Bethany House Publishers, 1985 rev.).

Martin, Walter, The Warnings of God (Kenneth Copeland's False Prophecy) (San Juan Capistrano, CA: CRI, 1987), audiotape #C-210.

Martin, Walter, You Shall Be As God, in Michael Horton, ed., *The Agony of Deceit* (Chicago: Moody Press, 1990).

Martinez, Sylvia, Tilton sues ABC News, PrimeTime, *Dallas Morning News* (11 November 1992), 29A, 33A.

Mattingly, Terry, 'Prosperity Christian' sings a different tune, *Rocky Mountain News* (16 August 1992), 158.

Mattox, Kent, Orlando Christian Center, telephone interview by Renee Hooley Munshi, for *Bookstore Journal* (1 September 1992).

McAlister, Rev. Jim, telephone interview by CRI-Canada (30 August 1992).

McAteer, Michael, Debunkers Put No Faith in Healer's Miracles, *Toronto Star* (24 September 1992), A2.

McConkie, Bruce R., *Mormon Doctrine* (Salt Lake City: Bookcraft, 2d ed. 1974 reprint [1966]).

McConnell, Daniel R., *A Different Gospel* (Peabody, MA: Hendrickson Publishers, 1988).

McConnell, Daniel R., *The Kenyon Connection: A Theological and Historical Analysis of the Cultic Origins of the Faith Movement* (master's thesis, Oral Roberts University, 1982).

Melton, J. Gordon, *Encyclopedic Handbook of Cults in America* (New York: Garland Publishing, Inc., 1986).

Melton, J. Gordon, *The Encyclopedia of American Religions* (Detroit: Gale Research Inc., 3rd rev. 1989).

Mérat, Pierre, M.D., Critical Study: Anatomy and Physiology of the Shroud, *The Catholic Counter-Reformation in the XXth Century*, no. 218 (April 1989), 1-6.

Metzger, Bruce M., *A Textual Commentary on the Greek New Testament* (London & New York: United Bible Societies, 1975 rev.).

Michel, Otto, Faith, in Colin Brown, gen. ed., *The New International Dictionary of New Testament Theology* (Grand Rapids, MI: Zondervan, 1975 Eng. transl.).

Miller, Elliot, *Healing: Does God Always Heal?* (San Juan Capistrano, CA: CRI, 1979).

Moberg, David O., *The Church As a Social Institution* [Englewood Cliffs: Prentice-Hall, Inc., 1962).

Monteros, Laura, The Rebirth of Morris Cerullo, *Los Angeles Herald-Examiner* (18 November 1978).

Munshi, Renee Hooley, Benny Hinn: An Enigma, draft article for *Bookstore Journal* faxed to CRI and Hinn Ministries (31 August 1992).

Munshi, Renee Hooley, Benny Hinn: An Enigma, revised draft article for *Bookstore Journal* faxed to CRI and Hinn Ministries (2 September 1992).

Munshi, Renee Hooley, telephone interview with CRI (1 September 1992).

National & International Religion Report, 1:18 (21 September 1987), 4.

Neuman, H. Terris, *An Analysis of the Sources of the Charismatic Teaching of Positive Confession* (unpublished paper, Wheaton Graduate School, 1980).

Neuman, H. Terris, Cultic Origins of Word-Faith Theology Within the Charismatic Movement, *PNEUMA: The Journal of the Society for Pentecostal Studies*, 12:1 (Spring 1990), 32-55.

New World Translation, The *Christian Research Newsletter*, 3:3 (1990), 5.

Nicoll, W. Robertson, ed., *The Expositor's Greek Testament* (Grand Rapids, MI: Eerdmans, 1979 reprint).

Noss, John B., *Man's Religion* (New York: Macmillan, 4th ed. 1969).

Ogata, Mamoru Billy, A Comparison Between Paul Yonggi Cho's Church (Korea), and the Soka Gakkai (Japan), [Appendix A] in Ogata, *A Comparative Study of Church Growth in Korea and Japan with Special Application to Japan* (Fuller Theological Seminary, thesis, 1984).

Onken, Brian, The Atonement of Christ and the Faith Message, *Forward* 7:1 (1984), 11-12.

Orange County Register (24 January 1992), O6.

Osborn, T.L., and Daisy, *She & He Photo-Book—Go For It!* (Tulsa, OK: Osborn Foundation, 1983).

Osborn, T.L., *Faith Digest*, XXII:E34-77.

Osteen, John, *The 6th Sense . . . Faith* (Houston, TX: John Osteen Publications, 1980).

Paulk, Earl, *Satan Unmasked* (Atlanta: K Dimension Publishers, 1984).

Peck, M. Scott, *The Road Less Traveled* (New York: Simon & Schuster, 1978).

Peel, Robert, *Christian Science* (New York: Henry Holt, 5th ed. 1959).

Pinsky, Mark I., FCC Reviewing Trinity's Minority Subsidiary, *Los Angeles Times* (29 September 1991), B7.

Pinsky, Mark I., He Wished Death on Foes: Theologians Fault Prayer by Crouch, *Los Angeles Times* [Orange County ed.] (16 February 1989), II-1, II-10.

Piper, John, *Desiring God* (Portland, OR: Multnomah Press, 1986).

Polino, Gene, personal interviews by Hanegraaff and CRI Vice-President–Research Robert Lyle (21 August 1992).

Polino, Gene, telephone interview by Renee Hooley Munshi, freelance reporter for *Bookstore Journal* (1 September 1992).

Poynter, Mrs. Jim, telephone interview by CRI-Canada (13 September 1992).

Price, Betty, A Praise Report, *Ever Increasing Faith Messenger*, 12:3 (Summer 1991).

Price, Betty, Health Update . . . then . . . and . . . now from Betty Price, *Ever Increasing Faith Messenger*, 13:4 (Fall 1992), 5.

[Price, Betty], Radio Interview: An Intimate Look at Betty Price, *Ever Increasing Faith Messenger*, 8:1 (January 1987), 8.

Price, Frederick K.C., *Ever Increasing Faith Messenger* (June 1980), 7.

Price, Ever Increasing Faith program on TBN (1 May 1992), audiotape #PR11.

Price, Ever Increasing Faith program on TBN (16 November 1990).

Price, Ever Increasing Faith program on TBN (23 November 1990).

Price, Ever Increasing Faith program on TBN (9 December 1990), available from Crenshaw Christian Center (audiotape #CR-A2).

Price, Ever Increasing Faith program on TBN (29 March 1992).

Price, Ever Increasing Faith program on TBN (1 May 1992), audiotape #PR11.

Price, Ever Increasing Faith program on TBN (3 May 1992).

Price, *Faith, Foolishness, or Presumption?* (Tulsa, OK: Harrison House, 1979).

Price, *How Faith Works* (Tulsa, OK: Harrison House, 1976).

Price, Identification #3 (Los Angeles: Ever Increasing Faith Ministries, 1980), audiotape #FP545.

Price, Identification #8 (Los Angeles: Ever Increasing Faith Ministries, 1980), audiotape #FP550.

Price, Identification #9 (Los Angeles: Ever Increasing Faith Ministries, 1980), audiotape #FP551.

Price, Is God Glorified Through Sickness? (Los Angeles: Crenshaw Christian Center, n.d.), audiotape #FP605.

Price, *Is Healing for All?* (Tulsa, OK: Harrison House, 1976).

Price letter to B.G. [name withheld for privacy] (14 October 1992).

Price, Name It and Claim It! What Saith the WORD?...*Ever Increasing Faith Messenger*, 10:3 (Summer 1989), 2.

Price, Paul's Thorn #1 (Los Angeles: Ever Increasing Faith Ministries, 1980), audiotape #FP606.

Price, *Petition Prayer, or the Prayer of Faith* (Los Angeles: Ever Increasing Faith Ministries, 1991).

Price, Praise the Lord program on TBN (21 September 1990).

Price, "Prayer: Do You Know What Prayer Is...and How to Pray?" *The Word Study Bible* (Tulsa, OK: Harrison House, 1990), 1178.

Price, *Prosperity on God's Terms* (Tulsa, OK: Harrison House, 1990).

Price, *What Every Believer Should Know About Prayer* (Los Angeles: Ever Increasing Faith Ministries, 1990).

Pusey, Allen, Florida Couple Sues Tilton Organization: Suit Says Story Misrepresented, Funds Misused, *Dallas Morning News,* 14 November 1992.

Pusey, Allen, and Howard Swindle, Tilton Bankrolled 83 TV License Bids, Source and Files Say, *Dallas Morning News* (12 July 1992), 1A, 29A.

Pynkoski, Paul, telephone interview by CRI-Canada (14 September 1992).

Quimby, Phineas, ed., H.W. Dresser, *The Quimby Manuscripts* (New Hyde Park, NY: University Books, 1961 [1859 orig.]).

Ramm, Bernard, *Protestant Biblical Interpretation* (Grand Rapids, MI: Baker Book House, 1978).

Reed, David A., *Jehovah's Witnesses Answered Verse-By-Verse* (Grand Rapids, MI: Baker Book House, 1986).

[Religious News Service], TV Preachers Seen As Beggars: Public Dislikes Evangelists' Onscreen Methods, Professor Says, *Dallas Morning News* (21 November 1992).

Reston, James, Jr., and Noah Adams, "Father Cares: The Last of Jonestown," program on National Public Radio (23 April 1981).

Reymond, Robert L., *Jesus, Divine Messiah* (Phillipsburg, NJ: Presbyterian and Reformed Publishing, 1990).

Rhodes, Ron, Esotericism and Biblical Interpretation, *Christian Research Journal* 14:3 (Winter 1992), 28-31.

Richardson, James T., *The Brainwashing/Deprogramming Controversy: Sociological, Psychological, Legal and Historical Perspectives* (Toronto: Edwin Mellen Press, 1983).

Riss, Richard M. and Kenneth Copeland, in *Dictionary of Pentecostal & Charismatic Movements*, 226.

Robert, Risa, Tilton sent dead man personal mail, *Tulsa Tribune*, 27 February 1992, 7A.

Roberts, Oral, ed., *Daily Blessing: A Guide to Seed-Faith Living*, 24:1 (January–February–March 1982).

Roberts, Oral, *A Daily Guide to Miracles: And Successful Living Through SEED-FAITH* (Tulsa, OK: Pinoak Publications, 1975).

Roberts, Oral, direct-mail letter, undated (ca. 1 January 1985).

Roberts, Oral, direct-mail letter, undated (ca. 1 March 1987).

Roberts, Oral, God's Mandate to Me, *Abundant Life* (March/April 1987), 3.

Roberts, Oral, *How I Learned Jesus Was Not Poor* (Altamonte Springs, FL: Creation House, 1989).

Roberts, Oral, *101 Questions and Answers* (Tulsa, OK: Oral Roberts, 1968).

Roberts, Oral, *Oral Roberts' Best Sermons and Stories* (Tulsa: Oral Roberts, 1956).

Roberts, Oral, Praise the Lord show on TBN (6 October 1992).

Roberts, Oral, presentation at World Charismatic Conference, Melodyland Conference Center, Anaheim, CA, 7 August 1992, tape recording by CRI.

Roberts, Oral and Richard, direct-mail letter (August 1984).

Roberts, Patti, with Sherry Andrews, *Ashes to Gold* (Waco, TX: Word Books, 1983).

Roberts, Richard, direct-mail letter, undated (ca. 1 January 1987).

Robertson, Archibald Thomas, *A Grammar of the Greek New Testament in the Light of Historical Research* (Nashville: Broadman Press, 1934).

Robertson, Archibald Thomas, *Word Pictures in the New Testament* (Nashville: Broadman Press, 1930).

Robertson, Archibald Thomas, and W. Hersey Davis, *A New Short Grammar of the Greek Testament* (Grand Rapids, MI: Baker Book House, 1979 reprint [10th rev. 1933]).

Robinson, Stephen E., *Are Mormons Christians?* (Salt Lake City: Bookcraft, 1991).

Rossiter, Don, telephone interview by CRI-Canada (13 September 1992).

S.C. [name withheld for privacy], letter (25 September 1991).

Sarles, Ken L., A Theological Evaluation of the Prosperity Gospel, *Bibliotheca Sacra* 143:572 (October-December 1986), 338.

Savelle, Jerry, The Authority of the Believer, in *The Word Study Bible* (Tulsa, OK: Harrison House, 1990), 1141.

Savelle, Framing Your World with the Word of God [Parts 1–2] (Fort Worth, TX: Jerry Savelle Evangelistic Assn., n.d.), audiotape #SS-36.

Savelle, *If Satan Can't Steal Your Joy...* (Tulsa, OK: Harrison House, 1982).

Schaff, Philip, *The Creeds of Christendom* (Grand Rapids, MI: Baker Book House, 1985).

Schaff, Philip, *History of the Christian Church* (New York: n.p., 1888 [reprint n.p.: AP & A, n.d.]).

Schultze, Quentin J., *Televangelism and American Culture* (Grand Rapids, MI: Baker Book House, 1991).

Simmons, Dale H., *A Theological and Historical Analysis of Kenneth E. Hagin's Claim to Be a Prophet* (master's thesis, Oral Roberts University, 1985).

Simpson, Preston, M.D., medical analysis report (28 October 1992).

Simpson, Preston, M.D., telephone interviews by CRI (6 and 23 October 1992).

Sire, James W., *Scripture Twisting* (Downers Grove, IL: InterVarsity Press, 1980).

Smith, Joseph, The King Follett Discourse, in Joseph Fielding Smith, ed., *Teachings of the Prophet Joseph Smith* (Salt Lake City, UT: Deseret Book Co., 21st ed. 1972).

Smith, Joseph, The King Follett Sermon (7 April 1844), *History of the Church* (Salt Lake City, UT: Deseret Book Co., 8th ed. 1975), 6:305.

Smith, Joseph Fielding, in Bruce R. McConkie, ed., *Doctrines of Salvation* (Salt Lake City: Bookcraft, 1975 [1954]).

Special Report: Campmeeting '83, *Word of Faith*, 16:10 (October 1983), 3-11.

Sproul, R.C., *Knowing Scripture* (Downers Grove, IL: InterVarsity Press, 1977).

Spurgeon, Charles Haddon, "A Sermon from a Rush," in *Metropolitan Tabernacle Pulpit*, 63 vols. (Pasadena, TX: Pilgrim Publiclations, 1989).

St. Pierre, Nancy, Judge Rejects Tilton Bid for Restraining Order, *Dallas Morning News* (15 May 1992), 1A, 8A.

St. Pierre, Nancy, Judge Rejects Tilton's Suit Against Foes (25 June 1992), 29A, 32A.

St. Pierre, Nancy, Man Sifted Tilton's Trash for Evidence, *Dallas Morning News* (6 March 1992), 1A, 6A.

St. Pierre, Nancy, 2nd Widow Sues Tilton over Letters, *Dallas Morning News* (18 March 1992), 28A.

St. Pierre, Nancy, Tilton's Lawyer Has Key Role, *Dallas Morning News* (17 February 1992), 1A, 14A.

St. Pierre, Nancy, Tilton's Wife Tells of Finances, *Dallas Morning News* (5 March 1992), 1A, 7A.

St. Pierre, Nancy, U.S. Court Judge Criticizes Morals in Tilton Inquiry *Dallas Morning News* (19 March 1992), 1A, 13A.

Stevenson, Kenneth E., and Gary R. Habermas, *The Shroud and the Controversy* (Nashville, TN: Thomas Nelson, 1990).

Strang, Stephen, The Ever Increasing Faith of Fred Price, *Charisma & Christian Life* (May 1985), 23.

Strang, Stephen, Marilyn Sweitzer Hickey, in *Dictionary of Pentecostal & Charismatic Movements*, 389.

Swindle, Howard, Tilton Letters to Dead Man Prompt Widow to File Suit, *Dallas Morning News* (28 February 1992), 1A, 18A.

Swindle, Howard, and Allen Pusey, Tilton Ends Syndication of His Sunday Services, *Dallas Morning News* (13 August 1992), 1A, 28A.

Swindoll, Charles R., *Growing Strong in the Seasons of Life* (Portland, OR: Multnomah Press, 1983).

Synan, H. Vinson, Capps, and Charles Emmitt, in *Dictionary of Pentecostal & Charismatic Movements* (Grand Rapids, MI: Regency/Zondervan, 1988), 107.

Synan, Vinson, The Faith of Kenneth Hagin, *Charisma & Christian Faith*, 15:11 (June 1990), 68.

Talmage, James E., *Jesus the Christ* (Salt Lake City: Deseret Book Co., 1969).

Tasker, R.V.G., *The Second Epistle of Paul to the Corinthians* [*Tyndale New Testament Commentaries*] (Eerdmans, 1977 reprint [1958]).

Tenney, Merrill C., The Gospel of John, in Frank E. Gaebelein, ed., *The Expositor's Bible Commentary* [vol. 9] (Grand Rapids, MI: Zondervan, 1981).

Thayer, Joseph Henry, *The New Thayer's Greek–English Lexicon of the New Testament* (Peabody, MA: Hendrickson, 1981 rev. [1889 rev.]).

Thomas, Mike, The Power and the Glory, *Florida* [weekly magazine of *Orlando Sentinel*] (24 November 1991), 12-18.

Tilton cuts back, *Dallas Morning News* (22 November 1992).

Tilton Ministries, PrimeTime Lies, program broadcast in place of Robert Tilton's regular Success-N-Life television program (18 August 1992).

Tilton, Robert, direct-mail letter with enclosures (1990).

Tilton, Success-N-Life television program (18 October 1990).

Tilton, Success-N-Life television program (27 December 1990).

Tilton, Success-N-Life television program (18 July 1991).

Tilton, Success-N-Life television program (22 November 1991).

Tilton, Success-N-Life television program (n.d. [ca. 1991]), video on file at CRI.

Torrey, Reuben A., *The Power of Prayer* (Grand Rapids, MI: Zondervan Publishing House, 19th ed. 1981).

Treat, Casey, *Renewing the Mind* (Seattle, WA: Casey Treat Ministries, 1985).

Tregelles, Samuel P., trans., *Gesenius' Hebrew and Chaldee Lexicon to the Old Testament Scriptures* (Grand Rapids, MI: Eerdmans, 1976 reprint [1857]).

Tribbe, Frank C., *Portrait of Jesus?* (New York: Stein & Day, 1983).

Trinity Foundation release, Does Word of Faith = Wheel of Fortune? (9 December 1991).

Trinity Foundation release, Tons of Tilton Prayer Requests Discovered in Recycle Center (9 December 1991).

Troeltsch, Ernst, transl. Olive Wyon, *The Social Teaching of the Christian Churches*, 2 vols. (London: George Allen and Unwin, 1931).

Turner, Nigel, *Grammatical Insights into the New Testament* (Edinburgh: T. & T. Clark, 1977).

Unger, Merrill, rev. Gary N. Larson, *The New Unger's Bible Handbook* (Chicago: Moody Press, 1984).

Van Gorden, Kurt, The Unity School of Christianity, in Ronald Enroth, ed., *Evangelizing the Cults* (Ann Arbor, MI: Servant Publications, 1990).

Vaughan, Curtis, and Virtus E. Gideon, *A Greek Grammar of the New Testament* (Nashville: Broadman Press, 1979).

Villanueva, Eric, Viewpoint: Territorial Spirits and Spiritual Warfare: A Biblical Perspective, *Christian Research Journal*, 15:1 (Summer 1992).

Vine, W.E., *An Expository Dictionary of New Testament Words* (Old Tappan, NJ: Revell, 1966 reprint).

Wagner, C. Peter, School of World Missions, Fuller Theological Seminary, CRI telephone interview (30 July 1992).

Watson, Merv and Merla, telephone interviews by CRI-Canada (30 August 1992).

Watt, G.D., ed., *Journal of Discourses* (Liverpool, Eng.: F.D. Richards, 1855).

What the Mormons Think of Christ (Salt Lake City: Deseret News Press, n.d.).

White, Russ, Congregation keeps the faith with spellbinding Benny Hinn, *Orlando Sentinel* (11 October 1987), F6.

Wilckens, U., *hysteros*, etc., in Geoffrey W. Bromiley, ed., *Theological Dictionary of the New Testament* [abridged ed.] (Grand Rapids, MI: Eerdmans/Paternoster Press, 1985), 1240-41.

Wilson, Bryan, *Religious Sects*, World University Library Series (Englewood, NJ: McGraw-Hill, 1970).

Wilson, Dwight J. and Paul Yonggi Cho, in *Dictionary of Pentecostal & Charismatic Movements* (1988), 161.

Wilson, Ian, *The Mysterious Shroud* (Garden City, NY: Doubleday, 1986).

Wilson, Ron, Executive Director, Evangelical Press Association, CRI telephone interview (24 July 1992).

Woodward, Kenneth L., and Lynda Wright, The T Stands for Troubled, *Newsweek*, 99:13 (30 March 1992), 60.

Word Study Bible (Tulsa, OK: Harrison House, 1990).

Yancey, Philip, and Tim Stafford, *The Student Bible* (Grand Rapids, MI: Zondervan, 1986).

Yesterday, Today, and Tomorrow: 15 Years of Covering the Earth With the Word, *Outpouring*, 15:1 (special edition), [3].

Yinger, J. Milton, *Religion, Society and the Individual* (New York: The Macmillan Company, 4th printing 1962 [1957]).

Yogi, Maharishi Mahesh, *Meditations of Maharishi Mahesh Yogi* (New York: Bantam, 1968).

Yonggi Cho Changes His Name, *Charisma & Christian Life*, 18:4 (November 1992).

Young, Brigham, Discourse..., June 8th, 1873, *Deseret News* [Salt Lake City, UT] (18 June 1873), 308.

Young, Brigham, The Gospel: The One-Man Power, discourse delivered 24 July 1870, reported by D.W. Evans and John Grimshaw, *Journal of Discourses* (London: Horace S. Eldredge, 1871 [reprint 1966]).

Young, Brigham, *Journal of Discourses* 13:271 (24 July 1890).

Young, Brigham, sermon (9 April 1852), in G.D. Watt, ed., *Journal of Discourses* (Liverpool, Eng.: F.D. Richards, 1855), 1:50.

Zoe College, Jacksonville, Florida, advertisement, *Charisma & Christian Life* (May 1992), 82.

Scripture Index

Old Testament

──────── *New Testament* ────────

Subject Index

A

aberrant (or aberrational) doctrine 12, 14, 17, passim
Abraham (or Abram) 23, 24, 55, 92, 97, 139, 212, 213, 214, 241, 364, 372, 381, 395, 396, 400
Adam 21, 22, 23, 24, 25, 26, 37, 77, 85, 108, 109, 116, 119, 125, 126, 129, 131, 132, 133, 134, 137, 139, 169, 211, 212, 241, 314, 338, 342, 346, 354, 368, 379, 380, 381, 391
adultery 33, 258, 334
African-American 34
Allen, A.A. (Pentecostal healer) 30, 31, 385
amen 57, 285-287
angels, angelic 22, 38, 44, 94, 131, 132, 169, 247, 259, 296, 314, 315, 321, 358, 380, 381, 389
anointing 30, 33, 202, 207, 224, 253, 335, 336, 341, 342, 343, 344, 351, 363, 364
apologetics (defense of the Christian faith) 57, 187, 309, 310, 314, 348, 367
archangel 44
Archbishop of Canterbury 49
Assemblies of God (Pentecostal Christian denomination) 31, 352, 386
Atlanta, Georgia 41, 48
atonement 47, 110, 145, 151, 152, 153, 154, 161, 174, 175, 185, 205, 250, 251, 252, 347, 360, 396, 418
Augustine (early church father) 47, 304, 395
Avanzini, John (Faith teacher) 35, 108, 109, 187, 188, 199, 200, 201, 208, 209, 222, 223, 262, 310, 337, 347, 348, 349, 359, 381, 382, 417
avatar (Hindu/New Age concept) 44, 320

B

Bakker, Jim 214, 215
baptism 47, 185, 229, 304, 343, 375
Berkhof, Louis (theologian) 70
biblical economics 35, 347
"big house" (Avanzini phrase) 35, 187, 188, 208, 348, 381
Billheimer, Paul E. (author-teacher) 164, 383
birth out of the side, giving (Hinn concept) 23, 34, 46, 341, 380
blasphemy 37, 44, 108, 109, 116, 132, 135, 138, 141, 155, 156, 157, 175, 332, 354, 381
born again 23, 26, 32, 41, 132, 153, 170-177, 332, 380, 382, 383
brainwashing 43
Branham, William (Faith healer) 30, 331, 384

breastplate, ceremonial (Hickey device) 36, 203, 351
Buddha, Buddhism 36, 37, 82, 83, 312, 352, 353, 369, 388

C

Cady, H. Emilie (early metaphysical teacher) 30, 392
California 48, 199, 344, 413
Calvary Assembly (Orlando, Florida) 49
Calvary Chapel of Costa Mesa, CA 48
cancer 31, 34, 78, 237, 238, 239, 245, 246, 248, 256-258, 262, 263, 337, 341, 346, 363, 408, 412
Capps, Charles (Faith teacher) 37, 66, 68, 77, 85, 89, 94, 98, 109, 117, 133, 134, 141, 142, 170, 212, 333, 354, 355, 357, 379, 381-383, 392, 396, 417
"carbon copy" (Faith concept) 21, 139
Carey, George (Archbishop of Canterbury) 49
Cerullo, Morris (Faith teacher) 11, 38, 109, 122, 199, 200, 357-359
charismatic 47, 48, 49, 50, 264, 331, 343, 344, 386, 401
child abuse 62
Cho, Paul (now David) Yonggi (Faith teacher) 36, 37, 82-84, 352, 353
Christian Research Institute (CRI), International 4, 12, 34, 44, 48, 61, 249, 262, 337, 340, 341, 344, 345, 360, 394, 406, 411, 413
Christian Research Journal (CRI publication) 49
Christian Science, or First Church of Christ, Scientist (metaphysical cult) 14, 29, 32, 111, 246, 247, 332, 392
Christianity in Crisis 4, 13, 15, 70, 282, 324
Christianity Today (evangelical magazine) 33, 124, 343, 344, 345, 393, 395, 398, 412
Church of Jesus Christ of Latter-day Saints (see Mormon Church)
colon 34, 341
coma 62
conceiving an image (Faith concept; see also visualization) 68
confession brings possession (Faith concept) 36, 352, 406
containers, spiritual (see spiritual containers)
context 53, 55, 70, 97, 113, 115, 117, 158, 205, 206, 209, 217, 220, 222, 223, 224, 251, 257, 298, 363, 364, 387, 393, 400, 405, 406

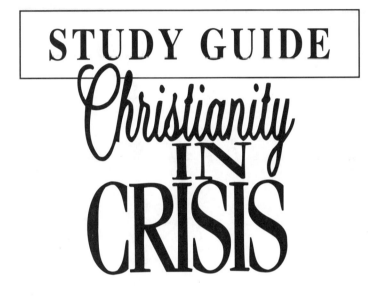

STUDY GUIDE
Christianity IN CRISIS

How to Use
This Study Guide

The *Christianity in Crisis Study Guide* has been carefully designed so it can be used independent of everything except Scripture. All quotations are faithfully reproduced and fully documented in the bestselling book *Christianity in Crisis*.* To derive maximum benefit from your study, it is highly recommended that you:

1. Read *Christianity in Crisis*, and

2. Listen to the *Christianity in Crisis Audiobook*

This study guide features 27 lessons, and can be adapted to a 13-week curriculum by combining the individual sessions as follows:

Week One:	Studies 1 and 2
Week Two:	Studies 3 and 4
Week Three:	Studies 5 and 6
Week Four:	Studies 7 and 8
Week Five:	Studies 9 and 10
Week Six:	Studies 11 and 12
Week Seven:	Studies 13 and 14
Week Eight:	Studies 15 and 16

---

* Shortly after the publication of *Christianity in Crisis* in 1993, Benny Hinn stated that he has revised his views on certain of his teachings. However, Hinn's views as articulated in the latest editions of his works, including *Good Morning, Holy Spirit*, are presented in this study guide until material to the contrary is available.

To help facilitate both *study guide leaders* and *students*, each lesson is arranged as follows:

- Spiritual Flaws*
- Study Questions**
- Scriptural Insights
- Summary Statement
- Supplementary Study Questions

The content of the study guide is carefully designed to build believers up in the faith "once for all entrusted to the saints." Truly, today as never before, it is incumbent for Christians to be so familiar with the truth that when a counterfeit looms on the horizon they will know it instantaneously.

---

* In study guide sessions 23–27, the *Spiritual Flaws* section is instead entitled *Spiritual Facts*.

** Note: It is not necessary to cover every single study question during group-study sessions.

Testing Doctrine Is God's Idea

*I*t is very common today to hear certain television and radio preachers warn their audiences against critiquing the preacher's "anointed" ministry. You will hear them make comments such as the following:

Spiritual Flaws

> There are people attempting to sit in judgment right today over the ministry that I'm responsible for, and the ministry that Kenneth E. Hagin is responsible for. . . .
>
> Several people that I know had criticized and called that faith bunch out of Tulsa a cult. And some of 'em are dead right today in an early grave because of it, and there's more than one of them got cancer.
> —Kenneth Copeland
>
> I think [heresy hunters] are damned and on their way to hell; and I don't think there's any redemption for them.
> —Paul Crouch

451

> The Lord said to me, "If I give you a message for an individual, a church, or a pastor, and they don't accept it, you will not be responsible. They will be responsible." There will be ministers who don't accept it and fall dead in the pulpit. I say this with reluctance, but this actually happened in one place. . . . I told the pastor . . . that man will fall dead in the pulpit. And just a very short time after, he did. Why? Because he didn't accept the message that God gave me to give him from the Holy Spirit.
>
> —Kenneth Hagin

To give a spiritual tone to their threats, these teachers typically twist Psalm 105:15: "Touch not mine anointed, and do my prophets no harm." Their audiences are expected to trust what they say simply because they claim to be "God's anointed."

But is this biblical? Is it indeed a sin to carefully examine the claims of preachers and teachers, or does God's Word command us to do so?

Harvest Audiobook Before moving on to the *Study Questions* below, it is suggested that participants listen to the introductory section of the *Christianity in Crisis Audiobook.* For maximum benefit, students should listen to the "Faith Fable" directly following the introductory section before moving on to session #2.

Study Questions

1. Who are God's "anointed"? How do you know for sure?

2. Are God's "anointed" likely to make threats against their critics? Why or why not?

3. How do you evaluate someone's teaching biblically? What is the goal of such an evaluation? What is to be the spirit of such an evaluation?

Scriptural Insights

1. Read 1 John 2:20-27.

   A. According to verse 20, who has "an anointing from the Holy One"? What does this "anointing" accomplish?

   B. What are the main truths that Christians are to safeguard, according to verses 22-25?

   C. What was John trying to accomplish in verse 26? How does this verse relate to our current study?

   D. Who has "the anointing," according to verses 26,27? If all Christians have this anointing and do not need to be taught, then what is John teaching them through this letter?

2. Read 2 Peter 2:1-3.

   A. What warning does the apostle give in this passage? What danger does he point out?

B. What are the results of failing to heed the apostle's warning? What ramifications does this suggest for us today?

3. Read Acts 20:17-38.

A. List the activities Paul engaged in with the Ephesian church. How do these activities demonstrate the heart of a true servant of God?

B. List the activities Paul says he purposefully *refrained* from doing. How does this demonstrate the heart of a true servant of God?

C. What instructions does Paul give the Ephesian elders? Why are these important?

D. What prediction does Paul make concerning the Ephesian church? What warning does he give the church? How does he instruct the church to respond?

4. Read Acts 17:10-12.

A. Why were the Bereans said to be "of more noble character than the Thessalonians"? What did they do differently from the Thessalonians?

B. How do you think Paul reacted to the Bereans searching "the Scriptures every day to see if what he said was true"?

How does this compare with the Faith teachers' quotes on pages 451 and 452 of this study guide?

5. Read 1 Thessalonians 5:21 and 1 John 4:1-3. What commands are given to all Christians in these two passages? How do we fulfill these commands in practice?

Summary Statement

No one's teachings or practices are beyond biblical evaluation—especially those of great influence. According to the Bible, authority and accountability go hand in hand (Luke 12:48). The greater the responsibility one holds, the greater the accountability to both God and to His people.

Supplementary Study Questions

Read pages 41-46 and 363-365 in *Christianity in Crisis*, then answer the following questions:

1. Why is it so important to distinguish between false teachers and those who may have unwittingly become involved in their ministries (pages 41-42)?

2. A cult may be defined both *sociologically* and *theologically*. What are these definitions (pages 42-44)?

3. What is the difference between the words "cult" and "cultic" (pages 44-45)?

4. Why is it important to recognize the existence of "an error continuum" (pages 45-46)?

5. What is the difference between evaluating someone's teaching biblically and judging him or her hypocritically (pages 363-365)?

2

Charismatic or Cultic?

*I*t would be a grave error to equate the Faith movement with
the charismatic movement. The Faith movement is not charismatic; it is cultic.

The issues discussed in this study do not involve an in-house
debate among committed Christians over such matters as the perpetuity of spiritual gifts. This study is not about whether one
speaks in tongues or whether God still heals today. It is about
*calling the church's attention to the grave threat posed by the
unbiblical doctrines of the Faith movement.*

Sincere and dedicated believers can differ in good conscience
when it comes to peripheral issues. They cannot do so, however,
when it comes to the primary doctrines that separate Christianity
from the kingdom of the cults. When it comes to such matters as the
fabric of faith, the nature of God, and the atonement of Christ, there
must be unity. As Saint Augustine so aptly put it: "In essentials,
unity; in nonessentials, liberty; and in all things, charity."

Spiritual Flaws

Harvest Audiobook Before moving into the *Study Questions* below, it is
suggested that participants listen to the remainder
of tape #1 of the *Christianity in Crisis Audiobook.*

Study Questions

1. What are the "essentials" that Augustine talked about? What are some examples of "nonessentials"? What does it mean to express "charity" in "all things"?

2. Discuss the following statement: "Unity must be maintained at all costs." Do you agree? Disagree? Why?

3. Based on what you know already, what differences can you name between the doctrines of the Faith movement and those of charismatic Christians?

Scriptural Insights

1. Read Romans 14.

   A. What does Paul mean by "disputable matters" in verse 1? What example does he use to illustrate his point in verse 2? What other example does he use in verse 5?

   B. How do verses 10-12 keep us "honest" in the way we deal with those whose opinions differ from our own?

   C. What general guideline is given to us in verse 22 about "disputable matters"?

D. What overarching principle in verse 23 should control our Christian behavior and beliefs?

2. Read Colossians 2:8-17.

A. About what danger does the apostle warn us in verse 8?

B. What is the core of the Christian faith, according to verses 9-15? How does this core shape our life of faith?

C. How is the command of verse 16 related to the main idea of Romans 14? In what way is it the "flip side" of Romans 14?

3. Read Jude 3,4.

A. What does it mean to "contend for the faith"? How do we do this?

B. If the faith was "once for all entrusted to the saints," what does this say about "new doctrines" that some teachers want to promote?

C. How did the false teachers mentioned in this passage get their platform? What two primary errors did they promote?

D. How does this passage relate to the present day?

Summary Statement

For the most part, charismatics and noncharismatics are unified when it comes to the essentials of the historic Christian faith. Their primary differences involve nonessential Christian doctrine. The Faith movement, however, has systematically subverted the very essence of Christianity so as to present us with a counterfeit Christ and a counterfeit Christianity. Standing against the theology of the Faith movement does *not* divide; rather, it unites.

Supplementary Study Questions

Read pages 47-50 in *Christianity in Crisis*, then answer the following questions:

1. Why is it a tragic error to use the teachings of the Faith movement to discredit the charismatic movement (page 48)?

2. Who are some of the leading charismatic thinkers and writers on the scene today (pages 48-49)?

3. Why does it take great courage today to stand against the unbiblical theology of the Faith movement (pages 49-50)?

The Force of Faith

At the core of the Faith movement's deviation from biblical Christianity is its teaching about faith—what it is, what it does, how it is used, and who uses it. In this study we will look at the movement's belief that *faith is a force.*

The Faith teachers claim that faith is a force and words are the containers of the force. Through the power of words, you create your own reality and make the laws of the spirit world function. Here's how the Faith teachers put it:

Spiritual Flaws

> Faith was the raw material substance that the Spirit of God used to form the universe.
> —Kenneth Copeland

> God cannot do anything for you apart or separate from faith [because] faith is God's source of power.
> —Kenneth Copeland

> Some think that God made the earth out of nothing, but He didn't. He made it out of something. *The*

substance God used was faith. . . . He used His words as a carrier of that faith.

—Charles Capps

Harvest Audiobook   Before going on to the *Study Questions* below, participants should listen to the "Force of Faith" section on tape #2 of the *Christianity in Crisis Audiobook.*

Study Questions

1. In your understanding, what is faith?

2. What do you think these teachers mean when they say faith is a "substance"? Do you think they're right? Why or why not?

3. What do you think of the statement "Faith is God's source of power"?

4. Does our faith (or lack of it) so completely restrict God's activity on our behalf as the above quotes assert? Explain.

Scriptural Insights

1. Read Hebrews 11:1 in a modern translation.

   A. How does this text define faith?

B. How does this definition differ from that of the Faith teachers?

C. Who must exercise faith, according to this passage?

2. Read Romans 5:1,2.
   A. What does faith accomplish, according to this passage?

   B. How does faith work, according to this passage?

   C. In what (or whom) is faith placed, according to Paul?

3. Read James 2:14-18.
   A. What does faith do, according to this passage?

   B. How can you identify true faith, according to James?

Summary Statement

Far from being a tangible material, faith is a channel of living trust—an assurance—which stretches from man to God. True biblical faith is only as good as the object in whom it is placed—God is both the object and the origin of true biblical faith.

True biblical faith has three essential elements: Knowledge, Agreement, and Trust. You may *know* that a candy bar is laced with cyanide; you might even *agree* that eating it would result in instant death, but if you ate it anyway, your action would prove that you did not *trust*—and therefore had no real faith.

Supplementary Study Questions

Read pages 65-71 in *Christianity in Crisis*. Then discuss the following questions:

1. What do the Faith teachers mean when they liken "God's source of power" to a coin? How could this also be likened to a car battery? What is wrong with this understanding (page 66)?

2. How is the Faith movement's teaching on faith similar to New Thought metaphysics (pages 67-68)?

3. How have the Faith teachers misunderstood and misused the King James translation of Hebrews 11:1 (pages 69-70)?

4. What difference does a proper understanding of faith make (page 71)?

4

The Formula of Faith

In Faith theology, formulas are the name of the game. Faith teachers insist that verbal confessions unlock the force of faith and activate spiritual law. Positive confessions activate the positive side of the force; negative confessions activate the negative side. Here is how they put it:

Spiritual Flaws

> If anybody, anywhere, will take these four steps or put these four principles into operation [i.e., "Say it, Do it, Receive it, and Tell it"], he will always receive whatever he wants.
> —Kenneth Hagin

> Words create pictures, and pictures in your mind create words. And then the words come back out your mouth. . . . And when that spiritual force comes out it is going to give substance to the image that's on the inside of you. Aw, that's that visualization stuff! Aw, that's that New Age! No, New Age is trying to do

this; and they'd get somewhat results out of it because this is spiritual law, brother.

—Kenneth Copeland

It took the devil over 900 years to kill [Adam], but now the devil has programmed his language into the human race, until people can kill themselves in about 70 years or less, by speaking his words.

—Charles Capps

Harvest Audiobook Before going on to the *Study Questions* below, participants should listen to the "Formula of Faith" section of the *Christianity in Crisis Audiobook.*

Study Questions

1. Why do you think Hagin's quote above has a great appeal to people? How does it strike you? Why?

2. What can you deduce about the "spiritual law" Copeland speaks of in the quote above? Does it bother you that the "results" he describes come with or without a relationship to the living God? Why or why not?

3. If Capps' contention were true in the quote above, what would that say about the life expectancy of the Faith teachers? Do you think they will match Adam's record? Why or why not?

Scriptural Insights

1. Read Matthew 6:7-13.

A. How do "pagans" pray? Why do they think they will be heard? Why should we *not* follow their example?

B. Was Jesus suggesting a "formula" in verses 9-13? How does this pattern differ significantly from Hagin's formula?

2. Read Isaiah 59:1,2. Does this passage suggest that unbelievers can tap into God's power, as Copeland suggests? Why or why not?

3. Read 2 Thessalonians 2:9-12.

A. Are all miracles, signs, and wonders from God? Explain.

B. What is the end of those who refuse to acknowledge God's truth?

4. Read 1 Samuel 1:9-20 and Nehemiah 2:1-8. In Faith theology, silent prayer is said to be ineffectual, because no words are spoken. How do the two passages above demonstrate the falsity of this Faith doctrine? How do these two examples violate Faith formulas?

5. Read Romans 8:26,27.

A. How does this passage refute the Faith understanding of faith? How does it refute the Faith understanding of prayer?

B. How are "words" specifically excluded in the kind of divine prayer described in this passage? How is this intended to give us great hope?

Summary Statement

If God could be controlled through positive confessions, He would be reduced to the status of a cosmic servant subject to the formulas of faith. You would be God and He would be your bell-hop! You would sit on the throne of a universe centered around your own ego. And you would wind up with a puny view of God and a bloated view of man.

The god of the Faith movement is no God at all. He is merely a faith being, bound by the impersonal force of faith. In this strange universe, Faith is king and God is its servant.

Supplementary Study Questions

Read pages 73-85 in *Christianity in Crisis*. Then answer the following questions:

1. Why does Kenneth Hagin teach his followers to have faith in their faith rather than faith in God (pages 73-74)?

2. Describe the "formula" that Hagin supposedly received from Jesus (pages 74-75).

3. What Scripture "proof" does Hagin provide for his formula? What is wrong with this "proof" (pages 76-77)?

4. How does the Bible respond to such twisting of Scripture (pages 79-80)?

5. How are such "Faith formulas" similar to occult practices (pages 80-84)?

6. How do Faith teachers abuse Proverbs 18:21 (pages 84-85)?

7. What do you think of Frederick K.C. Price's comment reproduced on page 85?

5

The Faith of God

Critics of the Faith movement have often referred to its God as the impersonal god of the metaphysical cults. In fact, the Faith teachers present a personal God in principle, but in practice they teach a metaphysical God. This God cannot operate outside the universal laws by which even He is governed.

In Faith theology, it is not the true God who reigns supreme. In Faith theology, the real heroes of the faith are those who learn to work in harmony with the force of faith—and all of this is "sanctified" through the use of the name of Jesus. Here are some examples of the Faith doctrine about the "faith of God."

Spiritual Flaws

> A more literal translation [of Mark 11:22] is "Have the God kind of faith," or "faith of God." . . . God is a *faith* God.
>
> —Charles Capps

> God is a faith being. You are born of God. You are a faith being. God does not do anything outside of

470

faith. With His faith living in you, you are to operate the same way.

—Kenneth Copeland

Jesus Christ was born of a virgin through the miraculous conception of faith—the God-kind of faith.

—Charles Capps

Harvest Audiobook Before going on to the *Study Questions* below, participants should listen to the "Faith of God" section of the *Christianity in Crisis Audiobook*.

Study Questions

1. How would it change your conception of God if He really depended on faith, as the Faith teachers claim?

2. Is it true that "God does not do *anything* outside of faith"? Explain.

3. What is the difference between saying that God is "faithful" and that God "has faith"? What difference does this make?

Scriptural Insights

1. Read Psalm 135:5-18.

   A. Does the God described in this passage sound like a God powered by faith? Why or why not?

B. Does the God described in this passage sound like a God who can operate on earth only when someone's faith allows Him to? Explain.

2. Read Daniel 4:28-37.

A. What lesson did Nebuchadnezzar learn about God in this passage? Do you think he thought of God as a being dependent upon faith? Explain.

B. Focus on verse 35. Does this sound as if God needs someone's permission to act? Explain.

3. Compare 2 Corinthians 5:7 with Hebrews 4:13.

A. Note that Paul contrasts "faith" with "sight." What is the point of the contrast? Why are "faith" and "sight" mutually exclusive?

B. Note that the writer of Hebrews says that "nothing in all creation is hidden from God's *sight*." How does this make faith unnecessary for God?

4. For an important critique of the Faith teachers' use of Mark 11:22 and Hebrews 11:3, discuss the material in *Christianity in Crisis* on pages 87-93.

Summary Statement

In Christian theology God is portrayed as the Sovereign of the universe. He is described as "spirit," perfectly wise, self-sufficient, omnipotent, and omniscient.

Not so in the cultic theology of the Faith movement. In these dreary environs, God is merely a "faith being" and man is deemed a sovereign. God is portrayed as a puppet at the beck and call of His creation. This god is impotent rather than omnipotent, limited rather than infinite. In other words, the god of the Faith movement is not the God of the Bible.

Supplementary Study Questions

Read pages 87-95 in *Christianity in Crisis*. Then answer the following questions:

1. How do the Faith teachers "strip God of His omnipotence and rob Him of His omniscience" (page 87)?

2. What do A.T. Robertson and several other Greek authorities say about the meaning of Mark 11:22 (pages 90-91)?

3. How do the Faith teachers misuse Hebrews 11:3 to claim that God is a faith being? What is wrong with their interpretation of the passage in question (pages 91-93)?

4. In what way is the Faith teachers' god a god of impersonal laws (pages 93-95)?

6

The Faith Hall of Fame

"Then the LORD said to Satan, 'Have you considered my servant Job? There is no one on earth like him; he is blameless and upright, a man who fears God and shuns evil. And he still maintains his integrity, though you incited me against him to ruin him without any reason.'"

—Job 2:3

Spiritual Flaws

Job's mouth was his biggest problem.
—Benny Hinn

You know what? We've said this a million times and it's not even scriptural—all because of Job: "The Lord giveth and the Lord taketh away. Blessed be the name of the Lord." I have news for you: that is not Bible, that's not Bible. The Lord giveth and *never* taketh away. And just because he said, "Blessed be the name of the Lord," don't mean that he's right. When he said, "Blessed be the name," he was just being religious. And being religious don't mean you're right.

—Benny Hinn

Job talked his world into destruction.

—Jerry Savelle

Harvest Audiobook Before going on to the *Study Questions* below, participants should listen to the "Faith Hall of Fame" section of the *Christianity in Crisis Audiobook*.

Study Questions

1. What do you think it would take to be inducted into the "Faith Hall of Fame"? What qualities would it require?

2. Which biblical characters do you think might be inducted into the Hall of Fame? Which nonbiblical people? Why would they be inducted?

3. What is your impression of Job? Where did you get this impression?

Scriptural Insights

1. Read Job 1:1,8; 2:3; 42:7-9.

   A. What is God's evaluation of Job at the beginning of the book? How does He characterize Job?

B. What is God's evaluation of Job at the end of the book? How does He communicate His evaluation?

2. Read Job 1:21,22; 2:10; 13:15; 19:25. How would you describe Job's comments in these passages? Does he sound like a man of faith or a man worthy of disdain? Explain.

3. Read Hebrews 11:32-39.

   A. How did the people mentioned in verses 32-35a demonstrate their faith? What happened to them?

   B. How did the people mentioned in verses 35b-38 demonstrate their faith? What happened to them?

   C. According to verse 39, how many of those mentioned in verses 32-38 were commended for their faith? What does this teach us about the nature of faith?

4. Read 2 Corinthians 6:3-10; 11:16–12:10.

   A. List Paul's qualifications for the Faith Hall of Fame, as described in these passages.

   B. How well do these passages fit with the Faith teachers' understanding of triumphant faith? Explain.

Summary Statement

The Faith Hall of Fame will surely not be bedecked with the glitz and glamour of those who mock the biblical concept of faith. Rather, it will be filled with the men and women who follow in the train of those who willingly gave their lives in service to the King of kings—those who like Gideon, Barak, Samson, Jephthah, David, Samuel, and the prophets through faith conquered kingdoms; who have been tortured, jeered, and flogged; who have been chained and put in prison; stoned and put to death; destitute; persecuted and mistreated, yet were commended for their faith—because their faith was not fixed on circumstances but on God.

Supplementary Study Questions

Read pages 97-102 in *Christianity in Crisis*. Then answer the following questions:

1. Why does Job have to fall in order for the Faith message to flourish (pages 97-99)?

2. How does God Himself refute this understanding of Job (pages 99-100)?

3. How is Job a worthy member of the Faith Hall of Fame (pages 100-102)?

The Deification of Man

" 'To whom will you compare me? Or who is my equal?' says the Holy One. Lift your eyes and look to the heavens: Who created all these? He who brings out the starry host one by one, and calls them each by name. Because of his great power and mighty strength, not one of them is missing."

—Isaiah 40:25,26

Spiritual Flaws

> Man...was created on terms of equality with God, and he could stand in God's presence without any consciousness of inferiority....Man lived in the realm of God. He lived on terms equal with God.
>
> —Kenneth Hagin

> God's reason for creating Adam was His desire to reproduce Himself....He was not a little like God. He was not almost like God. He was not subordinate to God even.
>
> —Kenneth Copeland

God duplicated *Himself* in kind!...*Adam was an exact duplication of God's kind!*
—Charles Capps

Dogs have puppies and cats have kittens, so God has little gods.
—Earl Paulk

Harvest Audiobook Before going on to the *Study Questions* below, participants should listen to the "Deification of Man" section of the *Christianity in Crisis Audiobook*.

Study Questions

1. What do you think of Kenneth Hagin's statement that man "could stand in God's presence without any consciousness of inferiority"?

2. What do you think of Kenneth Copeland's statement that Adam "was not subordinate to God even"?

3. If you had to pick a word to describe Capps' statement above, what would it be?

4. What do you think of Paulk's analogy in the quotation above?

Scriptural Insights

1. Read Isaiah 40:6-26.

   A. What comparison is made in this passage between men and God? Do you think the men in this passage would have any "consciousness of inferiority" to God? Explain.

   B. Focus on verses 15,17,22,23. Do these people seem to be "subordinate" to God? Why or why not?

   C. Focus on verses 25,26. To whom does God think He should be compared?

2. Read Isaiah 44:6-8. Who does God think is like Him? Do you think He approves of people comparing themselves to Him? Why or why not?

3. Read Numbers 23:19. How similar does the prophet think God and man are?

4. Read Psalm 82.

   A. In what sense is God using the word "gods" in this passage? To whom is He speaking?

   B. What is the point of the sharp distinction made from verse 6 to verse 7? What is being emphasized?

C. Who is the final judge of all, according to verse 8?

4. Read Isaiah 14:12-15.

A. What was the sin of the person described in this passage? How is verse 14 a summary of his sin?

B. How did God react to this sin in verse 15?

C. What lesson can we learn from this passage in regard to the current study?

Summary Statement

The fact is that the Bible nowhere teaches the "little gods" doctrine. God is infinitely and eternally exalted above humankind. It is the height of arrogance to think that humans can come close to approximating God in His awesome holiness and majesty. Yet this is precisely what the proponents of Faith theology are eager to do.

Supplementary Study Questions

Read pages 107-120 in *Christianity in Crisis*. Then answer the following questions:

1. How is Satan's lie, "you will be like God," still being spread today (pages 107-108)?

2. How is the Faith teaching that believers are "little gods" too radical even for Mormon scholars (pages 109-110)?

3. What do the Faith teachers mean by their "little gods" doctrine (pages 110-111)?

4. How do Faith teachers use John 10:31-39 (and therefore Psalm 82) to justify their "little gods" doctrine? What is wrong with this understanding of the passage (pages 112-115)?

5. How do Faith teachers use 2 Peter 1:4 to justify their "little gods" doctrine? What is wrong with this understanding of the passage (pages 115-116)?

The Demotion of God

" 'For my thoughts are not your thoughts, neither are your ways my ways,' declares the LORD. 'As the heavens are higher than the earth, so are my ways higher than your ways and my thoughts than your thoughts.' "

—Isaiah 55:8,9

Spiritual Flaws

> [God is] not some creature that stands 28 feet tall, and He's got hands, you know, as big as basketballs. That's not the kind of creature He is.... A being that is very uncanny the way He's very much like you and me. A being that stands somewhere around 6'-2", 6'-3", that weighs somewhere in the neighborhood of a couple of hundred pounds, little better, [and] has a [hand] span of nine inches across.
>
> —Kenneth Copeland

> [T]he glory of God appeared. The Form that I saw was about the height of a man six feet tall, maybe a little taller, and twice as broad as a human body with no

483

distinguishing features such as eyes, nose, or mouth.

—Morris Cerullo

Now this is a shocker! But God has to be given *permission* to work in this earth realm on behalf of man. ...Yes! *You are in control!* So, if man has control, who no longer has it? God.... When God gave Adam dominion, that meant God no longer had dominion. So, God cannot do anything in this earth unless *we let* Him. And the way we let Him or give Him permission is through prayer.

—Frederick K.C. Price

I was shocked when I found out who the biggest failure in the Bible actually is.... The biggest one in the whole Bible is God.... Now, the reason you don't think of God as a failure is He never said He's a failure. And you're not a failure till you say you're one.

—Kenneth Copeland

Harvest Audiobook Before going on to the *Study Questions* below, participants should listen to the "Demotion of God" section of the *Christianity in Crisis Audiobook*.

Study Questions

1. Do you think the god of Kenneth Copeland has more in common with the Bible or with Greek mythology? Explain.

2. If God really had a physical body such as the Faith teachers claim, how would that change your perception of Him?

3. What do you think of the idea that God is a failure? If you had to choose one word to describe this idea, what would that word be?

Scriptural Insights

1. Read 1 Timothy 6:15,16.

   A. What description is given of God in this passage?

   B. What does this passage say about *anyone* actually seeing God (verse 16)? What does this mean for the claims by the Faith teachers?

2. Read John 4:23,24.

   A. What does this passage teach us about the nature of God?

   B. What does this passage imply about God having a physical body?

3. Read Psalm 17:8; Isaiah 49:16; Ezekiel 1:26-28; Revelation 1:14-16.

   A. What do all of these descriptions of God have in common? What is each image intended to convey?

B. What is the problem with taking these passages literally? What kind of God would you have if you took the passages literally?

4. Compare Jeremiah 32:17,27 with Matthew 19:26.

   A. What do these verses teach us about God?

   B. Do these verses describe a God who is a failure? Explain.

Summary Statement

A doctrine that shrinks God to the status of man destroys an essential of the historic Christian faith. No Christian should simply look the other way and pretend it doesn't matter. Once we allow teaching on the nature of God to be twisted to the extent that it has been by the Faith movement, we have departed from the kingdom of Christ and have arrived in the kingdom of the cults.

The God of the Bible is omniscient (Psalm 147:5; Romans 11:33; Hebrews 4:13) and nothing catches Him by surprise (Isaiah 42:9). He is self-existent, transcendent, and invincible. His dominion is eternal and His kingdom endures from generation to generation. He does as He pleases with the powers of heaven and the peoples of the earth, and His hand no one can hold back.

Supplementary Study Questions

Read pages 121-127 in *Christianity in Crisis.* Then answer the following questions:

1. How do Faith teachers take Isaiah 40:12 out of context to claim that God has a physical body? What is wrong with their interpretation of the verse (pages 121-124)?

2. What is wrong with "shrinking" God to the status of a mere man (pages 125-126)?

3. What lesson did Nebuchadnezzar learn about God that we must never forget (page 126)?

4. In sharp distinction from Faith theology, how does Scripture portray God (page 127)?

9

The Deification of Satan

"The God of peace will soon crush Satan under your feet."
—Romans 16:20

Spiritual Flaws

God's on the outside looking in. *He doesn't have any legal entree into the earth. The thing don't belong to Him.* You see how *sassy* the Devil was in the presence of God in the book of Job? God said, Where have you been? *Wasn't any of God's business.* He [Satan] didn't even have to answer if he didn't want to.

—Kenneth Copeland

The Bible says that God gave this earth to the sons of men...and when [Adam] turned and gave that dominion to Satan, look where it left God. It left Him on the outside looking in....He had no legal right to do anything about it, did He?...What Satan had intended for Him to do was to fall for it—pull off an illegal act and turn the light off in God, and subordinate God to himself.... He intended to get God into such a trap that He couldn't get out.

—Kenneth Copeland

When Adam bowed the knee to Satan, he shut God out. God found Himself on the outside looking in. His man, Adam, had lost his authority. Satan... had become the god of the world system.... Satan had gained ascendency in the earth by gaining Adam's authority, and God was left on the outside. God *couldn't* come here in His divine power and wipe them out. He had to move in an area where it would be *ruled legal* by the *Supreme Court of the Universe*.

—Charles Capps

Harvest Audiobook Before going on to the *Study Questions* below, participants should listen to the "Deificaton of Satan" section of the *Christianity in Crisis Audiobook*.

Study Questions

1. How does it make you feel to hear someone say that an important issue was "none of God's business"? Why do you feel this way?

2. What do you think "turn the light off in God" might mean? How does this idea make you feel?

3. Do you believe it is possible for God to fall into a trap that He couldn't get out of? Explain.

4. What do you think Charles Capps means by "the Supreme Court of the Universe"?

Scriptural Insights

1. Read Revelation 12:7-12; 20:1-3,7-10.

   A. What do these verses teach us about the destiny of Satan?

   B. Do you get the impression from these passages that Satan has "legal dominion" over the earth? Explain.

2. Read Romans 16:20.

   A. Who is the party in control here, Satan or God? What difference does it make?

   B. Does this verse sound as if God is constricted in His actions in any way? Explain.

3. Read John 16:11 and 2 Corinthians 4:4.

   A. Although Jesus calls the Devil "the prince of this world" (not *the* world), what else does He say about him? What does this imply about God's "legal right" to the earth?

B. In what sense is Satan called "the god of this age" in 2 Corinthians 4:4? In what sphere does this verse say he operates? Over whom does he exercise some control?

4. Read Psalm 50.

A. What picture do you get of God in this psalm?

B. According to verses 10-12, who owns the earth and everything in it?

C. According to verses 21,22, how does God feel about those who would try to "shrink" Him down to their size?

Summary Statement

The Bible nowhere deifies Satan. Far from being a sovereign power, Satan is but a created being (cf. Psalm 148:2,5; Colossians 1:16). He is an angel—not a god—and a fallen angel at that. The difference between God and Satan is analogous to the difference between a potter and his clay. Satan may be described as the prince of this world, but orthodoxy has always affirmed that Satan is a creature who is subject to the will of his Creator.

If God had no legal right to interfere in a world supposedly under the control of Satan, how could He have banished Adam and Eve from Eden or subsequently destroyed the world with the flood? And how could He still have the audacity to claim that "every animal of the forest is mine, and the cattle on a thousand hills. I know every bird in the mountains, and the creatures of the field are mine.... The world is mine, and all that is in it"? The truth is that God never gave up His throne to anybody—not in heaven and not on the earth.

Supplementary Study Questions

Read pages 129-135 in *Christianity in Crisis*. Then answer the following questions:

1. In what way does Faith doctrine embrace an "implicit dualism" (pages 129-130)?

2. Why, in Faith theology, is there no such thing as a distinct human nature (pages 130-131)?

3. What is flawed about the Faith doctrine that Satan won legal dominion over the earth (pages 131-133)?

4. How is it absurd to talk of God being subject to "the Supreme Court of the Universe" (pages 133-135)?

10

The Demotion of Christ

"Jesus said to them, 'My Father is always at his work to this very day, and I, too, am working.' For this reason the Jews tried all the harder to kill him; not only was he breaking the Sabbath, but he was even calling God his own Father, making himself equal with God."

—John 5:17,18

Spiritual Flaws

What [why] does God have to pay the price for this thing? He has to have a man that is like that first one. It's got to be a man. He's got to be all man. *He cannot be a God* and come storming in here with attributes and dignities that are not common to man. He *can't* do that. It's not legal.

—Kenneth Copeland

Had the Holy Spirit not been with Jesus, He *would have sinned.* That's right, it was the Holy Spirit that was the power that kept Him pure. He was not only sent from heaven, but He was called the *Son of Man*—

and as such He was capable of sinning. . . . Without the Holy Ghost, Jesus would never have made it.
> —Benny Hinn

God spoke it. God transmitted that image to Mary. She received the image inside of her. . . . The embryo that was in Mary's womb was nothing more than the Word of God.
> —Charles Capps

Harvest Audiobook Before going on to the *Study Questions* below, participants should listen to the "Demotion of Christ" section of the *Christianity in Crisis Audiobook*.

Study Questions

1. Comment on Copeland's statement that it wouldn't "be legal" for God to enter this world as a human with His divine attributes intact.

2. In your understanding, what does the term "Son of Man" mean?

3. What is the implication of a doctrine that states Jesus did not exist as a Person before He began growing in Mary's womb?

Scriptural Insights

1. Read John 1:1-3.

A. Who is "the Word" spoken of in this passage? What does this passage tell us about Him?

B. Notice that the passage calls this person "he," not "it." What bearing does this have on this study?

2. Read John 8:48-59.

A. What bold claim does Jesus make in verse 58? Why can His statement only mean one thing?

B. How did the Jews react to Jesus' statement? Why did they react this way?

3. Read Daniel 7:13,14.

A. Who is the "Son of Man" mentioned in this passage? What kind of person is He?

B. How do "men of every language" respond to Him? How is this appropriate only if the person is God?

C. When Jesus used this title, "Son of Man," to describe Himself, do you think it was an accident? Explain.

4. Read 1 John 4:2,3.

A. How does John say we can recognize "the Spirit of God"?

B. What is implied when someone denies that Jesus Christ came in the flesh? What part of His attributes is thereby under attack?

5. Read Philippians 2:5-11.

A. What claim does verse 6 make for Christ?

B. How do verses 7,8 make a clear distinction between "giving up" divine attributes and "veiling" them? What is the signficance of this distinction?

C. Compare verses 9-11 with Isaiah 45:22-24. What does this comparison reveal?

Summary Statement

Every orthodox scholar in the 2000-year history of the church has recognized that when Jesus called Himself "the Son of Man" He was indeed claiming to be God. During the incarnation, Jesus was 100 percent God as well as 100 percent man. He did not lay aside His divine attributes. To say that Jesus surrendered even one attribute of deity is to assert that Jesus Christ is less than God and is therefore not God at all. While Christ voluntarily veiled His divine *glory*, Scripture insists that He never surrendered His divine *attributes*.

Supplementary Study Questions

Read pages 137-143 in *Christianity in Crisis*. Then answer the following questions:

1. How does the Faith movement compromise the deity of Christ (pages 137-138)?

2. How does the Gospel of John in several instances refute the Faith teachers' claims about Christ (pages 138-139)?

3. In what way does Faith doctrine subtract from the deity of Christ (pages 139-140)?

4. What is wrong with the Faith understanding of the incarnation (pages 140-142)?

5. What difference does it make what we believe about the deity of Christ (pages 142-143)?

Re-Creation on the Cross

"When you were dead in your sins and in the uncircumcision of your sinful nature, God made you alive with Christ. He forgave us all our sins, having canceled the written code, with its regulations, that was against us and that stood opposed to us; he took it away, nailing it to the cross. And having disarmed the powers and authorities, he made a public spectacle of them, triumphing over them by the cross."

—Colossians 2:13-15

Spiritual Flaws

> Jesus Christ knew the only way He would stop Satan is by becoming one in nature with him. You say, "What did you say? What blasphemy is this?" No, you hear this! He did not take my sin; He *became* my sin. Sin is the nature of hell. Sin is what made Satan. . . . [Jesus] became one with the nature of *Satan*, so all those who had the nature of *Satan* can partake of the nature of God.
>
> —Benny Hinn

Spiritual death means something more than separation from God. *Spiritual death also means having Satan's nature....*Jesus tasted death—spiritual death—for every man.

—Kenneth Hagin

Somewhere between the time He [Jesus] was nailed to the cross and when He was in the Garden of Gethsemane—somewhere in there—He died spiritually. Personally, I believe it was while He was in the garden.

—Frederick K.C. Price

The righteousness of God was made to be sin. He accepted the sin nature of Satan in His own spirit. And at the moment that He did so, He cried, "My God, My God, why hast Thou forsaken Me?"

—Kenneth Copeland

Harvest Audiobook Before going on to the *Study Questions* below, participants should listen to the "Re-Creation on the Cross" section of the *Christianity in Crisis Audiobook*.

Study Questions

1. How do you react to the statement that Jesus became "one in nature" with Satan?

2. Does "spiritual death" require "having Satan's nature"? Explain.

3. Do you believe Jesus underwent "spiritual death"? Explain.

4. If Jesus died spiritually, why is there no mention of it anywhere in the Bible?

Scriptural Insights

1. Compare Leviticus 4:3,28 and Deuteronomy 15:21 with 1 Peter 1:18,19.

   A. What kind of sacrifice was acceptable in the Old Testament? What kind was unacceptable?

   B. What kind of sacrifice was Christ? How does this make the Faith position impossible?

2. Read Leviticus 6:24-29.

   A. How does this text describe the sin offering before it is sacrificed (verse 25)?

   B. How does this text describe the sin offering after it is sacrificed (verses 26-29)?

   C. What does this imply about Christ's sacrifice? What does it imply about the idea that the Savior "took on the nature of Satan"?

3. Compare Ephesians 5:2 with Isaiah 53:11.

   A. According to Ephesians, what kind of sacrifice was Christ?

   B. According to Isaiah, what kind of servant would the Messiah be after He completed His suffering?

   C. What do these two truths imply for the Faith teaching under examination?

4. Read Luke 23:34.

   A. How did Jesus address God while on the cross?

   B. How does this truth make impossible the Faith teaching under examination?

5. Read 2 Corinthians 5:21 and consider the discussion on pages 159-161 of *Christianity in Crisis*.

   A. What is this passage really teaching?

   B. Why could it not possibly mean what the Faith teachers claim it does?

Summary Statement

Truly, it was on the cross that we were pardoned through Christ's broken body and shed blood. In John 19:30 Jesus said, "It is finished!" He did not say, "It has just begun!" The Greek word used in the original text is *tetelestai*, which means "It is paid; the debt has been paid in full." The finality of Jesus' accomplishment upon the cross is made crystal clear by the tearing of the temple curtain that veiled God's earthly sanctuary, the Holy of Holies, from man, thus signifying that access to God had been restored at that precise moment (Mark 15:38; cf. Hebrews 9:1-14; 10:19-22).

Supplementary Study Questions

Read pages 155-162 in *Christianity in Crisis*. Then answer the following questions:

1. Summarize the various Faith teachers' contention that Jesus took on the nature of Satan (pages 155-158).

2. According to both Leviticus and Deuteronomy, why is this Faith teaching biblically impossible (page 158)?

3. What error have the Faith teachers made in their interpretation of 2 Corinthians 5:21 (pages 159-160)?

4. Name several biblical objections to this Faith teaching, as summarized on pages 160-162.

12

Redemption in Hell

"For Christ died for sins once for all, the righteous for the unrighteous, to bring you to God. He was put to death in the body but made alive by the Spirit, through whom also he went and preached to the spirits in prison."

—1 Peter 3:18,19

Spiritual Flaws

Do you think that the punishment for our sin was to die on a cross? If that were the case, the two thieves could have paid your price. No, the punishment was to go into hell itself and to serve time in hell separated from God.... Satan and all the demons of hell thought that they had Him bound and they threw a net over Jesus and they dragged Him down to the very pit of hell itself to serve our sentence.

—Frederick K.C. Price

The Father turned Him [Jesus] over, not only to the agony and death of Calvary, but to the satanic torturers of His pure spirit as part of the just desert of the sin of all the race. As long as Christ was "the essence of sin" he was at Satan's mercy in that place of torment.... While Christ identified with sin, Satan and the hosts of hell ruled over Him as over any lost sinner. During that seemingly endless age in the nether abyss of death, Satan did with Him as he would, and all hell was "in carnival."

—Paul Billheimer

He [Jesus] tasted spiritual death for every man. And His spirit and inner man went to hell in my place. Can't you see that? Physical death wouldn't remove your sins. He's tasted death for every man. He's talking about tasting spiritual death.

—Kenneth Hagin

Harvest Audiobook Before going on to the *Study Questions* below, participants should listen to the "Redemption in Hell" section of the *Christianity in Crisis Audiobook*.

Study Questions

1. What logical error(s) does Price make in the quotation above?

2. Do you think Jesus had to "serve time in hell" to pay for our sins? Why or why not?

3. How can Billheimer say the "pure spirit" of Jesus was turned over to satanic torturers if He had become one with the nature of Satan?

4. What do you think about the idea that "Satan and the hosts of hell" once "ruled over" Jesus "as over any lost sinner"?

Scriptural Insights

1. Read Luke 23:43.

   A. What did Jesus promise the thief in this verse? When did He say He would fulfill the promise?

   B. How should this verse alone be enough to disprove the Faith teaching of Jesus' redemption in hell?

2. Read Luke 23:46.

   A. Into whose hands did Jesus commit His spirit?

   B. How should this verse alone be enough to disprove the Faith teaching of Jesus' redemption in hell?

3. Read John 19:30.

   A. What did Jesus say in this verse?

   B. Does this verse in any way imply that Jesus' work of redemption was just beginning? Explain.

4. Read Colossians 2:13-15.

    A. According to verse 14, how did Jesus nullify the negative effects of the written code?

    B. What three things did Jesus do to the "powers and authorities," according to verse 15?

    C. Through what means did Jesus accomplish the three things mentioned above? What implications does this verse carry for the Faith doctrine under examination?

5. Read Hebrews 2:14,15.

    A. Why did Jesus come in human form, according to verse 14?

    B. How did Jesus destroy the devil, according to verse 14?

    C. What did Jesus accomplish by His death, according to verse 15?

Summary Statement

Remember that on the cross Jesus cried, "Father, into your hands I commit my spirit," not, "Satan, into your clutches I submit my being. Take me, I'm yours. Take me to hell."

If we are to take the Bible seriously, we must conclude that Jesus committed His spirit to the Father, not to Satan. The apostle Paul put it eloquently when he wrote of Christ, "Having disarmed the powers and authorities, he made a public spectacle of them, triumphing over them *by the cross.*" Jesus did not suffer horrible torture at the hands of Satan in the bowels of hell. Christ triumphed over the devil at the cross! It was His death on the cross that made possible our salvation.

Supplementary Study Questions

Read pages 163-167 in *Christianity in Crisis.* Then answer the following questions:

1. Summarize the Faith teachers' claim that Jesus suffered for three days in hell (pages 163-165).

2. Explain the true significance of Matthew 12:40 and Ephesians 4:9,10 (pages 165-166).

3. How do Luke 23:46, Colossians 2:15, and Hebrews 2:14,15 refute this Faith teaching (pages 166-167)?

13

Rebirth in Hell

"Jesus Christ is the same yesterday and today and forever. Do not be carried away by all kinds of strange teachings."
—Hebrews 13:8,9

Spiritual Flaws

Jesus was born again in the pit of hell. He was the firstborn, the firstbegotten, from the dead. He started the Church of the firstborn in the gates of hell.
—Charles Capps

In order to be made alive unto God and restored to fellowship with His Father, He [Jesus] had to be reborn—for He had become the very essence of sin. Since sin had totally alienated Him from the Father, the only way He could be restored to fellowship with the Father was through a new birth to new life.
—Paul Billheimer

He's [referring to Jesus] in the underworld now. God isn't there, the Holy Ghost isn't there, and the Bible says He was begotten. Do you know what the word begotten means? It means reborn. ... Don't let anyone deceive you. Jesus was reborn.

—Benny Hinn

Harvest Audiobook Before going on to the *Study Questions* below, participants should listen to the "Rebirth in Hell" section of the *Christianity in Crisis Audiobook*.

Study Questions

1. In the biblical sense, what does it mean to be "reborn"? Where do we get this terminology?

2. What do you think of the statement that Jesus was reborn "in the pit of hell"? Explain your reaction.

3. Discuss the implications of Benny Hinn's statement above.

Scriptural Insights

1. Read John 3:3-13.

   A. To whom was the phrase "you must be born again" directed? Is there any indication here that Jesus meant to use this phrase of Himself? Explain.

   B. How does Jesus set Himself apart from the rest of humanity in verses 12,13? How would this further call into question the Faith doctrine under examination?

2. Read John 5:26.

   A. In what way does this verse say the Son is like the Father?

   B. How does this verse refute the Faith teaching that Jesus was reborn in hell?

3. Read Hebrews 7:15,16,23-26; 9:11-14; 10:11-14.

   A. According to Hebrews 7:16, on what basis was Jesus made a Priest according to the order of Melchizedek? What is the length of His priesthood? What does this imply for the Faith doctrine under examination?

   B. How is Jesus described in Hebrews 7:26? Does this sound like someone who had to be "born again"? Why or why not?

   C. How is Jesus described in Hebrews 9:14? Does this sound like someone who had to be "born again"? Why or why not?

   D. Hebrews 10:12 makes it clear that Jesus was already our High Priest when He gave His life on the cross. When you combine this thought with Hebrews 7:26, what conclusion must you make about the Faith doctrine of Jesus' "rebirth in hell"?

4. Read Colossians 1:18 and 1 Peter 3:18, then consider pages 171-172 in *Christianity in Crisis*.

   A. What does "the firstborn from among the dead" mean?

   B. What docs "made alive by the Spirit" mean?

Summary Statement

To say that Jesus' nature underwent radical corruption which needed complete renewal is to overturn the biblical picture of God. For if Jesus truly became sin (in the sense the Faith teachers mean), then one Person of the Holy Trinity was ripped away from the Godhead. This necessarily implies that the triune God ceased to exist, at least at that point. It also requires the destruction of Christ's deity. Indeed, how could God, in the person of Christ, have the nature of Satan? Scripture rejects any such idea! God is an unchanging Being (Malachi 3:6; Hebrews 13:8) who has "life in himself" (John 5:26). The picture which Scripture paints of the atonement is infinitely more majestic, breathtaking, and exhilarating than any fiction the Faith teachers have espoused.

Supplementary Study Questions

Read pages 169-174 in *Christianity in Crisis*. Then answer the following questions:

1. What "trap" did Satan fall into, according to the Faith teachers? In what way do they teach he was freed from hell on a technicality (pages 169-171)?

2. Explain the true significance of Colossians 1:18 and 1 Peter 3:18 (pages 171-172).

3. Discuss the horrifying significance of the Kenneth Copeland and Benny Hinn quotations on pages 172-173.

4. What does the term "begotten" really mean (page 174)?

Reincarnation

"Just as man is destined to die once, and after that to face judgment, so Christ was sacrificed once to take away the sins of many people; and he will appear a second time, not to bear sin, but to bring salvation to those who are waiting for him."
—Hebrews 9:27,28

Spiritual Flaws

Every man who has been born again is an incarnation and Christianity is a miracle. The believer is as much an incarnation as was Jesus of Nazareth.
—Kenneth Hagin

[Commenting on the idea that Jesus defeated Satan in the underworld:] "That's when His [Jesus'] divinity returned."
—Paul Crouch

Harvest Audiobook Before going on to the *Study Questions* below, participants should listen to the "Reincarnation" section of the *Christianity in Crisis Audiobook*.

513

Study Questions

1. Take apart the word "reincarnation." What does it mean?

2. What do you think of the statement "The believer is as much an incarnation as was Jesus of Nazareth"?

3. What is necessarily implied in the idea that at some point Jesus' divinity "returned"? Why has orthodox Christianity always rejected this concept?

Scriptural Insights

1. Read Hebrews 13:8.

    A. What statement is made about Jesus in this verse? What is the time frame covered?

    B. How does this verse alone refute the Faith doctrine that Jesus at one point "gave up" His divinity?

2. Read John 1:14.

    A. What statements are made about Jesus in this verse?

    B. In what way does this verse proclaim Jesus to be absolutely unique? In what way can we never become like Him? What does this imply for the Faith teaching under examination?

3. Read John 20:17. What did Jesus instruct Mary to tell His disciples? Why do you think He distinguished between "*my* Father" and "*your* Father" and "*my* God" and "*your* God"?

4. Read Galatians 2:20.

   A. In what way should this verse be a model for all Christians? What did Paul mean in this verse?

   B. How can Paul say "I no longer live" but then turn around and say "the life I live in the body"? How is this verse a refutation of the "reincarnation" teaching of the Faith movement?

Summary Statement

If Jesus was reborn in hell, then a form of reincarnation is true. Each time a human being is born again, we have God coming again and again in the flesh, being reincarnated over and over. This would also mean that Jesus, who already has a body (Luke 24:39), would take on additional bodies each time someone comes to faith in Christ. The notion is absurd. Agreeing with the Faith movement means that we end up with a world full of gods. And the Bible utterly rejects polytheism.

The glorious message of the Christian gospel is that Jesus' work of redemption was completed on the cross at Calvary. All those who place their faith in the finished work of Christ will receive a rich welcome into the eternal kingdom of our Lord and Savior Jesus Christ.

Supplementary Study Questions

Read pages 175-177 in *Christianity in Crisis*. Then answer the following questions:

1. Why is it "patently unbiblical" to say that there was a point in time where Jesus' "divinity returned" (page 175)?

2. In what way was the incarnation of the Son of God absolutely unique (pages 175-176)?

3. What three major problems are raised by the Faith teaching that every born-again person is an incarnation of God (pages 176-177)?

Cultural Conformity

"Do not conform any longer to the pattern of this world, but be transformed by the renewing of your mind. Then you will be able to test and approve what God's will is—his good, pleasing and perfect will."

—Romans 12:2

Spiritual Flaws

Not only is worrying a sin, but being poor is a sin when God promises prosperity!

—Robert Tilton

[I'm trying] to get you out of this malaise of thinking that Jesus and the disciples were poor.... The Bible says that He has left us an example that we should follow His steps. That's the reason why I drive a Rolls Royce. I'm following Jesus' steps.

—Frederick K.C. Price

I don't know where these goofy traditions creep in at, but one of the goofiest ones is that Jesus and His

517

disciples were poor. Now there's no Bible to substantiate that.

—John Avanzini

Harvest Audiobook Before going on to the *Study Questions* below, participants should listen to the "Cultural Conformity" section of the *Christianity in Crisis Audiobook.*

Study Questions

1. How do you feel when you turn on the television and another televangelist is asking you to send in money? Why do you think you feel this way?

2. How do you think this doctrine would be received in the poorest countries of the Third World? Explain.

3. If Jesus were ministering in the flesh on earth today, do you think He would be driving around in a Rolls Royce? Explain.

4. What Bible verses can you think of that would indicate Jesus and His disciples were far from rich?

Scriptural Insights

1. Read Luke 12:15-21,33,34.

A. What warning does Jesus give in verse 15? How does Faith doctrine ignore this warning?

B. What two things are contrasted in verse 21? What is the significance of this distinction? What are the consequences of ignoring this distinction?

C. What instruction is given in the first part of verse 33? When was the last time you heard a Faith preacher comment on this command?

D. What kind of treasure are believers promised in verse 33? How do they receive this treasure?

E. What is the plain meaning of verse 34? How is it both a warning and a promise?

2. Read 1 Corinthians 4:9-13. How does Paul describe his circumstances in this passage? How does it stack up with the prosperity doctrine?

3. Read 1 Timothy 6:5b-10.

A. What error does Paul expose in verse 5? How does Paul characterize the minds of those who make this error? How does this relate to the Faith teachers' doctrine of prosperity?

B. What true prosperity is taught in verse 6?

C. How does verse 8 fly in the face of the prosperity gospel?

D. What warning is given in verse 9? What are the consequences of desiring to become rich?

E. What is the ultimate outcome for many who chase after riches, according to verse 10?

4. Read Luke 9:23-25.

A. What challenge does Jesus give in verse 23? What does He mean?

B. What does Jesus mean in verse 24? How does this relate to prosperity doctrine?

C. What possibility does Jesus warn us against in verse 25? Why do you think He chose to contrast these two particular items?

Summary Statement

Christ did not come to bring financial prosperity; He came to focus our attention on *eternal* prosperity. Even now the words of the Master ring with divine authority: "Do not store up for yourselves treasures on earth, where moth and rust destroy, and where thieves break in and steal. But store up for yourselves treasures in heaven" (Matthew 6:19,20).

The difference between serving self and serving the Savior is the difference between cultural conformity and conformity to Christ. Jesus said it best when He said, "If anyone would come after me, he must deny himself and take up his cross daily and follow me." A cross may not ride as well as a Rolls, but in the end it will take you a lot farther.

Supplementary Study Questions

Read pages 185-192 in *Christianity in Crisis*. Then answer the following questions:

1. Discuss Quentin Schultze's quotation on page 186.

2. In what way do the Faith teachers encourage believers to be conformed to the surrounding culture (pages 186-188)?

3. How do 1 Corinthians 4:9-13, 1 Timothy 6:9, Acts 20, and Philippians 3:7-9 refute the Faith teachers' doctrine that Jesus and the apostles were rich (pages 188-189)?

4. Summarize the biblical objections to the Faith doctrine of prosperity found on pages 189-191.

5. Does poverty equal piety (page 191)?

6. Comment on the Patti Roberts quotation found on page 192.

16

Cons and Cover-Ups

"For the appeal we make does not spring from error or impure motives, nor are we trying to trick you. On the contrary, we speak as men approved by God to be entrusted with the gospel. We are not trying to please men but God, who tests our hearts. You know we never used flattery, nor did we put on a mask to cover up greed—God is our witness."

—1 Thessalonians 2:3-5

Spiritual Flaws

Have a need, plant a seed.

—Oral Roberts

Give one house and receive one hundred houses or one house worth one hundred times as much. Give one airplane and receive one hundred times the value of the airplane. Give one car and the return would furnish you a lifetime of cars. In short, Mark 10:30 is a very good deal.

—Gloria Copeland

If you're broke, if you're at your wit's end, if you're out of a job, out of work, let me tell ya. Not only are we gonna bless the world and preach Christ to millions and multitudes around the world, but you can be saved, yourself, by planting seed in this fertile soil called TBN.

—Paul Crouch

SEND ME YOUR GREEN PRAYER CLOTH AND MY POINT OF CONTACT WITH YOU!...WHEN I TOUCH YOUR CLOTH...IT WILL BE LIKE TOUCHING YOU!... *When you touch this cloth, it will be like taking MY hand and touching me.* I want the anointing that God has put upon my life for miracles of finances and prosperity to come directly from my hand to yours.... *You can reign in life like a king!*

—Robert Tilton

Harvest Audiobook Before going on to the *Study Questions* below, participants should listen to the "Cons and Cover-Ups" section of the *Christianity in Crisis Audiobook.*

Study Questions

1. Do you think there is always a direct correlation between giving financially to the Lord and receiving financial blessings from the Lord? Why or why not?

2. What ploys have you seen aimed at getting people to send in money to televangelists? What proper methods have you seen?

3. How would you respond personally to an appeal like the one by Robert Tilton above? Explain.

Scriptural Insights

1. Read Mark 10:28-31.

  A. How does Peter's statement in verse 28 set the context for Jesus' statements in verses 29-31? How does Peter's statement demonstrate he was not rich?

  B. What kinds of "prosperity" does Jesus promise in verses 29,30? Why is it impossible to take His words in the literal sense?

  C. What "negative" item is promised in verse 30? In what way is this part of the package? Is it possible to "claim" the positive aspects of Jesus' promise without "claiming" the negative aspects? Explain.

  D. In what way should verse 31 warn us against "prosperity doctrine"?

2. Read 1 Corinthians 4:7,8.

  A. In what way is this passage an example of apostolic sarcasm?

B. In what way is verse 7 a question we should often ask ourselves? What is usually the result of asking yourself this question? Why?

C. What is Paul's point in verse 8? How does his comment relate to "prosperity preaching"?

3. Read 1 Corinthians 9:12-18; 2 Corinthians 11:7-15; 1 Thessalonians 2:3-9.

A. What is Paul's attitude toward his "rights" in 1 Corinthians 9:12-18? What are these "rights"? How is his attitude different from that of the "properity preachers"?

B. What was Paul's method in working with the Corinthian church, as described in 2 Corinthians 11:7-15? How does this differ from that of the "prosperity preachers"? Why did Paul operate in this way?

C. How did Paul *not* cooperate with the Thessalonians? How *did* he operate? Why did he operate in this way?

4. Read 2 Peter 2:1-3,13-19.

A. How does Peter describe these "false prophets" in verse 1? What impact do they have (verse 2)? What is one motivation for these teachers (verse 3)?

B. What is these teachers' destiny (verses 3,13)?

C. How do these teachers operate (verses 13-19)?

Summary Statement

Our motive for giving must always be based on gratitude, not greed. Thousands of people fall for the tactics of the Faith teachers because they do not test everything by the Word of God. The question ultimately is this: How well do Faith practices hold up when examined in the light of God's Word?

If practices such as the hundredfold message were fact, prosperity teachers would never again have to ask for money. Instead, they would be in the streets giving it away as fast as they could so they could get more. All poverty would be gone and every believer would live in a mansion. The "wealth of the wicked" would indeed be in the hands of the "King's kids." But that is fantasy, not fact. And Jesus' words still ring true: "In this world you will have trouble. But take heart! I have overcome the world" (John 16:33).

Supplementary Study Questions

Read pages 193-209 in *Christianity in Crisis*. Then answer the following questions:

1. What does the story of Johann Tetzel have to do with the modern-day Faith movement (pages 193-195)?

2. What is "seed-faith" (pages 195-198)?

3. Discuss Oral Roberts' fund-raising methods described on pages 196-198.

4. What is the "hundredfold return" promised by Faith teachers (pages 199-201)?

5. Describe the Faith teachers' "point of contact" approach to fund-raising (pages 201-204).

6. What is wrong biblically with the "seed-faith" approach (pages 204-206)?

7. What is wrong biblically with the "hundredfold return" approach (page 206)?

8. What is wrong biblically with the "point of contact" approach (pages 207-208)?

9. How does John Avanzini explain the failure of his prosperity formulas? Why are these explanations both outrageous and cruel (pages 208-209)?

17

Covenant-Contract

"Then the word of the LORD came to me: 'O house of Israel, can I not do with you as this potter does?' declares the LORD. 'Like clay in the hand of the potter, so are you in my hand.... If at any time I announce that a nation or kingdom is to be uprooted, torn down and destroyed, and if that nation I warned repents of its evil, then I will relent and not inflict on it the disaster I had planned. And if at another time I announce that a nation or kingdom is to be built up and planted, and if it does evil in my sight and does not obey me, then I will reconsider the good I had intended to do for it.' "

—Jeremiah 18:5-10

Spiritual Flaws

We have seen that prosperity is a blessing of Abraham and that poverty is under the curse of the law. Jesus bore the curse of the law in our behalf. He beat Satan and took away his power. Consequently, there is no reason for you to live under the curse of the law, no reason for you to live in poverty of any kind.

—Kenneth Copeland

Christ has redeemed us from the curse of the Law, that the blessing of Abraham might come upon us. ...How did God bless Abraham? With *cattle, gold, manservants, maidservants, camels, and asses. Abraham was blessed materially.*
—Frederick K.C. Price

Since God's Covenant has been established and prosperity is a provision of this Covenant, you need to realize that prosperity belongs to you *now*!
—Kenneth Copeland

Harvest Audiobook Before going on to the *Study Questions* below, participants should listen to the "Covenant-Contract" section of the *Christianity in Crisis Audiobook.*

Study Questions

1. Do you think prosperity is guaranteed under God's covenant with Abraham? Explain.

2. According to Scripture, do you think Abraham's primary blessing was material? Explain.

3. If a believer's prosperity is guaranteed under God's covenant, why does prosperity seem much more common in the affluent nations of the West than in the poor, third-world nations such as those in Africa, Asia, and South America?

Scriptural Insights

1. Read Genesis 15.

   A. Who seems to be the greater party of the two in this account, Abraham or God? How can you tell?

   B. In verses 10-18, who is the active party in making the covenant, Abraham or God? Explain.

   C. What idea of "covenant" do you get from this passage?

2. Read Romans 4:1–5:5.

   A. What blessing of God's covenant with Abraham does Paul focus on? How does this differ from what the Faith teachers say?

   B. In Romans 5:1,2, how does Paul summarize the blessing granted to Abraham and to us?

   C. In Romans 5:3, what else is promised to believers in the context of their great blessing?

   D. What "hope" does Paul mention in Romans 5:5? How does this emphasis differ from that of the Faith teachers?

3. Read Galatians 3:6-9.

   A. What was the blessing of Abraham, according to this passage?

   B. How were the nations to be "blessed" though Abraham, according to this passage?

4. Read Philippians 1:29,30; 2 Timothy 3:10-13.

   A. What two things have been granted to Christians, according to Philippians 1:29? How is this consistent with the blessing of Abraham?

   B. What promise does the Lord give us through Paul in 2 Timothy 3:12? How was Paul himself an illustration of this (verses 10,11)? What is the purpose of verse 13?

Summary Statement

The Bible is not a mere contract we can use to command God. Jesus is not a magic mantra we can use to open Fort Knox. God's covenant with Abraham is the proclamation of His sovereign plan to redeem humanity from its sin. The overarching message of Scripture is God's redemption of mankind. The covenant is not a bilateral contract that guarantees us wealth.

The difference between the Faith concept of covenant and the Christian concept of covenant is not a peripheral issue; it makes all the difference in the world. At stake is nothing less than the sovereignty of God.

Supplementary Study Questions

Read pages 211-215 in *Christianity in Crisis*. Then answer the following questions:

1. Explain the Faith teachers' understanding of covenant-contract (pages 211-212).

2. What is wrong with the Faith teachers' understanding of covenant-contract (pages 212-213)?

3. In what way does Jim Bakker say he erred on the Faith teaching of prosperity (pages 214-215)?

18

Context, Context, Context

"Then he said to them, 'Watch out! Be on your guard against all kinds of greed; a man's life does not consist in the abundance of his possessions.'"

—Luke 12:15

Harvest Audiobook Before going on to the *Study Questions* below, participants should listen to the "Context, Context, Context" section of the *Christianity in Crisis Audiobook.*

Spiritual Flaws

> [Let's allow God to] sort out all this doctrinal doo-doo.... "We can't have faith preaching." "You can't have confession stuff." "You can't do this, you can do that." Who cares? Who cares? Let Jesus sort that all out at the judgment seat of Christ. We'll find out who was right and wrong doctrinally.
>
> —Paul Crouch

Study Questions

1. Do you think Crouch's advice above is sound? Why or why not?

2. In a discussion about the Bible's teaching on wealth, why is the context so critical?

3. If you were asked to describe in a single paragraph the Bible's view of wealth and money, what would you say?

4. It is sometimes said that a person's attitude toward money tells as much about his or her spiritual state as any single trait. Do you agree? Why or why not?

Scriptural Insights

1. Read Psalm 24:1,2.

   A. Who owns the world? What is included in this ownership (verse 1)?

   B. What is the basis of this ownership (verse 2)? What effect did Adam's fall have upon this ownership?

2. Read Philippians 4:12,13; 2:3,4; 4:14-19; 3:18–4:1.

A. What attitude did Paul have toward prosperity (4:12,13)?

B. How are we to use our resources for others (2:3,4; 4:14-18)?

C. Does the word "need(s)" or "greed" appear in 4:19?

D. How does Paul describe some "enemies of the cross" in 3:18,19? Where is the Christian's true citizenship (verse 20)? When will we experience true prosperity (verse 21)? What does "standing firm" have to do with this knowledge (4:1)?

3. Read 2 Corinthians 9:6-11. What advice is given about finances in this passage? What promises are given? What is the purpose behind God making one of His children "rich" (verse 11)?

4. Read Hebrews 13:5,6.

A. What commands are given in verse 5? How should these commands alone disprove the Faith teachers' "prosperity" doctrine?

B. What reason is given for the commands in verse 5?

C. What results from obeying the commands in verse 5 (see verse 6)?

5. Read James 5:1-5.

   A. What warning is sounded in this passage? To whom is it directed?

   B. How is verse 5 both a description and a prediction?

6. Read 1 Timothy 6:17-19.

   A. What is commanded in this passage? What are we not to do? What are we to do?

   B. What is the result of obeying these commands (verse 19)? Where is this "treasure" laid up? What is it for?

Summary Statement

It's your choice. You can swallow the Faith preachers' nonsense about your right to wallow in self-indulgence, or you can set your heart on the deep satisfaction that can come only through using your resources generously to further the gospel and improve the lot of those around you. You can live responsibly as a steward of God's resources and expect to hear Him say, "Well done, good and faithful servant," or you can squander His gifts and let His awful words fall with full force upon your foolish soul: "I tell you the truth, you have your reward in full."

It's your bank statement in *heaven* that counts. If your hope is fixed on the one you have down here, you're bankrupt no matter how many digits you count next to your name.

Supplementary Study Questions

Read pages 217-231 in *Christianity in Crisis*. Then answer the following questions:

1. How could a parking lot point to the conclusion that the Faith doctrine of prosperity is false (pages 217-218)?

2. How do Faith teachers often react to challenges to their teaching (pages 218-219)?

3. What is the "literal principle" of biblical interpretation (page 220)?

4. What is the "illumination principle" of biblical interpretation (pages 220-221)?

5. What is the "grammatical principle" of biblical interpretation (pages 221-223)?

6. What is the "historical principle" of biblical interpretation (pages 223-224)?

7. What is the "teaching principle" of biblical interpretation (pages 224-225)?

8. What is the "scriptural harmony principle" of biblical interpretation (page 225)?

9. How is Psalm 24:1 a good place to begin a biblical view of wealth (page 226)?

10. How does the book of Philippians provide us with a sort of "primer" for a biblical view of wealth (pages 227-228)?

11. Discuss John Piper's quotation on pages 229-230.

19

Symptoms and Sickness

"We know that the whole creation has been groaning as in the pains of childbirth right up to the present time. Not only so, but we ourselves, who have the firstfruits of the Spirit, groan inwardly as we wait eagerly for our adoption as sons, the redemption of our bodies. For in this hope we were saved. But hope that is seen is no hope at all. Who hopes for what he already has?"

—Romans 8:22-24

Spiritual Flaws

The basic principle of the Christian life is to know that God put our sin, sickness, disease, sorrow, grief, and poverty on Jesus at Calvary. For Him to put any of this on us now would be a miscarriage of justice. Jesus was made a curse for us so that we can receive the blessing of Abraham.

—Kenneth Copeland

Sickness does not belong to you. It has no part in the body of Christ. Sickness does not belong to any of us. The Bible declares if the Word of God is in our life,

540

there will be health, there will be healing—divine health and divine healing. There will be no sickness for the saint of God.

—Benny Hinn

When you have developed your faith to such an extent that you can stand on the promises of God, then you won't need medicine. That's the reason I don't take medicine.

—Frederick K.C. Price

I believe that it is the plan of God our Father that no believer should ever be sick....It is not—I state boldly—it is not the will of God my Father that we should suffer with cancer and other dread diseases which bring pain and anguish.

—Kenneth Hagin

Harvest Audiobook Before going on to the *Study Questions* below, participants should listen to the "Symptoms and Sickness" section of the *Christianity in Crisis Audiobook*.

Study Questions

1. Discuss Copeland's statement that it would be "a miscarriage of justice" for God to allow a faithful believer to be sick.

2. Discuss Hinn's claim that "there will be no sickness for the saint of God."

3. Do you think a person of real faith ever needs medicine? Explain. What are the implications of rejecting medicine?

4. Do you think it is ever God's will that a believer should contract a disease? Explain.

Scriptural Insights

1. Compare Isaiah 53:4,5 with Matthew 8:16,17 and 1 Peter 2:24.

   A. If Isaiah 53:4 were really intended to promise physical healing through the cross, why should it not also promise freedom from all sorrow? Why do you think the latter claim is never made?

   B. According to Matthew 8:16,17, did Jesus fulfill Isaiah 53:4 before or after He went to the cross? Why is this significant?

   C. How does Peter understand Isaiah 53:5 (1 Peter 2:24)? Explain.

2. Read Galatians 4:13,15. Was God active in Paul's sickness as described in this passage? Explain.

3. Read Philippians 2:25-30; 1 Timothy 5:23; 2 Timothy 4:20; 2 Kings 13:14 (cf. 2 Kings 2:9-15). What do you learn about

believers and sickness in these passages? How is this evidence against the Faith teachers' claims?

4. Read Romans 8:21-25.

A. How is the "creation" in "bondage to decay"? Is this a present-tense condition? How does this matter?

B. What is Paul's response to this bondage (verse 23)?

C. In what way is hope a huge part of Paul's theology? How does this hope relate to his physical body (verses 24,25)?

D. What is to be our attitude while we wait for the "redemption of our bodies" (verse 23)? How does this differ from what the Faith teachers espouse?

Summary Statement

When it comes to symptoms and sickness, the cultic teachings of the Faith movement are in practice indistinguishable from such metaphysical cults as Christian Science, Religious Science, and the Unity School of Christianity. Cult leader Mary Baker Eddy taught adherents to ignore their senses as well as the physical symptoms of sickness. In *Science and Health*, the textbook of Christian Science, she writes, "When the first symptoms of disease appear, dispute the testimony of the material senses with divine Science.... 'Agree to disagree' with approaching symptoms of chronic or acute disease, whether it is cancer, consumption, or smallpox."

But even Faith teachers, in their more honest moments, have to confess that they themselves have experienced the ravages of sickness and disease. And despite their protests, they will in the end be stung by the ultimate sickness: death. As Dr. Walter Martin used to say, "The death rate is still one per person and we're all going to make it!"

Supplementary Study Questions

Read pages 241-253 in *Christianity in Crisis*. Then answer the following questions:

1. In general, what do the Faith teachers believe about sickness for the believer (pages 241-243)?

2. How do the Faith teachers regard symptoms of sickness or disease (pages 243-244)?

3. How can ignoring symptoms be deadly? In what way are symptoms a gift of God (pages 244-246)?

4. In what way are Faith teachings about sickness practically indistinguishable from such metaphysical cults as Christian Science (pages 246-248)?

5. In what way is Ephesians 5:23 sometimes mishandled to lend support to the Faith teaching about sickness? What is wrong with this use of the passage (pages 248-249)?

6. How is Isaiah 53:5 often mishandled by the Faith teachers, and how should it be interpreted (pages 249-251)?

7. Name several biblical heroes who were afflicted with disease and sickness (pages 252-253).

20

Satan and Sickness

"The LORD said to him, 'Who gave man his mouth? Who makes him deaf or mute? Who gives him sight or makes him blind? Is it not I, the LORD?'"

—Exodus 4:11

Spiritual Flaws

You have been trained since birth to speak negative, death-dealing words. Unconsciously in your everyday conversation, you use the words of death, sickness, lack, fear, doubt, and unbelief: *That scared me to death. That tickled me to death. I laughed until I thought I would die. I'm just dying to go. That makes me sick. I'm sick and tired of this mess. I believe I'm taking the flu. We just can't afford it. I doubt it....* You say these things without even realizing it. When you do, you set in motion negative forces in your life and the fire blazes.... Your words loosed the powers of Satan.

—Kenneth Copeland

Satan, you demonic spirits of AIDS, and AIDS virus—
I bind you! You demon-spirits of cancer, arthritis,
infection, migraine headaches, pain—come out of
that body! Come out of that child! Come out of that
man.... Satan, I bind you! You foul demon-spirits
of sickness and disease. Infirmities in the inner ear
and the lungs and the back. You demon-spirits of
arthritis, sickness, and disease. You tormenting
infirm-spirits in the stomach. Satan, I bind you! You
nicotine spirits—I bind you! In the name of Jesus!

—Robert Tilton

I don't look at cancer. I don't look at the tumor.... I
can't look at the natural and...say..."I'm sick."
Because when I say that, I've signed for the package. I
have taken authority for it, and it belongs to me
legally. Satan can enforce it upon my body. And he
will kill me with it.

—Frederick K.C. Price

Harvest Audiobook Before going on to the *Study Questions* below, participants should listen to the "Satan and Sickness"
section of the *Christianity in Crisis Audiobook.*

Study Questions

1. Do you think phrases such as "that scared me to death" put
in motion negative forces that loose the powers of Satan?
Explain.

2. What is your understanding of "binding and loosing"? On
what is your understanding based?

3. Do you think that admitting you're sick means you've "signed for the package"? Explain.

4. Do you think Satan is always responsible for sickness? Why or why not?

Scriptural Insights

1. Read Job 2:3-7; Luke 13:10-16.

   A. Who is in control in the Job passage? Explain.

   B. What limits did God set on Satan's activity in Job 2:6?

   C. Who afflicted Job in this story (verse 7)? Is it biblical to say that Satan is sometimes connected with sickness?

   D. What was the woman's problem in Luke 13? Whom does Jesus say afflicted her (verse 16)? What does this teach us about some sicknesses?

2. Read Exodus 4:11.

   A. Who created the deaf and the blind, according to this verse? Of what significance is this?

B. Given the context (Exodus 4:10-17), what is the Lord's point in 4:11? How does this relate to the issue under examination?

3. Read Matthew 18:15-18.

A. What general issue is addressed in this passage?

B. In this context, what is the point of verse 18? What things will be "bound" or "loosed"?

C. What authority does this passage give believers to "bind" Satan?

4. Read 2 Kings 15:5; Luke 1:19,20; Acts 12:21-23.

A. In each of the cases reported above, who did the afflicting?

B. Describe each of the men above. Were they believers or unbelievers? Of what significance is this?

5. Read Romans 8:18-20.

A. How does Paul relate suffering to glory (verse 18)?

B. What is the creation waiting for (verse 19)? What does this imply?

C. By whose choice was the creation subjected "to frustration" (verse 20)? What does this mean? How does this relate to the issue under consideration?

Summary Statement

We live in a cursed creation, with aging the primary sickness of humanity. As we get older we all get wrinkles, some of us need glasses, our muscles get shorter, and eventually we all die. While Scripture makes it clear that Satan is often the *agent* of sickness, he is certainly not always its *author*. Exodus 4:11 alone ought to prove the point: "Who gave man his mouth? Who makes him deaf or mute? Who gives him sight or makes him blind? Is it not I, the LORD?"

Supplementary Study Questions

Read pages 255-260 in *Christianity in Crisis*. Then answer the following questions:

1. According to the Faith teachers, what connection does Satan have with sickness (pages 255-256)?

2. What is the "1-2-3" answer for sickness, according to the Faith teachers (pages 256-257)?

3. What is the biblical meaning of "binding and loosing" (pages 257-259)?

4. What do Exodus 4:11, 2 Kings 15:5, and Luke 1:19,20 teach us about the origin of some disabilities or sickness (page 259)?

5. How do Faith teachers normally respond when someone is not healed of a disease (pages 259-260)?

21

Sin and Sickness

"As he went along, he saw a man blind from birth. His disciples asked him, 'Rabbi, who sinned, this man or his parents, that he was born blind?' 'Neither this man nor his parents sinned,' said Jesus, 'but this happened so that the work of God might be displayed in his life.'"

—John 9:1-3

Spiritual Flaws

It makes a great deal of difference what one thinks. I believe that is why many people are sick.... The reason they are not getting healed is that they are thinking wrong.... The thing that makes a believer a success is right thinking, right believing, and right confession.

—Kenneth Hagin

If your body belongs to God, it does not and cannot belong to sickness.

—Benny Hinn

When are we *all* going to wake up and learn God didn't allow the Devil to get on Job. *Job* allowed the

Devil to get on Job. . . . Job, himself, said he was *not* upright in the earth. He said, "I'm miserable. My tongue is disobedient."

—Kenneth Copeland

God intends for every believer to live completely free from sickness and disease. It is up to you to decide whether or not you will.

—Kenneth Copeland

Harvest Audiobook Before going on to the *Study Questions* below, participants should listen to the "Sin and Sickness" section of the *Christianity in Crisis Audiobook*.

Study Questions

1. Do you believe that many people are not healed because they entertain wrong thoughts? Explain.

2. Comment on Hinn's claim that "if your body belongs to God, it does not and cannot belong to sickness."

3. What is your opinion of Job?

4. Do you agree that "God intends for every believer to live completely free from sickness and disease"? Explain.

Scriptural Insights

1. Read 1 Corinthians 11:27-34.

   A. What does it mean to "eat and drink judgment" on yourself (verse 29)?

   B. What sometimes results from this judgment (verse 30)?

   C. How can you prevent this kind of judgment (verse 31)?

   D. What is the purpose of this judgment (verse 32)?

2. Read John 9:1-7.

   A. What question did the disciples expect Jesus to answer in this passage?

   B. What was Jesus' explanation for the man's blindness (verse 3)? How does His answer refute the Faith teachers' doctrine about sickness and sin?

3. Read 2 Corinthians 12:7-10.

   A. Why was Paul afflicted with his "thorn" (verse 7)?

B. What was the Lord's answer to Paul's earnest request (verse 9)? What does this suggest regarding God's will about some afflictions?

C. Why did God's power rest on Paul, according to verse 9?

D. Why would Paul "delight in" weaknesses, insults, hardships, persecutions, and difficulties (verse 10)?

4. Read 1 Corinthians 15:47-57.

A. According to verse 49, when will we "bear the likeness of the man from heaven"? What does this mean?

B. What event is described in verses 50-53? When does this take place?

C. When will death be swallowed up in victory? What does this imply about our bodies until this time?

Summary Statement

It is tragic that the Faith teachers have resorted to accusing sick followers of some secret sin. While the Bible does teach that some Christians are sick as a result of sin, Scripture makes it plain that sickness and suffering are not always the result of personal sin.

Since the fall of mankind, both the righteous and the unrighteous have been subject to disease and decay. In the book of Romans we read that "the whole creation has been groaning as in the pains of childbirth.... Not only so, but we ourselves... groan inwardly as we wait eagerly for... the redemption of our bodies" (Romans 8:22,23). Our frail and fragile bodies will not be changed now, but rather when we are resurrected from the dead. *"Then,"* says Paul, "the saying that is written will come true: 'Death has been swallowed up in victory.'"

And for that day we must wait—with eager anticipation.

Supplementary Study Questions

Read pages 261-269 in *Christianity in Crisis.* Then answer the following questions:

1. Comment on the letters described on pages 261-262.

2. How does Frederick Price explain Paul's "thorn in the flesh"? How does 2 Corinthians 12:9b,10 tend to refute his understanding (pages 263-264)?

3. Comment on Gordon Fee's quotation found on pages 264-265.

4. How can sickness be to the glory of God (pages 266-267)?

5. Other than sin, what are some other biblical reasons for sickness? When does the Bible indicate we *will* be freed from all sickness (pages 267-269)?

Sovereignty and Sickness

"I know, O LORD, that your laws are righteous, and in faithfulness you have afflicted me."

—Psalm 119:75

Spiritual Flaws

Never, ever, ever go to the Lord and say, "If it be thy will...." Don't allow such faith-destroying words to be spoken from your mouth. When you pray, "If it be your will, Lord," faith will be destroyed. Doubt will billow up and flood your being. Be on guard against words like this which will rob you of your faith and drag you down in despair.

—Benny Hinn

If you have to say, "If it be Thy will," or "Thy will be done"—if you have to say that then you're calling God a fool.

—Frederick K.C. Price

The religious idea that God chastises His own with sickness and disease and poverty is the very thing that has caused the church to go 1500 years without the knowledge of the Holy Spirit.

—Kenneth Copeland

Harvest Audiobook Before going on to the *Study Questions* below, participants should listen to the "Sovereignty and Sickness" section of the *Christianity in Crisis Audiobook*.

Study Questions

1. Do you believe the phrase "if it be Thy will" destroys faith? Explain.

2. Do you believe people are calling God a "fool" when they pray "if it be Thy will"? Explain.

3. Do you think God ever "chastises His own with sickness and disease"? Explain.

Scriptural Insights

1. Read Matthew 26:39; Acts 18:21; James 4:13-16.

   A. What did Jesus pray in Matthew 26:39? Did His prayer build or destroy His faith? Explain.

   B. How did Paul qualify his promise in Acts 18:21? Does the text represent this as a lapse of faith? Explain.

C. What error does James oppose in James 4:13,14? What is his remedy for this error (verse 15)? How does he characterize failure to follow his guidelines (verse 16)?

D. What do these verses suggest about the Faith doctrine under examination?

2. Read Psalm 119:71,75.

A. Who afflicted David, according to these verses?

B. What does David think about this affliction?

C. What did this affliction accomplish in David's life?

3. Read John 11:1-15,41-44.

A. What was the purpose of Lazarus' sickness, according to Jesus (verse 4)?

B. How did the Lord respond when He heard His friend was sick (verse 6)? Why do you think He did this?

C. How did Jesus react to the knowledge of Lazarus' death (verse 15)?

D. How do verses 41-44 fulfill Jesus' words in verses 4 and 15?

E. What does this story teach us about some events of sickness and even death? What is God's chief concern for us?

4. Read Revelation 21:1-6.

A. Describe the scene in this passage.

B. When will God do away with "death" and "mourning" and "crying" and "pain" (verse 4)? What does this say about those things for today?

Summary Statement

There is great peace in knowing that the One who created us also has every detail of our lives under control. Not only is He the object of our faith, but He is also the originator of our faith. Indeed, He is the originator of our salvation and even the originator of our prayers. When we pray the prayer of faith for healing and our will is in harmony with His will, healing will take place—every time, 100 percent of the time.

But when we pray earnestly as Christ did, "Nevertheless not my will but Thy will be done," we can rest assured that even in sickness and tragedy all things work together for good to those who love God and are called according to His purpose (Romans 8:28).

Supplementary Study Questions

Read pages 271-276 in *Christianity in Crisis*. Then answer the following questions:

1. How do the Faith teachers feel about praying, "If it be Your will"? How does the Bible contradict their teaching (pages 271-272, 406)?

2. How can the truth of God's sovereignty give us comfort and reassurance in difficult times (pages 272-273)?

3. Explain why faith is a channel of living trust rather than an imaginary force (pages 274-275).

4. Why is up always the best place to look (pages 275-276)?

23

Amen

Spiritual Facts

A represents the word "Amen." Amen traditionally comes at the end of every prayer, and prayer is our primary way of communicating with God.

Amen is a universally recognized word that is far more significant than simply signing off or saying, "That's all." With the word "Amen" we are in effect saying, "May it be so in accordance with the will of God." The word "Amen" is a marvelous reminder that any discussion on prayer must begin with the understanding that prayer is a means of bringing us into conformity with God's will, not a magic mantra that ensures God's conformity to our will.

Study Questions

1. How have you seen God move through prayer? Describe some examples.

2. What difficulties do you have with prayer? How can you address these problems?

3. If God knows everything anyway, why pray?

4. Describe someone you know who is a real "prayer warrior." What makes this person different from the "ordinary" Christian?

Scriptural Insights

1. Read 1 Thessalonians 5:17,18; Psalm 100:4,5.

   A. What is commanded in 1 Thessalonians 5:17? How is this possible? What is commanded in verse 18? How is this possible?

   B. What is commanded in Psalm 100:4? How is this related to prayer? How does verse 5 supply the reason for the command in verse 4? What tips does this passage give us for effective prayer?

2. Read John 15:7; 1 John 5:14,15.

   A. What promise does Jesus give in John 15:7? What are His conditions? What does this mean in practice?

   B. What promise is given in 1 John 5:14,15? What are the conditions? How does this compare to John 15:7?

3. Read Luke 18:1-8.

   A. What lesson was Jesus trying to teach in this passage (verse 1)?

   B. How did Jesus choose to illustrate this lesson? Does He mean God is like the judge? Or should we be like the widow?

   C. What does Jesus' question in verse 8 have to do with persistent prayer? How are faith and prayer related?

4. Read Ephesians 1:15-23.

   A. What elements of prayer do you find in this passage?

   B. What empowers this prayer (verses 19-23)?

   C. How similar are your prayers to this prayer? Account for the differences.

Summary Statement

No relationship can flourish without constant, heartfelt communication. This is true not only in human relationships, but also in our relationship with God. If we are to nurture a strong walk with our Savior, we must be in constant touch with Him. The way to do that is through prayer.

What is prayer? As stated earlier, prayer is a means of bringing us into conformity with God's will. Biblical prayer can be summarized through the acronym F-A-C-T-S:

F	aith
A	doration
C	onfession
T	hanksgiving
S	upplication

Supplementary Study Questions

Read pages 285-290 in *Christianity in Crisis*. Then answer the following questions:

1. What teachings about prayer made by Faith teachers are refuted on pages 285-287? What are the biblical answers to these errors?

2. In what way is it the *object of faith* that renders prayer effective (page 288)?

3. What does it mean to "adore" God (pages 288-289)?

4. What does it mean to "confess" our sins to God? Why is this important (page 289)?

5. Why is nothing more basic to prayer than thanksgiving (pages 289-290)?

6. What part does "supplication" play in an active prayer life (page 290)?

24

Bible

Spiritual Facts

If we fail to eat well-balanced meals on a regular basis, we will eventually suffer from malnutrition. What is true of the outer man is also true of the inner man. If we do not regularly feed on the Word of God, we will suffer spiritual malnutrition.

Jesus said, "Man does not live on bread alone, but on every word that comes from the mouth of God" (Matthew 4:4). Great physical meals are one thing; great spiritual meals are quite another. If we want our spirits to grow healthy and strong, we must make sure that we regularly partake of God's Word.

Study Questions

1. In what ways is physical malnutrition like spiritual malnutrition? How are they different?

2. Name several ways to get a good daily intake of God's Word.

3. How much of your typical week is spent interacting with God's Word? Are you satisfied with this situation? Explain.

4. Have you ever made yourself accountable to a friend for your Bible reading/study habits? Do you think this might be a good idea? Explain.

Scriptural Insights

1. Read 2 Timothy 3:16,17; 2 Peter 1:19-21.

   A. What does 2 Timothy 3:16,17 tell you about the Bible? Of what use is the Bible (verse 16)? What is the purpose of the Bible (verse 17)?

   B. Peter says we would "do well to pay attention." Pay attention to what? Describe the Bible's origin, according to 2 Peter 1:20,21. What difference should this make to us?

2. Read 2 Timothy 2:7,15.

   A. What command is given in verse 7? What promise?

   B. What command is given in verse 15? What will obedience to this command produce?

3. Read Joshua 1:8; Psalm 119:11; Proverbs 7:1-3.

   A. What was Joshua commanded in Joshua 1:8? What was the promised benefit?

   B. What practice did David describe in Psalm 119:11? What purpose did this practice serve?

   C. What instruction is given in Proverbs 7:1-3? What practical advice is given? What promise is given?

4. Read 1 Samuel 3:8-10; John 10:27.

   A. What advice did Eli give Samuel? How is his advice still good for us today?

   B. Who follows Jesus, according to John 10:27? What is required for them to follow?

5. Read Matthew 7:24-27; James 1:22-25.

   A. Is knowing the Bible enough, according to Matthew? Explain. What are the consequences of failing to put the Bible into practice?

   B. Is listening to the Bible enough, according to James? Explain. What are the consequences of failing to put the Bible into practice? What are the benefits of acting on it?

Summary Statement

The Bible not only forms the foundation of an effective prayer life, but it is foundational to every other aspect of Christian living. While prayer is our primary way of communicating with God, the Bible is God's primary way of communicating with us. Nothing should take precedence over getting into the Word and getting the Word into us. The acronym M-E-A-L-S provides a good guideline for effectively using the Bible for our spiritual growth:

M	emorize
E	xamine
A	pply
L	isten
S	tudy

Supplementary Study Questions

Read pages 291-300 in *Christianity in Crisis*. Then answer the following questions:

1. What are some benefits of Scripture memorization (page 292)?

2. Name several practical steps you can take toward memorizing portions of the Bible (pages 292-293).

3. Name several practical steps you can take toward examining the Word of God (pages 293-295).

4. What does it mean to "apply" the Bible to our lives? Why is this crucial (page 295)?

5. How do we "listen" to God's Word (page 296)?

6. Name several aids that would help you in your study of God's Word (pages 296-300).

25

Church

Spiritual Facts

Scripture exhorts us not to neglect the gathering of ourselves together, as is the habit of some. Sadly, multitudes today turn from the church and tune into television—and the impact of televangelism on the church has been massive. By and large, however, instead of conforming us to Christ, televangelism has conformed us to our culture. Worship has been replaced with entertainment, fellowship has been transformed into individualism, and the biblical concept of "every believer a witness" has been largely lost.

Getting back to basics means returning our focus to the church as the God-ordained vehicle through which *God* is worshiped, *oneness* is demonstrated, and through which we are equipped to make *disciples*.

Study Questions

1. What is your idea of the "perfect church"? What are you doing to help build it?

2. What do you least like about the church? What are you doing to help change it?

3. What purposes does the church serve? Where do you fit into its ministry?

4. Finish the sentence: "I come to church because _____."

Scriptural Insights

1. Read 1 Peter 2:5,9-12.

   A. How does Peter describe the church in verse 5? In verse 9?

   B. What is the purpose of the church, according to verse 9? According to verse 12?

   C. How is the church to fulfill the purpose stated in verse 12 (see verse 11)?

2. Read Hebrews 10:24,25.

   A. What is commanded in verse 25? Is it possible to "encourage one another" if you are not "meeting together"? What added incentive for meeting together is given in verse 25?

B. What is commanded in verse 24? Why does this take "consideration"? How well do we do this?

3. Read Acts 2:42-47; 4:32-35; 6:1-7.

   A. Describe the activity of the early church in Acts 2:42-47. What did it look like?

   B. Describe the activity of the early church in Acts 4:32-35. What did it look like?

   C. Describe the activity of the early church in Acts 6:1-7. What did it look like?

   D. What can we learn and emulate from the practice of the early church? What errors can we avoid?

4. Read Matthew 28:19,20.

   A. What command did Jesus give to the church in this passage? Of what elements does this command consist?

   B. How does this command go far beyond mere evangelism? To what degree does your church fulfill this command? To what degree do you participate in it?

5. Read Ephesians 4:11-16; 5:19-21.

A. What is the purpose of the church, according to Ephesians 4:12,13?

B. How does the church keep us from being "blown here and there by every wind of teaching" (verse 14)?

C. What should be the goal of every healthy church (verses 15,16)?

D. What practical guidelines does Paul give the church in Ephesians 5:19-21? How do each of these guidelines strengthen the church? Which do you find the most attractive? Which the most difficult? Why?

Summary Statement

In Scripture, the church is referred to as the body of Christ. Just as our body is one and yet has many parts, so the body of Christ is one but is composed of many members. Those who have received Christ as the Savior and Lord of their lives are already a part of the church universal. It is crucial, however, that we become vital, reproducing members of a healthy, well-balanced local body of believers as well. The acronym G-O-D can help to remind us of the crucial components of a healthy church:

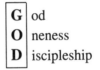

G od
O neness
D iscipleship

Supplementary Study Questions

Read pages 301-307 in *Christianity in Crisis*. Then answer the following questions:

1. What are the three main aspects of a healthy, well-balanced church (pages 301-302)?

2. How do prayer, praise, and proclamation help to nurture a strong church (pages 302-303)?

3. How do community, confession, and contribution help to unify a church (pages 303-304)?

4. How do the terms "love," "lips," and "life" remind us of what it means to be a true disciple of Jesus Christ (pages 305-306)?

26

Defense

Spiritual Facts

Getting back to basics means equipping yourself for the defense of the faith. The Cold War may be over, but the need to defend the Christian faith is just beginning to heat up. As we move into what has been described as post-Christian America, it is increasingly important for Christians to know *what* they believe as well as *why* they believe it. That is what the defense of the faith (apologetics) is all about.

The apostle Peter put it this way: "Always be prepared to give an answer [*apologia*] to everyone who asks you to give the reason for the hope that you have. But do this with gentleness and respect" (1 Peter 3:15).

The defense of the faith involves both *pre-evangelism* and *post-evangelism*. Christianity is not a blind leap into the dark, but faith founded upon fact. It is historic and evidential. And in a time when Christian leaders are falling all around us, it is encouraging to know that our faith is not based on the reliability of men but on the revelation of God.

577

Study Questions

1. Why should the faith have to be "defended"? Can't it take care of itself?

2. How would you respond to someone who said Jesus was a good moral teacher, but not God in the flesh?

3. In what ways do you think apologetics might be useful in pre-evangelism? In what ways do you think it might be useful in post-evangelism?

4. How versed are you in apologetics? Do you see the need for it? Explain.

Scriptural Insights

1. Read 1 Peter 3:15-17 and Jude 3.

   A. What is the beginning of good apologetics, according to the first sentence in 1 Peter 3:15? How does this control what follows?

   B. What does "preparation" have to do with apologetics, according to 1 Peter 3:15? What should all of us be prepared to do?

C. What did Jude urge his friends to do in verse 3 of his book? Why did he believe he had to do this? What does this have to do with apologetics?

2. Read Luke 1:1-4; 2 Peter 1:16-18; 1 John 1:1-3.

   A. What was Luke's purpose in writing his Gospel? What was his method?

   B. How do Peter's comments in 2 Peter 1:16-18 relate to apologetics? What is significant about his testimony?

   C. How do John's comments in 1 John 1:1-3 relate to apologetics? What is significant about his testimony?

3. Read Luke 24:36-43; Acts 1:3; 1 Corinthians 15:3-8,17-19.

   A. How is Luke 24:36-43 a good text for apologetics?

   B. How is Acts 1:3 a good text for apologetics?

   C. How is 1 Corinthians 15:3-8 a good text for apologetics?

   D. In what way might we say that 1 Corinthians 15:17-19 is a good text for "reverse apologetics"? What apologetic purpose does it serve?

4. Read Matthew 28:11-15.

   A. What "alternative explanation" for the resurrection of Christ is described in this passage? Is this explanation still popular today? Explain.

   B. How would you respond to such an "alternative explanation"? What other "alternative explanations" have you heard for the disappearance of Jesus' body? How would you respond to each of them?

Summary Statement

Too many people believe that the task of apologetics is the exclusive domain of scholars and theologians. Not so! The defense of the faith is not optional; it is basic training for *every Christian.* We must all be able to demonstrate three things:

   1. That the universe was intelligently designed by a Creator and did not evolve by random chance.

   2. That Jesus Christ is God and proved it through the undeniable fact of His resurrection.

   3. That the Bible is God-given rather than human in origin.

If you are looking for a real experience, try becoming a defender of the faith. Not only will you experience the power and presence of the Holy Spirit working through you, but you may just find yourself in the middle of an angelic praise gathering when a lost son or daughter of Adam finds his or her way into the kingdom of God.

Supplementary Study Questions

Read pages 309-314 in *Christianity in Crisis*. Then answer the following questions:

1. What does "apologetics" mean? Why does it *not* mean "to apologize for Scripture" (pages 309-310)?

2. Name three basic issues at the heart of defending the faith (page 310).

3. How can you demonstrate that the universe was created by God and did not evolve by random chance (page 311)?

4. How does the resurrection of Jesus Christ prove that He is God, and what difference does this make (pages 311-313)?

5. How can you demonstrate that the Bible is divine rather than human in origin (pages 313-314)?

6. What does each letter in the acronyms F-A-C-E, F-E-A-T, and M-A-P-S represent (pages 367-373)?

27

Essentials

Spiritual Facts

Sailors in days gone by fixed their course by the North Star. That star provided an unchanging reference point which guided their ships safely toward their destinations. The essentials of the Christian faith have likewise guided Christ's body through the doctrinal storms that have sought to sink it. While shooting stars may light the sky for a moment, following them leads only to shipwreck.

If we desire to build our faith on the solid rock rather than on sinking sand, we must look to the essentials for our starting point. Paul wrote:

> By the grace God has given me, I laid a foundation as an expert builder, and someone else is building on it. But each one should be careful how he builds. For no one can lay any foundation other than the one already laid, which is Jesus Christ (1 Corinthians 3:10,11).

Study Questions

1. Do you think it is possible to identify the essentials of the Christian faith? Explain.

2. What essentials of the Christian faith can you name?

3. How well-versed in the essentials of the Christian faith are you? Are you satisfied with this situation? Explain.

4. What happens to the church when it compromises the essentials? Have you seen this happen? If so, describe how.

Scriptural Insights

1. Read Galatians 1:6-9.

   A. What was the problem Paul addressed in the Galatian church?

   B. How seriously did Paul take this problem? Do you think his harsh language is justified? Why or why not?

   C. What does this passage have to do with the essentials of the Christian faith?

2. Read Colossians 1:19-23.

   A. What essentials can you identify in this passage?

   B. Why is it important for the church to stay glued to these essentials, according to verse 23?

3. Read 1 Corinthians 15:1-4.

   A. What is the core of gospel, according to this passage? How is this an essential?

   B. How does verse 2 remind you of Colossians 1:23?

4. Read 1 Timothy 4:13-16.

   A. How does Paul counsel Timothy to stay true to the essentials? What elements are critical?

   B. What is at stake in staying true to the essentials, according to verse 16?

5. Read 2 Timothy 4:3-5.

   A. What does Paul warn Timothy about in this passage? How is this warning also appropriate for us?

   B. What is the antidote to this danger, according to verse 5? How does this relate to us today?

C. How do you believe the Faith teachings relate to this passage? Explain.

Summary Statement

Unity in the church cannot exist apart from the essentials for which the martyrs spilled their blood. Christ warned us to beware of false prophets, and the history of the church has borne eloquent testimony to the necessity of the warning. The Bible throughout warns of false apostles and deceitful workmen who masquerade as apostles of Christ. Paul concludes that if Satan himself "masquerades as an angel of light," it should not surprise us that his disciples "masquerade as servants of righteousness" (2 Corinthians 11:14,15).

Even so, Jesus promised that the gates of hell would not prevail against the church. In His final commission He said, "Surely I will be with you always, to the very end of the age" (Matthew 28:20). The acronym A-G-E can serve as a reference point in getting back to basics:

A	thanasian Creed
G	ospel
E	ssential Christian doctrine

Supplementary Study Questions

Read pages 315-321 in *Christianity in Crisis*. Then answer the following questions:

1. What do we mean by the essentials of the faith? Why can true unity be achieved only in the context of these essentials (pages 315-316)?

2. How can the Athanasian Creed be a point of reference for the church (pages 316-318)?

3. Name five key points in communicating the gospel to a person who needs to hear it (pages 318-319).

4. What do Mormons, the New Age movement, and the Faith movement all hold in common (page 320)?

5. Name several good resources which develop some of the Christian faith's essential doctrines (pages 320-321).

6. How does essential Christian doctrine provide the key to successful Christian living (page 321)?

About the Author

Hank Hanegraaff is president of the California-based Christian Research Institute and host of the "Bible Answer Man" broadcast, heard daily throughout the United States and Canada by a potential listening audience of more than 120 million people.

As founder of Memory Dynamics, Hank has developed memorable tools to prepare Christians to effectively communicate 1) *what* they believe, 2) *why* they believe it, and 3) *where* cults deviate from historic Christianity. He has also developed fun and easy techniques for memorizing Scripture quickly and retaining it forever. Hank has become a popular conference speaker for churches, schools, and businesses worldwide.

Hank lives in Southern California with his wife, Kathy, and six children: Michelle, Katie, David, John Mark, Hank Jr., and Christy. He is the author of *Personal Witness Training: Your Handle on the Great Commission* and *Memory Dynamics: Your Untapped Resource for Spiritual Growth.*

To schedule a "Memory Dynamics," "Personal Witness Training," or "Contending for the Faith" workshop, or for information on Hank's books, tapes, and speaking schedule, address your request to:

Memory Dynamics
P.O. Box 667
San Juan Capistrano, CA 92693-0667
(714) 589-1504

Christianity in Crisis Audio Book

Statements by Faith teachers are at times so incredible and aberrant that, despite the well-documented evidence presented in *Christianity in Crisis*, you may be tempted to disbelief—until you hear the cultic doctrines of the Faith movement from the mouths of the Faith teachers themselves.

These audiotapes give a memorable overview of *Christianity in Crisis*, present an opportunity for *you to hear directly from the Faith teachers*, and provide an effective tool to reach people influenced by the Faith movement.